# Bound together

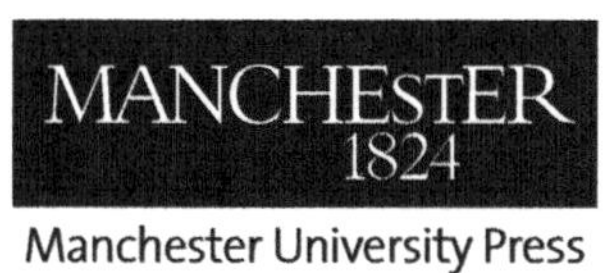

Manchester University Press

# rethinking
**art's** histories

SERIES EDITORS
Amelia G. Jones, Marsha Meskimmon

Rethinking Art's Histories aims to open out art history from its most basic structures by foregrounding work that challenges the conventional periodisation and geographical subfields of traditional art history, and addressing a wide range of visual cultural forms from the early modern period to the present.

These books will acknowledge the impact of recent scholarship on our understanding of the complex temporalities and cartographies that have emerged through centuries of world-wide trade, political colonisation and the diasporic movement of people and ideas across national and continental borders.

*Also available in the series*

*Colouring the Caribbean: Race and the art of Agostino Brunias*    Mia L. Bagneris

*Performance art in Eastern Europe since 1960*    Amy Bryzgel

*Art, museums and touch*    Fiona Candlin

*Staging art and Chineseness: The politics of trans/nationalism and global expositions*    Jane Chin Davidson

*Travelling images: Looking across the borderlands of art, media and visual culture*    Anna Dahlgren

*The 'do-it-yourself' artwork: Participation from fluxus to relational aesthetics*    Anna Dezeuze (ed.)

*Empires of light: Vision, visibility and power in colonial India*    Niharika Dinkar

*Fleshing out surfaces: Skin in French art and medicine, 1650–1850*    Mechthild Fend

*The political aesthetics of the Armenian avant-garde: The journey of the 'painterly real', 1987–2004*    Angela Harutyunyan

*The matter of miracles: Neapolitan baroque sanctity and architecture*    Helen Hills

*The face of medicine: Visualising medical masculinities in late nineteenth-century Paris*    Mary Hunter

*Glorious catastrophe: Jack Smith, performance and visual culture*    Dominic Johnson

*Otherwise: Imagining queer feminist art histories*    Amelia Jones and Erin Silver (eds)

*Addressing the other woman: Textual correspondences in feminist art and writing*    Kimberly Lamm

*Above sea: Contemporary art, urban culture, and the fashioning of global Shanghai*    Jenny Lin

*Photography and documentary film in the making of modern Brazil*    Luciana Martins

*After the event: New perspectives in art history*    Charles Merewether and John Potts (eds)

*Women, the arts and globalization: Eccentric experience*    Marsha Meskimmon and Dorothy C. Rowe (eds)

*Flesh cinema: The corporeal turn in American avant-garde film*    Ara Osterweil

*The ecological eye: Assembling an ecocritical art history*    Andrew Patrizio

*After-affects|after-images: Trauma and aesthetic transformation in the virtual Feminist museum*    Griselda Pollock

*Migration into art: Transcultural identities and art-making in a globalised world*    Anne Ring Petersen

*Vertiginous mirrors: The animation of the visual image and early modern travel*    Rose Marie San Juan

*The synthetic proposition: Conceptualism and the political referent in contemporary art*    Nizan Shaked

*The paradox of body, building and motion in seventeenth-century England*    Kimberley Skelton

*The newspaper clipping: A modern paper object*    Anke Te Heesen, translated by Lori Lantz

*Screen/space: The projected image in contemporary art*    Tamara Trodd (ed.)

*Art and human rights: Contemporary Asian contexts*    Caroline Turner and Jen Webb

*Timed out: Art and the transnational Caribbean*    Leon Wainwright

*Performative monuments: Performance, photography, and the rematerialisation of public art*    Mechtild Widrich

# Bound together

Leather, sex, archives, and contemporary art

**Andy Campbell**

Manchester University Press

Published by Manchester University Press
Altrincham Street, Manchester M1 7JA

www.manchesteruniversitypress.co.uk

British Library Cataloguing-in-Publication Data
A catalogue record for this book is available from the British Library

ISBN 978 1 5261 4280 1 hardback
ISBN 978 1 5261 4282 5 paperback

First published 2020

The publisher has no responsibility for the persistence or accuracy of URLs for external or any third-party internet websites referred to in this book, and does not guarantee that any content on such websites is, or will remain, accurate or appropriate.

Typeset by
Servis Filmsetting Ltd, Stockport, Cheshire
Printed in Great Britain by
TJ International Ltd, Padstow, Cornwall

*for*
*Jeanne Barney*

# Contents

# Plates

# Figures

Every effort has been made to obtain permission to reproduce copyright material, and the publisher will be pleased to be informed of any errors and omissions for correction in future editions.

# Acknowledgments

A heartfelt thank you to those who helped nurture this project, who were there from the beginning: Ann Reynolds, Chelsea Weathers, Laura August, and Tara Kohn; Henry Abelove, Cherise Smith, Neville Hoad, and John Clarke. And to those who encouraged and edited at Manchester University Press: Amelia Jones, Marsha Meskimmon, Emma Brennan, Rebecca Mortimer, Andrew Kirk, and the manuscript reviewers. My gratitude is truly without end.

To the leatherfolks who have helped in material and immaterial ways, I owe you a debt of gratitude, to be repaid under whatever terms: Gayle Rubin, Viola Johnson (and krewe), Jack Fritscher, Rick Storer, Patrick Califia, Gwen Hardy, Chuck Renslow, Camille O'Grady, Mark Hemry, Jennifer Tyburczy, and Jeanne Barney. Thanks also to the leatherfolks who humored me at conferences and chatted with me in bars.

To the artists appearing in this book, your work gives me life: Jaime C. Knight, Jonesy, Dean Sameshima, Patrick Staff, Monica Majoli, AK Burns, AL Steiner, Nayland Blake, Roy Martinez, Sean (John Klamik), Etienne (Dom Orejudos), Bill Ward, Tom of Finland, Robert Opel, and Camille O'Grady (again!). A special thank you to Ryan Hawk, who supplied, at the near last minute, a stunning cover for the book. I should also mention Christian Holstad, Nancy Grossman, Monica Bonvicini, Ivan LOZANO, Tom Burr, William E. Jones, Jacolby Satterwhite, Skylar Fein, and Ektor Garcia who all could have easily been discussed in these pages as well.

To the archivists—my favorite people to talk nerdy with: Mel Leverich, Jakob VanLammeren, Loni Shibuyama, Michael C. Oliveira, Bud Thomas, Cooper Moll; to the staff and leadership of the Leather Archives & Museum; GLBT Historical Society, the Lesbian Herstory Archives, ONE National Gay and Lesbian Archives, and everyone who opened their closets, garages, back houses, basements, and back rooms to me. Thank you.

To my colleagues (past and present): in critical studies, the dream team—Amelia Jones (again!), Karen Moss, Jenny Lin, Maura Brewer, Cecilia Fajardo-Hill, and Ceci Moss. Art and Design: Haven Lin-Kirk, Sherin

Guirguis, Nao Bustamante, Marisa Mandler, Edgar Arceneaux, Suzanne Lacy, Patty Chang, Jennifer West, Paul Donald, Tom Mueller, Ruben Ochoa, Karen Liebowitz, David Kelley, Ewa Wojchiak, Cindy Tsukamoto, Annie Watanabe, Lissa Sanders, Marcus Kuiland-Nazario, Katherine Guevarra, Jeff Cain, Alice Fung, Jason Ellenberg, Stephanie Sabo, Alexis Zoto, Brian O'Connell, Andrew Kutchera, David Evans Franz, and Alexis Zoto. Elsewhere in the university: Suzanne Hudson, Nayan Shah, Megan Luke, Hector Reyes, Amy Ogata, Vanessa Schwartz, Robin Romans, Nancy Lutkehaus, Bethany Montagano, Lexi Johnson, and Selma Holo. Texas State University: Erina Duganne, Jeff Cain, Joey Fauerso, M. Wright, Mary Mikel Stump, Ben Ruggiero, Gina Tarver, Heather Galloway, Diann McCabe.

To my students, current and former—particularly Hannah Grossman, Simone Krug, Brenna Ansley, Christina Houle, Shaun Bryan Ford, Carter Weeks, Kat Sarayath, Reed van Brunschot, Julia Oquera Bianco, Star Montana, Seymour Polatin, Alex Sizemore-Smale, Ana Briz, Josh Rains, Patrisse Cullors, Rachel Keller, Agnes Wu, Oscar David Alvarez, Loujain Bager, Eve Moeykins-Arballo, Paulson Lee. Your work sustains me; this world is better with you in it.

To the audiences at CAA, USC, the Fort Worth Museum of Modern Art, the Contemporary Austin, UT, and The Stud.

Houston/swamp friends: Laura August (again!), Nicole Burisch, Taraneh Fazeli, Ken Tam, Sondra Perry, Danielle Dean, Harold Mendez, Mike Wellen, Tsuyoshi Anzai, Julia Brown, Jason Byrne, Anahita Ghazvanizadeh, Rodrigo Valenzuela, Ivor Shearer, Mary Leclère, Pete Gerson, Lily Cox-Richard, Dean Daderko, Diane and Ryan Meyers, Cyril Amoin, Michelle White, Ryan Dennis, Ana Elise Johnson, Anna Walker.

Friends and extended colleagues: Kate Messer, Jo Labow, Jay Hodges, Kay Turner, Lucas Hilderbrand, Joshua Chambers-Letson, Dan Paz, Oli Rodriguez, Ivan LOZANO, Denise Markonish, Catherine Morris, Jennifer Burris, Kevin Quashie, Park McArthur, Sampada Aranke, Beatriz Cortez, Pavithra Prasad, Marcus Civin, Susanna Newberry, Daniel Villarreal, Masashi Niwano, Marcus Cruz Sanchez, Andrea Mellard, Leah DeVun, Ann Cvetkovich, Lisa Moore, PJ Raval, and Ann Johns.

Oberlin OGs: Wendy Kozol, Frances Hasso, Pat Mathews, Matthew Wright, Holly Handman, Amanda Smith, Matt Franks, Sarah Hallberg, Anna Eisenberg.

To family and kin (queer and natal): Cathy, Tom, Daniel, and also Al, Nenita, and Chris—I am so lucky to be in relation. Claudette and Jacob, Kate (again!) and Wendy, Jess and Beth, Jonesy (again!), Ted, and Rachel, Char, Ari, and Thea. A million hugs.

To everyone who aided, cajoled, argued, listened, enthused, and tolerated—especially those who I've forgotten to name here—thank you. If there is anything good and useful in this enterprise, you had a hand in it. Any missteps, mistakes, and misfires are my own.

And Jay: everything, everything.

Soon, the written history rejoins—has to rejoin—the insistent, tireless, repetitive beat of a cognitive form that has no end. The written history is a story that can be told only by the implicit understanding that things are not over, that the story isn't finished, can never be finished, for some new item of information may alter the account that has been given. In this way, history breaks the most ordinary and accepted narrative rule, and in this way also, the written history is not just about time, doesn't just describe time, or take time as its setting; rather, it embeds time in its narrative structure.

Carolyn Steedman[1]

The purpose of history, guided by genealogy, is not to discover the roots of our identity, but to commit itself to its dissipation […] to make visible all those discontinuities that cross us.

Michel Foucault[2]

This book considers historic gay and lesbian leather communities by way of two interrelated lines of enquiry; addressing the archives where leather histories and their attendant visual and material objects currently reside, while also examining the projects of contemporary artists who bring leather histories to the fore, making an implicit argument for their potential queer political force in the present.

Leather sexualities and cultures are, at their core, profoundly visual, having developed and transformed an astonishing set of visual signifiers. From the leather (and denim) garments that a leatherperson might wear—vest, pants, harness, cap, gauntlets, boots—to the darkened, yet nevertheless image-heavy, architectural spaces of the leather bar, nearly everything in the embodied performance practices of power exchange so central to leathersex's sexual expression are designed to visually declare their perverse, affinitive capacities. Historically, leather communities fostered and supported a number of artists, many of whom built artistic careers exclusively making work for other leatherfolks' eyes, libraries, and dungeons. For example, Dom Orejudos, a prolific leather artist working out of Chicago under the Europeanized pseudonym

Etienne, completed illustrations for leather publications (magazines, novels, catalogs, and newsletters), murals and logographics for leather bars, as well as original drawings and art prints derived from the former. Outside of leather communities his work is not recognized as artistically significant. It is a wonder and a shame that more scholastic attention has not been paid to the prolific visual productions of leather artists like Orejudos. I can only speculate that this is partially or fully the product of a sex-negative culture wherein images, photographs, and films representing sadomasochism and queer sex have been subject to intense and egregious litigation and censorship.[3] Such juridicial overreach (which is by no means limited to the United States, even though this study is) has broadly chilling effects, which can still be felt today from the newsstand to the academy.

This book seeks to change that in some small way by taking cues from contemporary artists who have quarried the archives, art, and visual and material cultures of historic gay and lesbian leather communities. They have been on the frontlines of research, and in my mind are greatly, if not wholly, responsible for the incipient recuperation of historic leather aesthetics we are witnessing today. It is through the work of artists like Dean Sameshima, Monica Majoli, Nayland Blake, Patrick Staff, A. K. Burns and A. L. Steiner, and the artist collective Die Kränken, that leather archives and certain strands of contemporary queer artistic practice are bound up with one another, and that each gives the other meanings that enrich and deepen their respective significance to their own times, communities, and, even, to culture at large.

My line of thought is really an extrapolation of Raymond Williams's observation that each generation constitutes and is constituted by its own structure of feeling forged in relation to a selective tradition of cultural touchstones.[4] Such affinitive relationships—Williams imagines them as lines—are never simply arbitrary, but inform the emergence and resultant interpretations of contemporary culture. About this process he writes,

> In the analysis of contemporary culture, the existing state of the selective tradition is of vital importance, for it is often true that some change in this tradition—establishing new lines with the past, breaking or re-drawing existing lines—is a radical kind of *contemporary* change. We tend to underestimate the extent to which the cultural tradition is not only a selection but also an interpretation.[5]

I make this argument at a moment when gay and lesbian leather aesthetics are being absorbed, often uncritically, into contemporary visual and popular culture. In 2015, for example, the pop singer Taylor Swift was photographed sporting a gray leather harness while out shopping with fellow celebrity singer Selena Gomez in Los Angeles. Such tabloid gossip is, on the surface, unremarkable in its quotidianess—a famous person went shopping with another famous person. Yet the coverage of the event didn't neglect to point out that the harness that Swift wore was produced by the American clothing brand Free People (the irony should escape no one), signaling that someone (or a group of someones) in some room decided that a leather harness would be an ideal fashion accessory for a young, bohemian fashion consumer. Leatherwear has, in other words, already been successfully commodified within a non-leather consumer market that trades, in large part, on the social and cultural capital of young people.[6] One tabloid covering Swift's fashion choice was predictably alarmist in its headline: '"I'm Ready to Get Extreme!" Taylor Swift Explains Her Bizarre Harness Accessory as Fans Question Her Fashion Choice.'[7] The authors of the story cycle between astonished and consultative tones, noting that if emulators wish to follow in the fashion footsteps of Swift, that they do so only with some caution, as the 'trend' of wearing harnesses 'can easily swerve into dominatrix territory.'[8] Implicitly positioning leatherwear as signifying sex work, which the authors believe should be avoided, is, I would argue, a common and uncritical elision (not to mention moral valuation) regarding leather aesthetics and sex work. As in many other instances where the sexually explicit comes into contact with the machinations of capitalism, the coverage of Swift's harness toggles between titillation and revulsion. Still, the harness is not without its charms—the author continues: 'While these leather harness [*sic*] serve no real function, they do manage to toughen up what would be a rather boring look.'[9]

This example of leatherwear appearing on the radar of pop-celebrity culture is not singular, and it points to the wide semiotic chasm separating the supposedly non-functional 'fashion choice,' and the garment that signals an overt and deep affinity with a particular culture (here leather communities). Indeed, the column misappropriates the garment as being intrinsic to sex work (the dominatrix), rather than leather communities and their visual and material cultures. Implicit in this bit of tabloid gossip is the fact that the authors' anxious frettings wouldn't be necessary if they didn't believe, on some level, that this gap was *not yet wide enough*.

Roy Martinez's *Sup Foo? #3* (2018) (figure 1.1) serves as a correlative and, in some ways, corrective to the glib mainstream flirtation with the visual and material cultures of gay and lesbian leather communities—of which fashion is only one component. Martinez, who also sometimes exhibits and sells clothing under the pseudonym Lambe Culo (literally 'lick-ass' in Spanish), offered the work for $150 on their website, where it was positioned promiscuously between the discourses of fashion and fine art in its description as a 'numbered and signed' shoulder harness. The pricepoint is equally evocative in its ambiguity, as the item is not much more than what a leather shoulder harness would otherwise cost in a leather shop, and not much less than an artist's multiple at a museum bookstore or gallery. Importantly, *Sup Foo? #3*

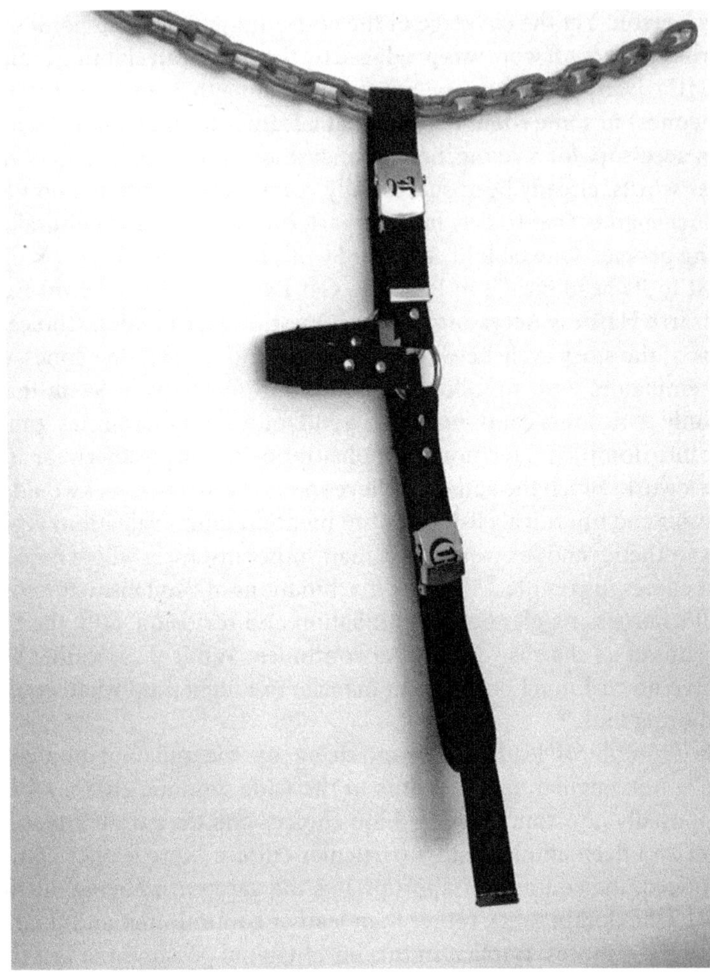

**1.1**     Roy Martinez, *Sup Foo? #3*, 2018.

is not made of leather, but cloth belting and plaque buckles riveted together. Martinez's two buckles are incised with the letters L and C (for Lambe Culo, no doubt) in the modernized Blackletter typeface colloquially known as 'Old English.' Akin to Swift's Free People folly, Martinez specifies on their website that the garment is 'not recommended for play,' perhaps due in large part to the structural fragility of the plaque buckles (unlike their more common, tongued counterparts in leatherwear). Whatever the reason, Martinez nonetheless collapses the current appeal of contemporary leather aesthetics to a middle-class, white fashion consumer and the hallmarks of cholo fashion, a subcultural and politicized mode of dress that delineates, among other things, a refusal to look and act like the ideal participant in white neoliberal capitalism.[10] The work, via its title, greets its viewer with culturally specific terms of endearment, and likewise proposes a cholo revision of the ur-material of kink: leather. At the same time it complicates what the artist identifies as the 'cis[-gender] het[erosexual] cholo subculture' as one in need of revision and a more inclusive reclamation for queer and gender non-binary people.[11] Picking up on Gayle Rubin's insight that 'fetishism raises all sorts of issues concerning shifts in the manufacture of objects, the historical and social specificities of control and skin and social etiquette, or ambiguously experienced body invasions and minutely graduated hierarchies,' Martinez refashions sadomasochism's reliance on leather as a primary material signifier of sexual power exchange.[12] Identity and its politics of contingency are central to any reasonable interpretation of this sculpture, which is cleverly photographed by Martinez in a state of suspension between strength and precarity, hanging from a rugged chain, which in turn is delicately pinned to the wall with a clear thumbtack. *Sup Foo? #3* conjures a kinky brown body—perhaps the artist's own, but also perhaps a more phantasmic one—and perversely plays with branding, adjustment, accommodation, and a history of racialized dress. In fashioning a particularized item of kinky dress and reimagining it within the parameters of latinx and gender non-binary cultural production, Martinez evokes 'tha multifaceted histories within a material / collective memory,' while also leveling a profound critique on a subculture that the artist identifies as too white and too narrowly masculine.[13]

I join artists like Martinez in insisting upon the depth and complications of the particular histories they access as a key component of claiming a politics of identity variously considerate of and irresponsible to a sense of a collective past—an acknowledgment that the 'then' of queerness is of enduring and foundational importance as one of the suppliers of metamorphic potentiality to queer life. Elizabeth Freeman suggests such archeological digging might even be intrinsic to the constitution of leather sexualities, as 'S/M relentlessly physicalizes the encounter with history and thereby contributes to a reparative criticism that takes up the materials of a traumatic past and remixes them in the interests of new possibilities for being and knowing.'[14] With epistemic and ontological projects deeply concerned with representing and imagining a kinky past, the artists discussed in this book access archives, or, sometimes, assemble them in the absence of publicly accessible archives while in pursuit of such queer possibility. Therefore, to fully think through their work demands a concomitant consideration of the joys and vicissitudes of archival work itself.

My methodology regarding the access and use of archives in this study has two interrelated components: by examining material and visual culture made by members of gay and lesbian leather communities, I trace their contextual meanings at the time of their making, as well as their continued ability to produce community-specific histories in archival repositories that may or may not be solely dedicated to leather communities. I also identify instances where the themes, materialities, and/or histories of like objects have become part of the work and politics of contemporary queer artists. This twofold methodology is represented in the structure of this book, as some of the following chapters combine readings of particular archives and the objects they contain with readings of contemporary artistic projects that are either tangentially or directly related to them and their histories.

I seek nothing less than to challenge, and potentially unseat, the orthodoxies of writing, structuring, and historicizing communities and artists that have heretofore been ignored, erased, destroyed, and decimated by the vagaries of discipline, illness, and a sex-negative society that stubbornly refuses to understand their contexts. My work does not sit alone in this task. The hard-won work of authors and cultural producers such as Gayle Rubin, Tony DeBlase, Pat Califia, Viola Johnson, Guy Baldwin, Larry Townsend, and Jack Fritscher has provided a foundation for thinking about leather cultures and communities, and I hope my work in turn opens out possibilities for other scholars and artists.

I have opted not to provide a comprehensive or encyclopedic history of gay and lesbian leatherfolks in the U.S.—in the vein of George Cauncey's *Gay New York* or Lillian Faderman and Stuart Timmons's *Gay L.A.*, each of which is remarkable for its thorough chronological accounting of geographically sited LGBTQ histories.[15] Instead, I stress something else, namely the state and scope of the archives of leather history, and the myriad ways in which that history has been accessed, understood, and remade by contemporary artists largely living and making work in the U.S. Tracking the sexual and racial politics of contemporary art alongside the visual cultures of historical leather communities is meant to illuminate the interconnected work of scholars, artists, and leatherfolks—bringing them into rare dialog. I have tried to structure this text to speak to each of these constituencies, knowing that some readers will claim membership in one or perhaps all of these groups.

## On 'leather' and 'fucking'

There are many ways to linguistically name the sex discussed in this book. I have chosen 'leather' as the term under which I organize the heterogeneous and multitudinous sexual practices discussed herein, ones that sometimes incorporate sadomasochism, power play, bondage, fisting, discipline, humiliation, flagging, flogging, fucking, and much more. To wit, leather also encompasses kissing, hugging, flirting, talking, and other practices that are often seen as sexually normative. Within contemporary BDSM communities these seemingly benign activities are positioned as 'vanilla,' but I would argue that these less-sensationalistic corporeal performances of the flesh become part-and-parcel of leathersexualities when coupled with practices usually associated with leather, or embodied by a self-identified leatherperson. A kiss means something different when it comes before, during, or after a consensual flogging. And as with all sex, it matters who is doing what with whom, and what they *make it mean together*.

I consistently use leather, instead of another term, for its broad applicability and elasticity; as Rubin has aptly noted, many fetishes are housed under the umbrella of 'leather.'[16] The term enjoyed wide dissemination during the period of leather's expansion and popularization, roughly 1964–84. It is to this period, non-coincidentally, that many of the artists discussed in this book turn when mining the ephemera and embodied practices of leather. There are many examples of 'leather' as the preferred term of this community. *Drummer* magazine, for example, one of the most remarkable repositories of information regarding leather communities in the late 1970s and 1980s, proclaimed its allegiance to 'leather' as a preferred term: from its earliest incarnation as an affinity organization called the 'Leather Fraternity,' to its masthead—'The one publication dedicated to the leather lifestyle for guys.' Another example would be the International Mr. Leather (IML) contest, which got its start in the late 1970s, and indexes leather as its preferred terminology via its title—sending-up the popular beauty contests of the era (such as the Miss America competition, or the earlier Groovy Guy contests put on by *The Advocate*), while simultaneously cohering fairly segmented and city-specific leather cultures. Both of these institutions of leather culture centered artists and their work as integral and necessary components of sexual lifeways. *Drummer*, for instance, published the artwork and illustrations of almost every leather artist working during its nearly 25-year-long run, marking it as an indispensable source for any visual historian of gay and lesbian leather communities. I would argue that IML's success could be attributed in large part to Etienne, who created the visual identity for the contest, populated the stage with giant, painted, cut-outs of leathermen, filled its programs and brochures with playful black-and-white illustrations, and not least of all served for over a decade as the contest's 'head judge.'

'Leather' is also a preferred archival term, and it is the most common descriptor used by institutions dedicated to displaying and preserving these histories. The Leather Archives & Museum in Chicago is the most obvious example (and is explored in greater detail in Chapter 4), and the same with the Carter/Johnson Leather Library (which is the subject of Chapter 6).

But leather was not the only term used in the 1970s; sadomasochism and its many initialisms (S&M, SM, S/M) were prevalent, too. These terms have their roots in a classificatory system that sought to pathologize sexual acts of dominance and submission—bringing them into a discourse that named and classified sexual normalcy and its constitutive aberrations. As many historians of sexual communities and cultures have rehearsed before, the terms sadism and masochism were the brainchild of Austro-German sexologist Richard von Krafft-Ebing, who first used them in his 1886 aggregation of case-studies, *Psychopathia Sexualis*.[17] In grouping together what he perceived to be similar pathologies, Krafft-Ebing created new taxonomic categories based on a sequence of eclectic case studies. Krafft-Ebing named two related, but (in his eyes) distinct desires—the desire to cause 'pain' through 'force,' and the desire to be willfully subjected to pain. In designing these paraphilias (the term for psychopathologies tied to sexual expression and sexuality), he name-checked the authors he felt most exemplified such desires in their literary works—the Marquis de Sade (1740–1814) and Leopold von Sacher-Masoch (1836–95), respectively. But Krafft-Ebing's formulations became, and in a more limited extent remain, orthodoxy within contemporary mental health diagnostic practice; the current DSM-5 contains entries for 'sexual sadism disorder' and 'sexual masochism disorder' as paraphilias.[18] It was only twenty years after Krafft-Ebing published *Psychopathia Sexualis* that Sigmund Freud wrote of sadism and masochism as related, continuous desires.[19] Eventually, his insight was clarified and popularized in the linguistic portmanteau 'sadomasochism.'

If I push against using sadomasochism because of its psychopathological roots, others within leather communities of the 1970s and 1980s believed that it should be used precisely because the term indicates something about leather's outlaw, and thus radical, status. Such voices are worth paying heed to. One particularly compelling counterargument is furnished in a book review of Geoff Mains's seminal leather text *Urban Aboriginals*. Published in *DungeonMaster*, the reviewer—most likely Tony DeBlase, who edited the periodical from his home in Chicago—excoriates the author's choice to use 'leather' over 'S&M,' stating that such a decision 'softens what he's writing about. "I'm into leather" could be easily viewed as a statement of a harmless quirk (Woody Allen got a joke out of that very quote in *Annie Hall*); "I'm into S&M" is a statement of radical politics.'[20]

That particular review was published in 1984, and now the terminology in the leather landscape is vastly different. I would refer any reader interested in more contemporary terminologies to the 'Note on Terminology' that opens Margot Weiss's performative materialist ethnography, *Techniques of Pleasure: BDSM and the Circuits of Sexuality*.[21] The thoroughness with which she traces the lineages of a variety of contested terms helped to further clarify the one I privilege in this study. In her book Weiss uses BDSM as her preferred term, as her study is focused on more contemporary, pansexual kink communities clustered around Silicon Valley. She notes that BDSM's etymology is of 'relatively recent (and, many suggest, Internet) coinage.'[22]

I also prefer 'leather' because it names one of the primary materials in the erotic arsenal of sexual practices that falls under its purview. Many leatherfolks have described leather as a 'second skin' and contemporary theorists have made much of this—especially in relationship to corporeal performances and embodiments of racialized bodies.[23] As a material used for garments, toys, equipment, and accessories, leather is still the clearest, but certainly not the only, material signifier of sadomasochistic practice (denim—particularly the wheat-colored denim used by early bike clubs—rubber, latex, and many other materials have had historic importance within leather communities). I also follow the lead of some of the most prominent writers within leather communities, such as Geoff Mains and Larry Townsend, and use portmanteaus such as 'leathersex' and 'leatherwoman,' connecting leather directly to what it describes or modifies. In this way I hope to tie together material and corporeal practices with identities via an already performative linguistics.[24]

It may be useful here to briefly set up some of the language I use to describe leathersex, language that is largely taken directly from of the archival material I work with. I do not always affect a researcher's 'objectivity' and cloak my discussions of sex in polite euphemism, or clinical, academic language. I use the word 'fuck' to generically cover a variety of embodied erotic practices, and this word comes with as much cultural baggage as does more seemingly benign phrasing. So let me be clear as to its meaning herein. To some, fucking may imply *only* penetrative sex—an interpretation I refuse for its limitations. To others, it may come to monolithically mean uncaring, unsympathetic, or anonymous sex—another association that in my estimation is too limited, and I reject it along with the moralizing tone that often accompanies this kind of usage. Fucking encompasses these things *and more*. I use 'fuck' as an umbrella term (not unlike 'leather'), inclusive of many kinds of affective sexual relationships. In this way I hope to extend Lauren Berlant's helpful framing of sex as 'not a thing of truth but a scene where one discovers potentiality in the abandon that's on the other side of abandonment.'[25] Within the imaginative possibilities of leathersex, fucking takes on a truly dynamic range: from a consensual agreement to sit in a chair while your lover(s) are in another room; or a devoted attention to the activity of shining a boot; to the piercing and suturing of flesh. Although I liberally use 'fuck/ing' throughout this book, I am also careful with such positionings of graphic language, for as Linda Williams points out in her overview of the field of pornography studies, there is a difference between sexualized terms and the comfortability or criticality they evince.[26] Therefore I theorize leather and fucking in terms of their most generous meanings and associations so that they might continue to be generative for leatherfolks, artists, and historians alike.

Positioning a wide variety of erotic activities under the linguistic sign of 'fucking' has its downsides, too. Once, while presenting some of the material contained in this book, a leatherman approached me after my lecture, and scolded me: 'You know,' he said, 'we make love too.' His point is not left unconsidered, especially in light of enriched theoretical reconsiderations of love—the writings of bell hooks and Sara Ahmed come to mind—and I hope that this book finds him, and that I've done justice to a myriad of sex practices as he (and others) experience them within leather communities.[27] It is in this book's conclusion that I will circle back to love, as a potential and productive site for surrogacy, encasement, and the reformulation of sexuality.

Finally, I concentrate on 'gay' and 'lesbian' leatherfolks, which is to say those people who most often had contacts with same or similar-gendered people. This may seem odd given that leathersexuality, in a profound way, questions the very foundations of affilliative and coalitional categories such as gay and lesbian. As Patrick (then Pat) Califia so clearly put it, 'Most of my partners are women, but gender is not my boundary […] If I had a choice between being shipwrecked on a desert island with a vanilla lesbian and a hot male masochist, I'd pick the boy.'[28] Some gay and lesbian leatherfolks fucked people of the opposite gender, while choosing to align themselves within the field of gay and/or lesbian identitarian categories that would seem on the surface to preclude such erotic affiliations. In writing a history of gay and lesbian leatherfolks I do so under the assumption of such fungible definitions of identity and their dynamic relationship to fucking—including processes of self-naming and affiliation.

In short, leather, for the purposes of this book, is proposed as a diverse sexual ecology that privileges fucking and improvisatory play, genital and non-genital pleasure, rules and their effacement—all under the rubric of a seemingly static visual iconography, which in actuality is always in the process of being amended, shored, repurposed, and obliterated. It is a live system of relationality, varied in its address. Powerful symbology—in the material form of leather and the visual forms of representation developed by artists, magazine editors, filmmakers, and others—aids a great deal in imagining the uses of the sensorium of the body, including, but not limited to, broader discourses of pain and haptic touch.[29] Notice that my working definition above says nothing of what is usually identified as leathersexuality's most prominent feature, the presentation of strictly dyadic relationships (top/ bottom, sadist/masochist). While common ingredients in leathersexuality's presentation and enactment, these relationships are not ossified identities, but temporary agreements that invest erotic significance in an agreement's terms and potential limits. Even the most rigid top or bottom would admit that within the relationality of fucking, dyadic positions are altered, transformed, and even flipped.

What Michel Foucault terms the 'strategic relationships' of leather have been read in a multitude of ways.[30] Leo Bersani, for instance, usefully describes leathersex as an 'X-ray of power's body,' while Geoff Mains places 'shared ritual and apotheosis' at the center of his definition.[31] I'll have much more to say about these ideas in the chapters that follow, but for now I want to suggest that we invest in both authors' notions as only a slice of a complicated terrain mapping out each person's relationship to fucking, power, and visual representation. This can be the foundation for addressing leather's 'interconnected social archipelago' with openness.[32] In response to Bersani, who famously surmised that sex's big secret is that 'most people don't like it,' I suggest a shift in the rubric of what counts as sex so as to supply a more expansive ground from which 'possibilit[ies] for creative life' (as per Foucault) might be built.[33] Then the question wouldn't be whether people like sex or not, but how it might address what Berlant identifies as the 'ongoing question of how living might be structured.'[34] It is this living that most interests and excites me.

## Archives, not 'The Archive'

Many have offered insights into the nature of archives. Archives are situated most basically as a 'non-random collection of things,'[35] which are 'grouped […] composed […] maintained,'[36] and which articulate 'memory's potential space,' a place where scholars can revel in the 'deep satisfaction of *finding things.*'[37] They are variously a 'centre of interpretation,'[38] or potentially a 'communication medium,' in and of themselves.[39] For some, archives engender a kind of disciplinary melancholy in that purgatorial present 'between the not-yet-known and the what-has-once-been.'[40] Others see them as fragmented sites that provide 'keys that unlock the door of historical background,' and yet we are often called upon to be wary (or at least aware) of their 'seductive' qualities and their 'daunting and distracting amount of information.'[41] Despite this, or, depending on whom you consult, precisely because of it, they are 'an everyday tool' of a radical politics that is 'inherent, practiced, and natural.'[42] An archive's work, broadly conceived, is to manage the 'morass of memory,'[43] where 'the remnants of someone's life' are 'numbered, filed, boxed and preserved for future generations.'[44] But maybe, in the end, they are just 'gigantic machines,' which are more or less organized, more or less agential, and we should therefore be more or less suspicious of them.[45]

An archive is both a 'temple and a cemetery.'[46]

In other words, archives are many things to many people—and the figuration of 'the archive' is by now overgeneralized to the point of requiring consistent clarification—a process Carolyn Steedman calls 'archivization.'[47] The preceding collage of statements, culled from a variety of disciplines, is meant to destabilize any singular claim that I, or any other, might wish to make about archives—while also pointing to some of the tropic language attached to writings focused on archives and archival work. How to make sense of it all? 'Theory is the price we pay,' historian Kathy E. Ferguson muses, 'to bring order to the archive, to make the archive speak.'[48] Indeed, theory supplies one answer for what many authors grapple with (and I am no exception), which is the unruliness of even the most strictly ordered archive. Part of this is our own fault: in accessing archives we enliven them with meaning, bringing their contents into the present—often in ways their creators and caretakers didn't intend. The historian Joan Wallach Scott worried about precisely this when she quipped, 'I'd rather be dead than misread.'[49] Archives consistently dramatize this prospect, and this is what my discussion of the appearance of the color yellow across the Leather Archives & Museum's collections (Chapter 4) is meant to reveal.

The implications of all this should be clear, that archives present a set of problems for any methodology that would seek to enact a standardized procedure for accessing, describing, and interpreting them. After years of research, the only thing I can say with any great certainty is that each archive I have encountered during the course of my research for this book is utterly unique, and demands to be taken on its own terms, with a set of methodological tools that can meet and convey its particular abilities to invigorate body and mind. Therefore, throughout this book I generally eschew the metonymic linguistic figuration of 'the archive,' even though many of the authors I have cited above use exactly this phrase. I find it difficult to use because it compresses that which only expands, singularizing that which I've always found to be multiple. By concertedly discussing particular leather archives and putting them in concert with contemporary artistic projects invested in accessing, reconstructing, repurposing, and exhibiting leather archives, I endeavor to impart some of the strangeness and satisfactions that accompany the temporal shifts at the foundation of archival work.

This book is caught between two disciplinary forms of thinking about archives. On the one hand, art historians have long used archives as sites for producing original scholastic contributions within their field(s). Roland Barthes describes the figure of the author in the popular imaginary as someone who nourishes a text, and in art history, at least operationally, archives are conceived of in similar terms—as nourishing scholarship.[50] Ernst van Alphen lays this out more schematically: 'what fieldwork is to anthropology, the archive is to art history.'[51] The importance of the archive is undeniable, even when it is unremarked upon within the body of an art historical text. Archives are, in this view, *things* that must be disciplined or mastered in some way to serve an author's argument (how's that for some academic S/M?!). This is especially true of the ways in which young scholars are made to account for the originality of their work, and it has now become a rite of passage for young art historians to consult archives, navigating and ultimately taming their pleasures and frustrations, thereby proving themselves methodologically worthy.

Hayden White, for example, famously critiqued this common understanding of archives as repositories of evidence, ceremoniously turned into 'the fictions of factual representation.'[52] Echoing White's suspicions, Alexander Nemerov counsels that when making sense of archival materials in all their heterogeneity (a process he usefully names 'envisioning the past') a historian needs to take both 'intuition and sentiment' into account.[53] Some of the research that grounds this text has been guided, at least in its early stages, by affect and by my desire to be transparent to a reader about how I have encountered, processed, and assembled the pieces of various archives that run throughout this study.

Queer, feminist, and POC projects are painfully aware that narrow definitions of archives increase the probability that racialized, queer, and gender non-conforming lives will be left uncollected, and therefore unconsidered in traditional scholarship. David Román, in writing about those who are 'undocumented and unexamined,' proposes that many archives exist 'in oral history, cultural memory, social ritual, communal folklore, and local performance—media that do not rely on print culture for their preservation.'[54] He adds, 'because this archive often exists outside of official culture, it is frequently undervalued or even derided. So too are most efforts to recover it.'[55] Whenever possible I have attempted to be attentive to these more embodied forms of archiving (what Diana Taylor terms a repertoire); when, for example, Viola Johnson identifies her primary role as a griot, or storyteller in the West African tradition, it means, in turn, that oral storytelling takes a central role in my chapter dedicated to her and her mobile archive.

Román's text could be included as part of the recent 'archival turn' in feminist and queer studies, which has usefully revisited what the archive might be, giving it new epistemic life. The net results of these inquiries have reinforced that we might better think of archives as a *function* or *mode* more than a discrete object of study. This view has an impact on how histories are told or written, and Leah DeVun and Michael Jay McClure point out that feminist and queer approaches to archival work can render the historical imagination 'promiscuous, multiple, and beyond finite reckoning.'[56] Making archives more inclusive by expanding upon what could potentially be considered an archive—often done by connecting the 'stuff' of particular archives to embodied knowledges of activism, pleasure, and the somatic sensorium of the body—means that feminist and queer enframings of archives thus claim a kind of radicality by centering performances of collecting, of reading and researching, of writing and presenting as enunciative and connected acts.

For some critics, this kind of openness pushes the utility of 'the archive' as an analytic category toward the outer limits of comprehensibility.[57] But in many ways this gesture of expanding what an archive might be makes sense as an outgrowth of feminist, queer, and critical race scholarship and methodologies which not only name, but reimagine the operations of power in a way that might better center the lives of folks who are consistently denied its claim. In attempting to reroute what exactly an archive can be, feminist, queer, and brown and/or black historians and archivists respond directly to the problem laid out in 1977 by historian Howard Zinn, who remarked that 'the most powerful, the richest elements in society have the greatest capacity to find documents, preserve them, and decide what is or is not available to the public.'[58] The connection between those with the power to access or assemble archives and what archives hold are enduring interests for queer, feminist, critical race, and postcolonial scholars.[59]

Many of the queer, feminist, and POC critiques and expansions of 'the archive' foreground the reading of one particular text, Jacques Derrida's *Archive Fever*, which, since its oration (in French) in 1994, and its publication (in English) in 1995, has continued to position the archive as an important node of power. Carolyn Steedman handily summarizes the common use of Derrida's argument: 'the *arkhe*—the archive—appears to represent the *now* of whatever kind of power is being exercised, anywhere, in any place or time.'[60] Power is apparent in the institutional act of collecting, and in the ways in which one might access and subsequently make use of the contents of an archive. But for many people working in queer, feminist, brown and/or black archives, this analysis is not enough. An archive's control is evident in its lists of collections, but also in those collections that go unaccessioned, unaccessed, and/or remain unprocessed. In most cases this is the result of sustained and systemic financial precarity. This is an important facet of power's relation to archives and archival processes, but one that reveals extrinsic cultural undervaluation and stigma, rather than the power that might issue forth from an archive.

Steedman, who carefully reviews Derrida's text and its implications, usefully rebuts Derrida's worry that archives are only accessed to find originary knowledge, and thus to solidify formations of power. She writes,

> Archives hold no origins, and origins are not what historians search for in them. Rather, they hold everything in medias res, the account caught halfway through, most of it missing, with no end ever in sight. Nothing starts in the Archive, nothing, ever at all, although things certainly end up there.[61]

And so we might also attach to archives and archival work a certain queer quality that José Esteban Muñoz writes about as the 'not yet here,' an open-ended proposition that whatever the work, it is never complete.[62] In thinking through the various archives discussed in this book, I take the advice of Kathy E. Ferguson, 'to give less credence to the alleged "eternal war" and more to the riotous unpredictability of archival excess.'[63] Ferguson's work, and the writings of Arjun Appadurai and Ann Cvetkovich, have helped me to conceive of the archive as 'an aspiration rather than a recollection.'[64] Therefore I see my task as drawing out the affective dimensions of archival work as a politically necessary activity tied to building non-reproductive genealogies of/for creative life.

If there is a gripe I have about queer, feminist, and critical race evaluations of archives, it is that beyond a cursory footnote, or a few lines in the acknowledgments of a book-length study, rarely are the labors of archivists and other cultural workers deeply acknowledged and made meaningful within the structure of an author's arguments. I am also guilty of this. Archivists are the ones most likely to have the clearest sense of the value, organization, and quotidian drudgery of archives, yet it is rare in the realm of academic publishing to hear directly from them. Kate Eichhorn and Lisa Darms, one an academic and the other an archivist, lay this out in a special issue of *Archive Journal* dedicated to 'Radical Archives.'[65] There, Eichhorn notes that academic peer-review limits and discourages participation from archivists, who may not be as invested in enduring scrutiny from non-archivist peers unfamiliar with the ins and outs of archival practices.

Although this might seem like inside baseball, the implications are profound. Grappling with this asymmetry requires some soul-searching on the part of academics who value and privilege certain kinds of knowledge over others, certain kinds of credentials over others, and certain kinds of labor over others. In my view this can lead to an abstract thinking about archives, declarations of archives as only unruly, or as simply another configuration of power/knowledge. By subscribing to these beliefs about archives, uninformed by the experiences of those who work within them day in and day out, I worry about inadvertently missing an opportunity to remark on all the ways that archivists interrupt these staid, and often falsely dichotomous, patterns of thinking. Yet archivists do this all the time, anyway, regardless of whether they are given credit or voice in academic journals and presses: sometimes through the important act of guiding a researcher toward content that would complicate pat theses, sometimes through the process of strategizing acquisitions, and through acts of refusal. Because archivists aren't typically given the room and/or resources in academic journals and presses to grapple with the philosophical implications of the knowledge projects they continue to contribute to (because, as mentioned above, archives face the pernicious and continual existential threat of defunding within educational and/or governmental organizations obsessed with tangible deliverables), their voices remain underconsidered. And this near silence from archivists intellectually impoverishes scholars and archivists alike.

One of the primary questions this study asks, and attempts to answer in turn, is: what are the archives of gay and lesbian leather history, and where can they be found? The easiest response would be to simply point to the Leather Archives & Museum (LA&M) in Chicago and be done with it. The LA&M is a grassroots institution founded upon the personal collections of the Chicago activist and photographer Chuck Renslow, and his primary partner for many years, Dom Orejudos. Since its founding in 1991, its scope has grown considerably, as evidenced by its mission, which is 'the compilation, preservation and maintenance of leather lifestyle and related lifestyles [including but not limited to the gay and lesbian communities], history, archives and memorabilia for historical, educational and research purposes.'[66] By its own count it has over 15,000 books, journals, and periodicals and over 60 collections of personal, organizational, and conglomerate records, all related to 'leather, fetish, kink, and alternative sexualities.'[67] I will return to this archive in Chapter 4—but for now I will only remark that it remains a focal point and a pilgrimage site for many leatherfolks and historians of leather cultures and communities.[68]

Gay and lesbian leather history also exists in archives dedicated to preserving a broader swathe of LGBTQ communities. Archives such as the GLBT Historical Society (San Francisco), ONE National Gay and Lesbian Archives (Los Angeles), and the Lesbian Herstory Archives (Brooklyn) contain the personal collections of leathermen and leatherwomen, as well as some organizational records and periodicals of interest to anyone wishing to write about leather communities and cultures. In such venues one is always highly aware of how leather sexualities are understood within the context of broader LGBTQ histories—an enframing that can be useful, but which can also minimize or subdue the voices and lives of gay and lesbian leatherfolks within the larger panoply of LGBTQ life.

Leather history is also kept hiding in plain sight—places where more official histories are told, often exclusive of any sustained consideration of leatherfolks and their lives. For example, two such places are the film collections of the Museum of Modern Art and UCLA's film and television archive, each of which contains a print of Fred Halsted's 'sadomasochistic, fistfucking faggot film,' *L.A. Plays Itself* (1972).[69] How it came to be in these collections, and how it was re-edited to conform to its archival home in MoMA, is the subject of my eighth chapter.

The sites where leather histories are kept and displayed—places that I'll be calling leather archives, regardless of whether their primary mission is to save or preserve leather history—are incredibly fragile. Feminist, queer, and black and brown perspectives on archives have consistently pointed to their contingent nature, highlighting their elusive and volatile conditions, aligning all too predictably with the fugitive and denigrated identities they purport to preserve.[70] Martin Manalansan, for example, in focusing on the 'un-HGTV dwellings of several undocumented queer households,' describes such archives as 'atmospheric states of material and affective disarray,' and understands that even the most quotidian object is subject to removal and destruction.[71] Leather archives, in particular, are at risk because the contents they often hold align with what Michel Foucault terms 'subjugated knowledges,' meaning 'a whole set of knowledges that have been disqualified as inadequate to their task or insufficiently elaborated: naïve knowledges, located down the hierarchy, beneath the required level of cognition or scientificity.'[72] In plain terms, this means leather archives face very real challenges in making an appeal for funding, space, and scholastic attention. They are more susceptible and vulnerable to changes in political regimes, to the destructive forces of natural disasters, and/or to the slow drain of resources, capital, and perhaps more ephemerally, engaged publics.

That there are leather archives at all is a miracle. There is an archive that disappeared during the course of my research, and it now serves as an example of the existential threats that many leather archives face, no matter their scale, or national or institutional affiliation. In the first years of researching this book I repeatedly consulted a website called 'The Colors of Leather.' The brainchild of Gwen Hardy, a Florida leatherwoman and a bootblack title-holder, 'The Colors of Leather' was a clearinghouse for information on leather clubs, their colors and pins, prominent leather artists, bars from across the United States, and a timeline of important events in the histories of gay and lesbian leather communities (amending Tony DeBlase's well-meaning, but sometimes specious, 'Leather History Timeline'). I found it indispensable for its hodge-podge of information—what year a particular club was founded, for example, or a random scan of a bar advertisement. It had the same mission that many archives do, which was 'to preserve the past, present, and future.'[73] What it gave me was a sense of the enormous scope and growth of leather communities during the 1970s; and so I came to value it for its gestalt as much as for the specifics I gleaned. I took its existence for granted.

One day I opened the website and was greeted with the following message: 'This web site is no longer being maintained. Any questions sent to the email may or may not be answered. Sorry but I am burned out.'[74] Admitting to being brought up short by the onerous demands of the archival labor she was performing—unpaid and unthanked—Hardy thought it better to cut her losses. By the summer of 2009 Hardy had taken the website down entirely. Today only a portion of the site's vast holdings can be retrieved from digital archeological sites such as the Internet Archive's 'Wayback Machine.' Hardy's decision to stop, and to let her site lapse, flew in the face of my (at the time, admittedly limited and naïve) conception of digital durabilities, as well as in opposition to Hardy's own utopic framing of her project as 'never-ending.'[75]

I miss 'The Colors of Leather' and feel loss in the wake of its disappearance. This is the death that Derrida described as underpinning archival enterprises, the potential death that foregrounds so many appeals for funding.[76] This book, in many ways, is a product of this and other archival absences in the present, of the possibility of archival extinction in the future, and of the pasts almost certainly already lost. For some this anecdote might provide proof that the only stable kind of archive exists within the framework of an institution and away from the whims of any single person; but that line of thinking misses what was so useful about Hardy's site, and specifically why it was valuable as a non-institutionally-affiliated archive. Arguably the Leather Archives & Museum in Chicago had much of the same material in its holdings, but at the time its website was difficult to navigate, and the amount of hard data was limited. I was a cash-strapped graduate student who couldn't afford a plane ticket to Chicago. Poverty circumscribed my research. Hardy's website was a much-needed, accessible, and dependable source in the face of the ever-present obstacles of class and mobility.

Gwen Hardy's 'Colors of Leather' is also a continuing reminder for me as to the presence and importance of women within historical leather communities. Throughout the period discussed in this book women played sometimes central and vital roles within leather social spaces, publications, and archives. Take, for example, the musician and performance artist Camille O'Grady, who performed her incantatory poems (the most famous of which was entitled 'Toilet Kiss') in some of the most popular leather bars on the East and West Coasts. With her friend and lover Robert Opel, she was a constant presence at his gallery, Fey-Way Studios, and did much to support and encourage her fellow artists. In Los Angeles, Jeanne Barney was the first editor of *Drummer* magazine, and in her role she crystallized the form and content of a magazine that would enjoy a nearly 25-year print run. In San Francisco, Cynthia Slater integrated women into the private, and up until that time exclusively male, play space of The Catacombs. She also founded the Society of Janus, a pansexual leather education and support group.[77] Agnes Hassett, who married Chuck Renslow so that he could obtain a liquor license for his bar the Gold Coast, was a frequent patron and continuing presence in the early history of the well-known leatherspace.[78] The list could go on; but the upshot is that women were a solid, if sidelined presence in leather communities that are often imagined (when they are imagined at all) to be only male. I have tried to be attentive to this as I assembled the roster of artists and archival sources for this book, while also remaining careful of overstating the presence of women in mostly male spaces and groups.

Archival dramas are always unfolding, even as this book goes to press.

On a Saturday in January 2019, Jeanne Barney's estate went up for sale. Many who knew Barney were caught off-guard, and only heard about the sale after the fact. The estate sale company that put Barney's belongings up for auction generated advertising copy to lure in potential buyers. It read (in part):

> 500+ RECORDS, MOSTLY ROCK & ROLL […] ACOMA PUEBLO POTTERY COLLECTION, STERLING SILVER, COSTUME JEWELRY, TONS OF VINTAGE CLOTHING, SHOES, PURSES … OVER 400+ VINTAGE SWEATERS OMG!!, […] 1000 BOOKS, LOTS OF EPHEMERA & VINTAGE POSTERS, ONE ENTIRE ROOM OF GAY/BONDAGE ARTWORK, PHOTOS, BOOKS, VINTAGE 1970'S ORIGINAL GAY MOVEMENT T-SHIRTS, MAGAZINES ETC. … OUR CLIENT WAS AN EDITOR FOR THE ADVOCATE MAGAZINE, DRUMMER MAGAZINE, NFL, TV GUIDE AND OTHER PUBLICATIONS. […] PACKED HOUSE AND EVERYTHING MUST GO.

There are many reasons why a person like Barney (whom the estate sale copy names as 'our client') would hire a company to liquidate their belongings, not the least of which is the real need for money in a country that still does not guarantee affordable physical and mental healthcare for the people within its borders (citizens and non-citizens alike). Or, like Hardy, she could just be over it—done with living in a house filled with accumulated stuff. It turned out that Barney had died, and her remaining family had put her effects up for public auction. Over the next few next weeks I was by turns enraged, disappointed, and mournful over the way in which Barney's archive of leather materials (including original photos, copy-edited issues of *Drummer* magazine, typescripts, and other ephemera) was put up for sale by eBay sellers named buffyoz123 (who posted his haul on Instagram a short time after he visited the estate sale) and sweetpickensvenice_2 (figure 1.2). A small group of friends and admirers of Barney (myself included) tried to purchase as much of her dispersed collections as possible, so that they might be donated to an archive. Because many eBay sellers were in Los Angeles and its surrounds, I visited a couple of them in their homes and tried to communicate my worry that Barney's effects would disperse and disappear, leaving a profound gap in our understanding about her role in coalescing national leather readerships and communities. My despair was all-consuming: didn't these people know what they were *doing*—the transaction became an obscenity too much to bear. For women, brown and black people, poor people, disabled people, and those otherwise on the margins of national politics and LGBTQ communities, this mourning and rage is more of the same; a story that illuminates whose lives are (de)valued and by whom.

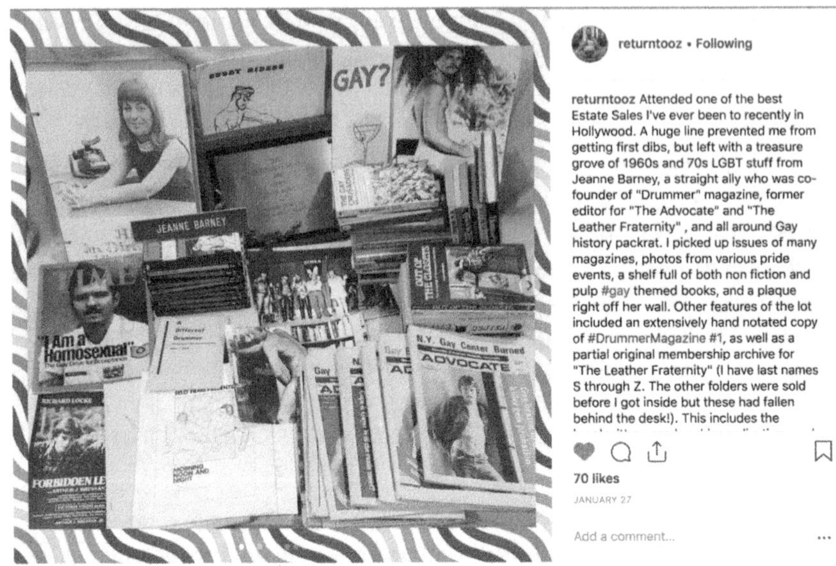



**1.2**     Returntooz, Attended one of the best… *Instagram*, 27 January 2019

## The unlaid

Nostalgia is a powerful drug and I am wary of any overly utopic rendering of leather history—those that represent these sexual livelihoods of the past as unmarked by pervasive societal homophobia, or pre-AIDS leatherspaces as uncomplicated sexual playgrounds. A comic published in *Drummer* magazine has reminded me many times of the vicissitudes of social sexual life (figures 1.3–1.5). Simple in concept and baroque in its execution, the comic trails a man across three multi-paneled pages as he cruises the busy interior of a leather bar. The artist, Bill Ward, virtuosically represents dozens of figures in each panel, densely populating a sexualized space whose actual architectural limits are only faintly discernible. Most are dressed in leather, although this is hardly the only fashion on display.

Our protagonist in this, and nearly every other comic drawn by Ward and published in *Drummer*, is a man by the name of Drum. He is depicted twice on the first page, once with his back to us, and once again to the right of the title, an autonomous figure in a well-defined panel. Ward enables his reader to follow Drum through this playspace by endowing him with a consistent iconography—a '10' patch on his left arm of his jacket, and the line of fringe running horizontally along the back of it.

The three pages of Ward's comic are a riot of bodies in motion. Men pose and dance, but hardly anyone—save for the bartender on the first page—is

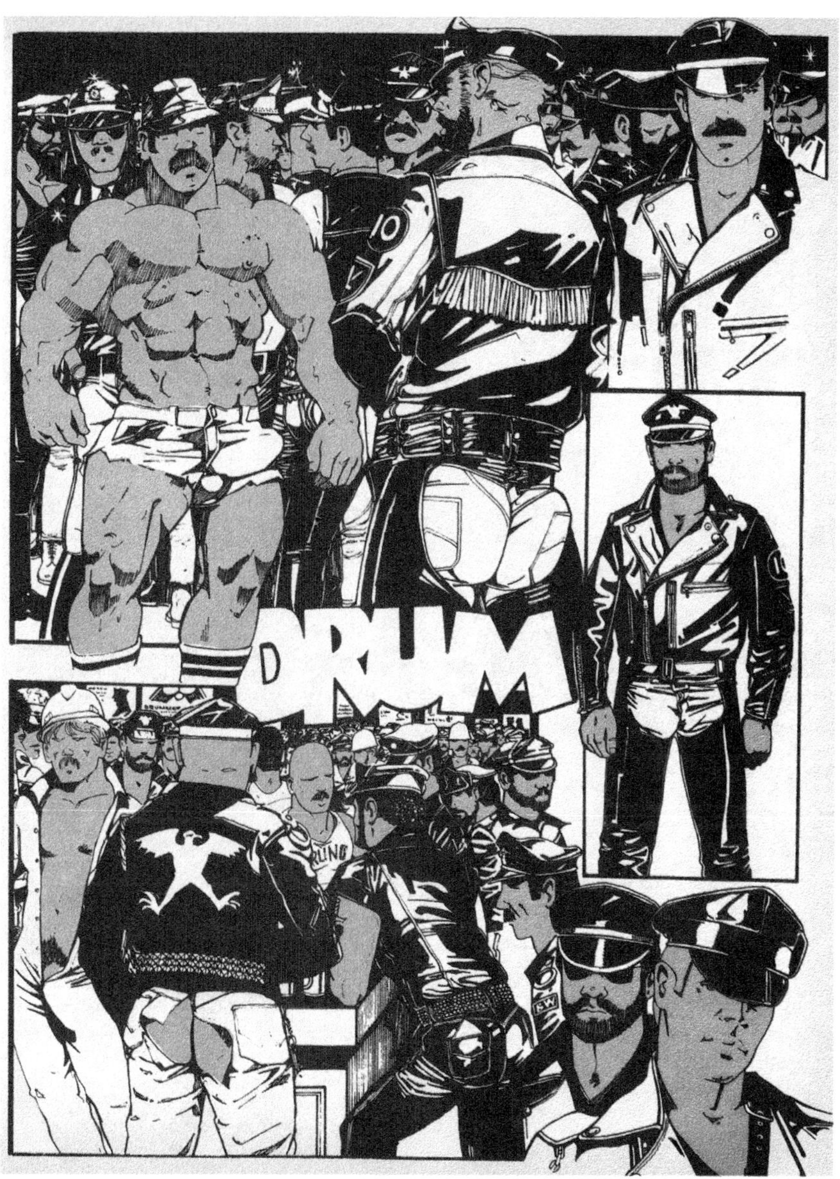

Bill Ward, 'DRUM', *Drummer*, 10:87 (1985), 91–3    **1.3**

talking. This is a noisy but wordless space, a place for looking and being seen, a site for what John Paul Ricco has dubbed the art of the consummate cruise.[79] Later, in the bathroom, signaled by an erect cock logogram on the door, Drum stands with other men at a piss trough. Lights blaze and cocks drip,

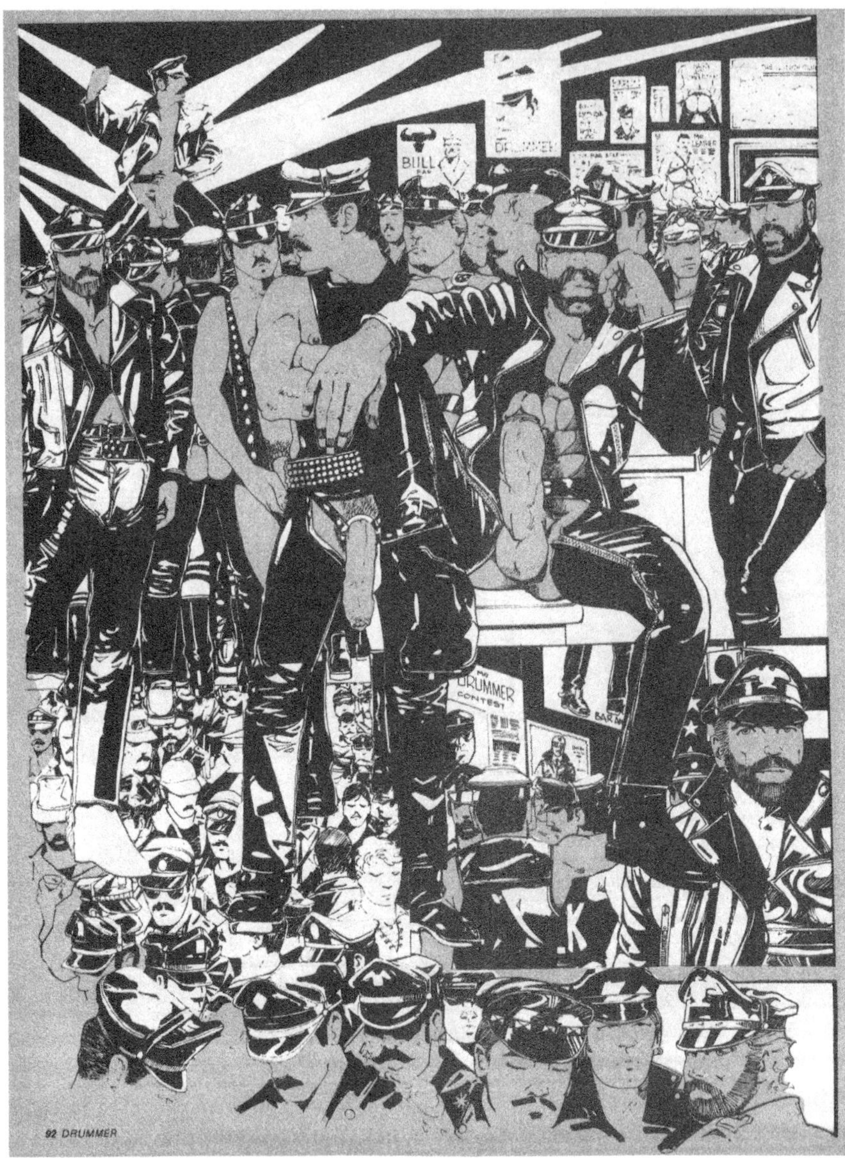



**1.4**     Bill Ward, 'DRUM', *Drummer*, 10:87 (1985), 91–3

and Drum looks out at a reader, as though cementing some pre-established bond. He continues his cruise from panel to panel, navigating the bodies that creep in from other registers. Sometimes we see him at a distance, and at other times close up, reminding a viewer of the uneven proximities and spatial

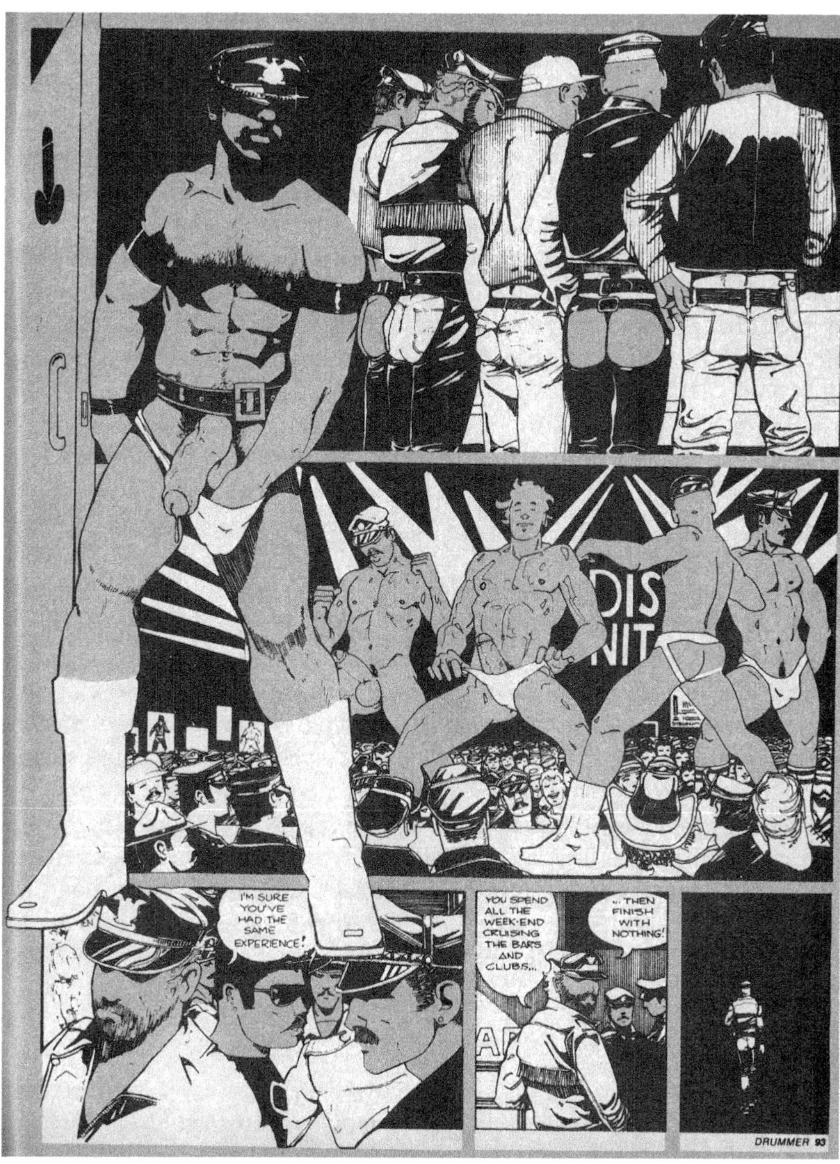



Bill Ward, 'DRUM', *Drummer*, 10:87 (1985), 91–3    **1.5**

choreographies of nightlife. We are deep in the cruise—navigating the tricky terrain of a bar. In this space filled with music and bodies, psychic and sensorial sagacity is shaken loose and reordered, evincing the 'voluptuous panic' of *ilinx* (vertigo) that Roger Caillois names as one of the four forms of play.[80]

But all of this sensuous abandon is upended in the final panels—a revelation foreshadowed by the boxed-in appearance of Drum on the first page. Here, in the last three frames, Drum breaks the fourth wall and speaks directly to the reader. He addresses us as a close confidant. He says, 'I'm sure you've had the same experience! You spend all weekend cruising the bars and clubs … then finish with nothing!' The last frame depicts Drum walking away; black of night, void exaggerating solitude.

Ward's comic is a reminder to be critical of fantasies solely filled with fucking—to cut off at the knees nostalgia about the 'glory days' of yore. It may be obvious, but not everyone got laid. Filled with loneliness and frustration (see those exclamation points?), Drum walks away from the action and goes home. His response comes at the end of a string of unlucky nights, and represents a puncture in an otherwise seamless and pervasive leather fantasy. This runs counter to nearly every other Drum comic, where he is the center of remarkable sexual escapades that confirm him (and in this he is like his forebear, Tom of Finland's Kake) as the embodiment of everything a leatherman should be: handsome, bearded, muscled, and with a closet at the ready and filled to the brim with leatherwear.

These pages were a departure, in both story and structure, for Ward and his beloved character. Going home alone is not how Drum's night is supposed to end, and subsequently not how the hypersexualization of leather culture is typically understood. This is why, in my mind, Ward's comic is an opportune object to think with, in that it entreats more questions and a more sophisticated sense of the lived experiences of leatherfolks. We know about the people who got laid—their tales are told in the pages of *Drummer*, in the pins dotting a leather vest or sash—but what of those who did not? Drum leaves the cacophonous space of the leather bar in the middle of the night, alone, not because he can't get laid (150+ comic strips prove otherwise), but because this time he doesn't. For whatever reason the explanation never comes, and likely never will.

✳ ✳ ✳

The chapters that follow track the archival repositories of U.S. gay and leather histories and the projects of contemporary artists interested in those histories. Two of the chapters are dedicated to institutions whose sole mission is to collect, preserve, and display leather history—the Leather Archives & Museum in Chicago (Chapter 4) and the mobile Carter/Johnson Leather Library (Chapter 6). In each case I detail the archives' history and propose methodologies for reading their collections. In the first instance I take the hanky code, a color-coded sexual signaling system developed in the 1970s, as an organizing principle, reading the appearances of the color yellow across the collections of the Leather Archives & Museum. What emerges, I hope, is a sense of both the depth and breadth of the institution's collections as well as a more atmospheric portrait of leather lifeways, particularly those tied to the erotics of pissing (golden showers).

In the chapter dedicated to the Carter/Johnson Leather Library I invest in the oral tradition that structures Viola Johnson's understanding of her role as archivist, librarian, and 'grandmom' to an array of 'kinklings.' As she travels the country with a group of POC familiars, setting up her books, magazines, and assorted ephemera at regional and national leather conferences, she transmits a notion of a shared history, and the importance of archival practices. Her leather pin sash (a piece of leatherwear of Johnson's own devising) is a metonymic object, serving as a reminder of these histories, some of which were experienced directly by Johnson, and others not. I read out the historical significance and context of one of the hundreds of pins and buttons that appear on and around her sash, a black button reading 'The L.A.P.D. FREED the Slaves April 10, 1976'—memorializing an especially devious police raid on a charity slave auction held at the Mark IV bathhouse in Los Angeles. The racial and sexual underpinnings of the auction provided the necessary cover for the L.A.P.D. to bust the event, and the ensuing public relations campaign waged by a broad coalition of Los Angeles' gay and lesbian communities ensured that the L.A.P.D. and their homophobic police chief, Ed Davis, were publicly shamed for their waste of public dollars.

The rest of the chapters here present archival collections (many nested within non-leather instutitions) in both direct and indirect coordination with contemporary artists' works. In the following chapter I discuss an installation by the artist collective Die Kränken, who made use of the Blue Max MC papers (owned by ONE National Gay and Lesbian Archives) in a wide-ranging installation that purported to translate a theatrical production staged yearly by the Southern California bike club. Performed for a group of familiars, the Blue Max's play, entitled 'The Rose of No Man's Land,' dramatized a popular early twentieth-century song extolling the bravery of Red Cross nurses during World War I. Invoking history, care, and relationality Die Kränken invests in the nurse as a figure of historical stewardship, providing intergenerational healing in the face of enormous loss.

Chapter 3 discusses the recent reception of Tom of Finland, perhaps the best-known artist within and outside of leather communities, and asks the question: What does Tom of Finland's work gain when it is collected by major art museums in the U.S.? In exploring a potential answer to this question, I explore the historical influences, reception, and distribution of the artist's work; a history that is now primarily told by the Tom of Finland Foundation. The Foundation, located in the artist's former Silver Lake house, is the primary subject of a video by artist Patrick Staff entitled, fittingly, *The Foundation* (2015). In it Staff explores the limits of normative leather masculinities, through verité footage of the daily activities at the Tom of Finland Foundation and a constructed studio scenario, wherein Staff and an older gay man (roughly fitting the 'gay daddy' type) dance together and explore their differences.

Dean Sameshima's painted appropriations of erotic connect-the-dots activities that appeared in the pages of *Drummer* magazine are the subject of the fifth chapter. Reading his interest in 'numbers' broadly—including the direct reference to John Rechy's 1967 novel of the same name—I discuss the work's capacities to frustrate handy readings of archival objects. One work in particular, *Bodily Fluids* (2007), is emblematic of these efforts, and I use it to read across Sameshima's oeuvre.

Attachments to historical and archival sources are at the center of Nayland Blake's 2012 installation at the Yerba Buena Center for the Arts in San Francisco. Entitled *FREE!LOVE!TOOL!BOX!*, the components of the exhibition, as well as one of its public programs (a piercing demonstration conducted by Blake and their long-time friend Lolita Wolf), is the subject of the seventh chapter. As a young artist Blake was a participant in San Francisco's changing arts landscape, and their relation to the massive development of the South of Market area (where YBCA is located, and also where many leather bars and institutions were established), structures their questions about San Francisco's leather histories. By literally attaching themselves to a reproduction of an iconic mural decorating one of San Francisco's earliest leather bars, Blake stages an encounter with history, exhorting their audience to participate in claiming historical networks and lineages.

Chapter 8, the longest in the book, discusses Fred Halsted's pornographic leather film, *L.A. Plays Itself* (1972), and traces its editing and exhibition history. Composed of two dissimilar sections—one focusing on urban cruising and fisting and the other on penetrative sex in the natural grandeur of the Malibu hills—Halsted switched the ordering of these sections in the early years of the film's exhibition history. His 1974 screening at the Museum of Modern Art in New York, and his subsequent gift of *L.A. Plays Itself* and two other films to the museum, became a point of pride for the director, who likely reordered his film to suit the narratives of Modernism pervasive in the museum's permanent collection installations. Decades later the artists A. K. Burns and A. L. Steiner watched Halsted's film in MoMA's screening room and it inspired the pair to make their own pornographic art video (also now owned by MoMA), *Community Action Center* (2010). In a sequence of polymorphously perverse scenes, Burns and Steiner directly quote *L.A. Plays Itself* and incorporate its gritty, experimental attitude with lesbian-feminist, queer, and trans performers and sources, assembling a heterogeneous pornographic archive in the process. In tracing the exhibition history of *Community Action Center* I argue that the switching and flexibility that marked the early exhibition history of *L.A. Plays Itself* is also a conceptual hallmark of the relationships depicted in Burns and Steiner's film and its earliest installations.

My conclusion ruminates on two series by the artist Monica Majoli, who sees her works as both 'surrogates' and 'envelopes' for herself. In luminous oil paintings of gay male piss orgies and monochromatic gouaches of suspended rubbermen, Majoli visualizes leather scenarios that center the masochist's body and experiences. Each extrapolates from an archive of lived experiences of an other, forcing Majoli to grapple with questions about subjectivity and sociality. Like Majoli, these paintings have become, over the years, 'surrogates' and 'envelopes' for myself as I think about the work of collecting, archiving, and entering the scene of leathersex. Connection begets connection, and the transmission of sexual gifts is discussed as a hallmark of leather and queer cultures more broadly.

Taken together I hope that the chapters of this book consistently ask a viewer to consider archives and contemporary artistic practice in dialog with one another—thereby situating how archives come to matter in the present, and how the present is unquestionably shaped by the past.

## Notes

1 Carolyn Steedman, 'Culture, Cultural Studies and the Historians,' in Simon During (ed.), *The Cultural Studies Reader*, 2nd edn (London: Routledge, 1999), p. 48.

2 Michel Foucault, 'Nietzsche, Genealogy, History,' in *Aesthetics, Method, and Epistemology*, vol. 2 of *Essential Works of Foucault, 1954–1984*, ed. James D. Faubion (New York: New Press, 1998), pp. 386–7.

3 Currently in the United States something can be considered obscene if it passes the three-pronged test developed from the 1973 Supreme Court case *Miller v. California* (413, U.S. 15, 24–25). Using imprecise terms such as 'average person' and 'contemporary adult community standards,' it holds that if the matter under question, as a whole 1) 'appeals to prurient interests,' 2) 'depicts or describes sexual conduct in a patently offensive way,' and 3) 'lacks serious literary, artistic, political, or scientific value,' then it will be considered obscene and thus illegal. Famously, sadomasochism was one of several kinds of sexual activity (including 'homoeroticism,' 'the sexual exploitation of children,' and the more generic 'individuals engaged in sex acts') specified for disqualification for funds disbursed from the National Endowment for the Arts, the national arts funding program for visual and performing arts. For more, see Section 304(a) of the Interior Department and Related Agencies Appropriation Act, 1990 (Pub. L. No. 101–121, 102 Stat. 701, 741, 20 U.S.C. § 954).

4 Raymond Williams, 'The Analysis of Culture,' in Charles Harrison and Paul Wood (eds.), *Art in Theory: 1900–1990* (Oxford: Blackwell, 1992), p. 716.

5  Ibid.

6  As part of the global URBN group of brands (which includes Urban Outfitters and Anthropologie), Free People imagines its customer in the following way: 'a 26-year-old girl, smart, creative, confident and comfortable in all aspects of her being, free and adventurous, sweet to tough to tomboy to romantic. A girl who likes to keep busy and push life to its limits, with traveling and hanging out and everything in between. Who loves Donovan as much as she loves The Dears, and can't resist petting any dog that passes her by on the street.' Free People, 'Our Story,' https://www.freepeople.com/help/our-story (accessed 10 October 2018).

7  Chelsea White and Jennifer Pearson, '"I'm Ready to Get Extreme!" Taylor Swift Explains her Bizarre Harness Accessory as Fans Question her Fashion Choice,' *DailyMail.com*, 18 June 2015, http://www.dailymail.co.uk/tvshowbiz/article-3130856/I-m-ready-extreme-Taylor-Swift-explains-bizarre-harness-accessory-fans-question-fashion-choice.html (accessed 10 October 2018).

8  Ibid.

9  Ibid.

10  Victor M. Rios and Patrick Lopez-Aguado, '"Pelones y Matones": Chicano Cholo Perform for a Punitive Audience,' in Arturo J. Aldama et al. (eds.), *Performing the US Latina and Latino Borderlands* (Bloomington, IN: Indiana University Press, 2012), p. 384.

11  Roy Martinez, email correspondence with author, 20 November 2018. The artist continues: 'For me it also referenced tha overall "bondage" black and brown people navigate under white supremacy … and in particular when it comes to identity … whats imposed … whats erased … whats accepted … whats deconstructed and made anew with its remnants … being assigned male at birth … also has it kind of bondage to masculinity. It's def really complex … but l like how it could mean a singular thing to one … but also tha multifaceted histories within a material/collective memory.'

12  Gayle Rubin with Judith Butler, 'Sexual Traffic,' *Differences*, 6:2+3 (1994), pp. 78–9.

13  Roy Martinez, email correspondence with author, 20 November 2018.

14  Elizabeth Freeman, *Time Binds: Queer Temporalities, Queer Histories* (Durham, NC: Duke University Press, 2010), p. 144.

15  George Chauncey, *Gay New York: Gender, Urban Culture, and the Making of the Gay Male World 1890–1940* (New York: Basic Books, 1994); and Lillian Faderman and Stuart Timmons, *Gay L.A.: A History of Sexual Outlaws, Power Politics, and Lipstick Lesbians* (New York: Basic Books, 2006). I am also abstaining from doing this work because I know it is forthcoming in books from Gayle Rubin and Robert Bienvenue.

16  Gayle Rubin, 'The Valley of the Kings: Leathermen in San Francisco, 1960–1990,' Ph.D. diss, University of Michigan, 1994, p. 37.

17  Richard von Krafft-Ebing, *Psychopathia Sexualis* (1886) (Burbank, CA: Bloat Books, 1999). See Amber Jamilla Musser, *Sensational Flesh: Race, Power, and Masochism* (New York: New York University Press, 2014), pp. 3–8; Margot Weiss, *Techniques of Pleasure: BDSM and the Circuits of Sexuality* (Durham, NC: Duke University Press, 2011), p. 11; Larry Townsend, *The Leatherman's Handbook*

(New York: The Other Traveller, 1972), pp. 250–2; Pat Califia, 'Beyond Leather: Expanding the Realm of the Senses to Latex' (1984), in *Public Sex: The Culture of Radical Sex* (Pittsburgh, PA: Cleis Press, 1994), pp. 190–8; Harry Oosterhuis, 'Richard von Krafft-Ebing's "Step-Children of Nature": Psychiatry and the Making of Homosexual Identity,' in Vernon A. Rosario (ed.), *Science and Homosexualities* (London: Routledge, 1997), pp. 67–88; and Romana Byrne, *Aesthetic Sexuality: A Literary History of Sadomasochism* (London: Bloomsbury Academic, 2013).

18  American Psychological Association, *Diagnostic and Statistical Manual of Mental Disorders*, 5th edn (Washington DC: American Psychological Association, 2013). While this is a happy change from previous DSMs where sadism and masochism were listed as diagnosable paraphilias, the current edition is still not yet subtle enough. For example, in regards to what it terms 'Sexual Sadism Disorder,' it states that 'acts of sexual sadism may occur with a consenting partner, or as assault on a nonconsenting individual.' The gulf between these two is wide, non/consent being the fault-line between a leather scene and violent sexual assault. The entry for 'Sexual Masochism Disorder' seems to be more circumspect, as it remarks that, 'if the patient is not experiencing anxiety, guilt, shame or other negative feelings related to masochistic sexual desires, it is considered a sexual interest, not a disorder.' Still, in this definition there is no admission that it might be the person's cultural, religious, familial, and social contexts that may be the cause of such 'negative feelings.' Some queer theorists have turned this around—as Ann Cvetkovich asks, 'What if depression, in the Americas at least, could be traced to histories of colonialism, genocide, slavery, legal exclusion, and everyday segregation and isolation that haunt all our lives, rather than biochemical imalances?' Ann Cvetkovich, *Depression: A Public Feeling* (Durham, NC: Duke University Press, 2012), p. 115.

19  Sigmund Freud, *Three Essays on the Theory of Sexuality (the 1905 edition)*, trans. Ulrike Kistner (New York: Verso, 2017). See also Byrne, *Aesthetic Sexuality*, p. 6 n.1.

20  T. R. Witomski, [review of *Urban Aboriginals*, by Geoff Mains], *DungeonMaster*, 26 (August 1984), p. 9.

21  Weiss, *Techniques of Pleasure*, pp. vii–xii.

22  Ibid., p. vii.

23  See Geoff Mains, *Urban Aboriginals: A Celebration of Leathersexuality* (San Francisco: Gay Sunshine Press, 1984), pp. 27–31; Jennifer Tyburczy, 'Queer Curatorship: Performing the History of Race, Sex, and Power in Museums,' *Women and Performance*, 23:1 (2013), pp. 107–24; and J. Lorand Matory, *The Fetish Revisited: Marx, Freud, and the Gods Black People Make* (Durham, NC: Duke University Press, 2018).

24  See J. L. Austin, *How to Do Things With Words*, 2nd edn, ed. J. O. Urmson and Marina Sabisà (Cambridge, MA: Harvard University Press, 1975).

25  Lauren Berlant and Lee Edelman, *Sex, or The Unbearable* (Durham, NC: Duke University Press, 2014), p. 56. Throughout her dialog with Edelman, Berlant uses the terminology of the scene, which in her view is 'a setting for actions, a discontinuous space that appears navigable for moving around awkwardly, ambivalently, and incoherently, while making heuristic sense of what's becoming-event'

(pp. 99–100). I find that language to be incredibly useful because scene also prag-
matically names the consensual agreement between sexual partners regarding the
genre of their interaction: for example, a cop scene, or a sailor scene.

26 Linda Williams, 'Pornography, Porno, Porn: Thoughts on a Weedy Field,' *Porn
Studies*, 1:1 (2014), pp. 24–40.

27 bell hooks, *All About Love: New Visions* (New York: Perennial, 2001); Sarah
Ahmed, 'In the Name of Love,' *borderlands*, 2:3 (2003), http://www.borderlands.
net.au/vol2no3_2003/ahmed_love.htm (accessed 10 October 2017).

28 Pat Califia, 'A Secret Side of Lesbian Sexuality,' *The Advocate*, 27 December
1979.

29 For more, see Elaine Scarry, *The Body in Pain: The Making and Unmaking of the
World* (Oxford: Oxford University Press, 1985).

30 Michel Foucault, 'Sex, Power and the Politics of Identity,' in *Ethics: Subjectivity
and Truth*, vol. 1 of *Essential Works of Foucault, 1954–1984*, ed. Paul Rabinow,
trans. Robert Hurley (New York: New Press, 2001), p. 170. See also Musser,
*Sensational Flesh*, pp. 8–14.

31 Leo Bersani, *Homos* (Cambridge, MA: Harvard University Press, 1995), p. 89;
Mains, *Urban Aboriginals*, p. 30.

32 Robert B. Marks Ridinger, 'Things Visible and Invisible: The Leather Archives &
Museum,' *Journal of Homosexuality*, 43:1 (2002), p. 3.

33 Leo Bersani, 'Is the Rectum a Grave?,' *October*, 43 (winter 1987), special issue,
'AIDS: Cultural Analysis/Cultural Activism,' ed. Douglas Crimp, p. 197; Foucault,
'Sex, Power,' p. 163.

34 Berlant and Edelman, *Sex*, p. 104.

35 James T. Hong, 'The Suspicious Archive, Part I: A Prejudiced Interpretation of
the Interpretation of Archives,' *E-flux*, 75 (September 2016), www.e-flux.com/jour
nal/75/67172/the-suspicious-archive-part-i-a-prejudiced-interpretation-of-the-
interpretation-of-archives (accessed 10 October 2017).

36 Michel Foucault, *The Archaeology of Knowledge* (New York: Pantheon Books,
1972), p. 129.

37 Carolyn Steedman, *Dust: The Archive and Cultural History* (New Brunswick, NJ:
Rutgers University Press, 2002), pp. 83, 10.

38 Thomas Osborne, 'The Ordinariness of the Archive,' *History of the Human
Sciences*, 12:2 (1999), p. 52.

39 Siva Vaidhyanathan, *The Anarchist in the Library: How the Clash between Freedom
and Control is Hacking the Real World and Crashing the System* (New York: Basic
Books, 2004), p. 121.

40 Michael Ann Holly, 'What is Research in Art History, Anyway?,' in Michael Ann
Holly and Marquard Smith (eds.), *What is Research in the Visual Arts? Obsession,
Archive, Encounter* (Williamstown, MA: Sterling and Francine Clark Art Institute,
2008), p. 10. Holly cites Maurice Blanchot's thoughts on writing and dread to arrive
at this formulation. For more, see Maurice Blanchot, 'From Dread to Language,' in
*The Station Hill Blanchot Reader: Fiction and Literary Essays*, trans. Lydia Davis,
Paul Auster, and Robert Lamberton (Barrytown, NY: Station Hill Press, 1998), pp.
343–58.

41 Elizabeth Bakewell, William O. Beeman, and Carol McMichael Reese (eds.), *Object, Image, Inquiry: The Art Historian at Work* (Santa Monica, CA: J. Paul Getty Trust, 1988), pp. 22–3.

42 Kim Schwenk, 'Another World Possible: Radical Archiving in the 21st Century,' *Progressive Librarian*, 36:7 (2011), pp. 51–8, 110.

43 Martin F. Manalansan, 'The "Stuff" of Archives,' *Radical History Review*, 120 (fall 2014), p. 103.

44 Anna McNally, 'All That Stuff! Organising Records of Creative Process,' in Judy Vaknin, Karyn Stuckey, and Victoria Lane (eds.), *All This Stuff: Archiving the Artist* (Faringdon: Libri Publishing, 2013), p. 107.

45 Pierre Chaunu, quoted in Michel de Certeau, *The Writing of History*, trans. Tom Conley (New York: Columbia University Press, 1988), p. 74; Matthias Winzen, 'Collecting—So Normal, So Paradoxical,' in Ingrid Schaffner and Matthias Winzen (eds.), *Deep Storage: Collecting, Storing, and Archiving in Art* (Munich: Prestel, 1998), p. 31.

46 Achille Mbembe, 'The Power of the Archive and its Limits,' in Carolyn Hamilton et al. (eds.), *Refiguring the Archive* (Dordrecht: Kluwer, 2002), p. 19.

47 Steedman, *Dust*.

48 Kathy E. Ferguson, 'Theorizing Shiny Things: Archival Labors,' *Theory & Event*, 11:4 (2008).

49 Joan Wallach Scott, *The Fantasy of Feminist History* (Durham, NC: Duke University Press, 2011).

50 Roland Barthes, 'Death of an Author,' in *Image – Music – Text*, trans. Stephen Heath (London: Fontana, 1977), p. 145.

51 Ernst van Alphen, 'Archival Obsessions and Obsessive Archives,' in Michael Ann Holly and Marquard Smith (eds.), *What is Research in the Visual Arts? Obsession, Archive, Encounter* (Williamstown, MA: Sterling and Francine Clark Art Institute, 2008), p. 65.

52 Hayden White, *Tropics of Discourse: Essays in Cultural Criticism* (Baltimore, MD: Johns Hopkins University Press, 1978), p. 122.

53 Alexander Nemerov, 'Seeing Ghosts: *The Turn of the Screw* and Art History,' in Michael Ann Holly and Marquard Smith (eds.), *What is Research in the Visual Arts? Obsession, Archive, Encounter* (Williamstown, MA: Sterling and Francine Clark Art Institute, 2008), pp. 13–32.

54 David Román, 'Visa Denied,' in Joseph A. Boon et al. (eds.), *Queer Frontiers: Millennial Geographies, Genders, and Generations* (Madison, WI: University of Wisconsin Press, 2000), p. 351.

55 Ibid.

56 Leah DeVun and Michael Jay McClure, 'Archives Behaving Badly,' *Radical History Review*, 120 (fall 2014), p. 124.

57 Kate Eichhorn, 'Introduction: Radical Archives,' *Archive Journal* (November 2015), www.archivejournal.net/essays/radical-archives (accessed 10 October 2017).

58 Howard Zinn, 'Secrecy, Archives, and the Public Interest,' *Midwestern Archivist*, 2:2 (1977), pp. 20–1. Zinn's proposed fix was to 'open all government documents to the public,' and to insist that archivists 'take the trouble to compile a whole new

world of documentary material, about the lives, desires, needs, of ordinary people' (p. 27).

59 Both Gayatri Spivak and Ann Laura Stoler, for example, have described how archives are often places where sanctioned histories of a state's own deployments of power are housed, reiterated, amended, obscured, and obliterated. Ann Laura Stoler, *Along the Archival Grain: Epistemic Anxieties and Colonial Common Sense* (Princeton, NJ: Princeton University Press, 2008); Gayatri Chakravorty Spivak, 'The Rani of Sirmur: An Essay in Reading the Archives,' *History and Theory*, 24:3 (1985), pp. 247–72; Antoinette Burton (ed.), *Archive Stories: Facts, Fiction, and the Writing of History* (Durham, NC: Duke University Press, 2005); Rebecca Comay (ed.), *Lost in the Archives* (Toronto: Alphabet City Media, 2002); Francis X. Blouin (ed.), *Archives, Documentation, and Institutions of Social Memory: Essays from the Sawyer Seminar* (Ann Arbor, MI: University of Michigan Press, 2006).

60 Steedman, *Dust*, p. 1.

61 Carolyn Steedman, 'Something She Called a Fever: Michelet, Derrida, and Dust,' *The American Historical Review*, 106:4 (2001), p. 1175.

62 José Esteban Muñoz, *Cruising Utopia: The Then and There of Queer Futurity* (New York: New York University Press, 2009), p. 1.

63 Ferguson, 'Theorizing Shiny Things.'

64 Arjun Appadurai, 'Archive and Aspiration,' in Joke Brouwer and Arjen Mulder (eds.), *Information is Alive* (Rotterdam: V2 Publishing/NAI Publishers, 2003), pp. 14–25; Ann Cvetkovich, *An Archive of Feelings: Trauma, Sexuality, and Lesbian Public Cultures* (Durham, NC: Duke University Press, 2003).

65 Eichhorn, 'Introduction: Radical Archives.'

66 Leather Archives & Museum, 'Mission Statement,' www.leatherarchives.org/about_.html (accessed 10 October 2017).

67 Leather Archives & Museum, 'Frequently Asked Questions,' www.leatherarchives.org/faq.html (accessed 10 October 2017).

68 Tyburczy, *Sex Museums*, p. 178.

69 Paul Alcuin Siebenand, 'The Beginnings of Gay Cinema in Los Angeles: The Industry and the Audience,' Ph.D. diss., University of Southern California, 1975, pp. 200–1.

70 Daniel Marshall, Kevin P. Murphy, and Zeb Tortorici, 'Editors' Introduction: Queering Archives: Historical Unravelings,' *Radical History Review*, 120 (fall 2014), p. 1.

71 Manalansan, 'The "Stuff" of Archives,' 94–5.

72 Michel Foucault, 'Two Lectures' (1976), in *Power/Knowledge: Selected Interviews and Other Writings, 1972–1977*, ed. Colin Gordon (New York: Pantheon Books, 1980), p. 82.

73 Gwen Hardy, 'Home,' *Colors of Leather*, Wayback Machine, 20 January 2007, https://web.archive.org/web/20070120072147/http://www.colors-of-leather.com:80 (accessed 10 October 2017).

74 Ibid.

75 Gwen Hardy, 'About,' *Colors of Leather*, Wayback Machine, 20 January 2007, http://colorsofleather.com:80/About/about.htm (accessed 10 October 2017).

76 Jacques Derrida, 'Archive Fever: A Freudian Impression,' trans. Eric Prenowitz, *Diacritics*, 25:2 (1995), p. 51.

77 Carol Truscott, 'San Francisco: A Reverent, Non-Linear, Necessarily Incomplete History of Its SM Community,' *Sandmutopia Guardian*, 8 (1990), pp. 6–12.

78 Tracy Baim and Owen Keehnen, *Leatherman: The Legend of Chuck Renslow* (Chicago: Prairie Avenue Productions, 2011), pp. 100–1.

79 John Paul Ricco, 'The Art of the Consummate Cruise and the Essential Risk of the Common,' *FeedBack*, 4 February 2016, http://openhumanitiespress.org/feedback/sexualities/the-consummate-cruise-2 (accessed 10 October 2018).

80 Roger Caillois, *Man, Play, and Games*, trans. Meyer Barash (Urbana, IL: University of Illinois Press, 2001), p. 23.

# 2    The work of the Master's hand

*Archives*: *Band of Bikers* album; ONE National Gay and Lesbian Archives
*Artwork*: Die Kränken, *Sprayed with Tears*, 2017

The art dealer, poet, and found photography collector Scott Zieher tells the following story:

> In the spring of 1999, I was doing laundry when my superintendent greeted me coming off the basement elevator with the estate of a man who'd recently passed away. He had apparently lived on my floor, though I'd never seen any elderly neighbors. I had no prior knowledge of this apartment, but its contents lay before me in a human-sized pile on the garbage room floor. It was an entire, pristine life in the trash, and I couldn't resist the temptation to rescue something.[1]

Zieher took (his preferred terms are 'rescued' and 'found') from this anthropomorphically scaled pile two items: a stamp collection and an album of photographs. While he deemed the former merely 'a novice collection … [adding] up to a couple hundred dollars worth of valid U.S. postage,' he felt differently about the album. Thumbing through it he encountered photographs of a 'man with [a] trim, lean body,' surrounded by motorcycles and 'the beautiful smiles of the men with whom he shared his weekend.'[2] Assessing this second collection, Zieher strikes a more lyrical tone, identifying its value as evidence of a 'celebration of communion in a heady time.'[3] One collection's value is clear as an impoverished commodity of exchange, while the other is more nebulously cultural, an example of a social way of life that Zieher sees as all but vanished. As Zieher readily admits later in his essay introducing the album and its subsequent exhibition at his Manhattan gallery, 'I am a better collector than scholar. I decided that research wouldn't enhance the mystery. The images are evidence enough.'[4]

This refusal to investigate the life of his deceased neighbor is a convenient, and I would argue dangerous, position to take, not because of its explicit anti-intellectualism (which is alarming), but for the absolution that such a stance

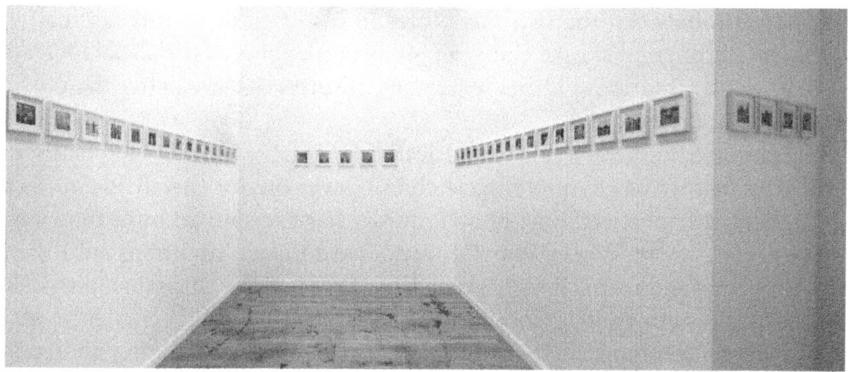

Installation of 'Band of Bikers,' Western Exhibitions, Chicago (20 May–2 July 2011)          **2.1**

affords Zieher in putting the effects of his neighbor's life up for exhibition and sale. In other words, he gives himself a pass to do what he eventually does with the album, which is to separate the photographs from their (admittedly anarchival) adhesive pages, frame them one by one, and hang them on his gallery's walls (figure 2.1). Even if the photographs were not for sale, pulling the contents of this deceased man's photo album into the realm of art commerce unquestionably changes the shape and force of the potential interpretations of the photographs, and as a consequence short-circuits the need to evaluate whether they should even be exhibited as 'art' in the first place. Zieher's transformative gesture reveals his understanding of the photographs as the aesthetic effluvia of a communal loss that he can only understand in general terms—collapsing the death of his neighbor onto the broader traumatic loss of gay men in the years since the AIDS pandemic started. As Zeiher recently conveyed to me: '[the album] was a great fantastic mystery.'[5] Specificity or extended analysis is foreclosed so that Zieher and his various publics (the visitors to his gallery, the readers of his book) might ultimately project whatever they wish upon the photographs. It is easier to idealize and essentialize a past than to reckon with its knotty particularities, the numerous profound and fecund strangenesses that interrupt and refute as much as they bolster and support.

Here is why this is a problem: as a result of Zieher's framing, the men in the album's photographs become merely *emblematic* of a whole way of life and culture, and in this generalized state there is no apparent need to do right by them or their living kin, to set them within a specific historical and social context. Perhaps this is the methodological fork in the road where historians and poet-gallerists diverge, but I don't necessarily think it has to be this way. In pitting poetry and history needlessly against one another, Zieher has missed an exceptional opportunity to suggest a more sensitive relationship between the two modalities in his exegesis of this fascinating group of photographs. Bike clubs, an important engine of the social lifeways and aesthetic programs of broader leather cultures, deserve better than to be shrouded in mystery.

Historians, anthropologists, and leatherfolks have written eloquently of the early history of gay motorcycle clubs. Gayle Rubin, Guy Baldwin, Jack Fritscher, and, most recently, Jenn Tyburczy have recounted how 'returning service men [from World War II] translated military traditions into their civilian social and sexual lives,' in the form of motorcycle clubs that 'provided leather men with mobile social spaces where they could experience new risk-taking adventures partially modeled after the experiences they shared in war.'[6] As one of the most important pieces of the assemblage of early leather social institutions, motorcycle clubs provided their members the unique opportunity to physically escape the repressive police regimes of cities. Gay motorcycle clubs would often sponsor annual or semi-annual 'runs,' inviting neighboring clubs to ride out into the wilderness and participate in a weekend of motorcycle competitions, ceremony, eating, drinking, socializing, and fucking. As described in *Wheels*, the newsletter/magazine of the New York-based Cycle MC, a run is 'a full weekend of planned activities outside of a major city (home base), where the entire group is housed and lives as a closed commune and independent of urban activity.'[7]

The first motorcycle club, the Satyrs of Los Angeles, was founded in 1954, and by 1972 Larry Townsend (author of *The Leatherman's Handbook*) estimated that over a dozen similar clubs were in existence in the Los Angeles area alone.[8] Their activities pierced the propriety of gay and straight presses, which all viewed the motorcycle clubs in extreme terms—as the 'far-out fringe of the "gay" world.'[9] Eventually, leather aesthetic programs, which included everything from vestments to DIY sex furniture, extended into a host of institutions that welcomed leathermen irrespective of whether they owned a motorcycle—bars, clubs, bathhouses, and private play spaces. The growth of motorcycle clubs as well as broader gay and lesbian leather communities in the U.S. during the 1960s and 1970s was both remarkable and exponential.

But none of this history, which I have only sketched out schematically, is present in Zieher's discussion of his dead neighbor's album. By crowing about his refusal to research the album, Zieher avoids coming to terms with the ethical implications of his steal. First among these questions, I'd argue, must be the very real conditions of the death of his neighbor, which predicates Zieher's scavenging. The potential reasons why his dead neighbor's possessions were thrown into the garbage rather than picked up by family members or friends, donated to local archives, or to the living members of the motorcycle club (the Praetorians of New York City, founded in 1970) pictured in the photographs are left unexplored.

Perhaps Zieher's dead neighbor had no immediate kin—a not uncommon situation for gay men of the album owner's generation, who were more often than not physically, emotionally, and psychologically exiled by their families for their perceived transgressions against heteronormative sexual mores and familial structures; or perhaps the landlord felt an opportunistic compulsion to clean the apartment before any family arrived—also frighteningly common. Whatever the reason, as a result we will likely never know if Zieher's dead neighbor was planning to donate his materials to family (chosen or biological) or to an LGBTQ archive. We don't even know if there existed a will that might have stipulated such a thing.

In an interview publicizing the exhibition and book release of the photographs, Zieher remarked that while he planned to show the photos at his gallery and art fairs, he would be interested in 'donat[ing] a few of the photographs to select institutions where they might be best preserved and appreciated.'[10] As of this book's writing Zieher has not done this, but in suggesting that *a few* photographs be donated to archives Zieher reveals two things: his ambivalence about whether he should own the photographs in the first place, and his lack of understanding as to the significance of the album (*in toto*) he currently possesses. While his intentions are laudable, he overestimates the value of individual photographs, seeing them as removeable component parts of an album, whose gestalt would otherwise be crucial to any subsequent historical contextualization and interpretation. I don't want to be entirely critical of Zieher's treatment of the album he found; great credit is due to Zieher for rescuing the album from its imminent deportation to a landfill. But this is not enough. In the alchemical transition from his neighbor's property to a potential art commodity, he fails to imagine another, different life for the album. Why any of this didn't occur to Zieher is a mystery far greater than the one he attributes to the photographs themselves.

All of this is obscured by the aesthetics of Zieher's book, entitled *Band of Bikers*, which attempts to approximate the album's original format, and largely falls short on this count as well. With few exceptions the images are laid out one per page, on a ground that mimics an old album, tacky yellowed glue defining shallow horizontal ridges. Some images are reproduced at full-bleed, and this loosely tracks with a handful of photographs that were printed at a larger size by the album's original owner.[11] Zieher also reproduces three intertitle pages, preserving some of structure governing the album. In this way the book gives a partial sense of the photographs' initial context. These intertitle pages bear the names of annual events, runs put on by various MCs; Marathon (put on by the Spartan MC), Bass River (put on by the Cycle MC), and Leif Erikson (put on by the Viking MC, naturally). It is worth noting that none of these events were sponsored by the Praetorians, which was a fairly small club, the product of a breakout group of members from the Wheels MC.[12] Regardless, it is difficult, given Zieher's layout, to know whether the album's initial owner intended certain photographs to be seen in groups or clusters (the usual format for albums of this type). In isolating each image—uncoincidentally similar to how art is presented on museum and gallery walls—the particular social connections between friends, lovers, and club members are left obscured.

One man recurs in Zieher's photographs with some regularity, and this person Zieher suggests is the album's owner. He appears in various kinds of leather dress—casual (boots, T-shirt, and jeans), formal (leather cap, button-up shirt, and leather tie), and overtly erotic (boots, cap, and leather g-string). What is his name? Zieher doesn't say.

Still, some information can be gleaned from the photos themselves. In addition to the album's hunky protagonist and potential owner, a few men in the album wear vests emblazoned with a patch featuring a yellow geometric clover design on a black background (figure 2.2). Inside each of the four 'leaves' is a red letter, spelling out AMCC. The acronym stands for the Atlantic Motorcycle Coordinating Council, which was founded in 1969 and continues to provide support for its member clubs today.[13] This small detail suggests a more sophisticated institutional and organizational history of gay MCs; as regional and national groups were founded and organized to support ever-more interconnected fraternities of men, solidifying common social forms (the bike run, the beer bust) and aesthetic programs (club colors and innovations in leather dress). Alongside a burgeoning crop of nationally distributed leather periodicals (*Drummer* and *DungeonMaster*, for example), organizations such as AMCC did much to regionalize and nationalize leather culture and communities—hailing their members and subscribers into publics and imagined communities connected across state lines.[14] As well as instantiating and supporting the 'fraternity' that club members no doubt felt for one another, organizations such as the AMCC signaled the beginnings of the administrativization of leather, leading to what Margot Weiss has suggested is BDSM's current entrenchment within neoliberal ideologies.[15]

A final point about *Band of Bikers*: In telling of his find Zieher also reveals an attitude toward historical material as direct and unmediated historical evidence. As he would have it, the 'weathered, chartreuse photo album' and the photographs inside are self-evident. Why his dead neighbor's stamp collection doesn't also qualify for this heuristic model is a question that lingers. But as everyone from Raymond Williams to Joan Wallach Scott reminds us, such documents are never autonomous; rather they are contingent on the selective traditions and visions of those in the present reading them.[16] The men in these photographs are not emblematic of all motorcycle clubs, but

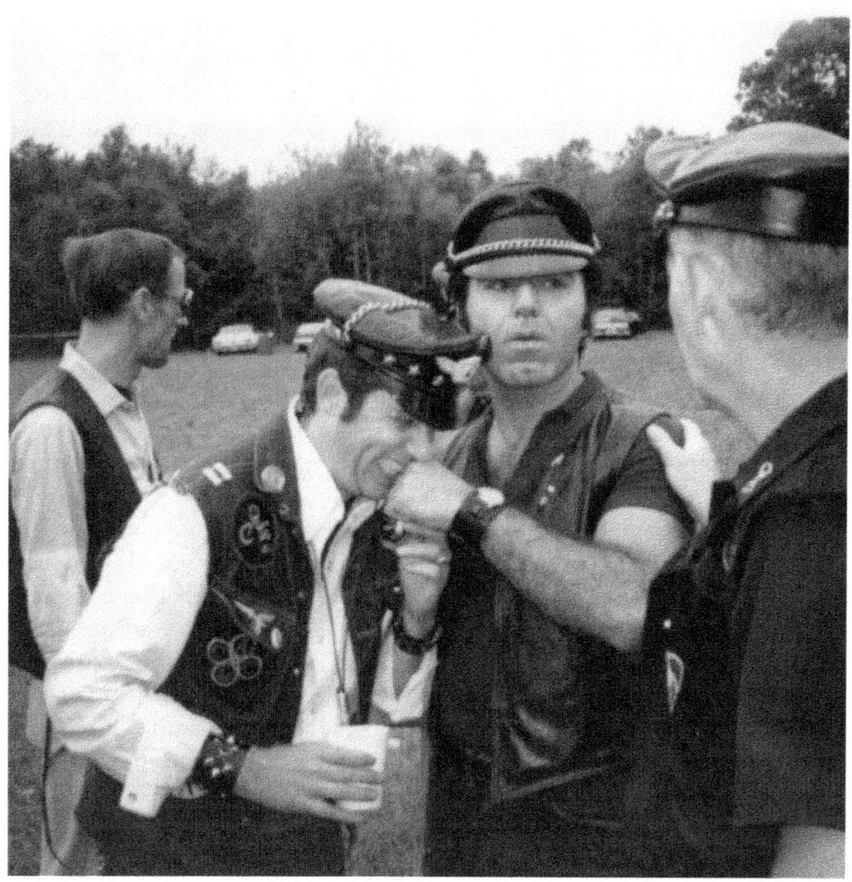

Photograph from *Band of Bikers*    **2.2**

are specific people with names, belonging to specific clubs with their own traditions.

Compounding the problem of historicity, clubs such as the Praetorians and the Blue Max MC of Los Angeles formed their own relationships to prior histories—oftentimes romanticized versions of autocratic or semi-dictatorial states of both recent and ancient vintage. The Praetorians' name, for example, is an allusion to the elite escort guard of ancient Roman emperors. Their primary symbol—an eagle with its wings outstretched and feathers splayed—appears with regularity in the photographs on banners, back-patches, and in one case tattooed across the chest of the ostensible owner of the album. The emblem is common among many historical European imperial entities, from the Byzantine and Holy Roman empires to modern Germany. The Blue Max MC, a roughly contemporaneous motorcycle club based in Los Angeles, also played fast and loose with history, taking the Prussian figurehead of Kaiser Wilhelm II as well as the famed German World War I fighter pilot Manfred Albrecht Freiherr von Richthofen (commonly known as the Red Baron) as symbolic and visual touchstones. While there is certainly a camp element to these choices (photographs housed in the Blue Max MC's collection at ONE National Gay and Lesbian Archives present the club's membership dressed in WWI-era Prussian costumes as well as in the more ubiquitous leather gear), there is also, undoubtedly, a reliance on patriarchal authority. Historical quotations of the kind made by the Praetorians and the Blue Max MC require attention, especially as to whether their masculine camping of history adds up to a critique of those historically repressive regimes (whose commonality is a hostility to all kinds of outsiders), a full-throated embrace of them, or, more likely, an ambivalent suspension between the two—in the words of Eve Kosofsky Sedgwick, 'kinda subversive, kinda hegemonic.'[17]

To really pressurize these histories and organizations, much more information and documentation is needed than the photo album itself provides. It is at this crossroads between the known and unknown, between the lost and found, that contemporary artists have made important and necessary interventions in the ways we approach such documents. The archive of the Blue Max MC was the subject of one such intervention, when, in 2017, the West Coast-based artist collective Die Kränken (German for 'the sick') sought to engage and recreate one of the club's most-beloved and long-standing traditions—a semi-yearly pageant known as 'The Rose of No Man's Land.'

Donated by Hal Hegge, an early Chancellor (leader) of the Blue Max MC, the bike club's archive is like many other organizational collections at ONE National Gay and Lesbian Archives. Spread across a number of boxes of various sizes, the collection contains administrative records (such as meeting minutes and correspondence), flyers for runs and beer busts, as well as photographs, slides, and videotapes of many of these same events. The collection also contains a box of realia—a kind of archival object that doesn't neatly fit into any of the previously mentioned categories, but is inclusive of things like costume pieces, awards, and trophies. Certain items, such as a group of cheeky Christmas cards made by Hegge, mark this collection as a partial and somewhat personal accounting of the history and activities of the club. For example, administrative records are most complete during the years Hegge sustained a leadership position within the club, and trail off in the years after he left the leadership. Blonde and barrel-chested, Hegge appears in many of the photographs throughout the collection, and therefore the collection tells us just as much about Hegge as the club he belonged to.

The Blue Max MC collection also contains a photo album assembled by Hegge. ONE's treatment of Hegge's album provides an instructive alternative to Zieher's handling the Praetorians album. While both the archivists at ONE and Zieher removed the photographs from their respective albums' adhesive backings, the photographs of Hegge's album are purposefully kept together in plastic sleeves. Where appropriate, the processing archivists (Rachel Roque and Loni Shibuyama) included printed scans of the original orientation of the photographs on the album's page, allowing any researcher to quickly reconstruct the vibrant interplay between photographs.

The members of Die Kränken no doubt saw this deconstructed album as they pored over the Blue Max collection in preparation for their 2017 exhibition at ONE. Commissioned by ONE's curator, David Evans Frantz, the centerpiece of Die Kränken's eventual installation was a single-channel video projection entitled *Sprayed with Tears* (also the title of exhibition). The video begins with Master Jones, played by erstwhile punk musician Jonesy (one of the members of Die Kränken), dressed in full leathers: cap, jacket, pants, boots, gloves, and aviator sunglasses (figure 2.3). He is seated in front of a painted backdrop of gray stones surrounding a hefty-looking door—a

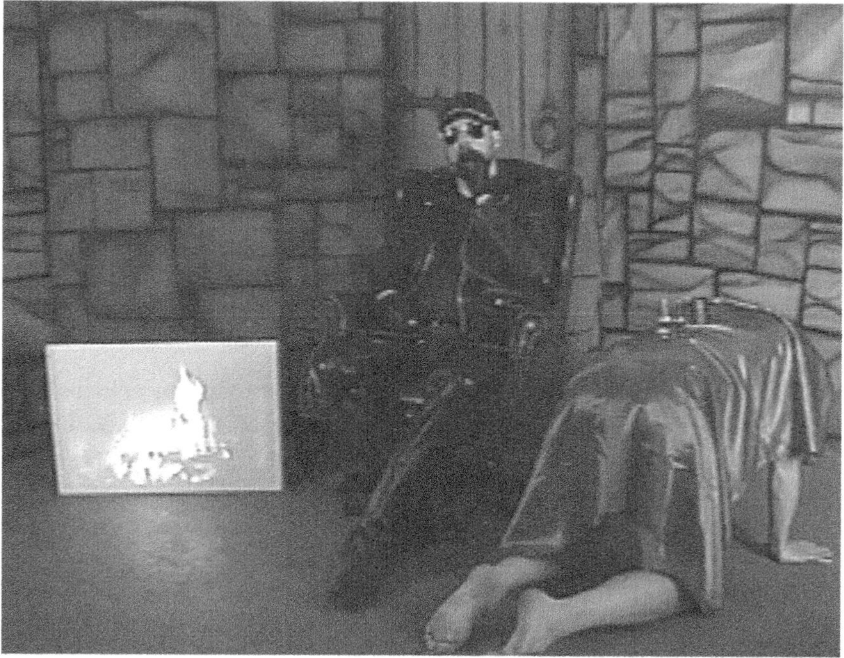

Die Kränken, video still from *Sprayed with Tears*, 2016, digital transfer of single channel VHS, 21 minutes     **2.3**

cartoonish imitation of a castle. Master Jones tokes his cigar. To his right a fireplace emits its kitschy glow on a small television screen. To his left a man draped in a red satin tablecloth does his best impression of a four-legged side-table, remaining motionless on his hands and knees. A cocktail and ashtray are purposefully placed on the straight of his back. Even before a word is spoken, *Sprayed with Tears* communicates that all interactions within the video will be deeply tied to the hallmarks of leathersexuality—a dynamic performance of dominance and submission, display and materiality. Fire crackles as ice clinks in the glass that Master Jones retrieves off the back of his slave. He addresses the audience directly: 'Hello, perverts.'

Hailing his audience and welcoming them into the realm of 'the sick,' this opening speaks to the collective ambitions of Die Kränken and to the stakes that anchor their critical representations of the particular leather histories they cite. Indeed, after greeting the viewer, the first thing that Master Jones relates is a kind of history: 'Gewgaws and gimcracks. Butt plugs and Tin Pan Alley. Legend has it, a long time ago, from 1967 to 1983 [*sic*] a group of distinguished leathermen known as the Blue Max Motorcycle Club gathered in the California High Sierras for the Annual Badger Flats Motorcycle Run.' It might be useful to relay here that all of the actors' voices in *Sprayed with Tears* are overdubbed, resulting in an almost imperceptible but nevertheless felt and sensual gap between the visual apprehension of the enunciative body and the language that tells, or speaks of, history. The Master breaks from his narrative to smack his human table with a riding crop ('Bad! Daddy has guests!'), and the table comically 'moos' in response. Theirs is a sexual scene whose rules we can only guess at. He continues:

> Each year the club reenacted the tale of a WWI fighter pilot, shot down in battle, and brought back to life by a red cross nurse. Entitled 'The Rose of No Man's Land,' each iteration of the play reflected the climate and happenings of the passing years. Tonight, Die Kränken presents their own version of the play, 'Sprayed With Tears.' Enjoy.

As Master Jones rubs his riding crop over the ass-crack of his table he asks, 'You want some of this?' and the screen fades to black as Die Kränken's reenactment begins.

You want some of this?

'This' is the crop. 'This' is history retold. 'This' is an archive performed inside the political present.

Master Jones is largely right. *Sprayed with Tears* reimagines 'The Rose of No Man's Land,' a play mounted yearly (sometimes more frequently) from 1968 to 1993 by members of the Blue Max MC. The play took its name from the title of a song written in the waning months of World War I by Jack Caddigan and James Alexander Brennan. Its subject is a Red Cross nurse (the eponymous 'rose of no man's land') who rescues wounded soldiers.[18] The song was as a constant touchstone for the Blue Max, often serving as musical accompaniment to the club's plays and ceremonies. Die Kränken, taking their cues from their historical source material, use the Caddigan/Brennan song twice in *Sprayed with Tears,* connecting the narrative structure of rescue and revival in the song to their own artistic ambulations within the archive. The song's last verse features an apotheosis of wartime care: 'It's the one red rose the soldier knows, / It's the work of the Master's hand; / Mid the War's great curse, Stands the Red Cross Nurse, / She's the rose of "No Man's Land."'[19] In the 1918 Caddigan/Brennan song the work of the Master's hand is imagined as a *deus ex machina* appearance of the nurse on the battlefield. In Die Kränken's video the work of the Master's hand is left more ambiguous.

The Blue Max MC was not the first organization of its kind in Los Angeles, but it was certainly unique among MCs for its striking visual and symbolic identifiers. Taking its name and insignia from a German and Prussian military decoration in use from 1740 through 1918, the Blue Max MC mined the visual culture and linguistics of World War I, often glorifying the reign of Kaiser Wilhelm II, who was a central figure in the events that precipitated the war. The Kaiser was also a noted antisemite.

Leather culture's reliance on the language of submission and dominance is perhaps by default ensnared in shared traumas such as war and slavery—even when the sense and the burden of such 'sharing' is often grossly asymmetrical among various groups. Unpacking this is foundational to understanding the intricacies of power play that have historically been both embraced and critiqued by scholars and leatherfolks alike.[20] It is therefore probably unsurprising that while there have always been leathermen and leatherwomen of color in MCs, as well as in non-motorcycle club leather groups, their membership numbers have been historically slim. Leather author John Preston confirms the idea that leather communities were racially or economically exclusive when he writes, 'for all practical purposes [the leather clubs are] composed of the same men in racial, class, and economic terms as Rotary and Lions in the straight world.'[21] For their part, the Blue Max MC seemed to largely ignore all but the most superficial aesthetics tied to their namesake. It is important to note here that while many early members of the Blue Max MC had fought or were otherwise involved in the war efforts of World War II, few, if any, of the club's members had been alive for the preceding world war. This historical distance meant that Blue Max members often abstracted the politics and the ethics of reproducing and glorifying the visual and material cultures of World War I. Die Kränken, in restaging the Blue Max theatrical production, do away with some of the club's troublesome iconography—a revisionary move  that evacuates the political ambiguity that accompanies certain archival material from the motorcycle club's collection.

'The Rose of No Man's Land' was thus an integral component of the Blue Max MC's visual identity, extending a broader deployment of World War I iconography. Divided into 'chapters'—with each new performance marking the next chapter—'The Rose of No Man's Land' essentially presented the same story every time. A typed list of the first twenty-eight chapters can be found among Hegge's archives. Producing up to four chapters a year, the Blue Max MC riffed on the play's basic premise by parodying literature and film (*Gone with the Wind* [ch. 17], *Dracula* [ch. 11], and *Oedipus* [ch. 21]) and fairy tales (*Snow White* [ch. 16] and *Hansel and Gretel* [ch. 18]). At its base the play is a story of heroism and derring-do, but in practice these performances were thinly veiled opportunities for club members to dress in drag and lip-sync to popular standards and showtunes, often with little or no relation to the overarching story.

The only dialog consistently employed in 'The Rose of No Man's Land' was spoken by a narrator whose task was to relate the two most dramatic moments of the structuring story—the pilot's collapse ('The proud WWI fighter pilot staggers … and still clutching his good conduct medal … sinks … slowly … to the ground…') and his eventual rescue ('But what's this? … out of the darkness … can it be? … a Red Cross nurse'). Relying on as few lines of dialog as possible allowed these performances to be more improvised than practiced, reducing the need for the performers to rehearse at great length and increasing the likelihood of audience participation in co-speaking the lines along with the narrator. This campy participation was a contrast to the highly choreographed events that usually preceded 'The Rose of No Man's Land': the presentation of club colors, official changes in club leadership, and yearly awards ceremonies.

But even though 'The Rose of No Man's Land' was spontaneous and some-what ad hoc, it was not an amateur affair. Key members of the Blue Max MC were employed in Los Angeles' film, music and theater industries, and so the play, although staged in the woods, featured professional theatrical lighting, costumes, sets, and sound design.

A VHS recording from 1993, one of the final years the Blue Max MC performed their long-running show, documents the preparations and per-formance of 'The Rose of No Man's Land.' The video begins with footage shot by Buddy (née Jim) Ball, a Southern California record producer and videographer whose papers are also held at ONE. Ball's POV cinematography illuminates the larger context of the club run. He interviews club members and is interviewed by them in return ('You're supposed to have one of the biggest dicks in L.A. County, is that true?'). He captures participants cooking, eating, and lounging by a large moving van that likely transported the stage sets, lighting, and sound equipment. He bugs the sound tech as he checks his levels. Ball even makes a personal appeal to one of the performers, cutting him down to size with a backhanded compliment: 'This is your swan performance tonight, you know, you've been on stage a long time and you've never known when to get off, but finally you do, so I want to congratulate you on finally waking up and realizing that.'

An intertitle abruptly announces the start of the show, which begins with a lip-synced rendition of Caddigan and Brennan's song. Faces of Blue Max members appear through porthole apertures in the stage set, to audible peals of laughter from the audience. A dance number follows, featuring half a dozen club members dressed up as World War I fighter biplanes, their arms operating as wings, decorated with the German black cross. The song they haphazardly dance to is 'Let's Go Flying,' from the 1991 musical *The Will Rogers Follies*. When the stage lights go out the edges of their arm-wings light up, and their dance becomes an abstract play of rising and falling dots—summer camp talent show meets avant-garde dance. As the song fades, the lights on each member's costume are turned off one by one until the stage is left in total darkness. The sounds of a plane dogfight (*BrrrrRRRRrrrr*; *RATTATTTAT*) and an eventual crash landing fills the darkness. One audience member tellingly and preemptively screams 'Crash!'

When the lights come up two angels dressed in blue babydoll dresses flutter out from the wings; one is recognizable from Ball's pre-performance segments. They lip-sync and dance to the 1968 novelty song by the Magistrates, 'Here Comes the Judge.' Their high-energy dance is more polished and successful than the previous number, and the audience begins to clap to the beat in response. The lyrics ('order in the courtroom / here comes the judge') are meant to describe the narrative onstage, as the downed fighter pilot has by this point stumbled out on stage to find himself before a judge. Is he dead or in some cosmic limbo? The situation is not made immediately clear, and frankly, it doesn't really seem to matter to anyone. As the court is called into session, the pilot and the two angels sit on the sidelines … and the floorshow begins.

What follows is a succession of nearly a dozen musical numbers, most featuring club members lip-syncing in drag. They run the affective gamut: some are charismatic and hold the audience in rapt attention; others are less so, and boredom prevails. An entire MC, the Constantines from San Francisco, get up and lip-sync a group number—they are the only performers who perform in their leathers. One of the acts is a duet of white men performing in yellowface as geishas, revealing and reminding any current-day viewer of the sanctioned racism that prevailed within the mostly white group of run participants.

The first of these variety acts is worth mentioning in detail because it exposes the way in which MC members were cognizant of the inherent contradictions of leather identities, often publicly presented within the strictly dyadic Master/slave paradigm. In this musical number two men appear on stage: one wears leather boots, chaps, and a black jock, and the other wears jeans, a flannel shirt, a pink scarf, a sparkly black baseball cap on his head and a gym bag on his arm. Two 'types' of gay man are put into relation in this number: one is the epitome of leather while the other is a fluff—a form of gay masculinity whose performances of effeminacy were often overtly or implicitly banned from leather events and spaces.[22] The leatherman stands still for most of the musical number as the more effeminately coded man preens over him, dressing him up as he might a mannequin, in a prop leather harness and vest. He lip-syncs to a song from the breakout musical of that year, Kander and Ebb's *Kiss of the Spider Woman*, which dramatized the relationship between two prisoners held in a Latin American prison—a homosexual window dresser and a Marxist revolutionary. In the musical, the window dresser, Luis Molina, sings a song ('Dressing Them Up') boasting of his professional aptitude for dressing mannequins in store windows. Midway through the song Molina recounts placing a Balenciaga scarf inside of a mannequin's purse, hiding it from direct display. Although questioned by his superiors about the effectiveness of such counterintuitive placement, Molina's aesthetic decision stands, affirming that what is hidden is perhaps more powerful than what is left out in the open. Onstage in the Blue Max's play, the man playing Molina takes the scarf from around his neck (one wonders if it, too, is a Balenciaga) and stuffs it in the jock of his model, charging the play with a ribald sexuality.

The revelation is transitive, as the performance remarks on the construction of leather identity and visual symbology through the radical incorporation of what it often purports to abhor—effete designer aesthetics and feminine gay presentation. This musical number succinctly counters the misapprehension that leather identities are inscrutable in their coding, and rigidly exclusionary in their gendered presentation. Performed in front of an audience of leathermen, this becomes an acknowledgment of the complexities inherent in the presentation of leathersexuality. As the mannequin comes to life and tangos with Molina, they together illustrate something about the codependence of otherwise seemingly oppositional gendered performances of gay masculinity and effeminacy

After the musical numbers have finished, the pilot gets up and lip-syncs to the 'Highest Judge of All' from Rodgers and Hammerstein's musical *Carousel*. The judge is affirmed to be St. Peter at the gates of heaven. As dramatic movie music fades in, the pilot stumbles to the ground and dies, leaving the metaphysical zone of the heavenly court and returning to the obdurately corporeal ground of the battlefield. Offstage, a performer with a mic begins to read the lyrics of 'The Rose of No Man's Land,' while an angel with a Red Cross nurse's hat runs in and begins to revive the pilot. She checks the pilot's pulse (through his crotch, naturally) and, finding the source of his ailment, administers a shot. She then sits on his face, and convinces the life back into him. After the customary bow, the entire cast of the show poses with a giant photograph of Kaiser Wilhelm II, and sings an encore rendition of Brotherhood of Man's 'United We Stand.'

Certain elements of this performance reappear, albeit transformed, in Die Kränken's *Sprayed with Tears*. In the video Jaime C. Knight (another collective member) plays the Soldier, a character modeled after the pilot in the 'Rose of No Man's Land.' He emulates the pilot's dance at the beginning of the Blue Max play. In the group's exhibition at ONE this connection was strikingly clear, for alongside Die Kränken's projected video a smaller monitor on the floor played synced elements from the 1993 Blue Max performance I've just described. Against a moonlit backdrop, Knight bounces along to Robin Gibb's 'Trash,' giving a viewer ample time to notice that his wings (arms) are decorated with the German black cross, and its edges illuminated with small white lights (figure 2.4). Perversely appropriated from the 1978 Sesame Street parody album *Sesame Street Fever*, the inclusion and repetition of Gibb's chorus ('Trash / I love it') amplifies the meanings of Die Kränken's moniker

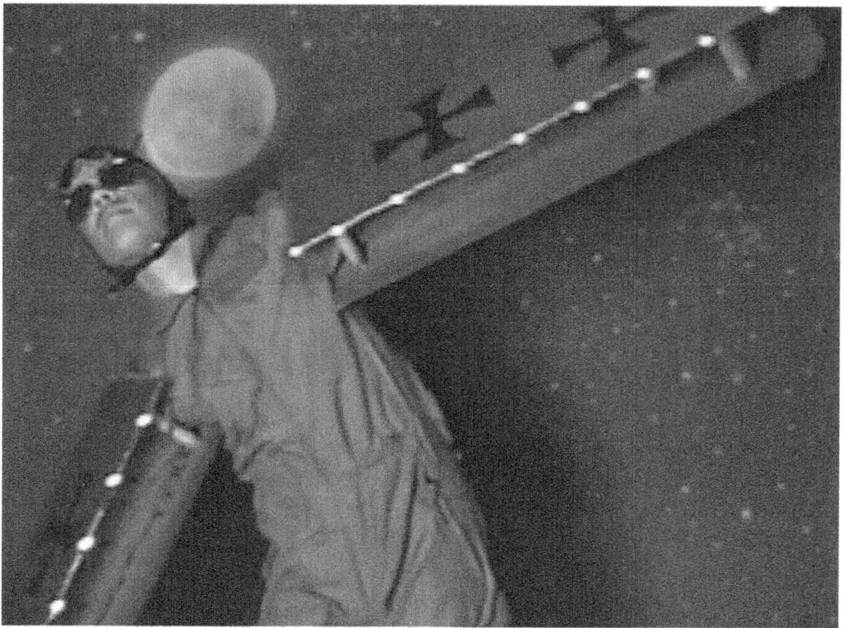

Die Kränken, video still from *Sprayed with Tears*, 2016, digital transfer of single channel VHS, 21 minutes    **2.4**

while also lovingly pointing to the collective's relationship to the Blue Max MC's 'The Rose of No Man's Land.'

Mirroring the politics apparent in the choreographed number from *Kiss of the Spider Woman*, Die Kränken subvert the strongly gendered roles often understood to be essential to gay leathermen and their sexual practices. The Soldier's primary interlocutor is a character dressed in a pink tutu and silver go-go boots named Rose (played by collective member and poet Luke Munson, who penned the script of *Sprayed with Tears*). Throughout the video the Soldier and Rose speak a kind of discombobulated, spastic poetry that vacillates between the willfully antisocial ('Most people are just abortions that didn't take') and the earnest ('I just wanted you to know me')—refracting some of the most salient debates in contemporary queer theory, from the affective turn to queer negativity, and parroting the language of interpersonal conflict. The narrative revolves around Rose and the Soldier speaking to, and often past, one another, as they work together on a mysterious biomechanical heart/machine that at various moments births a number of symbolic attributes: a gold-sequined double-helix, a three-headed Red Cross nurse, an image of Master Jones on his motorcycle, and a rotating black rose.

The arrival of the Red Cross nurse (played by Kelly Marie Martin) signals a change in the narrative flow of *Sprayed with Tears*. At first appearing as an apparition, the Nurse solemnly intones the lyrics of 'The Rose of No Man's Land' in unison with the Soldier. Once fully incarnated she produces a dismembered arm—a casualty of war, the Master's hand?—and proceeds to read its plastic palm. Miraculous and auratic, the Nurse has a messy agency that the rigid gender roles of the original 1918 song flatly denies. In this way Die Kränken amend their source material, instead of unthinkingly reiterating it. After carefully tying Rose to a fetish bench, the Nurse speaks some of the most crucial text of the video. Lifting her femme submissive's guazy tutu to reveal a jock-strapped ass, the Nurse is illuminated by a projecting light that pours out from Rose's asshole. She gathers this light to her like a Jewish matriarch who has just lit the Sabbath candles, and incants:

> This body is a prison, this body is a hole,
> this body is a ladder, this body is a wheel,
> this body is an obstacle and the way through,
> this body is a sounding chamber,
> this body is an unlicked envelope, this body is a hole onto a hole.

Filled with potential ('an obstacle and the way through') and absence ('a hole onto a hole'), her monologue splits the heart/machine, and it explodes, leaving a mass of costume accouterments—wigs and fake body parts—in its wake. A diminutive image of Master Jones astride his motorcycle floats up from its core. The Master, who soon materializes in person, joins the Nurse

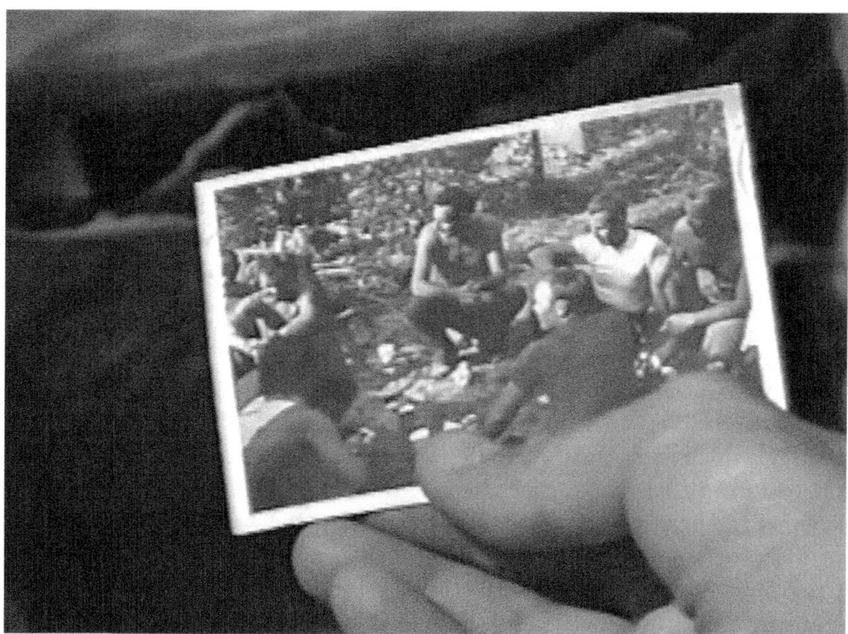

Die Kränken, video still from *Sprayed with Tears*, 2016, digital transfer of single channel    2.5
VHS, 21 minutes

in mounting his wooden cut-out motorcycle and drives away in a herky-jerky sequence of cut-stop frames, reminiscent of Jonesy's previous experimental animated video work. As Rose and the Soldier pick through the remains of the heart/machine, a recording of 'The Rose of No Man's Land' plays. Among the rubble they find a photo reproduced from the Blue Max MC archive. It depicts some of the Blue Max members attending the Badger Flats run—the large, regional Southern California bike run where many chapters of the Blue Max's play were performed (figure 2.5). An archival object temporarily appearing outside the confines of the archive that houses it, this photograph becomes a touchstone for memory. As they pore over this visual document, it triggers a set of emotional and nostalgic responses from Rose and the Soldier ('We were so pretty then' and 'It smells like him' and 'This was supposed to be different'). Unlike the photographs of Zieher's album, which can only be *emblematic* of a whole way of life, this photo is overtly personal, conjuring a 'we' and a 'him.' Rose and the Soldier's affect spills out like all the pieces of detritus from the heart/machine. As they cry—their faces literally sprayed with tears—Master Jones and the Nurse ride off into the sunset to an accelerated soundtrack of 'Say a Prayer For Me Tonight' from the 1958 musical *Gigi*.

Die Kränken's work in and around the Blue Max MC collection is a transformative reading project akin to certain types of history writing—in that they attempt to simultaneously acknowledge an intricate history and ferret its import into contemporary constructs. They align with the Jesuit historian and theorist Michel de Certeau who writes that 'all historiographic research is articulated over a socioeconomic, political, and cultural place of production.'[23] The abstract dialog of Munson's script is the clearest sign that Die Kränken are not merely reenacting a Blue Max performance, and yet the collective's words channel the undercurrents of affect and sexual tension *coursing through* the Blue Max MC's performances. Narratives are layered—Die Kränken's video alongside the Blue Max play and the Caddigan and Brennan song that inspired it—and so ritual and mythology are amplified through translation and iteration. Irresponsible to conventional history writing, which in its most Platonic (and naïve) form purports to re-narrate the past in an objective way, Die Kränken's work at the ONE Archives retains some of the hallmarks of their source material—the visually striking format of VHS, for example, or the particular characters of the Soldier and the Red Cross Nurse—and leaves others by the wayside. Expectations are consistently countered: the hetero pairings of the Soldier and Rose, and Master and Nurse, are subverted by their queer gender and sexual politics. Lines are not spoken but dubbed, in simultaneous adherence and difference to the lip-sync performances of the Blue Max members. Identity is rarely ossified, and nearly always in a temporal transit between then, now, and some apocalyptic future.[24]

The final moments of *Sprayed with Tears*, a direct homage to the use of Broadway musical scores in the Blue Max performances, ask a viewer to fulfill the request of the final lines of the *Gigi* song: 'Bow your head and please / Stay on your knees tonight.' *Sprayed with Tears* finally positions sex as a spiritual practice, an invocation of the losses and pleasures of queer historical memory. In this way Die Kränken support and reiterate the narrative nut of rescue and revival so crucial to their source material, confirming Saidiya Hartman's insight that 'history is how the secular world attends to the dead.'[25]

Die Kränken's installation at ONE National Gay and Lesbian Archives, the institution that houses the collections directly tapped in the making of this particular body of work, was much more expansive than the video I've just described. The exhibition included another video entitled *Die Kränken Black Pipe Intervention* (2016), intercutting an interview with the Reverend Troy Perry, founder of the Metropolitan Community Church and a self-identified leatherman, with a performance action staged on the streets of Los Angeles. Four nurses—Robert Acklen, Jacob Greenberg, Jaime C. Knight, and Luke Munson—carry a leatherman (Jonesy) on a stretcher, stopping at the former site of The Black Pipe, a gay bar made infamous by a 1972 raid conducted by the Los Angeles Police Department. As they process the nurses carry a banner decorated with Die Kränken's logo and that of The Black Pipe. Two dates appear on the banner—exactly forty-five years apart—the year of the L.A.P.D. raid and the (then-present) year of the collective's subsequent memorial action. While Perry narrates the history of gay motorcycle clubs, the nurses stop their memorial march to socialize, roast weenies, and talk convivially. Critically confusing documentary film techniques, whose generic hallmarks include the talking head interview, with a more quixotic performance action calls Hartman to mind again, and her method of 'critical fabulation' in which historical and archival work are supported by strategies most commonly associated with fiction.[26] Facsimile posters of the Summer Festival at The Black Pipe (the event that the L.A.P.D. raided) appear on the brick wall behind the convivial nurses, reminding a viewer that such modes of socializing were profoundly vulnerable to police intervention, a reflection of their supposed legal and moral authority to enforce vice laws. These nurses—figures located importantly *under* the authority and pedigree of the doctor, but historically central to the unfolding of the Blue Max's club mythology—are positioned as the palliative caregivers of communal history, memorializing and recasting the effects of a police action that brazenly sought to ruin lives and destroy a vibrant and complicated culture. The nurses' mostly silent march ends with interpersonal connection; their outfits mark them less as outlaws and more as helpers, caregivers, and custodians of the leather body politic. Like the revisionary absence of certain strands of racism and misogyny that appeared in the original Blue Max MC's plays, the turn toward socializing in this somber memorial march is meant as a reparative gesture, one that seeks to connect the semiotic and symbolic significance of the figure of the Red Cross nurse with the historical legacies and tailings of surveillance, repression, incarceration, and death.

In the collective's installation at ONE this video appeared on a monitor hung above a custom-built bar. The installation was meant to imitate the popular form of the video bar, a nightlife architectural assemblage wherein programmed video content sets and amplifies the mood of the bar while providing visual distraction from the sometimes anxious scene of sociality. In the grimiest (i.e. best) gay bars the video content is invariably pornography. Moseying up to Die Kränken's bar and watching the video, I felt a haunting of history. There is a striking gap between being in a gay bar and being in an exhibition approximating a gay bar. In a bar people talk and drink, touch and laugh, argue and watch from the sidelines. Here I was listening intently with headphones, an anathemic concentration given the usually loud, thumping music of a bar. Exhibitions require different kinds of performance and bodily attention; the space between the bar and the gallery rhyming with the temporal gap between the Black Pipe raid and Die Kränken's performance action.

Outside of ONE's main exhibition space Die Kränken displayed items related to their project *LA/ATX Pocket Expo: The New Rules of Flagging* (2015), which was initially conceived as a project for OUTsider Fest in Austin, Texas. During the run of the queer performance and film festival, Jonesy and Jaime C. Knight asked participants to fill out a questionnaire inquiring as to one's gender(s), sexual identit(ies), and sex practice(s). After careful review participants were assigned a hanky from the collective's newly constructed hanky code—the hanky code being a historical system conceived to wordlessly signal sexual interests and roles via carefully placed colored handkerchiefs (more on this in Chapter 4). Unlike the hankies of the original code, Die Kränken's code aligned with the sexual ethics of what festival organizer Curran Nault described as the 'beyond-the-binary 2010s,' with colors and their silkscreened designs dedicated to 'butch tears,' 'PrEP warrior,' 'original plumbing,' 'wymin power,' and, of course, 'leather.'[27] Once assigned a hanky, the participant would then be taught a choreographic sequence, developed by Austin-area dancer and choreographer Lindsey Taylor. Participants were asked to perform these movements in front of a green screen. Later, Die Kränken developed these scenes into a mesmerizing video compilation of Taylor and the various festival participants claiming their colors against the background of their hanky's design.

Taken as a whole, Die Kränken's exhibition at ONE presented a deep dive into archival holdings that collect, preserve, and present the histories of particular groups (*Sprayed with Tears*), events (*Die Kränken Black Pipe Intervention*), and lifeways (*LA/ATX Pocket Expo: The New Rules of Flagging*). It remains, for me, an example of the rigorous work artists can enact among, and in relation to, archival material—and an enduring illustration of this book's central thesis, which concerns the ongoing relationship between archival sites where gay and lesbian leather histories are kept, and the contemporary artists who tap these archives to create a queer politics of the present.

Ultimately, Die Kränken are engaged in a form of historical work—not history as rigidly defined by academic disciplinary methodologies, but, as the postcolonial theorist Tilottama Rajan would have it, 'history as the condition for an internal distanciation and for self-reflection on what we do,' thereby presenting alternatives to a discipline's 'routinized, even commodified […] repeatable techniques.'[28] In their specific address of leather histories and archives (unlike Zieher's album of motorcycle club photographs), the collective offer viewing and interpreting publics gifts that can aid in illuminating the polymorphous perversity of the pleasures and losses intrinsic to leather-sex, history, and community.

You want some of this? Moo.

Notes

1  Scott Zieher, *Band of Bikers* (New York: powerHouse Books, 2010), n.p.

2  Ibid.

3  Ibid.

4  Ibid.

5  Scott Zieher, phone conversation with author, 22 February 2019.

6  Tyburczy, *Sex Museums*, p. 185. See also Gayle Rubin, 'The Valley of the Kings,' *Sentinel USA*, 13 September 1984, pp. 10–11; and Guy Baldwin, 'Old Guard: Its Origins, Traditions, Mystique and Rules,' *Drummer*, 150 (September 1991), pp. 23–5. The desire to find camaraderie extending from a shared experience is also noted by cultural theorist Raymond Williams, who, reflecting on his return from World War II, recounts how a post-war run-in with a fellow service member begat an epiphany concerning the 'new and strange world' they found themselves in, exclaiming that the rest of the world did not 'speak the same language': 'When we come to say "we just don't speak the same language" we mean something more general: that we have different immediate values or different kinds of valuation, or that we are aware, often intangibly, of different formations and distributions of energy and interest.' Raymond Williams, *Keywords: A Vocabulary of Culture and Society*, rev. edn (Oxford: Oxford University Press, 1983), p. 10.

7  'The Inner Cycle,' *Wheels* (September 1971), n.p.

8  Townsend, *The Leatherman's Handbook*, p. 147.

9  Paul Welch, 'Homosexuality in America,' *LIFE*, 26 June 1964, p. 68.

10  'The Nitty-Gritty: Band of Bikers by Scott Zieher,' *Port Authority Los Angeles*, http://portauthorityla.blogspot.com/2010/04/nitty-gritty-band-of-bikers-by-scott.html (accessed 10 October 2018).

11  Scott Zieher, phone conversation with author, 22 February 2019.

12  'Praetorians,' *Wheels* (October 1971), n.p.

13  Atlantic Motorcycle Coordinating Council, 'FAQ and AMCC Documents,' http://www.amcc76.org/amccdocs.html (accessed 10 October 2018).

14  Benedict Anderson, *Imagined Communities: Reflections on the Origin and Spread of Nationalism* (London: Verso, 1991).

15  Weiss, *Techniques of Pleasure*.

16  Williams, 'Analysis of Culture,' p. 716.

17  Eve Kosofsky Sedgwick, *Tendencies* (Durham, NC: Duke University Press, 1993), p. 15.

18  Jack Caddigan and James Alexander Brennan, *The Rose of No Man's Land* (Boston, MA: Jack Mendelsohn Music, 1918).

19  Ibid.

20  There is a robust literature on this topic; what follows is only a cursory sampling: Weiss, *Techniques of Pleasure*; Musser, *Sensational Flesh*; Viola Johnson, 'The Love That Dare Not Speak Its Name: Playing With and Against Racial Stereotypes,' *Black Leather in Color* (1994), pp. 8–9; Samois, *What Color is Your Handkerchief? A Lesbian S/M Sexuality Reader* (San Francisco: Samois, 1979); Kobena Mercer, 'Skin Head Sex Thing: Racial Difference and the Homoerotic

Imagination,' in Bad Object Choices (eds.), *How Do I Look? Queer Film and Video* (Seattle, WA: Bay Press, 1991), pp. 169–210; and Robin Ruth Linden et al. (eds.), *Against Sadomasochism: A Radical Feminist Analysis* (East Palo Alto, CA: Frog in the Well Press, 1982).

21 John Preston, 'What Happened?,' in Mark Thompson (ed.), *Leatherfolk: Radical Sex, People, Politics, and Practice* (Boston, MA: Alyson Publications, 1991), p. 219.

22 For example, The Mineshaft, a leather club in New York, which was open from 1976 to 1985, had regulations regarding dress posted on the outside of the club, which, in its own words, were 'designed for particular men who compose the core of our club.' While 'Cycle leather & western gear' were allowed, there were to be 'No colognes or perfumes […] designer sweaters […] disco drag or dresses.' Mineshaft Board of Directors, 'The Mineshaft Dress Code' (1976), in the collection of The Leather Archives & Museum, Chicago.

23 de Certeau, *The Writing of History*, p. 58.

24 I'd like to thank Beatriz Cortez and Nao Bustamante for introducing me to this particular notion of identity instability. See also Irene Gedalof, 'Identities in Transit: Nomads, Cyborgs and Women,' *European Journal of Women's Studies*, 7:3 (2000), pp. 337–54.

25 Saidiya Hartman, *Lose Your Mother: A Journey Along the Atlantic Slave Route* (New York: Farrar, Straus, and Giroux, 2007), p. 18.

26 Saidiya Hartman, 'Venus in Two Acts,' *Small Axe*, 26 (June 2008), p. 11.

27 Curran Nault, 'Hanky Code 2.0: LA/ATX Pocket Expo—The New Rules of Flagging,' in David Evans Frantz (ed.), *Die Kränken: Sprayed With Tears* (Los Angeles: ONE Archives, 2017), p. 53.

28 Tilottama Rajan, 'Introduction: Imagining History,' *PMLA*, 118:3 (2003), special issue, 'Imagining History,' p. 428.

*Archive*: The Tom of Finland Foundation
*Artwork*: Patrick Staff, *The Foundation*, 2015

Tom of Finland, whose name is now synonymous with the burly, smiling, big-dicked men he drew for over forty years, presents something of a problem for historians of leather art and visual cultures. While his influence was, and remains, undeniable in the ongoing development of leather aesthetics—via his drawn figures' dress, affect, and range of sexual activity—he was hardly the only leather artist working in the latter half of the twentieth century. Etienne, A. Jay, Rex, Chuck Arnett, Martin of Holland, Robert Opel, Bishop, Bill Ward, Sean, Hun, Olaf, Luger, and many others contributed to the growing and mutating visual aesthetics of leather cultures between the 1960s and the 1990s. Yet today it is Tom of Finland's work, and his work alone, that is placed on the podium of widespread institutional acceptance in modern and contemporary museological and popular cultural contexts, and it (along with certain Robert Mapplethorpe photographs) is fast becoming a synecdochical place-holder for all art and visual culture tied to historic gay and lesbian leather communities.[1] In other words, his work has crossed over 'from the locked drawer to the coffee table,'[2] and in doing so it has been brought fully into a system of art display and exchange whose values are often at odds with the work's original contexts. This needs to worry more people than it currently does.

Most are happy to simply celebrate the fact that original drawings by the master's hand now reside in the permanent collections of select art museums—the Museum of Contemporary Art in Los Angeles and the Museum of Modern Art in New York are two notable examples. The five pencil on paper drawings now in MoMA's permanent collection were acquired in 2005 as part of a larger bequest from the Judith Rothschild Foundation's collection of contemporary drawings.[3] The single drawing (c. 1968) in MOCA's collection was acquired in the immediate wake of the duographic exhibition held in 2013–14, focusing on Tom of Finland and his frequent commissioner, the photographer Bob Mizer, founder of the Athletic Model Guild and its mail-order magazine, *Physique Pictorial*. Acquisitions such as these are certainly authorizing gestures, recognized not only by a general public, who might be safely titillated by the odd Tom of Finland drawing that appears in the context of larger collections-based exhibitions, but also by those who have been historically close to Tom and his work. Durk Dehner, co-founder and president of the Tom of Finland Foundation, noted that with the entry of Tom's drawings into MoMA's collections, the artist's 'message is permanently fused into the fabric of modern-day culture.'[4] While I wouldn't quibble with Dehner's assessment of the ubiquity of Tom's imagery (something which he, the staff, and many volunteers of the Tom of Finland Foundation can take partial credit for), I question the meaning of the milestone. I wish to ask: What exactly does Tom of Finland's work gain from being incorporated into extant histories of art as told by large-scale collecting institutions? Or, put another way, what aspects of his work are left by the wayside when he is positioned as *the* leather artist of note in U.S. museums?

Asking this question is not meant to lead into some separatist, and ultimately retrogressive, argument about whether or not Tom of Finland is *worthy* of MOMA or MOCA, or even worse, if his work is art or not. In fact, I think the question should be flipped and we should be asking whether MOCA or MoMA are worthy of Tom of Finland—and whether their curators and staff are equipped to collect and display his work with the sophistication demanded by the multiple instances in which his works have been historically seen, experienced, circulated, collected, and understood. MOCA and MoMA have both acquired, and thus made an explicit valuation of, Tom's original drawings over other kinds of print media produced by the artist such as photographs of drawings, lithographs, and/or books. When these latter products do enter into the hierarchical space of the museum or gallery, sites that sociologist Tony Bennett calls exhibitionary complexes, wherein knowledge and power are coordinated to produce viewing publics, they are almost always displayed in ephemera cases.[5] This relegates them to an adjunct status within the exhibition, and they become supporting documents—ephemera from an archive—rather than works worthy of contemplation in and of themselves. I readily admit that this is a difficult model to stray from, and that it might be perplexing, and perhaps much less visually satisfying, for a viewer to encounter a blurry photograph of a drawing by Tom of Finland instead of an actual drawing.[6] The photograph here (figure 3.1), really a photograph of a photograph of a drawing (one can see the edges of the initial photograph laid atop the grain of a wood surface), is a good example of the sometimes blurry images that circulated during the time Tom was working—black paper patches on the reverse of the photograph indicate it was once placed in a photo album. Displaying this photograph would highlight the conditions under which many men first encountered, and owned, the work of Tom of

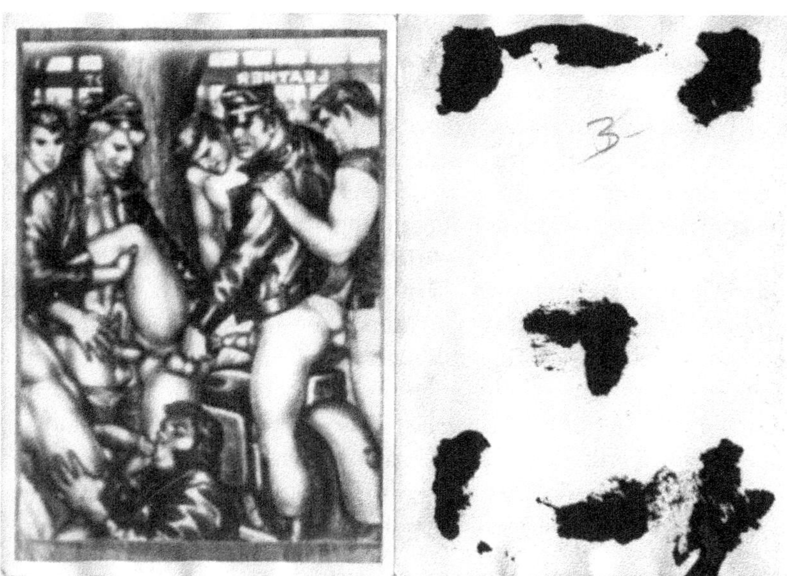

Touko Valio Laaksonen / Tom of Finland, *Untitled*, n.d.    **3.1**

Finland, and perhaps illuminate the fugitive and furtive circulation of images during the 1950s and 1960s, when such images were under the juridical surveillance of the U.S. Post Office.[7]

Currently, there are two book-length monographic studies dedicated to Tom of Finland, not counting the more showy, expensive art books published by the German publisher Taschen. The first was authored by F. Valentine Hooven III in 1993, and the other by art historian Micha Ramakers in 2000; both were released by the same publisher.[8] Hooven's text does an able job of tracking Tuoko Laaksonen's life, describing his childhood and time in Finland as an adult, his first published appearance in the spring 1957 issue of *Physique Pictorial*, his eventual semi-permanent move to Los Angeles, and his final years and eventual death in 1991. It is a biography that interprets Tom's work almost solely in relation to the events of the artist's life—a dearly held tactic of art history that cultural critic Mieke Bal identifies as biographism.[9] In understanding the shape of some artist's oeuvres, this is not a bad way to proceed, but a primary pitfall of such enframing is that a reader will only understand an artist's work through the teleological ordering of events in the life of the artist. That these kinds of exegeses often take on the work of describing the psychosexual impulses of the artist would seem to be a natural fit for a biography dedicated to Tom of Finland, an artist whose primary artistic subject was gay male sexual fantasy. A biographic approach has the potential to yield insights regarding the development of Tom's particular iconography, which legitimately shifts over the decades he was active.

Ramakers's text is something of an antidote to Hooven's, and its exploration of Tom of Finland's work is more generous and open. Ramakers engages in an iconographic analysis of Tom's images, and commits to discussing gaze and critical race theories, as well as notions of gender, camp, and patriarchy. Comparative examples such as Kenneth Anger's *Fireworks* (1947) and Edward Burra's *Silver Dollar Bar* (1955) are briefly brought to bear in his analysis. This positions Tom more intently as part of a larger networked world of queer image-makers. Of course, this tactic can go too far as well—Taschen's 2009 tome, appropriately titled *Tom of Finland XXL* (for both the large size of the book itself and the size of Tom's figures and their endowments), compares Tom's work to that of Michelangelo, Rosso Fiorentino, Paul Cadmus, and Japanese *shunga* artists. While these comparisons might be apt to greater or lesser degrees, their primary purpose in Taschen's case is to situate Tom of Finland *within* the boundaries of already accepted canons of art.

Between these two studies there is not yet a text whose primary aim is to examine the circulation, display, and reception of Tom's work in great detail. Nor is there an accounting of the kinds of skills and knowledge that Tom of Finland, who worked for nearly twenty years for the advertising agency McCann Erikson—first as a trainee illustrator and eventually as a senior art director—brought to bear in the branding, promotion, and dissemination of his own work. Tom's day job is often mentioned as an interesting biographical fact but remains understudied. What might a design history scholar, for example, make of U.S. and Finnish advertising cultures of the 1960s, and Tom's relationship to the many campaigns he no doubt oversaw or had a hand in designing?[10] Artist and scholar Ken Gonzalez-Day mentions Tom's work as an ad man in his entry on the artist for *The Queer Encyclopedia of Visual Arts*, noting that Tom's work was not exhibited in galleries or museums until he quit his job in advertising in 1973.[11] Thus the illustration and design work completed by Tom of Finland and his erotic art are temporally cordoned off from one another—providing a structural break in the discourse around Tom, keeping his advertising and erotic work essentially separate.[12] Pushing this point might reveal the relationships between the process of developing and executing a set of consistent signifiers (something we might now refer to as a brand identity) and the creation of a sexual type of masculine, hypersexualized man, one that Edward Lucie-Smith rightly points out nourished the iconography and lifeways of countless leathermen in the second half of the twentieth century, 'alter[ing] the way gay men thought about themselves.'[13] Little Tom of Finland logos, variously rendered as a single cock, two cocks touching at their tips, or the artist's name imaged into the form of a motorcycle, populate his drawings and are no doubt an extension of his many years as a workaday ad man.

So, to return to my question: What does Tom's work gain today when it is brought into the realm of the museological, and thus within spitting distance of certain canons of art? The most obvious answer is broader visibility. When a museum like MoMA displays a Tom of Finland drawing many people are likely to see it. But visibility is hardly analogous to understanding, and, as Michel Foucault famously warned, it can be a kind of trap.[14] I would argue that Tom of Finland's work potentially loses a great deal from such institutional acceptance and positioning. This is because the role in which he is so often uncritically cast is, depressingly for those of us who have taken to heart the lessons of Linda Nochlin's 1971 essay 'Why Have There Been No Great Women Artists?,' that of the great (male) genius artist.[15] Such a positioning continues old, tired patterns in the discipline of art history, which, as Griselda Pollock notes, 'produces the artist as the subject of the art work and the art work as the means of contemplative access to that subject's "transcendent" and creative subjectivity.'[16] Mostly, this comes in the form of commentary on Tom's drawing technique, consistent across a wide swathe of sources. A press release for MOCA's Tom of Finland/Bob Mizer exhibition calls the artist's drawings and collages 'masterful,' and further praises them for their 'deft skill.'[17] The exhibition's co-curator, Richard Hawkins, likewise describes Tom's works as 'the most exquisite pencil drawings of probably the most radical kinds of sexuality,'[18] and a review of the exhibition calls attention to the artist's 'old-fashioned academic style of drawing.'[19] Tom's one-time gallerist Hudson described his figures as 'somewhere between fading reality and the glowing fantasy,' noting that 'it has been a pleasure to see the artworld begin to acknowledge and accept the genius, the almost incomparable skill and, even today, the radical content of Tom of Finland's drawings.'[20]

When these two things are placed into coordination—the *skill* of the artist and the *radical content* of the images—it should be apparent that the former is trotted out to ameliorate any anxiety that might be caused by the latter. Similar arguments were made in court about the leather photographs of Robert Mapplethorpe.[21] In this way, one reviewer of the 2017 Tom of Finland biopic gets it wrong when they claim the ground upon which we might stake Tom's significance, describing the artist's drawings thusly: 'Their mad dynamism of line was a revolt against "proper" art the way gay lib was a revolt against "proper" sex.'[22] Besides being a person who was not particularly interested in the field of gay politics as it pertained to U.S. or international gay liberation movements, Tom of Finland's 'mad dynamism of line' only continues to support common understandings of the constitution and output of the great artist.[23] Indeed, if we did away with the necessity to position Tom's work as masterful or skilled, we could approach the conditions under which he measured his own success. In a quote reproduced in nearly every biography and coffee-table book dedicated to the artist, he declared that a drawing was only worthy, and thus good, if it gave him an erection while he was *completing* it.[24] He joins his contemporary, fellow leather artist Chuck Arnett, in this thinking. As Arnett put it, 'Galleries are funeral parlors for art work … I show my work in a bar because that's where the people who know me go and can get off on what I do and sometimes even buy something.'[25] Both Arnett's and Tom's work is deeply pornographic, not because of its sexually graphic content *per se*, but because it adheres to what Richard Dyer identifies as the central tenet of the genre, which is to produce 'sexual arousal in the spectator.'[26] Tom's work might be better interpreted and encountered in the space of a home, or in the cruising grounds of a bar. than in a museum.

So while museums and art critics alike assess Tom of Finland's *greatness* via his mastery of the techniques of drawing, for writers of leather periodicals such as *Drummer* and other folks attuned to leather communities, Tom's worth is measured in this other way, in terms of its capacities to arouse. That art is meant to cause something to happen in the body of the spectator is as much an *idée recue* in the history of art as the enduring belief in the genius of artists. Yet not all bodily affects are treated with equal reverence. We can be brought to tears by art,[27] morally uplifted by its messages,[28] or fascinated by the strangeness of its excesses,[29] but overt queer sexual arousal is often left out of this equation. Yet as the artist Nayland Blake reminds us, in what is one of the finest pieces of writing on Tom of Finland to date, 'what we arouse ourselves with speaks eloquently about who we are.'[30] And they are not alone in this belief: recently scholars such as Jennifer Tyburczy and Tan Hoang Nguyen—trained in cultural studies, queer theory, feminism, and critical race theory—have been reinvesting in art and film's capacities to induce the 'frenzy of the visible' attached to the genre of pornography (as per Linda Williams).[31]

Leatherfolks (and perhaps some non-leatherfolks, too) might be dismayed at my line of argument here, for Tom of Finland's work is understandably greatly admired and treasured in leather communities. This is because there *is* a radical aspect to Tom's work, and it is exactly what Dehner and others identify, namely that 'his megastuds exalt in a happy, healthy self-confidence of who and what they are.'[32] While Dehner and, by extension, the Tom of Finland Foundation promote such narratives of the 'genius' of Tom, the Foundation's activities to support itself and its mission by printing and disseminating the work of Tom of Finland on postcards, stickers, bed sheets, T-shirts, leather apparel, and in sizeable and often expensive books reproducing the artist's work, is arguably much closer to the mode in which Tom's work was seen, bought, and received during the artist's lifetime.[33]

I first encountered Tom of Finland in this way, on the front of a greeting card (figure 3.2). It was one of many displayed on the stands of Lobo, a gay

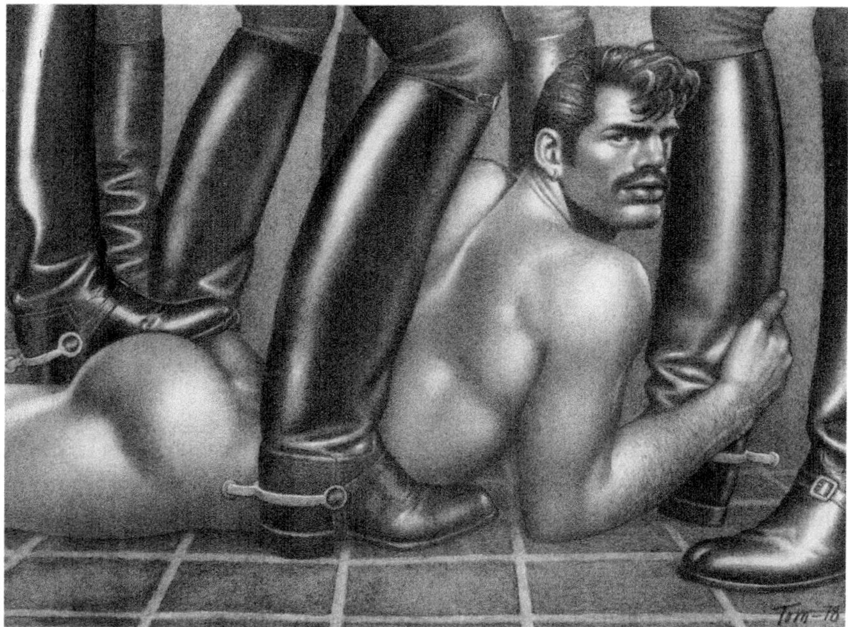

Touko Valio Laaksonen / Tom of Finland, *Untitled*, 1978                    **3.2**

bookstore located in Austin, Texas, where I grew up and was, at the time, attending high school.[34] The drawing, dated 'Tom – 78' in the lower right-hand corner, features a naked man lying on a tiled floor, his ass prominently on display, and his stoic face turned out towards a viewer. His dark hair falls onto his forehead in a waterfall of wavy curlicues. Black boots populate the image like a copse of trees—the high reflective shine along their shafts indicate that they are well cared for. One of these boots is placed on and slightly in the man's ass-crack; but the lack of any registered pressure on the almost comically round butt-cheek supplies only the merest of suggestion of a dominant/submissive relationship. Preparation sketches for this drawing reveal this to be a compositional device not present in the initial image's design. The spurs on many of the boots feature smooth disc rowels—a type common in dressage—instead of the spiked wheels of their cowboy counterparts. The man grasps the back of the lower calf of a booted figure standing in front of him. Another straddles the man's lower torso, while another hangs back, a temporary voyeur, perhaps, watching the scene but not directly involved in its unfolding.

While this scene portrays a naked man literally brought to heel by a group of men, this is really an image that a viewer completes with their own fantasies, and in this way it is an invocation for further fantasizing. Are these men who stand around the naked man kissing? Are they bare-chested or in full leathers? Are they even men? Is their focus the man on the floor, or is he meant to be ignored and incidental, and if so, properly debased within the scene of leathersex?

My brief encounter with this greeting-card reproduction of a drawing by Tom of Finland hews closely to what Durk Dehner recalls as his first encounter with a 'little tiny drawing on a bulletin board at the Spike bar in New York City.'[35] Elsewhere the item and location is described differently, as 'a postcard tacked up in the Eagle leather bar in New York,' or as 'a little ad with Tom's work.'[36] There is no way to know for sure what exactly Dehner saw, but it was probably not an original drawing. Instead, it was likely a photograph or postcard of the artist's work. Dehner eventually got in touch with Tom through a mutual contact, Dom Orejudos, who was by that time well-known as the Chicago-based artist Etienne. What this information suggests to me is how Tom's drawings, whether in the form of an advertisement, a postcard, a photograph, lithograph or otherwise, had the capacity to open out the field of identification, to become a shared point of contact in the scene of erotically networked relations.

At first, Tom displayed his drawings selectively to the tricks he brought home. In these encounters he would sometimes give the drawings away, and they were then passed along a network of personal sexual contacts. He also reproduced his drawings as photographs in a small home darkroom—and these were eventually circulated in the late 1950s through Bob Mizer's *Physique Pictorial*, a publication that at one point had a circulation of thirty thousand.[37] The quality, size, and medium of these reproductions varied widely, but their format enabled collectors to keep them either in small, hidden-away places, or stored in photographic albums and binders.[38] One such binder can be found in the Jim Kane Papers at the Leather Archives & Museum (figure 3.3), and elucidates how photographs of Tom of Finland drawings often joined and abutted other mail-order material—beefcake photographs of young men in posing straps. Although clearly photographs of drawings, Tom's work, in this context, is a tentacular extension of the photographic—a fantastical exaggeration of the kinds of qualities sought out in the models of Bob Mizer's Athletic Model Guild, Chuck Renslow's Kris Studio, or later, by Lou Thomas's Target Studios.

Regardless of the fuzziness of some of these reproductions, by the mid-1970s Tom's work was available from several mail-order sources, some of which were authorized by the artist and others not. Throughout the late 1960s and 1970s Tom's drawings were used in bars and in advertisements for motorcycle club runs and leather events. For example, Tom's work first appears in the second issue of *Drummer* illustrating an ad for the magazine's subscription membership service, the Leather Fraternity. It is important to

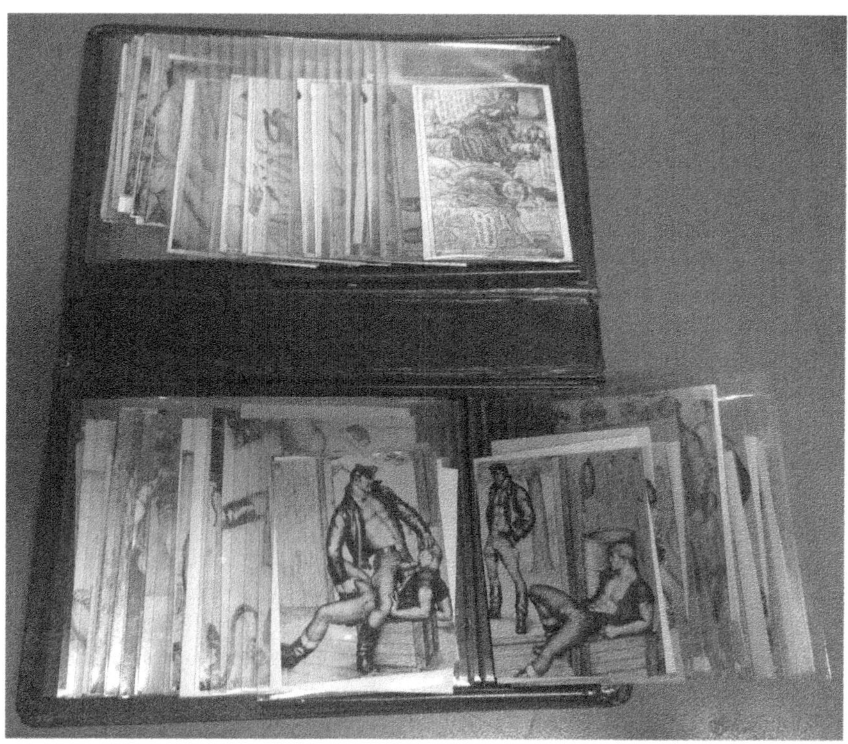

Binder with Tom of Finland photographs. Jim Kane Papers at the Leather Archives &          **3.3**
Museum

realize that by this time, his work was already well-known to a U.S. leather audience, as his drawings populated the semi-public and private spaces (clubs, bars, houses, apartments) in which leathermen socialized and lived. Another, but altogether different, measure of the artist's growing mainstream importance was a brief mention in Margaret Walters's compendium *The Nude Male: A New Perspective*, where she mostly denigrated the artist's figures as 'hulking brutes.'[39] This ambivalence about the cultural meanings of Tom's figures—especially as they relate to normative models of masculinity—remains a hallmark of their interpretation to this day.

Through his publishers in Sweden (Revolt Press) and Denmark (DFT), Tom of Finland began to release a series of comic books that followed the sexual exploits of a character named Kake. These comics did much to popularize the image of the archetypal leatherman, in scenarios filled with what Camille Paglia once described as 'assertive, theatrical figures' with cocks like 'Dionysian maypoles.'[40] The first of these wordless comics, entitled 'The Intruder' tells the narrative of a leatherman (Kake) who spies on a young (ostensibly straight) blonde man (in the second frame he is shown reading a porn magazine exclusively dedicated to images of women). Eventually Kake comes in to the young man's bedroom through his window, giving him head and fucking him anally. Near the end of the comic they are discovered by the young man's father, who, as Kake tries to escape, traps him in a vulnerable position by closing the window on his lower back. The father then fucks Kake as the son watches, masturbating to completion. The series continues thusly, in loosely connected narratives that usually feature a surprise or twist comical ending. Between 1968 and 1986 Tom completed twenty-six such episodes, making it the longest-running comic series he produced.

In the midst of this series, Tom had his first gallery shows in the United States—and this broadened the scope of the kinds of items produced from his work. For his 1978 solo shows at Fey-Way Studios (a short-lived San Francisco space owned and operated by photographer and performance artist Robert Opel), and Eons Gallery in Los Angeles, Tom showed thirteen drawings that were to be reproduced as plates in a dedicated calendar for that year. The drawings on display, each an image for the calendar, featured pairs of clothed and naked figures—a lifeguard and his rescue (June), for example, or a naval officer and his shirtless seaman (July).[41]

Later that same year Tom was given a duographic exhibition along with Etienne at Stompers, a Greenwich Village boot shop that had a modest gallery at the back of the store. For this show Stompers and Tom produced a portfolio of four poster-sized lithographs (13½ x 19¼ in.), in a large edition of four hundred. These four images came in a signed and numbered black folder with the names of the artist and the gallery emblazoned on the front. One of the four images in this poster set is the one I initially saw as young man in Austin. These sets were sold out of the gallery, and the remainders would be sold many years later through the Tom of Finland Foundation's catalog. The idea was that Tom's images would disseminate to private residences and bars, taking up important visual real estate. The advertisement for the lithographic set calls forth the potential buyer who 'know[s] *quality* and appreciate[s] *size*,' remarking on both the fidelity and scale of the reproduction, as well as the fidelity and scale of the drawn figures' endowments.

These four posters appear in a photo-spread dedicated to a New York home dungeon that appeared in a 1983 issue of *DungeonMaster*. The owner's play space features high, dark beams that anchor a variety of hanging leather gear (figures 3.4, 3.5). Dangling stirrups and other cowboy ephemera code this dungeon space with a generic Western ambience. Two of the photographs in the spread depict the four Stompers Tom of Finland posters *in situ*, framed and hung in a cruciform pattern on the far wall. Beyond remarking that the art on the walls 'leaves little to the imagination,' the author's captions make no mention of the Tom of Finland posters—they are assumed as a natural part of the décor, and thus not particularly noteworthy. For me, this points to how Tom of Finland's imagery was already understood as part of a shared visuality. Like people who hang posters of art exhibitions up in their homes instead of original works, the owner of this New York dungeon likely did not place value on the auratic originality of the works hanging on his wall—they are not the original drawings now exclusively prized by U.S. museums. Rather, they are depicted as a component of larger signaling systems of material, gear, images, and architecture that could encourage and extend the sexual livelihood of the apartment's occupant. In this regard the posters are used in perfect alignment with the intentions of the artist—as aids for getting off.

Tom's work adorned bars, populated catalog pages, was passed between lovers, collected into albums, and even sometimes hung on the wall. Tracking the various appearances of Tom's art illuminates its circulation within the common gay cruising areas of bars, bookstores, magazines, catalogs, membership sex clubs, and private dungeons. Arguably it was this complex circulation of Tom's work—made possible by its multiple material manifestations—that did more to solidify his place within leather visual cultures than the artist's own travels and timeline (i.e. his biography).[42] If his work is of importance to leather cultures of the 1970s and 1980s, and I believe it is, it is because of this and not because it has been recognized as art by a non-leather artworld. Understanding this means coming to terms with the unruly materiality of Tom's work—which often lies somewhere beyond the neat museological collecting categories of drawings, prints, and/or photography. When museums and galleries invest in Tom of Finland's work they primarily collect and display his drawings, and rarely the lithographic prints, which were seen, owned, and treasured by leatherfolks from the 1950s to the 1980s.

There's a final twist to this story, and it is that the museological has inflected the ways that Tom of Finland's work circulates today. Dehner and the Tom of Finland Foundation have called Tom and his work into the circuits of capitalism in playful, and sometimes troubling ways. Currently in the Foundation's online store, for example, one has the opportunity to buy a replica of Kake's cock in the form of a suction-cup backed dildo (figure 3.6).[43] Boasting that the twelve-inch dildo is 'hand sculpted exclusively from Tom of Finland original artwork,' products like this made under the aegis of the Tom of Finland Foundation have the potential to both light up and close down the erotic circuits of imagination so important to his work. By presenting the opportunity to be fucked by a fictional character, the dildo would seem to realize a fantasy. But I would argue that what Kake's silicone cock really does, via its rubbery materiality and hefty pricepoint ($425), is to bring the fantasy into a particularly classed arena of commodity fetishism. While other dildos for sale on the Tom of Finland Foundation's site are black or tan-colored,

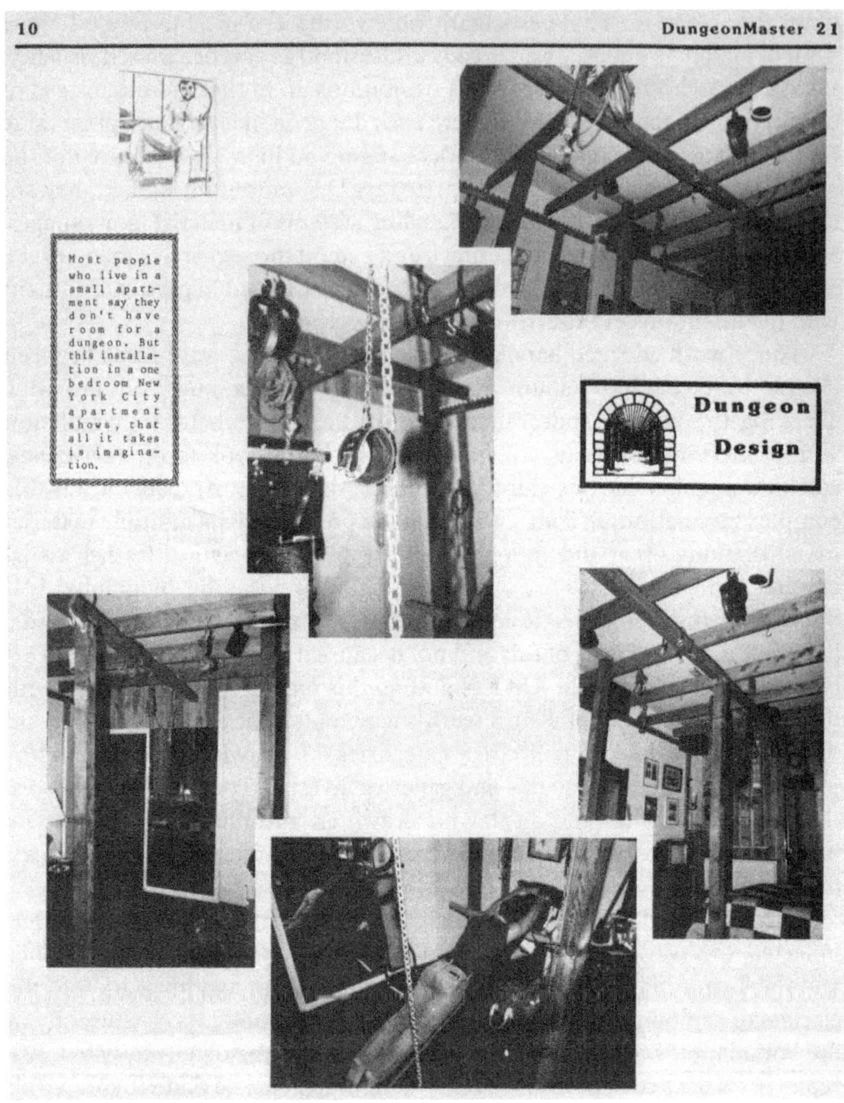


**3.4**    'Dungeon Design: New York City,' *DungeonMaster*, 21 (1983)

employing race as one driver of erotic experience, this one is a marbled silvery-gray. At the base of the shaft, the Tom of Finland Foundation's logo is imprinted into the design, meaning that the foundation's name would potentially be visible during play, interpolating the bodies of participants, the artist, his most recognizable fictional character, and the artist's foundation together in a scene of sexual encounter. That's a lot to get into the sling with,

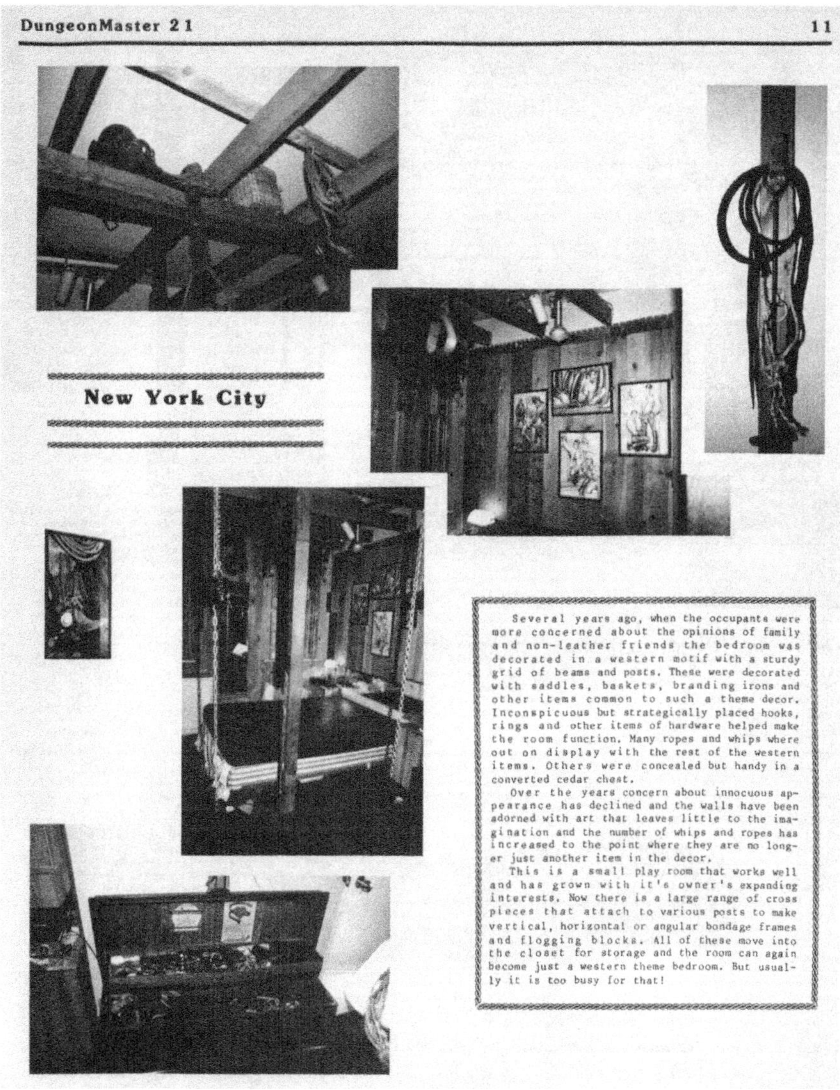



Several years ago, when the occupants were more concerned about the opinions of family and non-leather friends the bedroom was decorated in a western motif with a sturdy grid of beams and posts. These were decorated with saddles, baskets, branding irons and other items common to such a theme decor. Inconspicuous but strategically placed hooks, rings and other items of hardware helped make the room function. Many ropes and whips where out on display with the rest of the western items. Others were concealed but handy in a converted cedar chest.

Over the years concern about innocuous appearance has declined and the walls have been adorned with art that leaves little to the imagination and the number of whips and ropes has increased to the point where they are no longer just another item in the decor.

This is a small play room that works well and has grown with it's owner's expanding interests. Now there is a large range of cross pieces that attach to various posts to make vertical, horizontal or angular bondage frames and flogging blocks. All of these move into the closet for storage and the room can again become just a western theme bedroom. But usually it is too busy for that!

and because the dildo is more expensive than many other similarly styled and sculpted dildos, it limits the experience to only the most affluent appreciators of Tom of Finland's work. Indicative of its status as a high-value object, the dildo comes with a plexiglass display case, an etched dog tag, and a 'collector print' of a drawing of a group of guys getting off together. Thus the circuits of display and distribution are connected by this particular offering of the Tom of Finland Foundation, for it appropriates the authorizing modes of museum

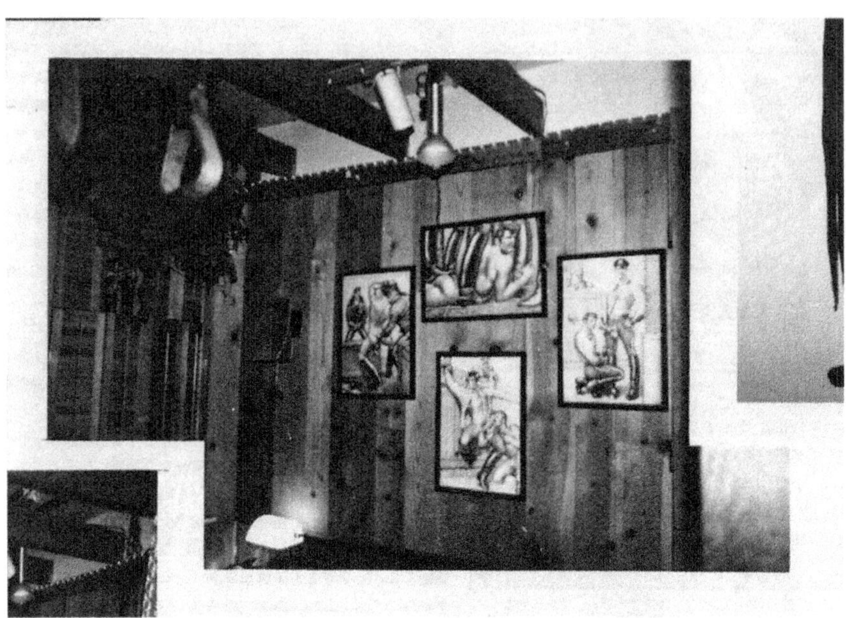

**3.5**     Detail from 'Dungeon Design: New York City,' *DungeonMaster*, 21 (1983)

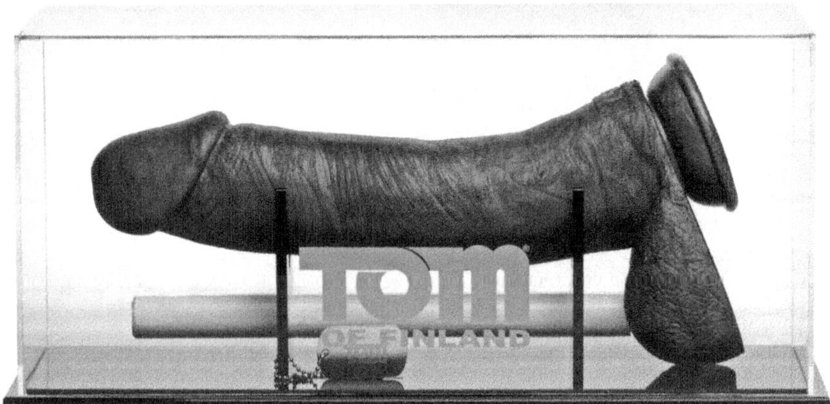

**3.6**     Touko Valio Laaksonen / Tom of Finland, 'Tom of Finland Kake's Cock, 12 Inch Silicone Dildo,' Tom of Finland Foundation

display in the service of realizing, and literalizing, the fantasy of Tom of Finland's fictional universe.

I want to turn now to a contemporary project that deals with these aspects of Tom of Finland's work and evinces what Lauren Berlant calls the 'scene of relationality's hard pleasures and hard knocks,'[44] reinforcing the potentialities and capacities of leather archives. Patrick Staff's experimental documentary *The Foundation* (2015) was filmed, in part, at the Tom of Finland Foundation, a house in Echo Park where the famed leather artist lived out the last decade of his life. Tellingly, one does not get from *The Foundation* a sense of who Tom of Finland was, either as an artist or a person. I invest in this absence as a conscious decision on Staff's part to make a film that encircles what *remains* of his life, art, and social attachments, instead of providing a biographical accounting of the Finnish artist's life and work as I have attempted to sketch it out above. In doing this Staff happily moves away from enframing Tom of Finland within the cult of the 'great male artist,'[45] leaving his work open to critique and reassessment. I find Staff's film to be an important and generous way of proceeding because it allows for a more open approach to the ongoing social conditions that both sex and archives occasion. Staff creates a film that is as much about processes of observation, iteration, and difference as it is about Tom of Finland's art.

*The Foundation* begins with establishing shots of the Tom of Finland Foundation's basement, bedroom, living room, and interior hallways. In fact, the whole first half of Staff's film is oriented toward capturing the house's various functions as living space, archive, community center, and business complex (figure 3.7). Light filters in through blind-drawn windows, its subtle invasion drawing attention to every surface it touches: a row of boots on a windowsill, scummy and worn; rows of binders organized by subject ('Faces 1, Faces 2, … Sexual Outlaws'); a subterranean landing, an entry to

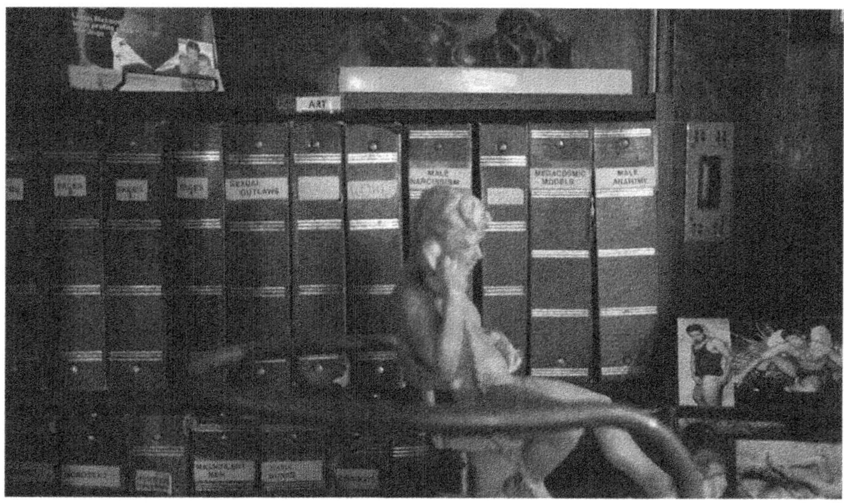

Patrick Staff, video still from *The Foundation*, 2015     **3.7**

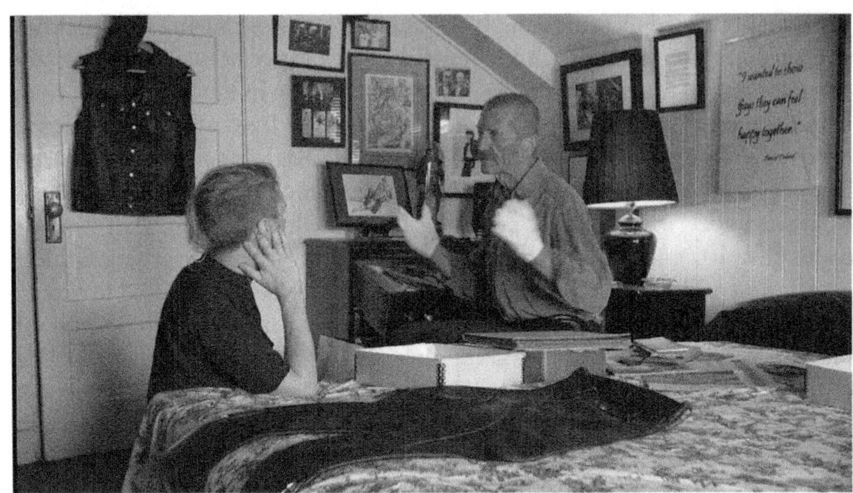



**3.8**    Patrick Staff, video still from *The Foundation*, 2015

an unidentified elsewhere. When a living, moving person finally comes into Staff's frame, the awkwardness of his transgression (Staff can be heard off-camera telling the man: 'we are shooting with sound') underlines that despite the fantasy of its cinematic premise, this is not a hermetically sealed place. People live and work in these environs, and they get in the way. Furthermore, it is clear that Staff and their film crew are only there on the good graces of those who make their home in this space—they have made arrangements, and these arrangements structure the kinds of activities that Staff captures.

In one sequence Staff and Durk Dehner sit together on the late artist's bed (figure 3.8). Archival material is spread out on the coverlet. In a recorded voice-over Dehner tells the story of the Foundation, which I reproduce here in its entirety:

> So the house, I bought the house in 1979 with a group of brothers, and then Tom became part of that family. And so this was always his room. And actually … [Staff: How many of you were living here?] Oh, it varied, but there was at least five or six of us. So what happened is that, and he was always grateful because, he was in his sixties, my age, so he was my age and I was in my thirties, and we actually took him out and made him part of the community at that time, and that kept him young, and he was always grateful for that, because he was going out to the bars and to the nightclubs with us, and having fun, and then he'd come back here, you know, and it was quiet up here, and it was his retreat. So I just started to dig in and help him as a friend. And then by 1980 we realized we should start a business together here, and so we started a mail-order company. And actually I just was going through these drawers, this is

a photograph of the staff, and Richard managed the staff and everything, so this is how we all, we were all there, yeah, yeah. And that's Bud, Bud Hole, he became a porn actor, so there's all sorts of us here.

I have quoted Dehner at length to highlight the ways that notions of chosen family, intergenerational alliance, the compression and layering of time, as well as conflations of out/retreat and home/business structure Dehner's off-the-cuff history—one which I imagine he has rehearsed, in some form or another, countless times. During this monologue Staff intercuts shots of employees and volunteers of the Foundation at their workstations. Dehner's words to Staff are followed by some remarks he makes to a gathered crowd on the occasion of Tom's birthday. Here, on the Foundation's patio, where a porno (aged and magenta-tinged) is being projected onto a collapsible screen, its shutter speed providing a low-level soundtrack to the festivities, Dehner addresses the crowd, encouraging them to visit the Foundation more, and to 'make this your community center.'

In Staff's video that phrase is soon repeated by a bearded man whose bodily presentation roughly correlates with the trope of the gay 'daddy.' He speaks directly to camera. The setting in which he makes his remarks is different from the cozy homespace of the Foundation—a controlled soundstage kitted out with architectural elements intended to recall the Foundation's interior spaces shown earlier. Unlike the Tom of Finland Foundation where erotic art hangs everywhere, here empty picture frames hang over closed blinds, through which an artificial Fresnel light pours in. Together, Staff and this gay daddy initiate a dance to a plucky, pulsing beat—their movements are collapsed feints of the gendered performances associated with the ballet studio and the gym—lunges, squats, arm-raises (figure 3.9). They dance in synchronization, but not *with* each other as in a traditional, romantic choreographic duet. The music cuts out and the scene changes abruptly once more; although still on the soundstage, Staff and their partner now inhabit a replica of the archives room at the Foundation. Instead of the drawings, prints, and photographs that populate the flat files and binders in the Echo Park bungalow, they are handling blank sheets of white paper, hands greased with lube (figure 3.10). Touching the papers renders them translucent and luminous—as if use amplified their value, transmission a gift. This leads into a sequence wherein the daddy uses his hands, now black-greased, to position Staff's arms and face. Again, marks (this time on Staff's body) index haptic touch, in what is easily the most erotically charged and intimate act in *The Foundation*. When the two were dancing they were in accord, together but separate; but now, in the archives, Staff willfully gives up control of their own movements, and their partner responds with rigorous tenderness. One dominates and the other submits, bringing their relationship into the common dynamic language of

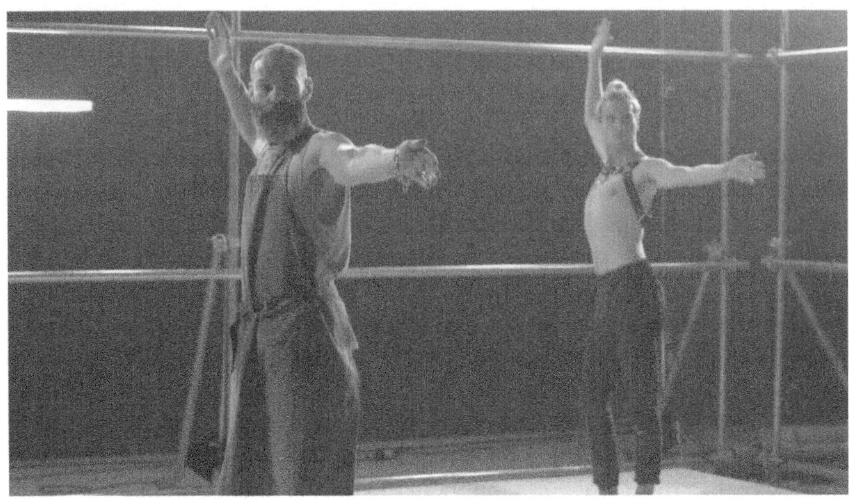

**3.9**    Patrick Staff, video still from *The Foundation*, 2015

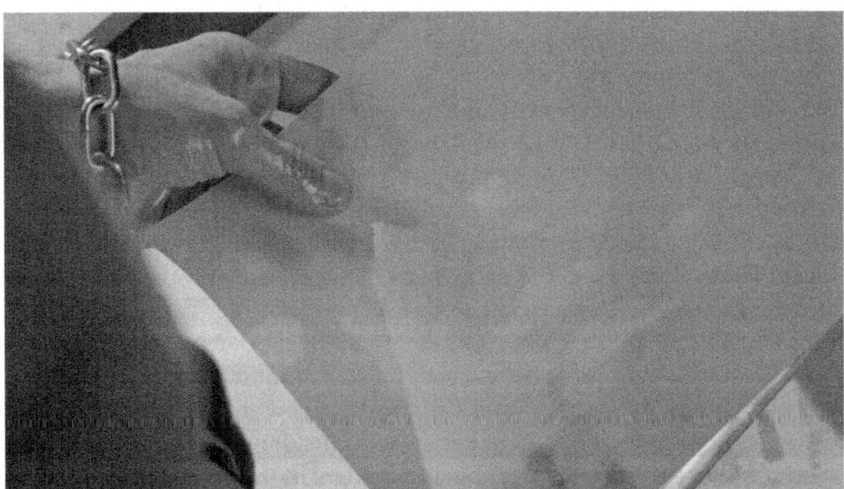

**3.10**    Patrick Staff, video still from *The Foundation*, 2015

leathersex, a horizontal power exchange wherein consenting parties exert will and its conditioned, temporary renunciation.

The second half of the film begins with a life-drawing class, held in one of the main spaces of the Tom of Finland Foundation. Though we never see the model, we see the participants' drawings of his body. Like the previous sequence this, too, is a willed, consenting posing of a body—its historical lineaments tied to art pedagogy and dating back at least to the nineteenth century.[46] Helen Reddy's rendition of the Beatles' 'The Fool on the Hill' plays as the men work on their drawings.

What follows is a sequence of still shots of the Foundation's dungeon, painted black and decorated with collages, prints, drawings, racks of uniforms, and a large leather sling. Its black-on-black arrangement is typical of dungeons in homes, private clubs, and leather bars. This sequence is paired with yet another analogous soundstage scene. Here the set is a kind of heightened and abstracted dungeon. Instead of the leather and metal belts and chains that hang off every surface of the Foundation's dungeon, here large drawings of chains are the backdrop; and a row of leather boots is placed on the ground, echoing the row of leather boots on the windowsill of the Foundation. The sex dungeon, a stereotypical scene for leathersex, is often a place where consensual pleasure is given and taken freely. In Staff's video this space produces some unwarranted advice. 'Don't worry,' says the gay daddy to a visibly uncomfortable Staff, 'you'll grow into it—being a man.' Staff is shown in counter-shot squeamishly receiving this admission ticket into normative masculinity. A smear of foundation makeup, visible in the harsh, theatrical lighting of the scene, appears on the gay daddy's face. The gay daddy's sentiment is one that Staff encountered in real life from an older gay man, after the artist confided that they might be trans.[47] The man's statement, rehearsed verbatim by the gay daddy in Staff's film, is an attempt to soothe the anxieties felt in response to Staff's potential gender transition. The statement only soothes the speaker, who still wants to believe that Staff will join the 'group of brothers' (as Dehner would have it) of the Foundation. Here the Foundation is revealed to be a place of growth and self-realization, with limits for those who transgress the ideals of masculinity promoted in Tom of Finland's drawings.

As if in answer to this revelation, the final two sequences of *The Foundation* imagine the sociality of leathersex away from the architectural conceit of the home-base of the Tom of Finland Foundation. In the first instance Staff appropriates footage of an erotic party thrown by the Foundation, wherein hundreds of men socialize, drink, and look at dozens of framed pieces of erotic art hung on the walls of the cavernous, and echoing, warehouse space. This is followed by the final appearance of the soundstage as a bedroom overrun by a thick, cloudy foam—issuing from the kind of machine used to pep up parties in gay bars (figure 3.11). As the foam starts to dry and evaporate, it leaves a damp wetness in its wake, soaking the room's mattress, clothes, boots, and blank pieces of paper.

For archivists this is a nightmarish sequence: waterlogged documents and realia invite mold, rot, and warping. Staff's camera lovingly hovers over the foam's valleys and peaks, in stark opposition to the floating dust motes of the romanticized archive. Leathersex's dynamic dyadic vocabulary of mastery

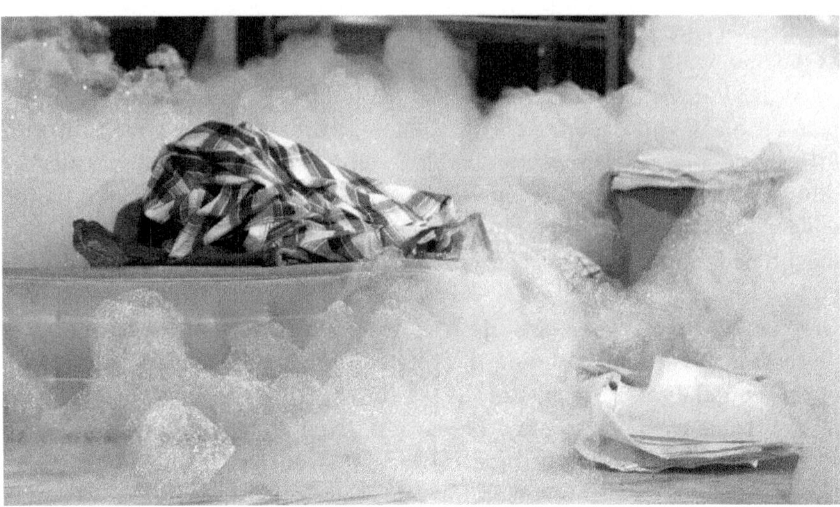

**3.11** Patrick Staff, video still from *The Foundation*, 2015

and submission is thus extended out into the realm of the archival—the will to preserve and the inevitability of destruction.

The two spaces that recur throughout Staff's video—the Foundation and the soundstage, the latter made to reflect and resemble the former—are places of human activity. The rooms of the Tom of Finland Foundation change very slowly, if at all, and are the kinds of spaces that are useful precisely because of their resistance to change. Without the people who inhabit the Foundation, it runs the risk of becoming a precious diorama of the life of a famous leatherman—a biographic museum. Meanwhile, the soundstage is presented as inherently flexible, akin to the drawing and erasing described in Freud's 'Mystic Writing Pad,' full of potentiality and possibility, and always bearing the trace of what it no longer is.[48] The architectural conceits of these two interrelated but distinct spaces allow for the opportunity to think about sex and archiving as interrelated practices, as both are given a domestic and theatrical enframing in Staff's video. The people at home in the Tom of Finland Foundation are lovers and archivists, artists and workers—a dedicated commune bound together by work and play, and their affinity for the work of Tom of Finland. Yet positioning themself against the 'romance' of this figuration of community, Staff doesn't demur from pointing out the ways in which their life experience and body is different to the homomasculine ideal of Tom of Finland's art, life, and legacy.[49] Instead of resting this disjunctive experience at the familiar doorstep of critique, Staff presents their own entrance into the space of the Foundation as representative of an archive's 'mixed ecologies,' an admission and acceptance of non-reparative loss or exclusion.[50] The concept to which the desires of Tom of Finland's art, and those who work in the Foundation, are so attached, namely, masculinity as a fairly narrowly and normatively defined ideal, is shattered by Staff's self-presentation. Staff implicates their hunky dance partner in their critique, and by leaving a smear of tan makeup visible on the gay daddy's face, subtly destabilizes the naturalized ontology of 'being a man.' *The Foundation* is comfortable with the homonymic multiplicity of its title—it is at once an ideological place, an architectural premise, and a form of writing with makeup on the body. Staff's video incorporates archives, and the histories and figures they purport to be dedicated to, in order to press the relationship between trans and gay male cultures and histories toward new ground and understandings.

Throughout *The Foundation* we are reintroduced to the soundstage again and again, and it is constantly repurposed toward new ends, made in the image of the Tom of Finland Foundation, but without succumbing to the tyranny of exact fidelity. 'There are only reintroductions, after all,' writes Berlant, 'reencounters that produce incitements to loosen, discard, or grasp more tightly to some anchors in the attunement that fantasy offers.'[51] This is as true of the hard-muscled figures that reappear throughout Tom's art as it is about the recurrent soundstage of Staff's film. Staff's work helps me to articulate what is so generative about archives and their relationship to contemporary artistic practice. Their film seems to acknowledge the primary tasks of an archive—sorting, viewing, and keeping documents—but reframes it as a process wherein things become marked and unevenly visible, naming the body as a potential repository for these knowledges along the way.

Staff's video is not about the historical person called Tom of Finland, nor about Tom's historicity. Rather, *The Foundation* tells us something about Tom after death, Tom in the present in and among his archives: namely, that his work is the occasion for a community's livelihood, in all its spectacular dailyness. I find it moving and completely apropos that the artist's archives are still in his home, instead of in a larger multi-focal or institutional archive. Here people eat, drink, sleep, fuck, and fight among the prints, collages, original drawings, and leatherwear that Tom produced and owned. Tom's work is a part of everyday life, and it is in this setting that we might come most fully into a historical sense of Tom of Finland.

## Notes

1 I do not take Robert Mapplethorpe as my example (although many have encouraged me to do so) because his work is ultimately quite varied—with only relatively few of the thousands of photographs he took directly addressing leather people and communities.

2 Guy Lodge, 'Film Review: Tom of Finland,' *Variety*, 11 February 2017, http://

variety.com/2017/film/reviews/tom-of-finland-review-1201983671 (accessed 10 October 2017).

3 The bequeathed collection was comprised of over 2,500 drawings, with the stipulation from Harvey S. Shipley Miller, the Judith Rothschild Foundation's sole trustee, that should MoMA wish to excise any of the artists in the assembled collection, the whole gift would have to be declined. Thus, we may rightly wonder if the acquisition of the Tom of Finland drawings was truly a priority for the institution or whether they entered MoMA's collection as a matter of convenience. Alex Mar, 'Paper Trail,' *New York Magazine*, 9 March 2013, http://nymag.com/nymetro/news/people/columns/intelligencer/9500/# (accessed 10 October 2017).

4 Durk Dehner, 'Afterword' to F. Valentine Hooven III, *Tom of Finland: Life and Work of a Gay Hero* (Berlin: Bruno Gmünder, 2012), p. 233.

5 For more on how knowledge and power are coordinated in the formation of viewing publics, see Tony Bennett, 'The Exhibitionary Complex,' *New Formations*, 4 (spring 1988), pp. 73–102.

6 In my own curatorial practice I have also had trouble pushing against the art/ephemera spatialized dynamic that structures so many exhibitions. In an exhibition I curated in the spring of 2016 entitled 'Dean Sameshima: Public Sex' I placed artists' books, contact sheets, and other items in a large display case, while keeping Sameshima's art on the walls.

7 For more on this history, see Rodger Streitmatter, *Unspeakable: The Rise of the Gay and Lesbian Press in America* (New York: Faber & Faber, 1995).

8 F. Valentine Hooven III, *Tom of Finland: His Life and Times* (New York: St. Martin's Griffin, 1993); Micha Ramakers, *Dirty Pictures: Tom of Finland, Masculinity, and Homosexuality* (New York: St. Martin's Griffin, 2000).

9 Mieke Bal, 'Autotopography: Louise Bourgeois as Builder,' *Biography* 25:1 (2002), pp. 180–202.

10 This fact, minus the name of the agency, appears in a press release of the monographic exhibition of Tom of Finland's work at Artist's Space in New York, and in many other publications and articles. During Tom's time at McCann Erikson the agency released their famous 'I'd like to buy the world a coke' campaign, and so I wonder if there are sites of connection between the way Tom understood Finnish and American visual/cultural systems, and if he exploited these knowingly in his drawings.

11 Ken Gonzalez-Day, 'Tom of Finland,' in Claude J. Summers (ed.), *The Queer Encyclopedia of the Visual Arts* (San Francisco: Cleis Press, 2004), pp. 330–1.

12 Tom of Finland's first gallery exhibition was in 1973 in the backroom of the Revolt Press Bookshop in Hamburg, Germany. It was another five years until his next solo exhibitions in San Francisco (Fey Wey Studios), Los Angeles (Eons Gallery), and Amsterdam (Rob Gallery). Ramakers, *Dirty Pictures*, p. 239.

13 Edward Lucie-Smith, 'Tom of Finland,' in Dian Hanson (ed.), *Tom of Finland XXL* (Cologne: Taschen, 2009), p. 21.

14 Michel Foucault, *Discipline and Punish: The Birth of the Prison*, trans. Alan Sheridan (New York: Vintage, 1995), p. 200.

15 Linda Nochlin, 'Why Have There Been No Great Women Artists?,' *ArtNews*, January 1971, pp. 22–39.

16 Griselda Pollock, 'Artists Mythologies and Media Genius, Madness and Art History,' *Screen*, 21:3 (1980), p. 59.

17 Museum of Contemporary Art, Los Angeles, 'Bob Mizer & Tom of Finland' [exh.], www.moca.org/exhibition/bob-mizer-tom-of-finland (accessed 10 October 2017).

18 'Richard Hawkins – Bob Mizer & Tom of Finland – MOCA U – MOCAtv,' video, 3:28, 22 January 2014, www.youtube.com/watch?v=tQF4qN-8uok (accessed 10 October 2017).

19 Christopher Knight, 'Review: Fun To Be Had in Works of Bob Mizer and Tom of Finland,' *The Los Angeles Times*, 5 December 2013, www.latimes.com/enter tainment/arts/culture/la-et-cm-review-bob-mizer-tom-of-finland-at-mocapdc-20131204-story.html (accessed 10 October 2017).

20 Hudson, 'Tom of Finland – An Appreciation,' in *Tom of Finland: Retrospective II* (Los Angeles: Tom of Finland Foundation, 1991), p. 5.

21 For more on Mapplethorpe and censorship, see Richard Meyer, *Outlaw Representation: Censorship and Homosexuality in Twentieth-Century American Art* (Oxford: Oxford University Press, 2002); and Mark Jarzombek, 'The Mapplethorpe Trial and the Paradox of Its Formalist and Liberal Defense: Sights of Contention,' *Appendix*, 2 (spring 1994), pp. 58–81.

22 Nigel Andrews, 'Tom of Finland—A Lugubrious Biopic,' *Financial Times*, 10 August 2017, www.ft.com/content/b2ee4372–7dd8–11e7-ab01-a13271d1ee9c (acc-essed 10 October 2017).

23 Tom of Finland, 'Tom of Finland Speaks at Calarts 1/2 & 2/2,' lecture, CalArts, 1988, video, www.youtube.com/watch?v=KmDfUkZC_wo (accessed 10 October 2017).

24 Dian Hanson, *Tom of Finland: The Comics, Vol. 1* (Cologne: Taschen, 2011), p. 7.

25 Robert Opel, 'Arnett: Lautrec in Leather,' *Drummer*, 1:4 (1976), p. 19.

26 Richard Dyer, 'Male Gay Porn: Coming to Terms,' *Jump Cut*, 30 (March 1985), pp. 27–9.

27 James Elkins, *Pictures and Tears: A History of People Who Have Cried in Front of Paintings* (London: Routledge, 2004).

28 Immanuel Kant, *The Critique of Judgment*, ed. Nicholas Walker, trans. James Creed Meredith (Oxford: Oxford University Press, 2007).

29 Jean-Francois Lyotard, 'Critical Reflections,' trans. W. G. J. Niesluchawski, *Artforum*, 24:8 (1991), pp. 92–3.

30 Nayland Blake, 'Tom of Finland: An Appreciation,' *Out/Look* (fall 1988), p. 37.

31 Tyburczy, *Sex Museums*; Tan Hoang Nguyen, *A View from the Bottom: Asian American Masculinity and Sexual Representation* (Durham, NC: Duke University Press, 2014); Tim Dean, *Unlimited Intimacy: Reflections on the Subculture of Barebacking* (Chicago: University of Chicago Press, 2009); and Linda Williams, *Hard Core: Power, Pleasure, and the 'Frenzy of the Visible'* (Berkeley, CA: University of California Press, 1989).

32 Dennis Forbes and Fred Bisonnes, 'Tom of Finland – An Appreciation,' in *Tom of Finland: Retrospective* (Los Angeles: Tom of Finland Foundation, 1988), p. 5.

33 To my knowledge the only non-leather or LGBTQ museum with a notable collection of leather material not comprised of original drawings by Tom of Finland is the Oakland Museum of California, which in 2008 incorporated the poster collections of Michael Rossman, a Free Speech Movement activist and progenitor of the 'All of Us or None' archive project. At least three of these posters feature images made by Tom of Finland and each is used to advertise something outside of the artist's own work (a black party, a Mr. Drummer contest, and a Mr. San Francisco Leather contest, respectively). Other posters showcase the work of Etienne, Pat Daley, Zach, and Rex.

34 For a brief history and bibliography regarding gay and lesbian bookstores in the United States, see Ruth M. Pettis, 'Gay and Lesbian Bookstores,' in *The GLBTQ Encyclopedia*, 2007, www.glbtqarchive.com/literature/gay_lesbian_bookstores_L.pdf (accessed 10 October 2017).

35 F. Valentine Hooven III, *Tom of Finland: Life and Work of a Gay Hero* (Berlin: Bruno Gmünder, 2012), p. 163.

36 Ibid., pp. 141–2; Neil Vazquez, 'At LA Pride Durk Dehner Talks Tom of Finland's Popular Resurgence,' *ArtSlant*, 7 June 2016, www.artslant.com/ny/articles/show/46019-at-la-pride-muse-durk-dehner-talks-tom-of-finlands-popular-resurgence (accessed 10 October 2017).

37 Ramakers, *Dirty Pictures*, pp. 78–9.

38 The photographs were initially sold in an 8 x 10 in. format (at $1.50 a piece—the magazine was sold at 35¢), but later Mizer produced them in smaller formats and slides.

39 Margaret Walters, *The Nude Male: A New Perspective* (London: Paddington Press, 1978), p. 297.

40 Camille Paglia, 'Sex Quest in Tom of Finland,' in Dian Hanson (ed.), *Tom of Finland XXL* (Cologne: Taschen, 2009), pp. 81–2.

41 Hooven, *Tom of Finland: Life and Work*, p. 161.

42 Tom of Finland did not travel to America until the late 1970s when his work was already well-known by U.S. leatherfolks.

43 'Tom of Finland Kake's Cock 12 Inch Silicone Dildo,' Tom of Finland Store, https://tomoffinlandstore.com/collections/xxx/products/tom-of-finland-kakes-cock-12-inch-silicone-dildo (accessed 10 October 2017).

44 Berlant and Edelman, *Sex*, p. 25.

45 Pollock, 'Artists Mythologies,' pp. 57–96.

46 Albert Boime, 'Curriculum Vitae: The Course of Life in the Nineteenth Century,' in *Strictly Academic: Life Drawing in the Nineteenth Century* (Binghamton, NY: State University at Binghamton, University Art Gallery, 1981), pp. 5–15.

47 Patrick Staff and Tess Edmonson, 'Patrick Staff "The Foundation",' *Vdrome*, n.d., www.vdrome.org/patrick-staff-the-foundation (accessed 10 October 2017).

48 Sigmund Freud, 'A Note Upon the "Mystic Writing Pad"' (1925), in *The Standard Edition of the Complete Psychological Works*, vol. XIX, ed. and trans. James Strachey (London: The Hogarth Press, 1961), pp. 227–32.

49 When I invoke community here, I think of Miranda Joseph, for whom the overuse of the term speaks to a romanticization of it, taking community-organizing

outside of the realm of economic/cultural power relationships. Miranda Joseph, *Against the Romance of Community* (Minneapolis, MN: University of Minnesota Press, 2002). While Joseph doesn't call for 'a complete abandonment of identity or community,' she does call into question the methods in which 'community' is invoked by non-profits, NGOs and activist collectives to represent their activities as fostering the 'cherished ideals of co-operation, equality and communion' (p. 174). Elided in this pervasive definition and representation of community are bad feelings, grudges, inequality, and an ever-present complicity with larger systems of oppression and hierarchical arrangement. Joseph positions community as an integral, but unrecognized, part of industrial-capitalisms (p. vii). The effect is that those writing after Joseph, like myself, are not able to take for granted, and thus romanticize the *idea* of community, which for anyone who has been involved in community organizing, maintenance, and dissolution is markedly different from the *experience* of community.
50 Staff and Edmonson, 'Patrick Staff.'
51 Lauren Berlant, *Desire/Love* (New York: Punctum Books, 2012), p. 3.

*Archive*: The Leather Archives & Museum

> It's curious that the great thing that's developed out of gay liberation, one of its most visible artifacts, is all those bars where guys go and piss on each other [...]
>
> Kate Millett[1]

It was a specific death that established the Leather Archives & Museum (LA&M). Dom Orejudos, the prolific leather artist who went under the pseudonym Etienne, died in the fall of 1991 from AIDS. Reading the obituary printed in the *Chicago Tribune*, however, one would be forgiven for thinking that Orejudos's primary contribution to culture was not as a leather visual artist but as a ballet dancer and choreographer. Although accomplished in both of these fields, the obituary omits his most significant contributions: his art and his role in establishing what was perhaps the U.S.'s first leather bar—The Gold Coast (1960)—as well as dozens of other business ventures founded with his lover Chuck Renslow—including the beefcake photography studio, Kris Studio, and in 1979, the International Mr. Leather contest, which still exists today.[2]

One of the many questions death begets is what will happen to a dead person's stuff? Upon Orejudos's passing, Renslow inherited much of his artwork, even though the artist had been living with another lover in Colorado full-time for nearly a decade. Renslow tried to offer it to art museums in Chicago, New York, and San Francisco, but to his dismay each wanted to 'pick and choose which pieces they'd accept into their collections.'[3] It was Tony DeBlase, then-publisher of *Drummer* and *DungeonMaster*, who suggested that Renslow's inheritance along with Renslow and DeBlase's personal collections could form the nucleus of a new organization that would be both archive and museum.[4]

As Gayle Rubin, who was involved in various aspects of the fledgling LA&M, points out, the notion of a leather archive and museum with non-profit status was 'more or less unthinkable' for many decades, due to ingrained cultural and academic associations of leather and kinky people with mental illness.[5] This meant, essentially, that institutions that would normally collect material and visual cultures in the U.S.—places such as municipal and/ or academic libraries and archives—did not regularly collect material from leather communities. Furthermore, biological families could not be counted upon to save materials that would be of interest to leather communities. These materials are often marginal and ephemeral both in their social valuation within normative culture and in their materiality. As Ann Cvetkovich notes, in collecting and displaying such things, institutions like the LA&M turn this system of valuation on its head, 'propos[ing] that affects—associated with nostalgia, personal memory, fantasy, and trauma—make a document significant,' instead of some claim to an official history.[6]

The terms under which documents or items in an archive become significant is the central focus of this chapter, which traces the history of the LA&M and gives a sense of its collections and display strategies by reading them 'on the diagonal,' via the coded signaling system of the hanky code. I propose this as a potential methodology when attempting to make sense of the wildly heterogeneous contents of an archive that collects subjugated knowledges and lifeways. To be sure, this methodology may only make sense in relation to this particular archive, or within this particular study (supported by other chapters with perhaps more recognizable methodologies). I contend here that taking methodological cues directly from archival collections has a revelatory potential. In particular, I will focus on the color yellow, one of colors of the hanky code whose meaning has remained fairly stable over the years, connoting the erotic activity of golden showers. In gathering yellow items from the LA&M's collections I find that a particular lifeway can be revealed through an assemblage of documents that would ostensibly have nothing else in common save for growing out of broadly defined national leather communities. Tracking the color yellow, then, is an arbitrary conceit that reveals histories that would remain unconnected otherwise, and as such serves as an opportunity to rethink research strategies as well as leather histories and identities otherwise.

Leather history itself became thinkable, in part, due to the efforts of leatherfolks in the early 1980s—especially the programming efforts of the Gay Male SM Activists (GMSMA), which sought to identify the history of leather cultures and communities by inviting men to speak about the motorcycle club cultures of the 1950s.[7] That this occurred at the same moment that the HIV/ AIDS pandemic was laying waste to LGBTQ communities is no accident, but an outgrowth of a recuperative drive—already in effect—to curtail the loss of so many leathermen and leatherwomen. Many a leatherperson's personal effects were lost in the pandemic, devalued and thrown out by family members or friends. In 1991 Rubin became involved in a leadership capacity in the National Leather Association—a political organization founded in 1986—and attempted to convince its membership to establish a 'historical society' whose purpose would be to preserve the memorabilia from 'the junk heap of history.'[8] When Rubin was invited to present on a panel at that year's Living in Leather conference, she happily discovered that DeBlase and Renslow had already incorporated a leather archive in the state of Illinois.[9]

For the first few years the LA&M did not have a stable or reliable physical space; its collections were shown in pop-up displays at leather events such as the International Mr. Leather contest. In 1996 Renslow and DeBlase cut a leather ribbon inaugurating the first physical space dedicated to the Leather Archives & Museum. This early brick-and-mortar incarnation of the LA&M was located at 5007 N. Clark, adjacent to Renslow's business offices and much-beloved bathhouse, Man's Country. Beyond the practicalities of such an arrangement—Renslow didn't have to travel far to keep an eye on two of his many ventures (he also lived nearby)—placing the LA&M next to a bath-house had deep symbolic resonance, suggesting that archival history adjoins contemporary sexual practice, each being integral to the other.

Tony DeBlase served as the museum's initial curator, and he set the tone for exhibition display tactics, many of which are still in use at the LA&M today (figure 4.1). As a mammologist who worked for Chicago's Field Museum (his pseudonym, *fledermaus*, is the German word for bat), DeBlase had consider-able experience thinking about display—at least within the exhibitionary model of natural history and ethnographic museums. Like those institutions, DeBlase densely populated several wood and glass display cases, closely

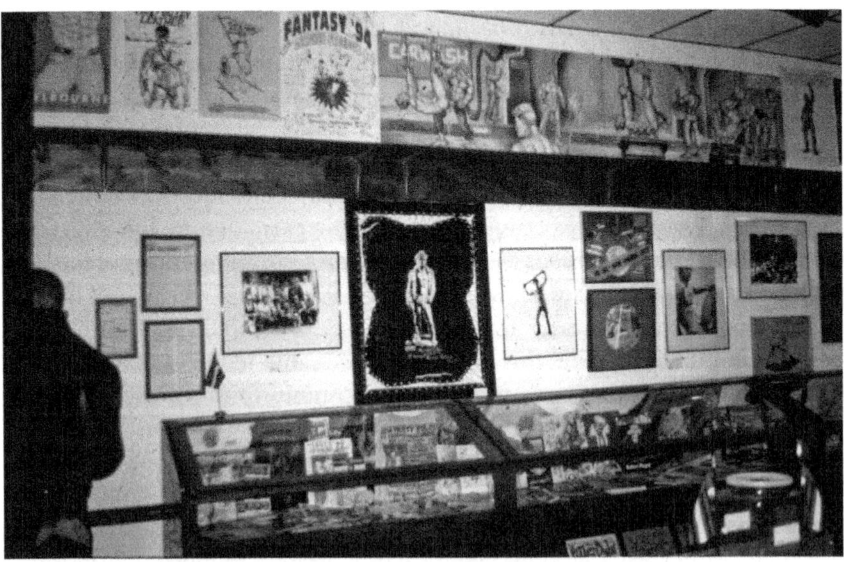

**4.1**    Exhibition display of Leather Archives & Museum (5007 N. Clark Street), c. 1996

hanging art prints and photographs, and even bringing in a mannequin and dressing it in leather garb. Here is DeBlase's description of the range and scope of the LA&M's collections at the time:

> The current exhibit is a wide range of items from the LA&M collections including books, magazines, posters, run pins, friendship pins, club colors, business promotional items, photography, original art, titleholder sashes, trophies and commemorative and memorial pieces as well as several leather items.[10]

The density of objects on the walls and in the cases of the first brick-and-mortar LA&M thus reflected the wealth of material already at hand from the earliest collections. The display of leather material at the LA&M points to the 'ghostly traces' of the curator's past, but also to similar modes of presentation found elsewhere within leather communities.[11] For example, another key influence on the early displays of the LA&M was no doubt the displays of objects, posters, periodicals, and sex toys in leather stores—most located in close proximity to leather bars and venues. Views of these early spaces of leather commerce are rare, but a few telling images of one particular store, A Taste of Leather, survive. Run by Nick O'Demus, whom Rubin describes as 'a Santa in black leather,'[12] A Taste of Leather was located upstairs from Fe-Be's, an early South of Market leather bar in San Francisco. A Taste of Leather kept similar hours to the bar, benefitting patrons who needed to purchase gear in a pinch. O'Demus published a series of foldout catalogs that sometimes featured images of the interior of his shop. He cheekily referred to his overwrought display as 'The Museum of Unnatural History' (figure 4.2), and in these photos one can see the hallmark *horror vacqui* of O'Demus's space. Chains hang from the ceiling and terminate in leather cuffs, gauntlets, and dildos. The mascot of Fe-Be's, known as the 'leather David,' appears in two forms, as a white plaster statue and as a design printed onto a hanging T-shirt. Created by artist and bartender Mike Caffee, the leather David became the primary graphic identifier of Fe-Be's, and, to some extent, the South of Market neighborhood where the bar was located. In O'Demus's store, every surface is covered with items for sale—from sex toys to novelty knick-knacks. Although not hung as densely as O'Demus's store, the new Leather Archives & Museum shared enough in common with leather stores for some early visitors to be confused as to whether the items in the museum were for sale or not.[13]

The display strategies of the early LA&M were also informed by the AIDS pandemic, which by the time the institution opened had claimed over 350,000 lives. One prominent item on display in the 5007 N. Clark space evidences this connection. It is a large banner, made to the approximate dimensions of the quilt panels aggregated into the Names Project's *AIDS Memorial Quilt*. In an early installation photograph (figure 4.3) one can see this banner hanging in

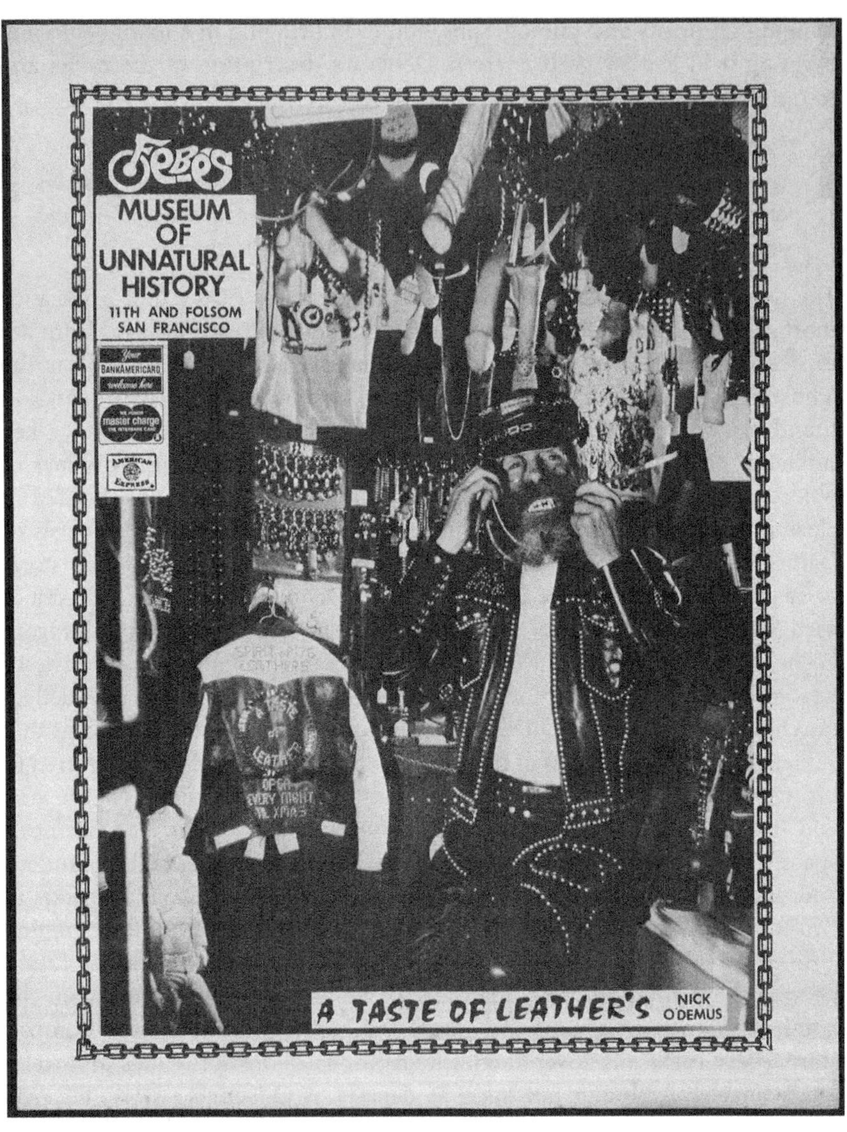




the corner of the LA&M's exhibition space, suspended by large rings attached around its perimeter. The name of the memorialized person, Randy Sauder, and his death date are inscribed at the bottom of the banner. Beyond this vital information the main design element appears in the form of the front and back of a leather vest, onto which various buttons and pins are attached. A

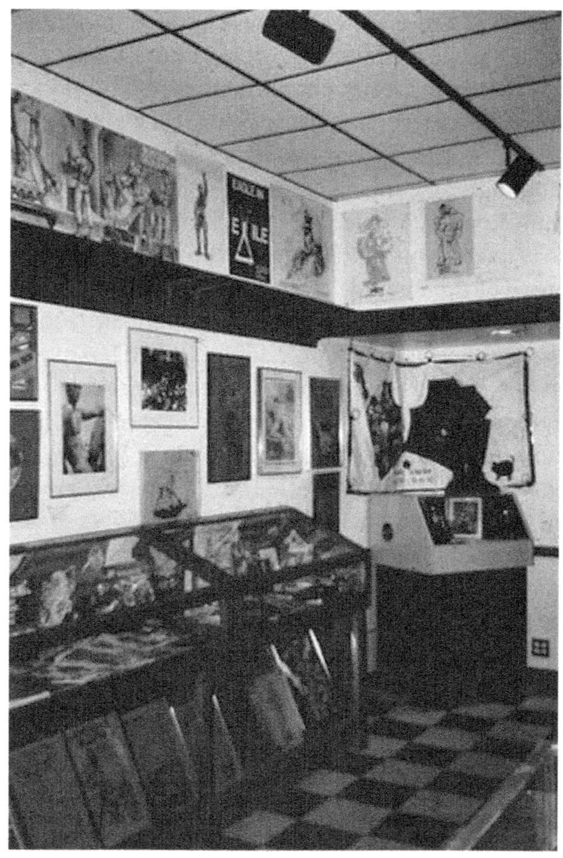

Exhibition display of Leather Archives & Museum (5007 N. Clark Street), c. 1996    **4.3**

silhouette of a little black pig also appears on the banner—perhaps a playful symbol of the 'sex-pig' parlance often attached to sexual voraciousness. The LA&M's finding aid for Sauder's collection, which was later combined with the collection of his lover, Gary S. DeNichilo, states that this object was created as a memorial tribute to Sauder (and 'all leathermen who had passed on from AIDS') at his home bar, The Stud in Fort Lauderdale, Florida.[14] The finding aid goes on to describe some of the contents of the collection:

> various pins and a button related to Randy and Gary's involvement with FFA [Fist Fuckers of America] and the Fort Lauderdale leather community, metal cock rings, 2 metal boot hooks made in England (similar to the Arcron boot hook, manufactured at the now defunct Gamage's London department store), and engraved metal Bentley lighter, and a 7th Broward County Dixie Awards [*sic*], Leathermen of the Year trophy won by Randy and Gary in 1991.

From this descriptive list a visitor to the LA&M immediately gets a sense of Sauder and DeNichilo's affiliations with leather organizations (the FFA), their standing within larger leather communities (the trophy), as well as their particular sexual interests (boots, fist-fucking, cock rings). The Sauder collection is listed as one of only four outside collections in a 1994 inventory of the LA&M's holdings—the others being the collections of Janet Ryan, Sailor Sid, and William Roosen. While the vast majority of the LA&M's holdings were related to leather communities in Chicago—Renslow and DeBlase's collections (inclusive of the Orejudos inheritance) formed the bulk of what the LA&M owned—some of the earliest collections were the result of a concerted effort on the part of Renslow, DeBlase, and the LA&M board to collect materials from across the United States. Shortly after its incorporation, the LA&M established regional coordinators to fundraise, represent the museum, and garner collections from their various home regions. Sauder's and Sailor Sid's collections came from the Southeast (Florida), Roosen's from the Southwest (Arizona), and Ryan's from the Midwest (Kansas City). It was remarkably forward-thinking of the institution to value regional representation as a major acquisition strategy even before the LA&M had acquired a permanent exhibition space, and bespeaks a noble ambition on the part of the LA&M's organizers to represent a variety of experiences of leather communities across the U.S.

A call for donations at the back of the LA&M's second newsletter lists the full scope of needs for the new organization: cash, published materials, insignia and logos (i.e. pins and club colors), commemorative pieces (title belts, trophies), original art, unpublished materials, uniforms and clothing, equipment (large, furniture-sized gear), archival equipment, and real estate.[15] The plea for acquisitions and funds was often made at the annual International Mr. Leather contests held in Chicago, so that attendees from all across the U.S. could not only hear about the LA&M, but also see for themselves that the museum's current space was bursting at the seams. Renslow hired the LA&M's first executive director, Joseph Bean, in late 1997, and he promptly began a capital campaign for a new building. In the interim, however, Bean oversaw the expansion of the LA&M's activities—including concerted efforts to collect club colors and pins, as well as running numerous fundraisers at bars and regional and national events. He also set an ambitious plan to rotate exhibitions at the 5007 N. Clark space quarterly, with exhibits on International Mr. Leather, women in leather, the photographs of George Platt Lynes, and leather images in mainstream media filling out the 1998–99 season.[16] Only the first two of these planned exhibitions were realized, and the rest were put on hold as the LA&M space was converted to be used exclusively for archival storage, due, in no small part, to the rapid growth of the collections.[17]

Recognizing the need for more space, and a permanent home for the

LA&M, Bean and the donors to the LA&M eventually raised enough funds to put a downpayment on a building in the Rogers Park neighborhood in Chicago that had once been a Jewish Orthodox synagogue (Kesser Ma'ariv) and then briefly a performing arts venue called Greenview Arts Center, which played host to John Kirk's Red Dress Theater Company and Defiant Theater's famed production of *Hamlet*. With much cajoling and creativity (Bean subjected himself to a shaving fundraiser in an event called 'Shave Da Bear,' and leatherwoman Viola Johnson similarly put her ponytail on the chopping block to raise funds), the staff and board of the LA&M were able to pay off the building's mortgage within five years—allowing for a much-needed sense of autonomy and security.[18] Traveling exhibits from the LA&M spread its mission to a broader audience at regional leather events, and Guy Baldwin, Gayle Rubin, and Rob Ridinger wrote and spoke at various venues about the need to preserve and center leather histories.[19]

Although I have already described some of the early influences on the display of the material and visual histories of U.S. leather cultures in the LA&M's first physical space, it is worth focusing more emphatically on the displays in its second, and current, home, paying some attention to the construction of what Svetlana Alpers identifies as the museum's primary function, which is to enframe a particular way of seeing.[20] The LA&M currently splits its collections between two floors: on the topmost floor is a reception desk; a locker-room where visitors can store their bags, which doubles as a display room for uniforms; an auditorium decorated with the portable murals (painted on Masonite) by Etienne, initially created for the many bars and businesses owned and operated by Renslow and him; a room used for collections-processing and volunteers; a library with reading tables; and the LA&M's administrative offices. On the lower floor are the archives, with smaller rooms dedicated to fiber and leather collections; a large open gallery space with temporary walls for exhibitions; as well as a museum store. Every space that a visitor encounters is hung tight with materials from the LA&M's collections—original artworks, club colors and banners, photographs, documents, leather gear, didactic panels, buttons, and so on. The display logics of the LA&M's first location were carried over nearly unchanged into its second.

Unlike the LA&M's previous space, the current building has much more room, and its spaces can be retooled for a variety of purposes. For example, within the first months of opening, the museum's auditorium played host to a monologue performance by Quentin Crisp, served as construction space for International Mr. Leather's set crews, became a meeting ground for the Chicago Hellfire Club and the Rogers Park Gay and Lesbian Neighborhood Association, and welcomed filmmaking students from the Art Institute of Chicago for a showing of their final projects.[21] From its first days in its new

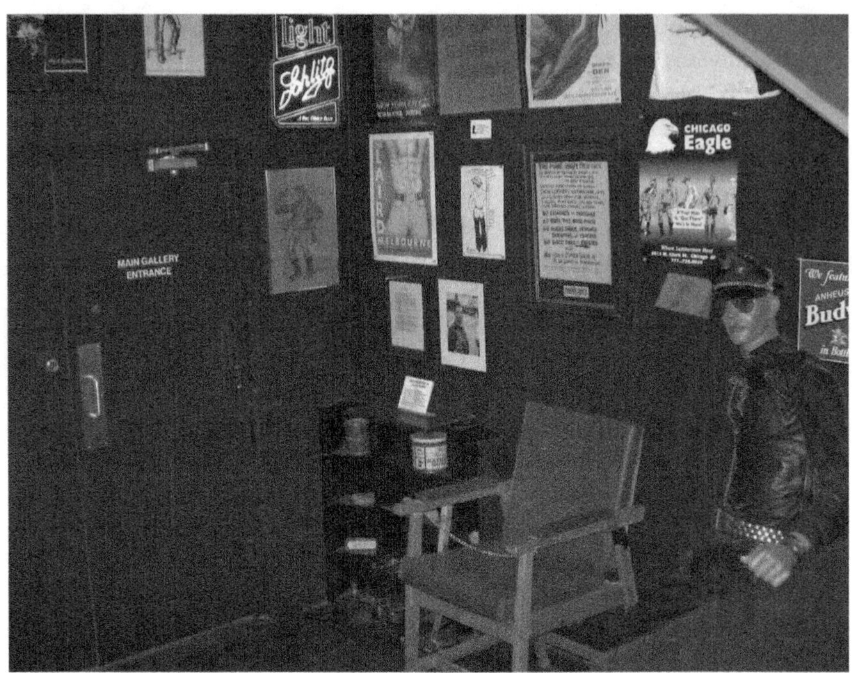



**4.4**    'The Leatherbar' [exhibition], The Leather Archives & Museum, Chicago

location Bean positioned the building not only as an archive and museum, but as a community center for leatherfolks and for artistic and local communities as well.

The spandrel of one of the LA&M's staircases—the space that is often used as a broom closet in domestic settings—contains a diorama-like installation that loosely replicates a leather bar. Displayed there are the kinds of items found in a leather bar: posters, cards, event fliers, matchbooks, T-shirts, neon beer signs, award plaques, a shoe-shine stand, and, as a proxy for the people who populate leather bars, one, sometimes two, mannequins dressed in leathers (figure 4.4). The overall effect is more humorous than erotic, perhaps because key components of social spaces such as bars—immaterial things such as lighting, bodies, music, temperature, and smell—are noticeably missing. Still, certain pieces of this exhibition are of continuing and historical interest, such as the posted dress code for The Mineshaft (a New York leather bar), which illuminates the sartorial policing that often ocurred at the entrances to leather bars ('No colognes or perfumes / No suits, ties, dress pants / No rugby shirts, designer sweaters, or tuxedos / No disco drag or dresses').

The main exhibition space hosts any number of exhibitions, and is rarely given over to a single one. Shows have been dedicated to marginalized identities within leather communities (such as the International Mr. Deaf Leather contest, Latinos/as in leather, or the Women's Leather History Project), single figures (such as Fakir Musafar), and, as Jennifer Tyburczy writes about, particular object histories that illuminate ongoing and critical debates in leather (such as the display of a leather sword sheath and whip that dates to the 1840s and was most likely used as a tool in the enslavement and genocide of black people in the antebellum South).[22] One of the more permanent displays in this area of the LA&M is a small, dimly lit room that is simply referred to as 'The Dungeon.' It houses sex toys and 'pervertibles,' quotidian objects that can be used in perverse ways within the structures of leathersex.

Just beyond the main exhibit space is the museum store which sells T-shirts, postcards, knick-knacks emblazoned with the leather pride flag (designed by Tony DeBlase), art books, and texts produced by the museum. During one of my visits to the LA&M the store sold leather paddles embossed with the museum's logo—a silhouette of a leather boot. This object is a novel extension of the usual museum store fare; an object crafted with the LA&M's primary audience of leatherfolks in mind. If one were to be hit with any great force by this paddle, the pattern of the museum's logo would likely register on the skin, connecting the institution with the somatic body in a visible and lasting way.

The items on display in the museum's varied exhibitions are pulled from its vast archival holdings of institutional, organizational, and personal collections. How one uses and accesses these collections shapes the kinds of histories that might be told from them.

* * *

Homosexuality is a historic occasion to reopen affective and relational virtualities, not so much through the intrinsic qualities of the homosexual but because the 'slantwise' position of the latter, as it were, the diagonal lines he can lay out in the social fabric allow these virtualities to come to light.
Michel Foucault[23]

Foucault's interest in reading the diagonal lines homosexuals trace in the social fabric could be handily connected to how he accessed archives. Historian Mike Featherstone has usefully described how Foucault used the 'French national libraries in highly unorthodox ways by reading seemingly haphazardly "on the diagonal," across the whole range of arts and sciences, centuries and civilizations, so that the unusual juxtapositions they arrived at summoned up new lines of thought and possibilities to radically re-think and re-classify received wisdom.'[24] Thus the insights stemming from texts such as *Discipline and Punish* and *The Birth of the Clinic* came into being only through Foucault's purposeful and strategically irresponsible method of accessing archives. For his capacity to read archives in this way Gilles Deleuze dubbed Foucault 'the new archivist,' and acknowledged his role in ushering in new, constellated forms of knowledge such as discourse analysis.[25]

I thought of Foucault when, in the summer of 2010, I cut a deal with the LA&M's executive director, Rick Storer. I had been given a fellowship to travel to Chicago for the summer to conduct foundational research for my dissertation. After finding a temporary sublet in Logan Square in the apartment gallery of a friend, I had little money left to obtain membership of the LA&M—something I considered a good show of faith in supporting a community archive I would rely heavily upon. I offered my time instead. With Storer's agreement I devoted mornings to doing the institution's work and afternoons to doing my own. I was upfront with Storer about not having any kind of formalized archival training, but I also conveyed that I was happy to learn, and could, at the very least, perform basic administrative tasks. He put me on sorting and filing incoming documents into the LA&M's vertical files—housed in a row of filing cabinets, and comprised of hundreds of subject folders dedicated to people, clubs, organizations, events, and general categories of interest ('flogging,' for example). This, in my mind, was good for the archives and good for me in equal measure; the archives were the beneficiary of my labor, and I would likely be put into contact with material that was not on my formal research agenda, greatly expanding my limited knowledge.

My intuition was right. While filing away various documents I encountered an astonishing array of material. I swooned over a clutch of letters that the English artist Bill Ward sent to his stateside beau—Ward's drawings animate the margins of his sweet prose, adding fantasy and hilarious commentary to his descriptions of longing nestled in the mundane activities of everyday life. I found, also, that I had a difficult time navigating the graphic design of flyers and event postcards of leather organizations from the late 1990s and early 2000s, when three-dimensional fonts and metallicized colors butted up against one another in what I thought was an overly noisy bid for attention. Occasionally, I flipped through the leather catalogs I encountered in the vertical files to get a sense of what kind of gear was available in the 1970s—the decade to which I initially limited my study. In other words, every day was a fresh encounter with something outside of the purview of what I knew.

Unlike the other researchers who came to the LA&M, I was allowed to do my work in the stacks of the archives—not in the library reading room where scholars and visitors were typically set up. To say this showed a high degree of trust on the part of the LA&M and its staff would be an understatement; and knowing this, I tried to prove throughout my stay that this trust was not misplaced. My special access was partly due to the fact that the previous archivist and programs manager, Jennifer Tyburczy, whose work on sex museums has been essential reading for me, had left only weeks before, leaving a gap in the day-to-day operations of the museum. I was a temporary, and reliable stand-in—at least until the summer was over and I returned to my graduate obligations.

Working in the archives for a season allowed me to sink into its collections—to open up the flat files and plumb the vertical files during my own work time. I kept a running list of items I found interesting or wanted to find more about. Soon I was keeping lists within lists. One such sub-list was a catalog of everything I came across that was the color yellow. Once the list grew past a few items I began to actively look for yellow things. Looking back at this document I cannot tell which items were added to my list from accidental encounter and which were the result of more purposeful looking. As I learned and consumed more, my looking habits became more sophisticated. This was an education in archival praxis, knowledge gathered in the doing.

The decision to keep a running list of yellow things emerged from a very specific form of document I encountered again and again in my work sorting papers into the LA&M's vertical files: the hanky code. There was a subject file dedicated to the hanky code, but I found many more examples of the code outside of it—in magazines and other subject files dedicated to groups like Samois, or bars such as The Gold Coast.

The origins of the hanky code have yet to be identified, even though many have made guesses or have produced anecdotal evidence.[26] As previously described in relation to Die Kränken's *LA/ATX Pocket Expo: The New Rules of Flagging*, the hanky code, broadly speaking, is a system of signaling or flagging a variety of sexual interests on the body using colored handkerchiefs or bandanas. Particular colors are aligned with particular sexual activities, and which rear pocket the hanky is placed in indicates a generally active or passive role. Contrary to the notion of a dominant right hand/side, the wearer places a hanky on the left side of her body to communicate dominance. A submissive relationship to a particular color-coded act is communicated through right side placement. The wearer of a hanky only has to know the colors of the hanky code that interest her. It is a system developed for *visual apprehension*.

Hal Fischer, a San Francisco-based photographer and art critic who was part of a group of West Coast conceptual photographers metastasized around the work and publishing efforts of Lew Thomas, created a series of photographs which eventually accompanied an essay on what he termed 'Gay Semiotics.' Identifying the signifiers of a male homosexual subcultural style that he was intimately familiar with from the streets of San Francisco, Fischer added wry texts to seemingly straightforward, taxonomic photographs of 'archetypal media image[s]' of gay men.[27] One of these photographs (figure 4.5) depicts the backsides of two men wearing jeans, with bandanas peeking out of their back pockets. Fischer's text (initially handwritten, and in

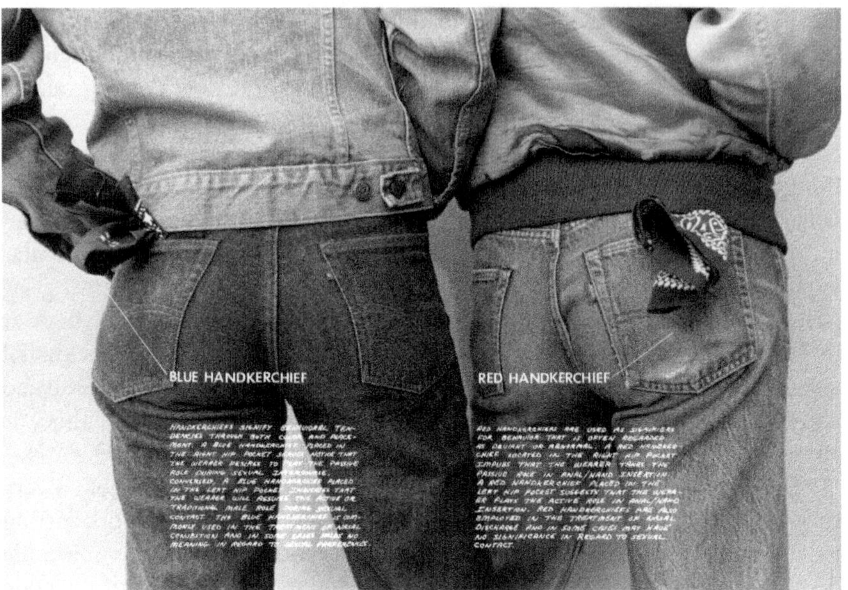



**4.5**   Hal Fischer, *Handkerchiefs*, from the series 'Gay Semiotics,' 1977, printed in 2014

subsequent editions typed) describes the meanings of both blue and red handkerchiefs. Although the photographs are printed in black and white, the words 'blue' and 'red' semiotically charge the photograph. With great wit Fischer assumes the tone of the academic ethnographer/semiotician, only to undermine this seriousness by the end of his text:

> Red handkerchiefs are used as signifiers for behavior that is often regarded as deviant or abnormal. A red handkerchief located in the right hip pocket implies that the wearer takes the passive role in anal/hand insertion. A red handkerchief placed in the left hip pocket suggests that the wearer plays the active role in anal/hand insertion. Red handkerchiefs are also employed in the treatment of nasal discharge and in some cases may have no significance in regard to sexual contact.

Like the competing meaning of fisting with the practical utilitarian purpose of taking care of 'nasal discharge,' the hanky code remained the subject of much debate during the 1970s (and even today). A letter to the editor in a 1976 issue of *Drummer* points out that the genesis of the 'media hoax' known as the hanky code was 'an article on S&M in New York's *Village Voice* [in] the summer of '75 […] they're still laughing about it back in the pressroom.'[28] Elsewhere the origin is attributed to a leather store in San Francisco called Leather and Things in early 1969, or to a distressed reporter for the gay entertainment magazine *Queen's Quarterly* who needed copy to make deadline and so invented the hanky code.[29] *Drummer* published a hanky code in 1977, but there were also earlier hanky codes published in 1974 and 1975 in the West Coast bar magazine *Scene and Machine.*

At issue in all of these accounts of the 'origins' of the hanky code are the anxious interactions between broader gay and lesbian publics, specifically commenced by print media, and the sites of leather commerce and cruising. The high cost of leather gear was already an issue within leather communities, as Gayle Rubin has pointed out.[30] A bandana was unique in that it was not a garment made of leather, and so it was much cheaper and provided an opportunity for those of limited economic means to enter into and participate in the signaling system of leathersex.

Regardless of the original intent of the code (as hoax, as copy, as humor, as earnest attempt at streamlining cruising), it was in fact used, to varying degrees, throughout the 1970s and 1980s. The versions of the hanky code are as numerous as the litanies of fetishes indexed in the longest of codes. Hanky codes, and their specific language, were often cannibalized and expanded based on a particular distributor's aims, with the result being a great accretion of codes that challenged the legibility of the system. Here's Rubin:

> At first, the major colors were red, black, yellow, and navy blue. [...] By the late 1970s the hankie codes had been elaborated and subdivided into every more byzantine categorizations of sexual tastes. But while there were individuals whose tastes undoubtedly ran the gamut, the more exotic colors were often worn more for humor than serious cruising.[31]

Sometimes these codes were tweaked to reflect the gendered position of the publisher, as is the case with the lesbian hanky code published by Samois, the first organization of lesbian leatherwomen, which adds the color maroon for menstruation fetish, and alters the meaning of pink (alternatively tit torture, dildo play, or piercing) to signify the activity of fondling breasts.[32]

Interesting to me, though, is that yellow does not change its meaning across various iterations of the code. Yellow always indicates golden showers—the act of releasing, drinking, and otherwise making recreative use of urine in an erotic context.[33] It may seem obvious, but this combination of color and activity is not arbitrary. So strong are the associations of the color yellow with urine that a great deal of the visual and material culture produced by leather communities that is yellow directly references golden showers.

But even though the associations between yellow and piss are strong, a practical use of the hanky code is challenged by the interior conditions of most leather bars. Many bars had little or very dim light, and this would make 'reading' the color of a particular hanky difficult, especially when trying to parse out subtle color gradations such as yellow, mustard, and rust. A letter to the editor of *Drummer*, written by a reader known only as Trooper, wanly weighs in: 'Is the man into piss? If there isn't a wet patch on his Levis, stand downwind from him and breathe deep, Dad. Or wet your leg. But don't look for a yellow hanky.'[34] Or as Jack Fritscher, then-editor of *Drummer*, writes in the magazine soon thereafter:

> Try walking up to a dude who drips with leather, chains, and six handkerchieves [*sic*], and you find the only way to get an honest reading these costumey nights is to ask him: 'Do you mean all those signals, or are they only junk jewelry?' Some of these frauds cruise under so many flags they look like the semaphore version of *Hello Dolly*.[35]

Fritscher's complaint is somewhat different from Trooper's; for Fritscher it is the excess of signals/flags that reveals a poseur. Trooper's issue with the hanky code is that it is a form of negotiation that replaces direct contact with the body—either visual or olfactory.

While working in the archives of the LA&M, I wondered what a history would look like if it took its cues from an organizing principle native to leather communities, such as the hanky code. I even thought about the possibility of letting the code structure my entire dissertation. Such a thought experiment led me to gather up instances of the color yellow in earnest, so as to evoke the 'anonymous murmur of statements' that 'bracket' the archival appearances of subjects.[36]

In using one color of the hanky code as a method to organize the material of the LA&M's collections, cutting against archival best practices and the system of subject headings already in use at the LA&M, I do not mean to suggest that this is the sole or even the *best* way of proceeding with archival research. Nor do I think it is particularly applicable outside the context of the LA&M's collections. What it reveals to me in a way that I have found non-replicable through other methodologies of archival research is a sense of the heterogeneity of material and visual culture that, in the case of leather archives at least, inevitably falls back into the body as the site of sensorial exchange and spatial-political experience.

To assemble my list I had to evaluate what I would *count* as yellow: for yellow itself is a plurality of multiple hues whose differences in value are elided. What color is it, exactly? Is it marigold? The deep amber, even brown, of a popper vial? And does the color yellow actually have to exist on the document or object itself, or is the word, or a representation of piss enough? Does piss automatically count as yellow – because, depending on how hydrated one is, it can be clear also?

I erred on the side of an expanded and inclusive definition of yellow, not just the color itself but the word, as well as black-and-white illustrations and photographs of golden showers. Doing so ensured that I encountered the color (or its proxy) in a variety of objects during my summer at the LA&M: in hanky codes, drawings of watersports, newsletters for watersport fetish groups, advertisements for poppers, descriptions of the light in leather bars (in both erotic pulp fiction and non-fiction), and in consistent reference to the liquid ingestible most often sold in leather bars—beer.[37] Together, these associations with the color yellow trace an evocative line through the body: from inhalation and ingestion to urination. As such, a generalized portrait of the leather body and some of its potentialities emerges from the adjacent placement of these documents and objects. Such a performative assemblage from the archive is meant to reflect a sampling of the hallmarks of leather visualities and spaces.

To give you some sense of what I mean, and how, indeed, these things come to mean, I reproduce here ten representative objects (plates 1–10) from my list of well over one hundred. It is an 'anthology of existences,' and I echo Foucault, who in 'The Lives of Infamous Men' confides, 'The selection here was guided by nothing more substantial than my taste, my pleasure, an emotion, laughter, surprise, a certain dread, or some other feeling whose intensity I might have trouble justifying, now that the first moment of discovery has passed.'[38]

These ten items were found in a variety of locations across the museum's collections and exhibitions—the Sean lithograph (plate 3) was on display in the main exhibition hall; the pulp novel and the popper advertisement from the back cover of an issue of *Drummer* are both from the library's collections (plates 7, 8). Other items were found in particular archival collections: the untitled Chuck Arnett drawing and the GSA newsletter (plates 4, 5). Two of the ten items are from the museum's fibers collection (plates 1, 2), and the two hanky codes are from the vertical subject file dedicated to the code (plates 9, 10). The 'Piss on Big Brother' poster (plate 6) was one of many similar posters located in the museum's flat files. To refind these items would necessitate a scavenger hunt through the various areas of the LA&M—and one of the items, the GSA newsletter, has yet to be refound from my first visit in 2010. In such an embodied mode of looking one would likely encounter other items and objects, in a process that would mirror my own experiences volunteering and working in the archives.

Each one of these items is distinct and served as the occasion for more research on my part. The Mandana tank top, for example, is a visual imagining of the otherwise exclusively textual hanky code (plate 1). Inside a frame of paisley, most commonly associated with industrially produced bandanas, are two concentric circles of cartoonish representations of men fucking. The men behave in ways that correspond to each respective colored quadrant. In the yellow portion of the shirt men drink beer and pee on one another. There is some indication of bleed, when, for example the figural group that crosses the yellow and red quadrants perform both the activities of golden showers *and* fisting. And yet there is another other yellow here, too, in the form of pale yellow stains below the screen-printed design, indicating a history of use.

Produced by a company punningly known as Soft Corps, advertisements for Mandanas show up in *Drummer* in late 1978 and 1979. One of these advertisements (figure 4.6) features three men in collective embrace, interrupting normative dyadic figurations of partner-based relationships.[39] In addition to their Mandana shirts, two of the men have a variety of colored hankies coming out of their back pockets. The advertisement performs the excess of signals that some of those within leather communities (such as Jack Fritscher and Trooper) worried about in previous and subsequent issues of *Drummer*. The ad copy conveys that even if a potential sexual contact is confused by the color worn on a Mandana T-shirt or tank top (the designs came in single colors, as well as the four-color design represented in the LA&M's collection), the figures would communicate the wearer's sexual desires.

The undated yellow hanky from The Gold Coast (plate 2) is marked with a reproduction of an ink drawing by Etienne. The face of the leatherman, half-obscured in shadow, is a reproduction of Etienne's portrait of Durk Dehner, used as the poster image for the first International Mr. Leather contest in 1979.[40] A large, wooden, painted cut-out of the image was used as stage decoration for the contest, and is currently on display in the Etienne Auditorium of the LA&M alongside the artist's other large-scale mural works. The vivid yellow of the hanky refers handily to several features of the illustrated image (the hair, the ankh, the circular halo that frames the head) as well as serving as a visual reminder of the name of Renslow and Orejudos's bar. The hanky was likely given away by the bar or sold near it, at Male Hide Leathers, which grew organically out of the Gold Coast's operations.[41] Of course, when worn on the body, this particular item could do double duty, signaling an interest in golden showers as well as an allegiance to The Gold Coast as a home bar.

Most of the items on my list illustrate the activity of watersports in a direct and unambiguous way. The Sean lithograph (plate 3), for example, represents two construction workers at play. One stands with a beer in his right hand, looking down at his companion who is skillfully drinking his piss. The hard hats, plain T-shirts, jeans, work boots, and metal lunchbox indicate their profession, in clichéd signs that are readily identifiable. Hanging out of the back-right pocket of the man being pissed on is a handkerchief—a necessity when working outside, but also, in this context, potentially signaling an interest in receiving golden showers. Happily, by virtue of the paper color, the hanky is yellow.

One of a set of five images, these lithographs were produced in an edition of 500 on 'top quality golden art stock.' These and similar art prints were often

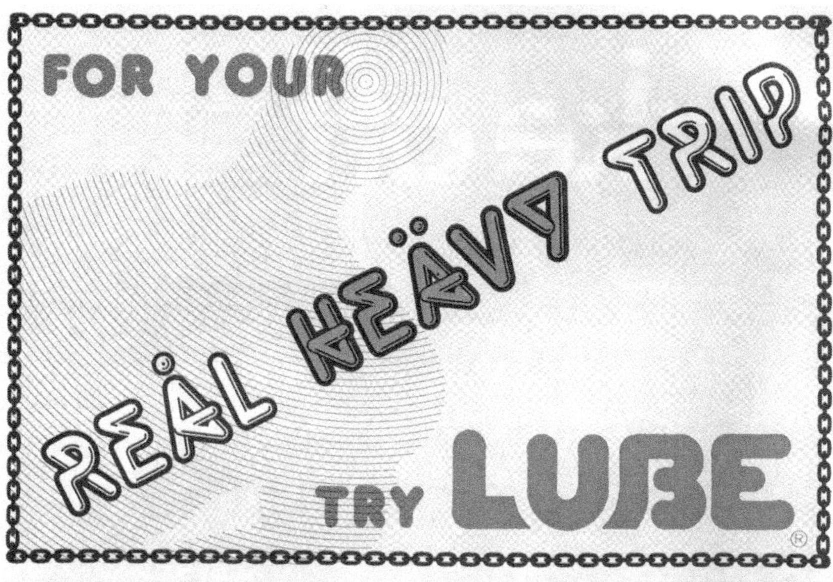


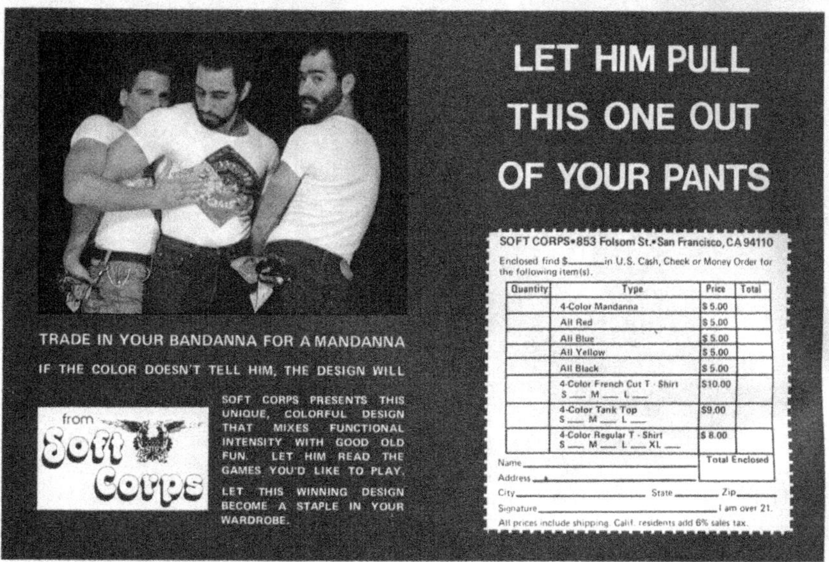


SOFT CORPS•853 Folsom St.•San Francisco, CA 94110

Enclosed find $_______in U.S. Cash, Check or Money Order for the following item(s).

| Quantity | Type | Price | Total |
|---|---|---|---|
| | 4-Color Mandanna | $ 5.00 | |
| | All Red | $ 5.00 | |
| | All Blue | $ 5.00 | |
| | All Yellow | $ 5.00 | |
| | All Black | $ 5.00 | |
| | 4-Color French Cut T - Shirt<br>S ___ M ___ L ___ | $10.00 | |
| | 4-Color Tank Top<br>S ___ M ___ L ___ | $9.00 | |
| | 4-Color Regular T - Shirt<br>S ___ M ___ L ___ XL ___ | $ 8.00 | |
| Name_______________ | | Total Enclosed | |

Address_______________
City_______________ State_______ Zip_______
Signature_______________ I am over 21.
All prices include shipping. Calif. residents add 6% sales tax.

Soft Corps, Mandana [advertisement], *Drummer*, 1978 [back cover]     **4.6**

sold through newsletters, leather organizations, leather shops, and magazines. An early advertisement for the five Sean lithographs depicting 'a most popular pastime' (read: golden showers) appeared in Larry Townsend's self-published *Leatherman's Workbook* in 1976, for example. Sean had a wide-ranging career,

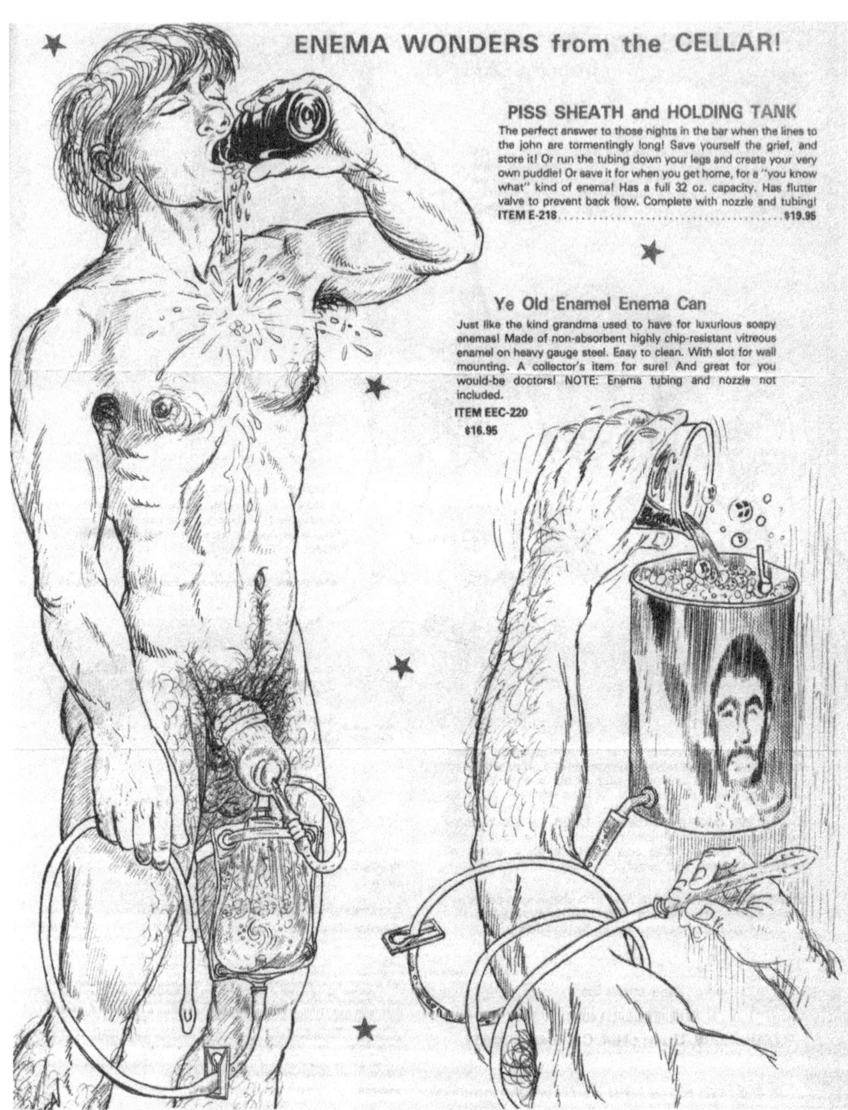


**4.7**    Sean, illustrations for The Cellar catalog, c. 1977

and was sometimes contracted out by leather goods companies and stores such as The Cellar to illustrate their catalogs (figure 4.7). In one particular image a man greedily drinks a bottle of beer, which cascades down his chest and has also already magically worked its way through his body, filling an enema bag attached to the man's cock. The product for sale is described as a 'Piss Sheath and Holding Tank' which includes a 'flutter valve to prevent back

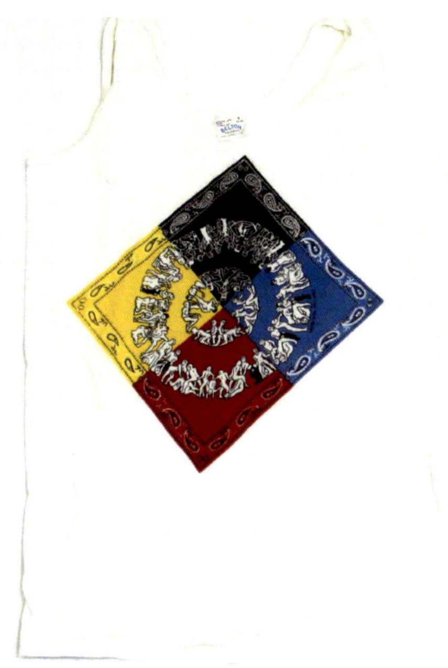

Soft Corps, Mandana [tank top], c. 1978                                                  **1**

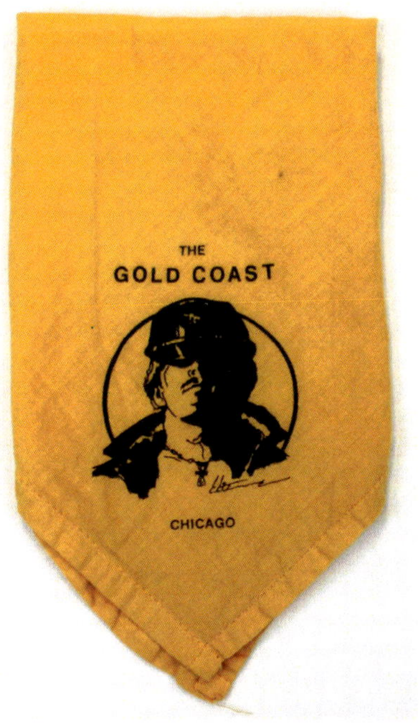


Etienne, Gold Coast Hanky, c. 1978                                                       **2**

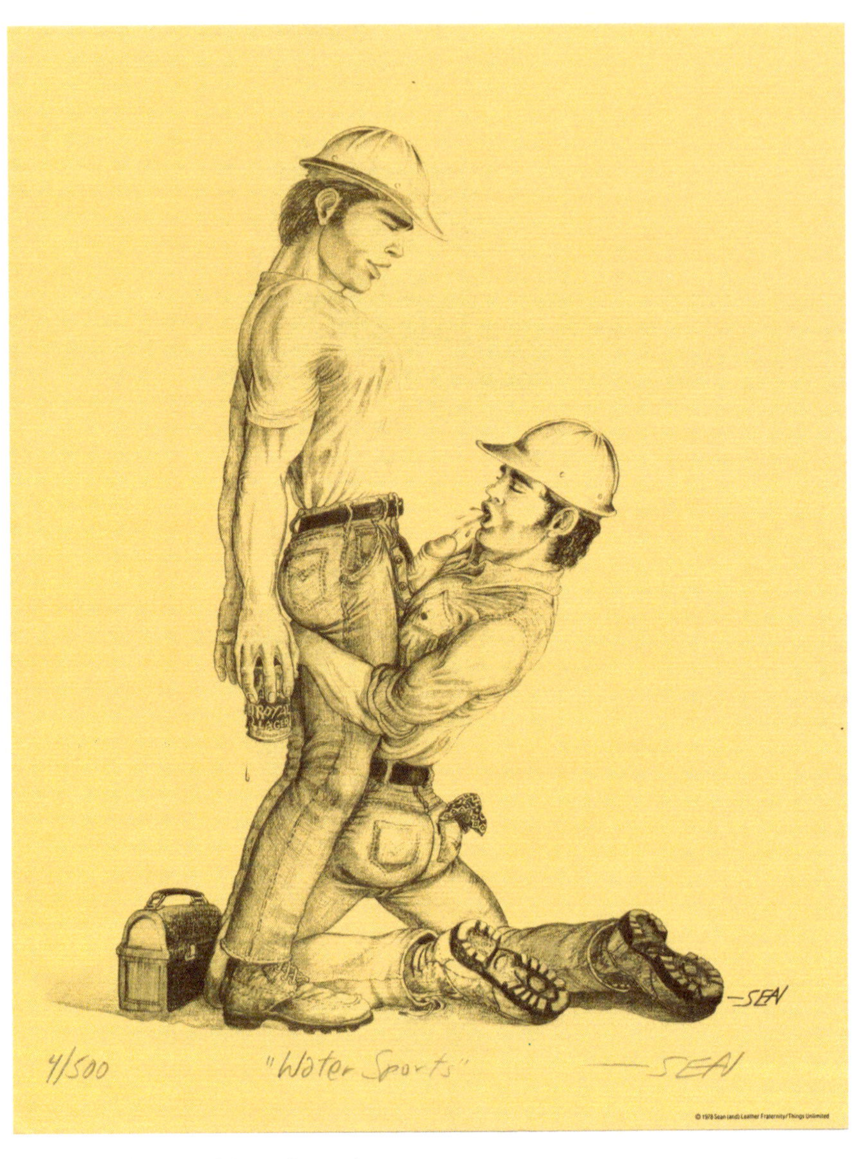



3    Sean, from the series 'Water Sports,' c. 1978

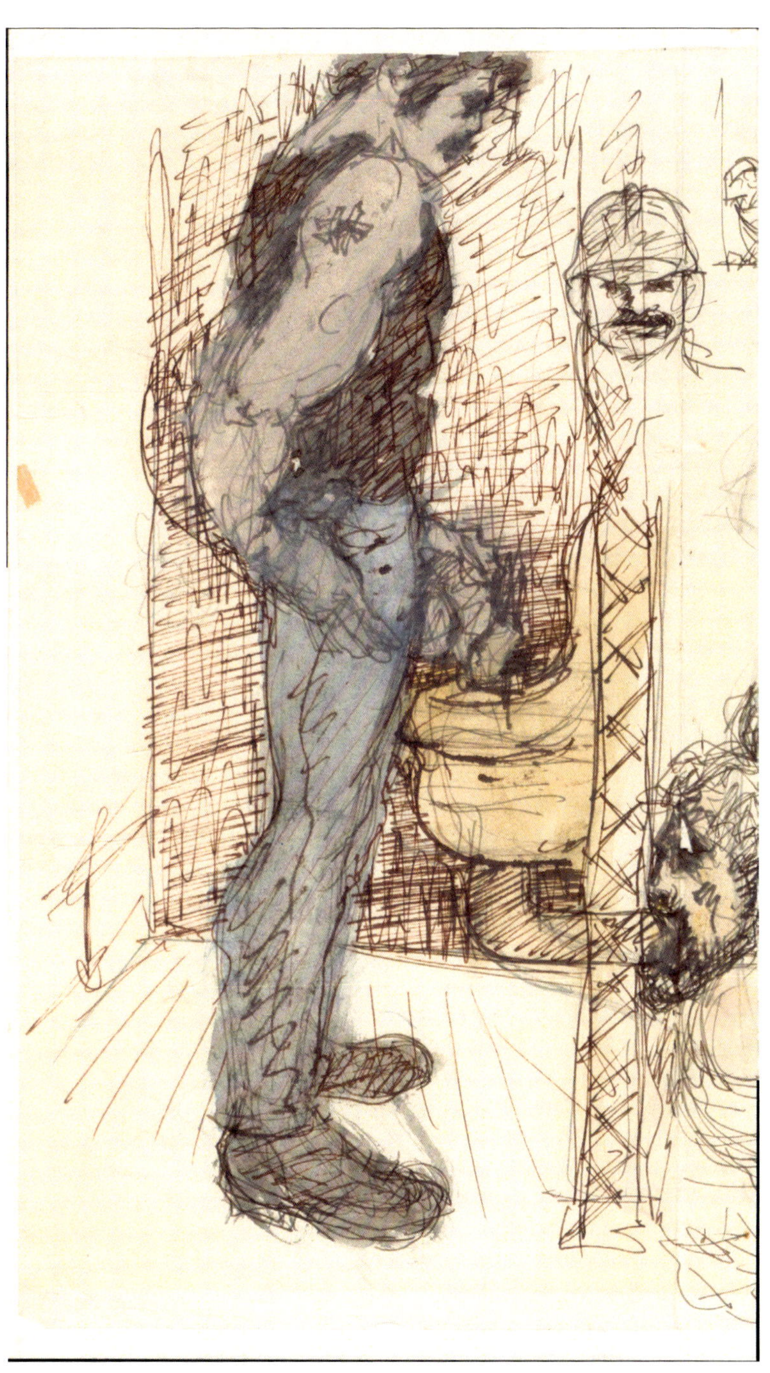

Chuck Arnett, *Untitled*, 1970

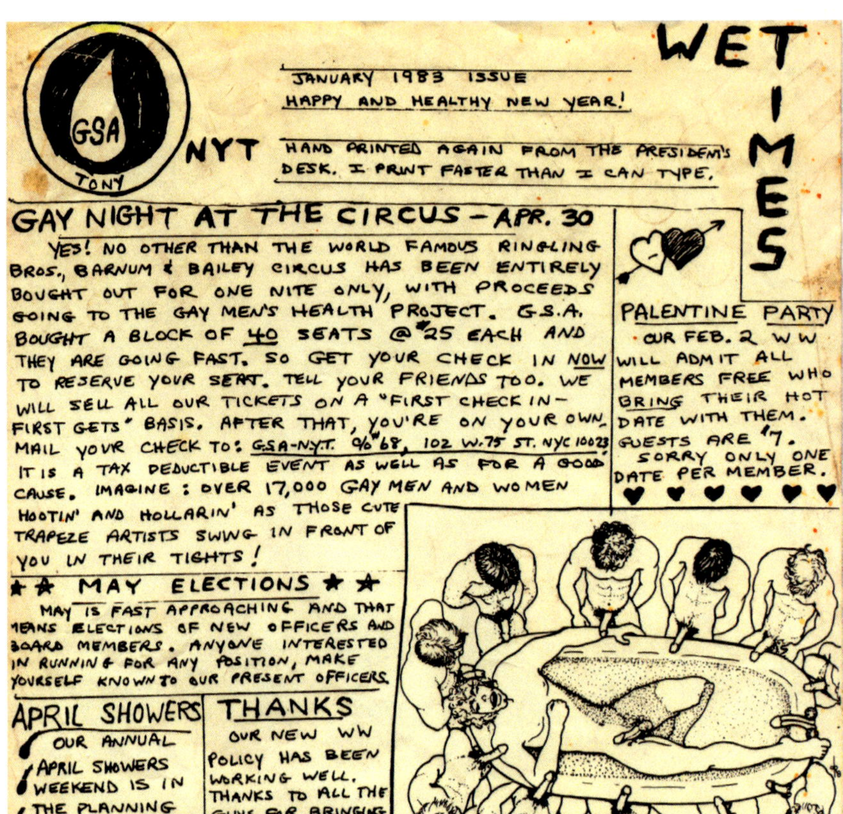

# WET TIMES



JANUARY 1983 ISSUE
HAPPY AND HEALTHY NEW YEAR!

HAND PRINTED AGAIN FROM THE PRESIDENT'S DESK. I PRINT FASTER THAN I CAN TYPE.

## GAY NIGHT AT THE CIRCUS — APR. 30

YES! NO OTHER THAN THE WORLD FAMOUS RINGLING BROS., BARNUM & BAILEY CIRCUS HAS BEEN ENTIRELY BOUGHT OUT FOR ONE NITE ONLY, WITH PROCEEDS GOING TO THE GAY MEN'S HEALTH PROJECT. G.S.A. BOUGHT A BLOCK OF 40 SEATS @ $25 EACH AND THEY ARE GOING FAST. SO GET YOUR CHECK IN NOW TO RESERVE YOUR SEAT. TELL YOUR FRIENDS TOO. WE WILL SELL ALL OUR TICKETS ON A "FIRST CHECK IN — FIRST GETS" BASIS. AFTER THAT, YOU'RE ON YOUR OWN. MAIL YOUR CHECK TO: G.S.A-N.Y.T. % 68, 102 W. 75 ST. NYC 10023. IT IS A TAX DEDUCTIBLE EVENT AS WELL AS FOR A GOOD CAUSE. IMAGINE: OVER 17,000 GAY MEN AND WOMEN HOOTIN' AND HOLLARIN' AS THOSE CUTE TRAPEZE ARTISTS SWING IN FRONT OF YOU IN THEIR TIGHTS!

## ★ ★ MAY ELECTIONS ★ ★

MAY IS FAST APPROACHING AND THAT MEANS ELECTIONS OF NEW OFFICERS AND BOARD MEMBERS. ANYONE INTERESTED IN RUNNING FOR ANY POSITION, MAKE YOURSELF KNOWN TO OUR PRESENT OFFICERS.

## PALENTINE PARTY

OUR FEB. 2 WW WILL ADMIT ALL MEMBERS FREE WHO BRING THEIR HOT DATE WITH THEM. GUESTS ARE $7. SORRY ONLY ONE DATE PER MEMBER.

♥ ♥ ♥ ♥ ♥ ♥



## APRIL SHOWERS

OUR ANNUAL APRIL SHOWERS WEEKEND IS IN THE PLANNING STAGE. SO KEEP APRIL 29-30, MAY 1 FREE FOR A "WET & WILD" WEEKEND, INCLUDING THE CIRCUS... DETAILS WILL BE OUT NEXT MONTH. WE'RE SURE SOME GUYS FROM THE G.S.A. MAINSTREAM IN D.C. WILL CUM UP TO JOIN US, SO IT'LL BE WILD!

## THANKS

OUR NEW WW POLICY HAS BEEN WORKING WELL. THANKS TO ALL THE GUYS FOR BRINGING EXACT AMOUNT OF DOOR ENTRY. IT SPEEDS UP THINGS. AND THANKS FOR DRINKING UP BEFORE ORDERING ANOTHER. IT KEEPS COSTS DOWN. ANYWAY WE ARE INTO RECYCLING — AREN'T WE?

— GEORGE B. — THANKS - I'LL THINK OF YOU IN San Francisco!

## Calendar

FEB. 2 — WW PALENTINE PARTY — CHECK-IN 9-10 M/S CLUB
MAR. 2 — WW TIDES OF MARCH PARTY 9-10 M/S CLUB
APR. — WW
APR. 30 — GAY CIRCUS AT MADISON SQ. GARDEN
APR. 30 — OUR ANNUAL APRIL SHOWERS PARTY FOLLOWING THE CIRCUS. DETAILS IN THE NEXT NEWS LETTER.

**5**  The Golden Showers Association, New York Tributary, *Wet Times Newsletter* (January 1983)

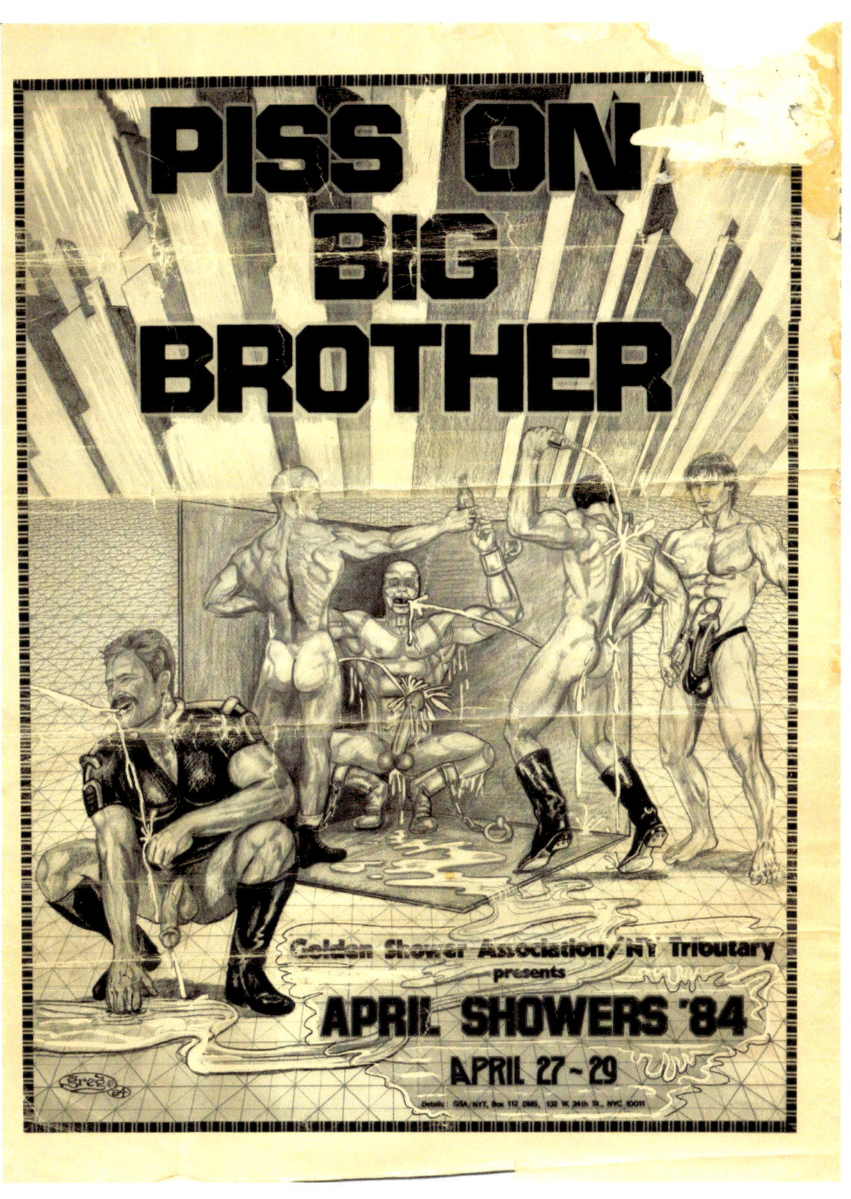


Greg, *Piss on Big Brother* [poster], 1984

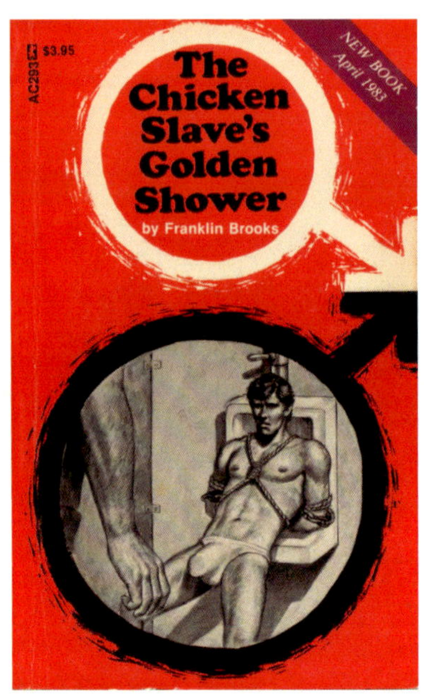


**7**    Cover of *The Chicken Slave's Golden Shower*, 1983

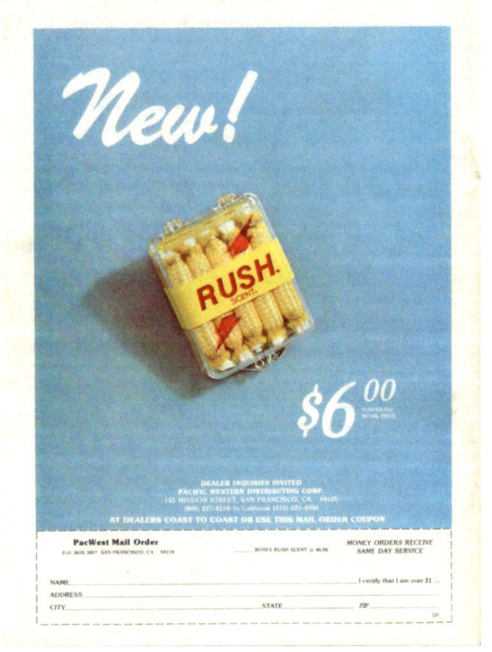


**8**    Pac-West Distributing, Rush [advertisement], *Drummer*, 1977

**COLOR**  **LEFT SIDE**   **RIGHT SIDE**

| COLOR | LEFT SIDE | RIGHT SIDE |
|---|---|---|
| Red | Fist Fucker | Fist Fuckee |
| Dark Blue | Anal Sex, Top | Anal Sex, Bottom |
| Light Blue | Oral Sex, Top | Oral Sex, Bottom |
| Robins Egg Blue | Light S/M, Top | Light S/M, Bottom |
| Mustard | Food Fetish, Top | Food Fetish, Bottom |
| Orange | Anything Goes, Top | Anything Goes, Bottom |
| Yellow | Gives Golden Showers | Wants Golden Showers |
| Green | Hustler, Selling | Hustler, Buying |
| Olive Drab | Uniforms/Military, Top | Uniforms/Military, Bottom |
| White | Likes Novices, Chickenhawk | Novice (or Virgin) |
| White Lace | Victorian Scenes, Top | Victorian Scenes, Bottom |
| Gray | Does Bondage | Wants To Be Put In Bondage |
| Brown | Shit Scenes, Top | Shit Scenes, Bottom |
| Black | Top, Heavy S/M & Whipping | Bottom, Heavy S/M & Whipping |
| | | |
| Purple | Piercer | Piercee |
| Maroon | Likes Menstruating Women | Is Menstruating |
| Lavender | Group Sex, Top | Group Sex, Bottom |
| Pink | Breast Fondler | Breast Fondlee |

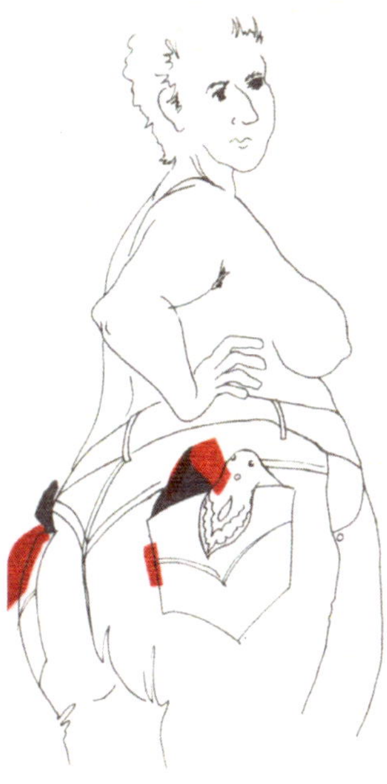

# HANDKERCHIEF COLOR CODE FOR LESBIANS

*a project of*

## samois

P.O. BOX 2364, BERKELEY, CA 94702

SAN FRANCISCO BAY AREA'S

LESBIAN-FEMINIST

S/M SUPPORT GROUP

1980


Samois, Handkerchief Color Code for Lesbians, 1980

# THE PLEASURE CHEST
## Introduces the World's Most Comprehensive Hanky Code

| HANKY COLOR | WORN ON LEFT | WORN ON RIGHT |
| --- | --- | --- |
| Light Blue | Wants Head | Expert Cocksucker |
| Robin's Egg Blue | 69-er | 69-ee |
| Medium Blue | Cop | Cop-sucker |
| Navy Blue | Fucker | Fuckee |
| Teal Blue | Cock & Ball Torturer | Cock & Ball Torturee |
| Red | Fist Fucker | Fist Fuckee |
| Light Pink | Dildo Fucker | Dildo Fuckee |
| Dark Pink | Tit Torturer | Tit Torturee |
| Dark Red | 2-handed Fister | 2-handed Fistee |
| Maroon | Likes Menstruating Women | Woman Menstruating |
| Mauve | Into Navel Worshippers | Has Navel Fetish |
| Magenta | "Suck My Pits" | Armpit Freak |
| Purple | Piercer | Piercee |
| Lavender | Likes Drags | Drag |
| Yellow | Pisser | Piss Freak |
| Pale Yellow | Spits | Drool Crazy |
| Mustard | Has 8" or More | Wants a Big One |
| Gold | 2 Looking for One | One Looking for 2 |
| Orange | Anything Anytime | Nothing Now |
| Apricot | Two Tons o' Fun | Chubby Chaser |
| Coral | "Suck My Toes" | Shrimper |
| Rust | A Cowboy | His Horse |
| Fuschia | Spanker | Spankee |
| Kelly Green | Hustler | John |
| Olive Drab | Military Top | Military Bottom |
| Hunter Green | Daddy | Hunting for Daddy |
| Lime Green | Dines off Tricks (Sex w/Food) | Dinner Plate |
| Beige | Rimmer | Rimmee |
| Brown | Scat Top | Scat Bottom |
| Brown Lace | Has Uncut Dick | Likes Uncut Dick |
| Brown Satin | Circumsized | Likes Circumsized Cock |
| Black | Heavy S&M Top | Heavy S&M Bottom |
| Gray | Bondage Top | Bondage Bottom |
| Charcoal | Latex Fetish. Top | Latex Fetish. Bottom |
| Gray Flannel | Actually Owns a Suit | Likes Men in Suits |
| White | "Beat My Meat" | "I'll Do Us Both" |
| Cream | Cums in Scum Bags | Sucks It Out |
| Red/White Stripe | Shaver | Shavee |
| Black/White Stripe | Likes Black Bottoms | Likes Black Tops |
| Brown/White Stripe | Likes Latino Bottoms | Likes Latino Tops |
| Yellow/White Stripe | Likes Oriental Bottoms | Likes Oriental Tops |
| White Lace | Likes White Bottoms | Likes White Tops |
| Paisley | Wears Boxer Shorts | Likes Boxer Shorts |
| Fur | Bestialitist. Top | Bestialitist. Bottom |
| Silver Lame | Starfucker | Star |
| Gold Lame | Likes Bottom Musclemen | Likes Top Musclemen |
| Leopard | Has Tattoos | Likes Tattoos |
| Tan | Smokes Cigars | Likes Cigars |
| Teddy Bear | Cuddler | Cuddlee |
| Kewpie Doll | Chicken | Chicken Hawk |
| Dirty Jockstrap | Wears a Dirty Jock | Sucks 'em Clean |
| Zip-Lock Baggy | Has Drugs | Looking for Drugs |
| Kleenex | Stinks | Sniffs |
| Handywipe | Gives HOT Motor Oil Massages | Wears It Well |
| Chamois | Rides a Motorcycle | Likes Bikers |
| Cocktail Napkin | Bartender | Bar Groupie |
| Doily | Tearoom Top | Tearoom Bottom |
| Mosquito Netting | Top for Sex Outdoors | Bottom for Same |

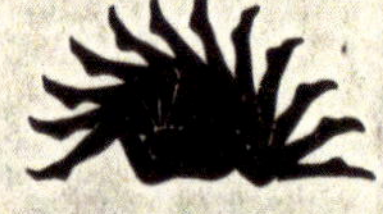

*The Pleasure Chest Ltd.*
7733 Santa Monica Boulevard
Los Angeles, California 90046
(213) 650-1022

 The Pleasure Chest, 'The World's Most Comprehensive Hanky Code,' c. 1985

flow.' Sean's drawing depicts a perverse circuit of the body—beer goes in, piss comes out, and then goes in again (via the enema bag).

A similar fantasy is imagined in the untitled and undated Chuck Arnett drawing (plate 4), wherein a man pisses into a urinal (which has been colored by the artist a bright yellow). On the other side of the wall a bearded man opens his mouth to accept the piss carried through the pipe. A ghostly figure of a construction worker—Arnett most likely reused an uncompleted sketch—floats above the scene, face partially embedded in the dividing wall that separates pisser from pissee. Arnette depicted golden showers many times throughout his career; perhaps the best-known example would be the promotional image he created for The Red Star Saloon (c. 1970), copies of which 'found their way onto the john walls of leather maniacs everywhere.'[42]

The Golden Showers Association's newsletter *Wet Times* is, in many respects, like any other organizational newsletter in the LA&M collections (plate 5). Handwritten and then photocopied onto pale yellow paper, it contains informational items germane to the organization's membership: announcements regarding upcoming events (a circus night to benefit the Gay Men's Health Crisis, an April Showers party, a 'wet and wild' weekend, and a 'Tides of March' party), news on elections, and personal announcements ('George B. I'll think of <u>you</u> in San Francisco'). Most everything is a riff on the basic premise of the organization, which is to support and facilitate those interested in golden showers. The anonymous drawing on the newsletter's first page dramatizes this activity. It depicts a group of men (shown in aerial perspective) gathering around the edge of a tub, in which a long-haired man, mouth open, relaxes in the stippled water. The formal design of the bathtub's faucet is echoed several times over in the cock and balls of the men surrounding the tub. Although liquid is not drawn coming out of the cocks of this circle of men (like in the illustrations on the Mandana), the caption helps a viewer imagine the act of urination by campily riffing on the lines of the famous 1952 musical-movie: 'I'm singing in the rain, just singing in the rain.'

A year later the group held its annual 'April Showers' party, and produced a poster that playfully referenced the dystopian George Orwell novel, *1984* (plate 6). The slogan of the party, 'Piss on Big Brother,' conflated the surveillance state of Orwell's novel with the linguistics of the gay male fraternity. For the event's poster, leather artist Greg depicts a city of skyscrapers dramatically falling away in two-point perspective. On a grid-like ground, whose horizon meets the city but doesn't adhere to its perspectival rules, five men drink and bathe in each other's piss. A sixth figure is implied via a stream of liquid coming from off-left. The central figure, the object of the attentions of two other men, is shackled in a half-cube, urine flowing off of his body and toward the bottom of the image, and forming an organic frame around the title of the weekend-long party.

If the illustration for the GSA's party is explicit, the cover for the pulp novel *The Chicken Slave's Golden Shower* (published in 1983) is less so (plate 7). The uncredited cover illustration, key-holed by one of two adjoined male symbols, depicts two figures. One is propped up against a urinal, bound by rope with his arms tied behind his back and his legs splayed. His erect cock almost bursts out of his tight underwear. He looks incredulously at a figure who faces him—only his hairy arm and waist are visible. It is implied that this man is about to give the chicken (the young man on the toilet) a golden shower. While this, and similar books' narratives are filled with orgasmic exclamations ('Do it, daddy, give my guts a golden shower!')[43] and improbable embodiments, a narrative version of its cover illustration appears nowhere in the book. It was not uncommon for the pulp novels published by Greenleaf or Surrey (two of the most popular gay erotic fiction publishers at the time) to use artwork, sometimes unlicensed, from artists unconnected to the narrative of the story.[44] Leather authors such as Larry Townsend and Jack Fritscher bucked this trend, by commissioning artists to create drawings specifically based on the narratives inside.

The advertisement for Rush poppers reproduced in full color on the back cover of *Drummer* #18 might not seem to conform to the other yellow objects previously described on my list (plate 8). Manufactured and distributed by Pac West Distributing (PWD), Rush poppers derived their name from the effects of amyl nitrite (and other other alkyl nitrites such as butyl nitrite); when inhaled, poppers relax smooth muscle tissue—including sphincter muscles. By relaxing the channels through which blood flows, poppers lower the heart rate and thus users experience a 'rush,' or flushed feeling. As described by *Time* magazine in 1978, 'the popper fad began among homosexuals, who first used amyl nitrite to enhance sexual pleasure.'[45]

The plastic case in the advertisement is screened with the product's logo and name—a combination of a yellow band with a red lightning bolt design. Inside of the case are five poppers—tiny glass ampoules concealed by cotton batting and held together with yellow netting bound at both ends, having the appearance of tiny corncobs. These would be broken, 'popped,' and inhaled directly or inserted into nasal inhalers, which would contain the vapor emitted from the broken ampoule, prolonging the use of each popper.

Rush poppers cornered a significant share of the poppers market by the late 1970s; in 1977 PWD reported retail sales in excess of $20 million.[46] This success may be attributable, in part, to the use of the advertising character of Captain Rush, a white, dark-haired superhero, whose outfit featured the iconic red and yellow colorway shared by Rush's logo and product design (figure 4.8).[47] In a series of short episodic advertisements bought by Rush to adorn the back cover of *Drummer* issues #12–15, Captain Rush worked tirelessly to defeat the Zorro-like Brandex and the silver-headed Bullit (a play

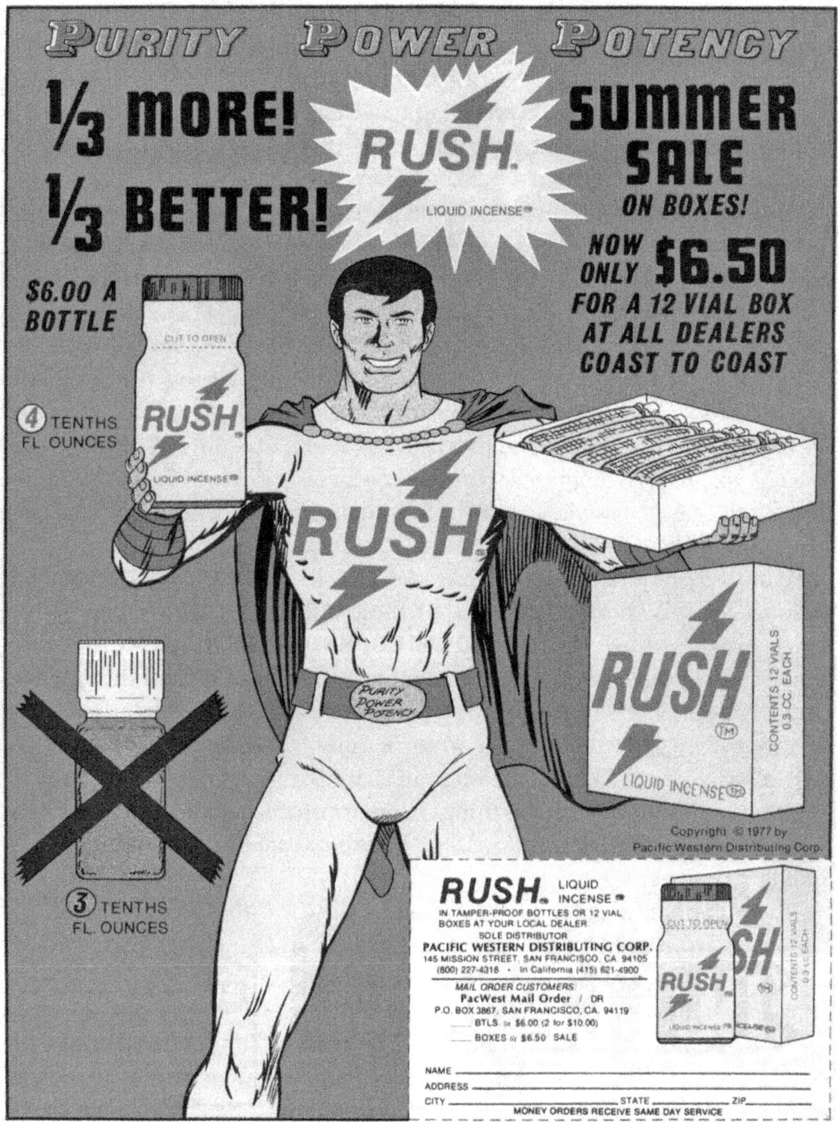



RUSH. LIQUID INCENSE ®
IN TAMPER-PROOF BOTTLES OR 12 VIAL
BOXES AT YOUR LOCAL DEALER.
SOLE DISTRIBUTOR
PACIFIC WESTERN DISTRIBUTING CORP.
145 MISSION STREET, SAN FRANCISCO, CA 94105
(800) 227-4318 · In California (415) 621-4900

MAIL ORDER CUSTOMERS:
PacWest Mail Order / DR
P.O. BOX 3867, SAN FRANCISCO, CA. 94119
____ BTLS. @ $6.00 (2 for $10.00)
____ BOXES @ $6.50 SALE

NAME _______________
ADDRESS _______________
CITY _______ STATE _____ ZIP_____
MONEY ORDERS RECEIVE SAME DAY SERVICE

Pac-West Distributing, Captain Rush [advertisement], *Drummer*, 15 (1977) [back cover] **4.8**

on a competitor brand of poppers that also employed a superhero figure to sell its product). The comic often played off of the perceived and real dangers of poppers. For example, in one episode Captain Rush saves helpless people from a fire started by the dastardly Brandex (low flashpoints are one of the risks of nitrites).

If Captain Rush looks familiar, it is not by coincidence. Meant to remind viewers of Superman, whose story would be revitalized a couple years later in the popular imagination via a series of films starring Christopher Reeve, some of Rush's competitors played off of Captain Rush's similarity to the iconic DC Comics superhero. One competitor brand in particular, Crypt Tonight, was a linguistic pun on Superman's weakness, Kryptonite.

The two hanky codes (plates 9, 10) in the clutch of ten objects I have chosen reveal how the hanky code was amended, and even extended past the point of usefulness. The Samois hanky code was first published in 1979 in the group's aptly named publication, *What Color is Your Handkerchief?* The Samois hanky code card reproduced here, from the LA&M's vertical files, was advertised in this booklet for 25¢ apiece, and features the same illustration that graces the cover of *What Color is Your Handkerchief?* In an explanatory paragraph below the hanky code, the booklet's author(s) explain that 'It is often difficult for S/M lesbians to identify themselves to one another [...] The Women in Samois thought the gay male style of wearing a bandana in one pocket or the other was handy, but didn't wish to adopt their code without alteration.'[48]

Samois attempted to sell *What Color is Your Handkerchief?* in local and national feminist bookstores. One of these bookstores, A Woman's Place, which was based in Oakland and collectively run, had initially carried the booklet with a disclaimer, but soon completely removed it from their shelves, citing the complaints of patrons who perceived the lesbian leather publication as encouraging violence against women. Samois responded with an act of civil disobedience, a 'mill-in,' wherein Samois members milled about the bookstore without buying anything. A report of this action, which included heated conversation, testimony, and debate, is detailed in the April 1980 Samois newsletter.[49]

The other hanky code was produced by the Pleasure Chest, a sex shop in California (with branches in Los Angeles and San Francisco), and it is aptly titled 'The World's Most Comprehensive Hanky Code.' It lists yellow as signifying 'Pisser' if worn on the left and 'Piss Freak' if worn on the right. It is by far the longest hanky code I have found to date, and this copy can be found in the LA&M vertical file dedicated to the hanky code. It contains many gradations of the color yellow: pale yellow is listed as signifying 'Spits' if worn on the left and 'Drool Crazy' if worn on the right; mustard is listed as signifying 'Has 8" or More' if worn on the left and 'Wants a Big One' if worn on the right; gold is listed as '2 Looking for One' if worn on the left and 'One Looking for 2' if worn on the right; yellow with white stripes is listed as signifying 'Likes Oriental Bottoms' if worn on the left and 'Likes Oriental Tops' if worn on the right; gold lamé is listed as signifying 'Likes Bottom Musclemen' if worn on the left and 'Likes Top Musclemen' if worn on the right. Yellow, pale yellow, mustard, gold, yellow with white stripes, and gold lamé are six of fifty-eight options.

Exhaustive in its scope this hanky code goes far beyond utility, pushing the very concept to absurd and farcical proportions.

The object descriptions and histories I have sketched here are schematic, but through careful examination and their new contextual placement in my virtual yellow archive, these ten objects touch the history of leather bars and contests, sex shops and bookstores, biographies of leather artists, leather organizations and support groups such as Samois and the GSA, commercialized drug use and advertising—most specifically poppers—and the consumption of erotic fiction. In essence, a whole world. What emerges, to return to Foucault's comment, is not just a collection of objects, but a way of life, yielding not only a 'culture and an ethics,' but also 'intense relations not resembling those that are institutionalized.'[50]

Indeed, in reading the LA&M's collections diagonally, using the hanky code as an organizing principle, I also have wound up arriving at what archival scholars Andrew Flinn, Mary Stevens, and Elizabeth Shepherd identify as the primary characteristic of community archives, which 'is the active participation of a community in documenting and making accessible the history of their particular group and/or locality *on their own terms*.'[51] That the terms reveal 'affective and relational virtualities' is a hallmark of both the profound pleasures of community-based archives like LA&M, as well as archival and research methodologies that centralize the systems and codes valued by those same communities.

## Notes

1  Mark Thompson (ed.), *Long Road to Freedom: The Advocate History of the Gay and Lesbian Movement* (New York: St. Martin's Press, 1994), p. 244.

2  Kenan Heise, 'Dom Orejudos, 58, Ballet Dancer and Artist Known as "Etienne",' *Chicago Tribune*, 2 October 1991, http://articles.chicagotribune.com/1991-10-02/news/9103300004_1_ballet-choreographer-and-principal-dancer-fantasy-art (accessed 10 October 2017).

3  Chuck Renslow, 'From the Founder: On 25 Years of Leather History,' in Jakob VanLammeren and José Santiago Pérez (eds.), *Leather Archives & Museum: 25 Years* (Chicago: Leather Archives & Museum, 2016), p. 17.

4  Baim and Keehnen, *Leatherman*, pp. 384–6.

5  Gayle Rubin, 'The Leather Archives & Museum: Some Pre-History,' in Jakob VanLammeren and José Santiago Pérez (eds.), *Leather Archives & Museum: 25 Years* (Chicago: Leather Archives & Museum, 2016), p. 25. Rubin points out that exceptions existed, such as the Kinsey Institute (Bloomington, Indiana), and what eventually became known as ONE (Los Angeles, California), and the Gay, Lesbian, Bisexual, and Transgender Historical Society (San Francisco, California). She also notes that all of these institutions were 'underfunded, poorly housed, had little to no staff, and were extremely unstable' (p. 27).

6 Cvetkovich, *An Archive of Feelings*, p. 244.

7 Rubin, 'The Leather Archives & Museum,' p. 25.

8 Ibid., p. 30.

9 Ibid., p. 31.

10 'LA&M Museum Opens in Chicago,' *The Leather Archives & Museum Newsletter*, 2 (April 1996), p. 1.

11 Tyburczy, *Sex Museums*, p. 21.

12 Gayle Rubin, 'The Miracle Mile, South of Market and Gay Male Leather 1962–1997,' in James Brooks et al. (eds.), *Reclaiming San Francisco: History, Politics, Culture* (San Francisco: City Lights Books, 1998), pp. 247–72.

13 Baim and Keehnen, *Leatherman*, p. 384.

14 'Finding Aid to the Randy Sauder and Gary DeNichilo Collection,' Leather Archives & Museum [PERS0021].

15 'Donations to the LA&M,' *The Leather Archives & Museum Newsletter*, 2 (April 1996), p. 4.

16 Joseph Bean, 'Executive Director's Report,' *The Leather Archives & Museum Newsletter*, 4 (April 1998), pp. 1–2.

17 Joseph Bean, 'The Ongoing Adventures of Mr. Bean!!,' *The Leather Archives & Museum Newsletter*, 6 (fall 1998), pp. 1–3.

18 See Chris Zimmerman, 'De-TAILing Vi,' *The Leather Archives & Museum Newsletter*, 11 (spring 2000), p. 2; Joseph Bean, 'We've Got the Keys!! Say, "Hello, Honey, We're Home!",' *The Leather Archives & Museum Newsletter*, 9 (fall 1999), pp. 1–2; and Rick Storer, 'LA&M Mortgage: GONE!!,' *Leather Archives & Museum Newsletter*, 22 (summer 2004), p. 10.

19 Robert B. Marks Ridinger, 'Things Visible and Invisible: The Leather Archives & Museum,' *Journal of Homosexuality*, 43:1 (2002), pp. 1–9.

20 Svetlana Alpers, 'The Museum as a Way of Seeing,' in Ivan Karp and Steven D. Lavine (eds.), *Exhibiting Cultures: The Poetics and Politics of Museum Display* (Washington DC: Smithsonian Institution Press, 1991), pp. 25–32. Alpers puts it succinctly: 'The taste for isolating this kind of attentive looking at crafted objects is as peculiar to our culture as is the museum as the space or institution where the activity takes place' (p. 26).

21 Joseph Bean, 'Busy Building, Growing Community, … and Thank You!,' *The Leather Archives & Museum Newsletter*, 12 (summer 2000), p. 6.

22 Tyburczy, *Sex Museums*, pp. 175–99.

23 Michel Foucault, 'Friendship as a Way of Life,' in *Foucault Live (Interviews, 1961–1984)*, ed. Sylvère Lotringer, trans. John Johnston (New York: Semiotext(e), 1989), p. 138.

24 Mike Featherstone, 'Archive,' *Theory Culture Society*, 23:2–3 (2006), p. 594.

25 Gilles Deleuze, *Foucault*, trans. Seán Hand (Minneapolis, MN: University of Minnesota Press, 1988), p. 1. This approach to archives is also reflected in Foucault's remarks on homosexuality. Recognizing homosexuality as something to be desired, rather than as a problem relating to how, or who, one desires, Foucault proposes that homosexuality opens out a different question, namely: 'what relations, through homosexuality, can be established, invented, multiplied, and modulated?'

(Foucault, 'Friendship as a Way of Life,' p. 135). Homosexuality here is not supposed as an object of study, but a manner of approach within the realm of the social.

26  See Bob Guenther, 'Four Early Hanky Codes,' *Leather Times* [formerly *The Leather Archives & Museum Newsletter*], 23 (fall/winter 2004), pp. 3–5; and Taylor of San Francisco, 'Signs: Their Meaning and Their History,' *DungeonMaster*, 16 (1982), pp. 6–7.

27  For more on subcultural style, see Dick Hebdige, *Subculture: The Meaning of Style* (London: Routledge, 1979).

28  A. Trooper, 'Malecall/ Dear Sir,' *Drummer*, 1:10 (1976), p. 4.

29  Guenther, 'Four Early Hanky Codes,' pp. 3–5. I have not yet found evidence that a hanky code appeared in one of the first issues of *Queen's Quarterly*, counter to Guenther's assertion.

30  Rubin, 'The Valley of the Kings' (Ph.D.), p. 224. Rubin then goes on to describe the implications of being a leather person of limited or low income: 'It is the poor and working-class men who staff many of the non-union (and low-benefit) leather businesses and who have few other employment options. It is the low-income leathermen who live in the most hostile or homophobic neighborhoods, where as visible homosexuals they face a disproportionate amount of violent gay-bashing. And it is these men who have the considerable courage it takes to ride public transportation in full leather regalia' (pp. 225–6).

31  Ibid., pp. 295–7.

32  Gayle Rubin, 'Samois,' *Leather Times* [formerly *The Leather Archives & Museum Newsletter*], 21 (spring 2004), pp. 3–6.

33  I don't use the term 'watersports' here, even though in today's parlance it is commonly elided with golden showers. This is because 'watersports' is an umbrella term, inclusive of fetishes that feature urine, but also other liquids, such as enemas.

34  Trooper, 'Malecall/ Dear Sir,' p. 4.

35  Jack Fritscher, 'Getting Off,' *Drummer*, 3:24 (1978), pp. 8, 72–3.

36  Giorgio Agamben, *Remnants of Auschwitz: The Witness and the Archive* (New York: Zone Books, 1999), p. 145.

37  For example, Brad Gooch describes entering The Mineshaft, a New York leather bar and sex club: 'He felt he'd walked into a pumpkin, black inside but artificially lit by red and yellow glows. It was that amber again, the amber of the movies, but mixed with coal dust.' Brad Gooch, *The Golden Age of Promiscuity* (New York: Knopf, 1996), p. 173.

38  Michel Foucault, 'Lives of Infamous Men,' in *Power: Essential Works of Foucault, 1954–1984*, vol. 3, ed. James D. Faubion, trans. Robert Hurley (New York: New Press, 2000), p. 157.

39  The advertisement I use is from *Drummer*, 1:4 (1978), p. 4.

40  Joseph Bean, *International Mr. Leather: 25 Years of Champions* (Chicago: Leather Archives & Museum, 2004), p. 9.

41  Baim and Keehnen, *Leatherman*, p. 106.

42  Opel, 'Arnett: Lautrec in Leather,' p. 19.

43  Johnny Ross, *Golden Shower Chicken* (San Diego, CA: Greenleaf Classics, 1984), p. 122.

44  See Streitmatter, *Unspeakable*.

45  'Rushing to a New High Poppers with a Risky Bang,' *TIME*, 17 July 1978, p. 16.

46  Ibid. For a comprehensive history of the medical, entrepreneurial and corporate development and sale of poppers, see David Reed, 'The Multimillion-Dollar Mystery High,' *Christopher Street*, 3:7 (1979), pp. 21–8. In his article Reed traces the ways in which juridical intervention (either general ignorance of nitrites being used as inhalants, or outright bans on poppers) worked in tandem with corporate advertising campaigns to corner a narrow market of gay men. Reed is, unlike most commentators on poppers, balanced in his approach. For example, he notes that 'Those who like poppers express surprisingly consistent reasons: feelings of power and aggressiveness, reduced fear and pain levels, giddiness, higher sensitivity to music and pulsing rhythms, increased sexual excitement and responsiveness, and a general sense of time being slowed down, leading to an illusion of prolonged orgasm,' while 'Those who dislike poppers report equally bad consistent reasons for their stand: bad odor, pounding headache, dizziness, nausea, disturbingly fast heartbeat, pressure on the eyes, and hacking cough' (p. 26). Poppers brands would advertise in unconventional ways; for example, Hardware Liquid Aroma sponsored a contestant's entry into the 1980 International Mr. Leather contest in Chicago, Joseph Lo Presti.

47  Reed, 'The Multimillion-Dollar Mystery High,' p. 22. Reed points to Rush's 'superman-type figure' (Captain Rush) as instrumental to PWD's success.

48  Samois, *What Color is Your Handkerchief?*, p. 36.

49  Newsletter, Samois Records and T-Shirts, 2003–37, The Gay, Lesbian, Bisexual, Transgender Historical Society, San Francisco.

50  Foucault, 'Friendship as a Way of Life,' p. 138.

51  Andrew Flinn, Mary Stevens, and Elizabeth Shepherd, 'Whose Memories, Whose Archives? Independent Community Archives, Autonomy and the Mainstream,' *Archival Science*, 9 (2009), pp. 71- 86. My gratitude to Jakob VanLemmeren for introducing this article to me via his essay, 'Memory and the Power of Place: Meditations on Archives and Community at the LA&M,' in Jakob VanLammeren and José Santiago Pérez (eds.), *Leather Archives & Museum: 25 Years* (Chicago: Leather Archives & Museum, 2016), pp. 55–9.

Numbers **5**

*Artwork*: Dean Sameshima, *Bodily Fluids*, 2007

As the novel *Numbers* (1967) opens, its protagonist, Johnny Rio, has been absent from the life of tricking in Los Angeles for a few years. Upon his return from Texas, and in a quest to find himself through the desire accorded to him by others, he decides to set a challenging goal for himself: to acquire thirty (mostly anonymous) tricks—they are referred to variously as 'youngmen' and 'numbers'—within the short time span of ten days. The novel traces this string of ten days, demarcated by the amount and quality of sex that Johnny has and his shifting relationship to his own desires.

Rechy shares a similar history with his protagonist, and in interviews and lectures the author has often positioned Johnny Rio as an analog to himself.[1] Both Rechy and his fictionalized self were born and raised in Texas border towns (El Paso/Juarez and Laredo/Nuevo Laredo, respectively), and fled at a young age to New York and then to Los Angeles. The cruising grounds of Pershing Square and Griffith Park covered by Johnny in *Numbers* were indeed the same cruising grounds that Rechy frequented.

A rumination on sexual expectations and the gap between experience and description, *Numbers* is also the inspiration for a series of paintings produced in the first decade of the twenty-first century by the artist Dean Sameshima. An Angelino who now lives in Berlin, Sameshima trod the same cruising grounds that Rechy writes about in *Numbers*; indeed, he was arrested as a 'youngman' in a tearoom in Alondra Park in Lawndale, California a month before the Los Angeles riots in 1992. He was booked for disorderly conduct under article 647(a) of the California Penal Code, which stipulates that any person 'who solicits anyone to engage in or who engages in lewd or dissolute conduct in any public place or in any place open to the public or exposed to public view.'[2] This chapter considers Sameshima's large 'Numbers' paintings, which are silkscreened appropriations of erotic connect-the-dots activities (called 'Erotic Dots') that appeared off and on in *Drummer* magazine during the late 1970s.[3] Aware of the many potential meanings of 'number,' the series title references Rechy's novel while also describing the representational content of the paintings: fields of numbered dots, left unconnected. The works' refusal to figure a specific desire in the form of a drawn picture, in contradistinction to the instruction to 'connect-the-dots,' is instead taken up by the paintings' coloration, which is an extension of the historic signaling system of the hanky code (used as an organizing principle in the previous chapter).

Sameshima's series of erotic dots appropriations provides an opportunity to reflect on the ways in which visual works can be optimal sites where reading practices are frustrated and negotiated, elucidating the connections and slippages between similar but distinct sexual communities. The 'Numbers' series bear a direct relation to particular texts (Rechy's *Numbers*, the hanky code, Sean's connect-the-dots activities), but inquire more deeply into the processes of remembering, forgetting, and projecting a sexual ethic of promiscuity in the present. Sameshima accomplishes this primarily through the deployment of archival source material, which, when seen in light of the artist's most recent 'Documentary Paintings,' become key components of the artist's personal archive. As a person who came of age during the HIV/AIDS pandemic, Sameshima's work often reflects on what has been lost, not just in terms of the sheer numbers of people, but also, as Douglas Crimp reminds us, 'a culture of sexual possibility: back rooms, tea rooms, bookstores, movie houses, and baths; the trucks, the pier, the ramble, the dunes.'[4]

Mention John Rechy to a leatherperson of a certain age and they'll likely flinch. That's because the author was largely dismissive of leather, claiming that 'most of it is charade.'[5] In a wide-ranging interview that appeared in *Drummer* magazine, Rechy argued that leathersex was a conduit for the violence and self-loathing he felt to be intrinsic to gay communities, and even worse, that he believed leathersex was ultimately 'based on the *imposed* mores of the straight world on the gay.'[6] Rechy's theories are too pat; he elides the symbolics of leathersex's power-play (as embodied by those who have been historically repressed) as a dumb copy of truly repressive systems. While I would argue that a leatherman dressed as a cop is not, in fact, a cop, for Rechy the distance is not great enough. Because Rechy was argumentative, if not openly hostile, about the terms and enduring iconography of leathersex, he is a strange figure to turn to in a book ostensibly dedicated to leather lives and their archives. Why waste the time? Rechy's positioning of leather as well as the subsequent criticism leveled against him within leather communities and publications marks an ambivalent node of tension and affinity between leather communities and the broader gay and lesbian communities they were apart from and a part of.[7]

Sameshima brings Rechy's work into dialog with the art of John Klamik, who produced cartoons and drawings under the pseudonyms Buckshot, Shawn, and Sean. As Buckshot/Shawn/Sean, Klamik contributed to widely circulating gay and lesbian publications—most notably *The Advocate* (Buckshot/Shawn)—as well as leather publications—*Drummer* (Sean)—for which he produced a suite of erotic connect-the-dots designs. It is these designs that Sameshima appropriates in his 'Numbers' paintings. One of these (which, when completed, illustrates a man sucking dick through a glory hole) appears in the same issue of *Drummer* as the contentious Rechy interview quoted above. That these two kinds of cultural production shared the same space within this leather magazine is notable in and of itself.

Picking up on the sexual ethics of Johnny Rio, and by extension, the autofictional strategies of John Rechy, Sameshima proposes that the visual experience of 'reading' a painting can be a pathway to autobiography, arousal, and activism.[8] In focusing my energies first on the interplay between Rechy's novel and Sameshima's paintings, I mean to foreground a lineage between two queers of color, removed by more than a generation, who nonetheless share and, in the case of Sameshima, re-render the sexual inhabitations of a prior generation.[9] To make this connection more clear, a rehearsal of a key narrative moment from *Numbers* is in order.

Near the end of Rechy's novel, as Johnny has just achieved his goal of thirty tricks in ten days, he considers quitting hustling. This is not a singular revelation in *Numbers*; throughout the novel Johnny vows to return home to Laredo after his task is accomplished. What interrupts this consideration is an invitation to a dinner party at the well-manicured Santa Monica home of Sebastian Michaels, and it is there that Johnny's host and the other guests at the dinner party (whom up until this point he has held in contempt because they are white gays representative of a normative homosexual intelligentsia) start to collaborate in reorganizing Johnny's sexuality as something safely within the boundaries of monogamous couplehood.[10] Sebastian makes his case to Johnny:

> But you still haven't explored … a further country, dear John. And until you do, you'll never know if *that* is *it*: yes, what could, just possibly could, make you happy. Until you do, you simply can't be completely—truly—free of a world you've explored only in part […] The country of sharing mutually of course, one for one […] and … perhaps … of finding *one* … number.[11]

Happiness and liberation are bound up in Sebastian's vision of coupling, 'sharing mutually … one for one.'[12] The divide between Johnny's sexual athletics and this alternative lifestyle proffered by Sebastian is tellingly and paradoxically pitched to Johnny as a foreign country, offered in an Orientalizing mode, whereby Johnny is meant to be tantalized by the exoticism of this intimate organization. Yet Sebastian's positing of coupling as a foreign country also reveals something to a reader about Johnny's subjectivity, and not only necessarily the cultural norms of the dinner-party gays. In the context of the dinner party Johnny is apprehended as an interloper—in both sexual practice and in ethnicity. Johnny, in another mirroring of Rechy, is represented in the novel as a Chicano character. Importantly, in having Sebastian pitch the monogamous life to Johnny in such a loaded way, Rechy presents the self-centered, short-term, mostly anonymous sexual practices of Johnny as a kind of place as well; his non-normative sexual practices and values are allegorized in terms of a homeland deeply resonant with diasporic configurations of the U.S./Mexico border. Monogamy is envisioned as a place for Johnny to colonize romantically, a place to be 'free of a world' that Sebastian can only see in restrictive and moralistic terms, as self-destructive and illogical.

Despite his condescension, Sebastian actually initiates something of a crisis of self in Johnny, who takes the older, white man's words to heart. It is here, in the context of this brief conversation with Sebastian, a seductive abutment with sex normativity, that a reader might begin to view Johnny as a deeply *un*happy hustler. Johnny quickly exhibits a newfound excitement in finding this '*one … number*.'[13] Soon after the dinner party ends, and in a passage that at first seems to confirm both Sebastian's moral superiority and sexual conservatism, as well as Johnny's drive for sex, he tricks again, this time with one of the guests from the dinner party.[14] Through this sexual experience, and having fully internalized Sebastian's expectations, Johnny gains an 'intimate knowledge of that further country.'[15] Persuaded by the belief that this guest (deliciously, he is named 'Guy') could be the 'one,' Rechy's narrative veers dangerously close to presenting a morality play about the reformation of a hustler—thus leaving the boundaries of the 'charmed circle' of normative sexual organization ultimately unchallenged, or perhaps further reinforced.[16] Thankfully, this knowledge, like many of Johnny's sexual contacts, is short-lived, and, in a masterful turn, it literally nauseates Johnny as he drives away from his encounter. Johnny vomits out the window: 'That country— … he thinks. It wasn't mine.'[17]

In a book littered with sexual climaxes, the moment of narrative climax is one of vomiting—an unambiguous marker of physical illness. In structuring his narrative in this way, Rechy deftly unmoors the socially ill body from a sexuality figured as deviant by the dinner-party gays, and insists on the corporeal harm normative sexual expectations produce. The idea and the enactment of monogamy makes Johnny sick to the point where his insides become his outsides. This is nothing short of a transformative realization of self, one that runs counter to Sebastian's assertion; relationships matter, but on Johnny's terms, within the borders of his home 'country.' After this incident Johnny continues to count his numbers/tricks past thirty. Laredo, it seems, is no longer on the cards. His is a drive that is insistent and unslakable. And why should it end? As Johnny dryly puts it, 'There never was a reason, I'm just here and that's all.'[18]

'I'm just here and that's all' could be the subtitle of an early series of photo-conceptualist works by Sameshima. In the mid-1990s the artist began photographing the cruising grounds that he covered in and around Los Angeles. Initially conceived as three separate bodies of work, but subsequently gathered under a single series title, 'Wonderland' explores these various spaces for cruising: hidey-holes in Griffith Park, recently closed bathhouses and sex clubs, and the scratchy graffiti on the stalls of tearooms (public restrooms). Each is carefully framed and documented. These photographs of places without people signal one of the core concerns of Sameshima's artistic career: the politics of identification as evidenced through the tension between surveillance and concealment—especially concerning sex in public and semi-public spaces. Sameshima says of these works:

> I felt the need/urge to document this stuff, and this was before I knew what kind of impact computers would have, before it all started to disappear. I don't mind the word nostalgia and I am not sure why people think it is such a bad thing in artwork. I no longer care much what others think. My work is very steeped in nostalgia. To me, the past was just so much more interesting.[19]

Locating his interest in the past, at least more so than in the present or future, Sameshima's 'Wonderland' photographs are emotionally rich precisely because they acknowledge and refuse the conditions of the present: the building located at 1064 Myra Avenue, for example, depicted in *Untitled (15 rooms, 1 locker room, 3 bathtubs, 2 leather slings 1995)* (1995/96), has been repurposed from its former life as The Nighthawk, a sex club (figure 5.1). In Sameshima's photograph a white sign proclaiming the business's name (B. &

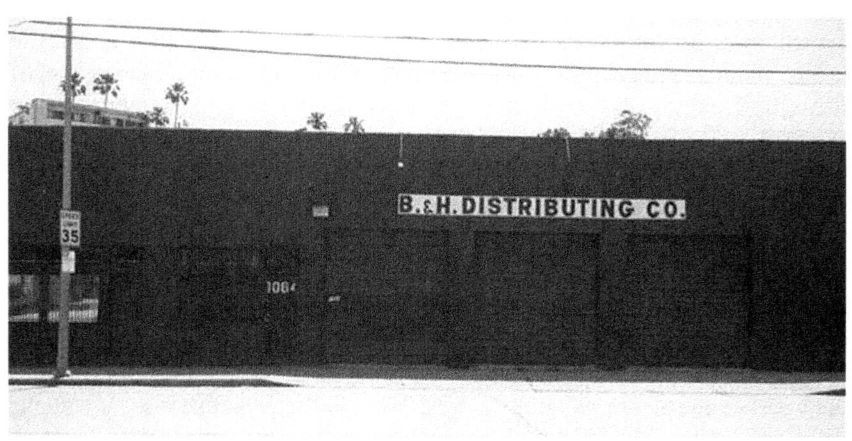


Dean Sameshima, *Untitled (15 rooms, 1 locker room, 3 bathtubs, 2 leather slings 1995)*, 1995/1996, c-print    **5.1**

H. Distributing Co.) is placed unceremoniously on the all-black façade. The tops of palm trees, ubiquitous in Silver Lake, peek out above the roofline. Sameshima's title is the only indication as to what the space used to offer its members, the two leather slings an unambiguous marker that leathermen were at least superficially courted by the club.

Another photo from this series, *Untitled (closed, 1995)*, relates through its titling what eventually became of these spaces. A 1997 article in the *Los Angeles Times* describes why so many sex clubs in Silver Lake and Hollywood were being shuttered—after the settlement of a years-long federal court case, Los Angeles started to enforce local zoning laws in 1995.[20] These regulations stated that adult entertainment businesses could not be within 500 feet of a residential zone, school, public park, or religious institution, and not within 1000 feet of a similar institution, thereby preventing the agglomeration of like businesses forming a red-light district. Many of the buildings that Sameshima photographed were cited and eventually closed under these regulations, and his photographs highlight buildings that were designed to be unremarkable from the outside. The 1995 enforcement of zoning laws left those who frequented the clubs without designated and concentrated spaces for cruising.

In documenting the outcomes of changing sex law enforcement (the laws may be zoning laws, but their target is unambiguously sex businesses), Sameshima arrived at what would become his primary visual strategy—depopulating the scene of sexuality. His series 'In Between Days (Without You),' from 1998, details the two weeks following a break-up, in which he visited one of the few remaining local bathhouses and rented a room there each night.[21] At the end of each visit Sameshima took a photograph of the bed in his rented room. What happened during his frequent visits is never directly depicted, but left only to inference. Sometimes the bed is wet and messy, sometimes it is nearly perfectly made—the pillow resting upright against the wall, providing back support for what one can only guess was a long period of sitting and waiting. These photographs are scaled small, and usually installed in a grid, a kind of visual calendar where beds stand in for numbered days. In this sense, 'In Between Days (Without You)' insists on the affective fullness of having and not having sex at the baths.

In these early photographic works Sameshima performs his own auto-biography while revealing the impoverished state of urban institutions dedicated to sexual encounter. Of course, depopulating the scene of sex is both a pragmatic and conceptual move in the series 'In Between Days (Without You)': pragmatic because the reality of taking pictures of people in the middle of cruising (whether in a park, tearoom, or bathhouse) is fraught with issues around consent and anonymity. These are spaces that are notori-ously allergic to photo-documentation. Sameshima's decision to leave the figure out of the picture (without evacuating its presence entirely) is also tied to an artistic strategy used by queer artists of Sameshima's generation, who came of age during the onset of the AIDS pandemic, as a way of visualizing loss through visual absence. Because of this Sameshima's works have usually been interpreted as taking on a melancholic cast—they mourn for possibilities foreclosed, lives lost, and the ultimate closure of bathhouses and sex clubs in Los Angeles.[22]

Like Rechy, Sameshima's focus is broadly queer, inclusive of but not exclusively representing practices easily identifiable as leathersex. But in a sequence of photographs produced with the cooperation of a local leather-man, Master Rich, Sameshima acknowledges the deep divide between the sexual encounter of leathersex and the photographic representation of it.[23] *Master Rich #1 (Cocoon)* (2004) (figure 5.2) depicts a man who has been hung from the cross-beams over a small stairway at The Gauntlet II, a leather bar

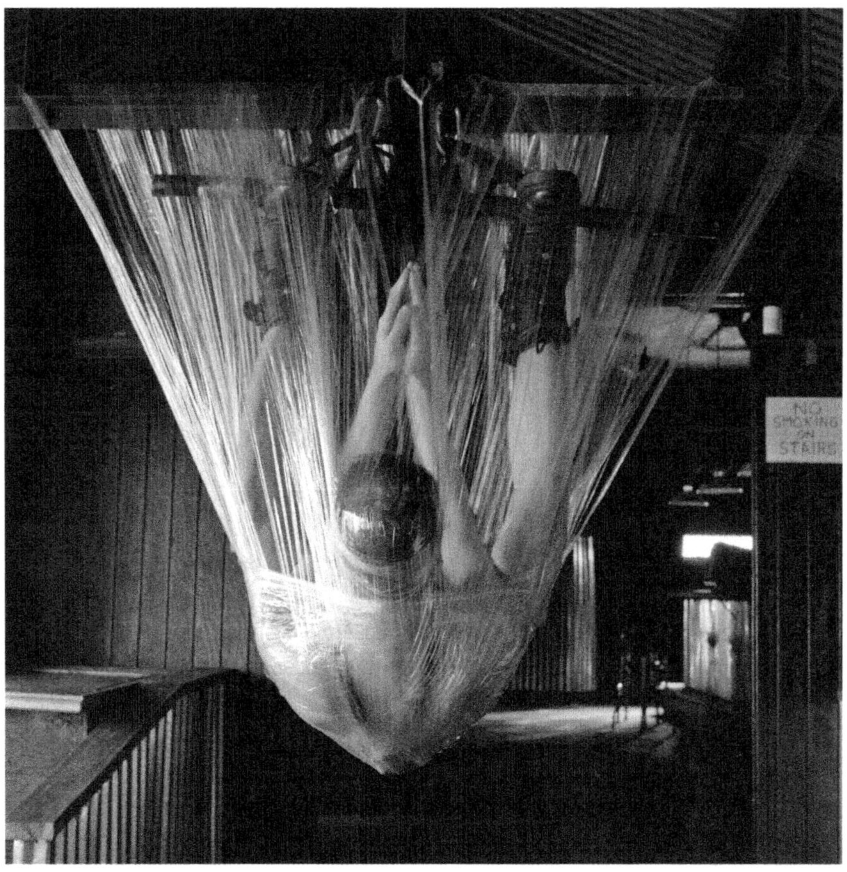


Dean Sameshima, *Master Rich #1 (Cocoon)*, 2004, fuji flex print          **5.2**

in Silver Lake, which survives today as The Eagle. He is hung in a passageway between the interior of the bar and a covered patio area (which is depicted in another Sameshima photograph, taken the year before, and entitled *Gauntlet II (O Daddy)*). Natural light spills in from the left, illuminating the yards of clear plastic wrap that have been used to bind, or cocoon, Master Rich's subject into a suspended and folded position. The suspended man's arms are extended out in front of him, as though in a parody of prayer. Sameshima's photograph acknowledges that Master Rich's practice is, at base, creative—as one has to marvel at the mechanics of this form of leathersex. This is a performance put on exclusively for Sameshima's camera, as the cocooned man is the only figure in a photograph shot in what would otherwise be a crowded leather bar. This runs counter to the sociality that would normally accompany a mummification demonstration such as this at a bar like The Gauntlet II, where plenty of people would gather around to watch, and might eventually engage and play with the suspended subject. Such was the scenario when Sameshima initially encountered Master Rich at the leather bar: 'I would just stand there and watch him bind, tie and sometimes hang his subjects. It was all so beautiful and elegant and quite performative.'[24]

In a triptych of photographs from the same year, Sameshima photographs Master Rich's work in a more domestic space. Here a white-painted brick fireplace and tall vertical blinds complement the light-colored carpet and bare, white walls (figure 5.3). Against this spare interior a figure is hung by ropes on a cross. The middle photograph in the triptych represents Master Rich's submissive frontally, standing on a small black stool. In the flanking photographs he hangs from the ceiling, free of any furniture anchoring him to the ground. His hands hang loosely from their wrist bindings in one photograph, and in another they languidly grasp the cross bar. The crucified man closes his eyes, his expression unpained. White bondage rope criss-crosses his body, flattening his cock against his stomach and pulling his balls out perpendicular to his

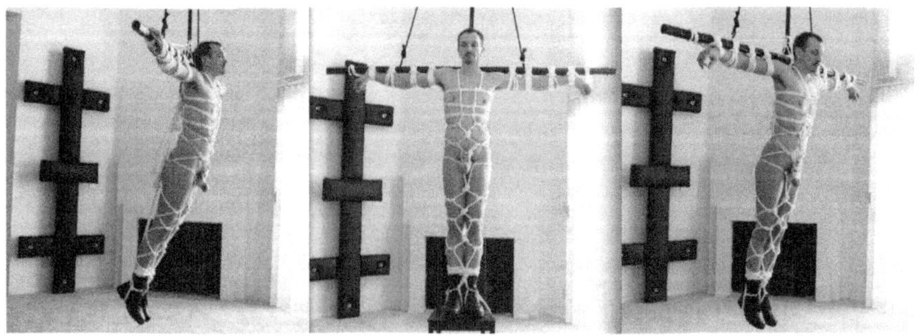

**5.3**    Dean Sameshima, *Master Rich #3 (Crucifixion)*, 2004, fuji flex prints

torso. To the man's left, echoing his bound position, a piece of padded, black bondage furniture is bolted to the wall. In this triptych and the photograph previously described, leather activity is presented as a form experienced singly—someone had to bind the people depicted in these photographs, and yet Master Rich appears nowhere. He is an absent interlocutor (not dissimilar to the format of Monica Majoli's large 'Rubbermen' works that are the subject of my conclusion).

Perhaps none of Sameshima's works are better at thinking through notions of sexual promiscuity, loss, nostalgia, and the archival than his series entitled 'Numbers.'[25] These were first exhibited in 2007, in a solo show at the artist's Berlin gallery, Peres Projects. Earlier that same year Sameshima had moved his life and practice from Los Angeles to Berlin, a city that was hailed by the *New York Times* as a bohemia for young artists.[26] One of the primary ways in which Sameshima's connect-the-dot paintings might be best understood is via that initial installation.

The exhibition put into coordination several distinct series of work: in the main gallery of Peres Projects, Sameshima installed seven colorful connect-the-dot paintings, some of which were diptychs (figure 5.4). One more connect-the-dot work, *Bodily Fluids*, was installed in an adjacent room facing a group of three small 'Safety Pin' paintings. These works, another continuing series of Sameshima's, are an exuberant visual collapse of sexual positions, punk aesthetics, and the languages of 'safe sex' that flowed from the HIV/ AIDS pandemic. Placed in another room were two white-on-white silkscreen appropriations of 'Toilet Talk' cartoons (also sourced from *Drummer*), in which two urinals engage in a jokey call-and-response regarding queer sexual

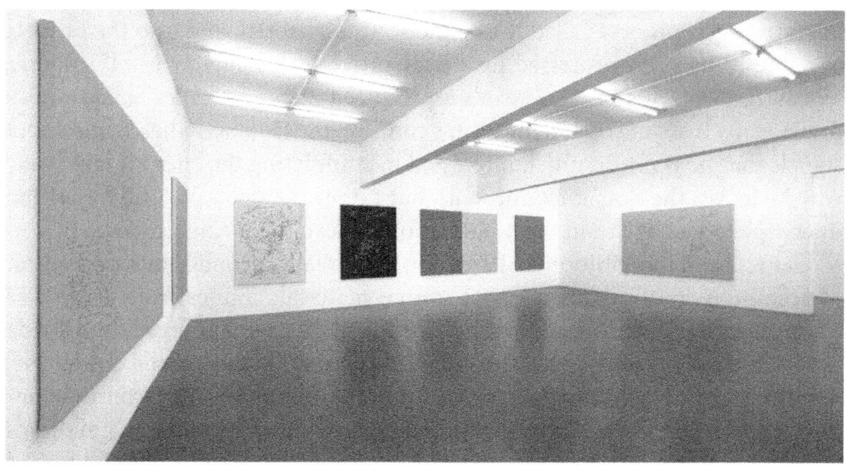

Dean Sameshima, 'Numbers' installation, Peres Projects, Berlin    **5.4**

practice and surveillance ('Q: How do you feel about Vice Cops? A: They piss me off!'). Finally, in the gallery that also served as the director's office, Sameshima installed a suite of photographic appropriations of pages from a 1964 report put together by the Florida Legislative Investigation Committee entitled *Homosexuality and Citizenship in Florida*. Sameshima's reproductions feature the handwritten annotations and corrections of the pamphlet's anonymous owner. Many of these photographs focus on the 'Glossary of Homosexual Terms and Deviant Acts' at the back of the report, which combines in-group lingo with pathologizing terminology. As is the case with such objects, it is at once a heinous artifact of public regimes of surveillance and a near-excellent manual for uninitiated homosexuals. One might learn, for example, that someone who is 'Piss Elegant' is 'a homosexual who brags or is outwardly conceited;' and that the definition of 'She' is actually a 'Male homosexual.'[27]

A quick note about Sameshima's process: in appropriating Sean's erotic dots designs the artist subtracts some key information. Sameshima excises Sean's signature, the design's heading of 'Erotic Dots,' and the printed tongue-in-cheek warning which reads: 'Warning! When completed this will be a sexually explicit drawing. If you will be offended by the content, do not connect the dots,' sometimes included in the bottom right of the design. This excision of the mechanical type and of Sean's signature hints at Sameshima's working method, which consists of tracing enlarged Xeroxes of Sean's connect-the-dot images onto acetate. Once done, the acetate is exposed to light over an emulsion-covered screen. The result is essentially a large negative (a silkscreen) that ink can be pulled through. Sean's erotic dots are not photomechanically reproduced to make a screen (i.e. Xeroxed directly onto large pieces of acetate), but are rather traced and drawn by Sameshima, perverting the process called for by the source material, and also the process of Sameshima's self-professed historical antecedent, Andy Warhol. In other words, through this process Sean's reproduced image becomes Sameshima's drawing. By insisting on tracing Sean's connect-the-dots activities, Sameshima signals that he is not so much interested in completing the latent image (thus why he leaves the dots unconnected), but rather the open possibilities of the uncompleted activity and the inhabitation of Sean's drawing process.

Sameshima's exhibition at Peres Projects was a cacophonous excavation of seemingly antinomous archival source material: comics from *Drummer* on the one hand, and the Florida report on the other. Whereas the Florida report is explicit, albeit in an overly clinical way, Sameshima's erotic dots paintings are notable for their playful inexplicitness. After all, connect-the-dots is a familiar form of participatory image-making, common to children's activity books and magazines such as *Highlights for Children*. The activity of connecting-the-dots is a straightforward one: a participant is asked to begin at the number one, sometimes indicated by the word 'start' or an arrow, and then draws a continuous line connecting progressive integers. Connect-the-dots activities provide an opportunity for cognitive skill building, a way of learning numbers and letters alongside using contextual clues to arrive at an image, often even before the activity is completed. Yet in some of the works in the 'Numbers' series, for example *Bodily Fluids*, Sameshima overlays two different (already overly complex) connect-the-dots activities, frustrating a viewer's ability to easily imagine a final drawn figure. This would be one way in which *Bodily Fluids* and the other paintings from the series are, as one reviewer of the Peres Projects installation puts it, 'far from childish.'[28]

Of course, the other way they are far from childish is in the sexual practices that are latent in Sean's designs: fisting, auto-fellatio/self-suck, blowjobs through glory holes, bestiality, and masturbating in front of a mirror.[29] In Sean's erotic dots, activity renders activity, and drawing is positioned as a form of sexual excitation in its own right—one where a reader of *Drummer* is not only a consumer of images, but a participatory maker as well. A poster campaign concurrent with the run of the exhibition at Peres Projects reproduced Sameshima's connect-the-dot paintings, wheat-pasting them around Berlin's urban environs. In response, some of those who encountered these posters on the street connected the dots and completed the images—answering the entreating appeal of Sean's activities.

In one of the few contemporary reviews of his Peres Projects installation, Berlin-based art critic Ana Finel Honigman introduced Sameshima's 'Numbers' paintings in the following way:

> Heterosexuals often gush about how internet dating simplifies the sticky, tricky process of flirting with a stranger: after looking at someone's profile, preliminary introductions become much more efficient. But lists of preferences and tastes are far more reticent and archaic than the direct color code system gay men designed decades ago for streamlined cruising.[30]

Honigman refers here to the hanky code. She tellingly makes a division between contemporary heterosexual dating technologies and historic gay systems of signaling potential sex partners, describing the latter anti-teleologically as more 'streamlined' and less 'archaic.' As covered in the last chapter, the hanky code's origins and permutations are difficult to trace. During the 1970s, and even now, as Sameshima, die Kränken and many other artists are recovering the hanky code as an important precedental figuration of queer sexual life, its cultural importance continues to mutate.[31] Examining the hanky code, and the numerous responses to it, reveals more than may at first be apparent, and has much to do with reading Sameshima's work alongside Rechy's *Numbers*: as a structure of recognition and difference, of seriousness and play as a mask and a mode of understanding the machinations of negotiating sex. Whether or not this system worked in the real world—its non-leather gay detractors sound like the badgering dinner-party gays in *Numbers*—the accounts from the previous chapter indicate the code was only marginally successful in practice, but was nevertheless an important cultural signaling system regarding the ways leathersex was represented and understood through visuality.

Sameshima and his gallery distributed Xeroxed copies of the Pleasure Chest's hanky code as a guide to the exhibition. Indeed, some of Sameshima's titles are directly transcribed from this comically long iteration of the code— works such as the orange-colored *Anything Anytime Nothing Now* and the gold-colored *2 Looking for 1 1 Looking for 2* (both 2007). Others are more coy in their reference to the Pleasure Chest hanky code, yet their perversions are nevertheless legible. *Regiment* (2006), for example, is an olive drab color, and a clear riff on military fetish even though it doesn't directly adopt the Pleasure Chest's language of 'Military Top' and 'Military Bottom.'

*Bodily Fluids* (figure 5.5), which in its initial gallery installation hung in an adjacent gallery to the rest of the series, breaks from its counterparts in noticeable ways. Like *Regiment*, in its titling the yellow and white painting suggests golden showers without pinpointing it as a specific activity, or even bodily fluid. The title is generic and could refer to any number of corporeal liquids—tears, semen, urine, spit, milk, blood, sweat, mucus. And because the Pleasure Chest's code is so long, there are potentially many readings of the yellow color of *Bodily Fluids*. The obvious would be to follow the customary alignment of the color yellow with the activity of golden showers; the Pleasure Chest's hanky code explains that yellow means 'Pisser' when worn on the left and 'Piss Freak' when worn on the right. But the placement of *Bodily Fluids* outside the room with the rest of the 'Numbers' paintings indicates that difference and exclusion may be more fundamental to its inter- pretation. This is true in many respects—for example, it is the only painting in the series where the coordinating color with the hanky code corresponds with the color of the numbered dots rather than the colored ground onto which the erotic dots design is silkscreened. This suggests that the white color of the ground is just as important as the color of the dots. Down toward the bottom of the Pleasure Chest's hanky code, the combination of yellow and white is labelled as 'Likes Oriental Bottoms' if worn on the left, and 'Likes Oriental Tops' if worn on the right.[32] I would argue that in *Bodily Fluids* Sameshima leaves the door open to the multiple significations indicated in the Pleasure Chest's hanky code.

Because the hanky code doesn't specify a particularized raced user, it might be tempting also to argue that it, like Rechy's dinner-party gays, assumes a white subject. Certainly, mobilizing the term 'Oriental' in the mid-1980s is a damning piece of evidence in this regard, considering that

Dean Sameshima, *Bodily Fluids*, 2007, acrylic and silkscreen ink on canvas, 70 x 60 in.    **5.5**

the term was a marked point of contention for Asian-American civil rights activists in the late 1960s and 1970s.[33] Read in this way, Sameshima's painting is an enactment of the racialization of subject-positions in white-dominant signaling systems. One might recall Zora Neale Hurston's insight that 'I feel most colored when I am thrown against a sharp white background.'[34] Here that 'sharp white background' is descriptive of both the ground of *Bodily Fluids*, as well as the exhibitionary complex of the gallery, which relies on the formulation of the white cube as a neutral 'ground' against which artistic productions are figured.[35]

The paintings in Sameshima's 'Numbers' series do not consist of a random assortment of colors from the hanky code, but according to critic Laura Allsop, 'reflect the artist's own sexual preferences.'[36] If the paintings in the 'Numbers' series are autobiographical in this manner—construed as an extended abstract portrait of the artist, in the manner that the 'Wonderland' and Master Rich photographs were loosely autobiographical—it might follow that *Bodily Fluids* could also be productively understood as a scene in which an Asian-American artist calls forth an Asian-American/Asian-European viewer.[37] The conjuring of such a gallery viewer is at odds with the exclusionary racialization of the gallery space. In encouraging a viewer to read the paintings as autobiographical, Sameshima slyly charges the space of the gallery as an arena for cruising, where we are all potential numbers … racialized figures on grounds.[38]

*Bodily Fluids*'s legibility is also challenged by the fact that its image is made by overlaying two different connect-the-dot designs. Because the connect-the-dot designs are left unconnected, they function as spaces for imaginative and wild projection. Sameshima's numbered dots thus facilitate different kinds of embodiment—collapsing numbers as both numerical signs and counted tricks (à la Rechy's *Numbers*). This allows the dots to become more than what they are: they are hundreds of men, schematically seen from above, populating the cruising grounds of Griffith Park (the ones used by Sameshima, Rechy, and the fictive Johnny Rio). Or they are an evocative and complicated map of social relations (former and future lovers). Who exactly is whose number is never clear. Which '3' follows which '2'? And are the imaginary lines drawn between dots descriptive of intensity of contact, distance traveled, or a chronological accounting?

These new lines that one might draw flow irrespective of numerical order, and begin to describe not a coalesced image, but an abstract net of possible social relationships. Uneven body traces are replaced with asymmetrical asterisks and chevron switch-backs. The relationships/connections between the numbered dots are descriptive of different choreographies, akin to what Jean-Luc Nancy dubs being-with.[39] *Bodily Fluids* not only entangles racialized subjectivities with historical sexual codes, but also intimates the ways in which we may be alone while also with others. The odd number, far afield from any other, acknowledges that some (due to any number of reasons ranging from shyness to uninterest) may never be with others—isolated in the sexual exchange—while some will have many sexual contacts. The numbers on this field of erotic possibility are always becoming, and bristling with potential. Yes, it is a call to action—to the activity of reading, but also to the activity of fucking, which may be similar to reading in its potential to shatter and constitute multiple senses of self. Sameshima's painting recognizes the potential and obstacles inherent in the gambit for public and leathersex—that all it takes is a group of queers to congregate in Griffith Park to 'shift lived worlds.'[40] *Bodily Fluids* is shot through with these same possibilities; the painting is ultimately an open-ended suggestion regarding sex, community, and historical lineage. Like Rechy, Sameshima argues that desire's latency might, in fact, be its most powerful feature.

* * *

Nearly a decade after the creation of the 'Numbers' paintings, Sameshima is now in the midst of an evolving series he calls 'Documentary Paintings.' The documents that he paints are a wild assortment: covers of books and journals, membership cards for bathhouses and sex clubs, a press release of a Felix-Gonzalez Torres exhibition, an intertitle from *Paris is Burning*, receipts of visits to Berlin porn theaters on the birthdays of significant queer figures, and even the artist's own arrest record from 1992. Unlike previous works where Sameshima employed silkscreen to complete his canvases, these are painstakingly hand-painted, enlarging his source material. This method reverses Warhol's historical move away from painting and illustration to the reproductive possibilities of silkscreen. Sameshima's new series emphasizes abstraction, dislocation, and reorientation, as he abstracts his original source documents during the long painting process. This ultimately enables a viewer to read the document again via the gestalt of his completed painting.

In *Against Nature* (2015), a five-canvas polyptych of the artist's arrest record, one can read the report of Sameshima's entrapment by the Los Angeles Sheriff Department's Metro Vice unit in a tearoom in Alondra Park (figure 5.6). The salaciousness of the reporting officer's description of his encounter with Sameshima functions not unlike the 'Glossary of Homosexual Terms and Deviant Acts' in the 1964 Florida Legislative Investigation Committee report reproduced by Sameshima earlier in his career; it damns as much as it teaches. But one can divine more than Sameshima's cruising habits from this carceral bit of re-presented juridical realia. Listed under Sameshima's place of employment is the MOCA bookstore, where he would have come into contact with many of the books that he reproduces as part of this new series, as well as a whole array of artists and artistic practices in Los Angeles during the early 1990s.

There are numbers at work here, too: Sameshima's driver's license, the officer's badge number, an accounting of the two toilets and two urinals in the park restroom, Sameshima's booking number, the ID number of the facility where he was taken. But these numbers are constituitively different than those enshrined by Rechy's novel, or in Sean's erotic dots designs, because there is no room to interpret them as anything but numbers cohering a subject under

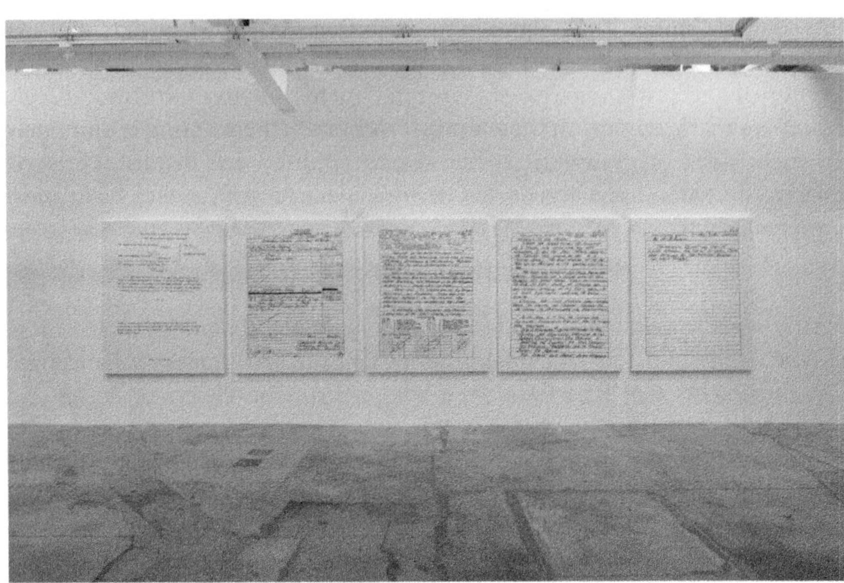

**5.6**    Dean Sameshima, *Against Nature*, 2015, acrylic on canvas, each canvas 62 x 51 in.

carceral subjugation—a response to that same subject's uncountable, and I would argue unfathomable, sexuality.

One of the 'documents' Sameshima reproduces is the cover of the issue of the journal *October*, which contains Douglas Crimp's essay, 'Mourning and Militancy.'[41] In it Crimp takes up Sigmund Freud's conception of profound and absorptive mourning, one which, Freud writes, 'leaves nothing over for other purposes or other interests.'[42] Pairing these insights regarding the psychology of mourning, Crimp applies it to his own community of activists in ACT-UP, at points writing through the scrim of an academic journal to speak to the real conditions of caregiving and emotional decimation during the first decades of the HIV/AIDS pandemic. 'We must recognize,' Crimp writes, 'that our memories and our resolve also entail the more painful feelings of survivor's guilt, often exacerbated by our secret wishes, during our lovers' and friends' protracted illnesses, that they would just die and let us get on with our lives.'[43] These are the affective threads pulled by Sameshima's work, inclusive of the project of mourning, but also of the militancy evidenced by a thorough critique of the systems of representation and display that can't or won't acknowledge the myriad ways in which our lovers and friends—dead, alive—are still absented from public discourse. Through their remarkable shift in scale and careful hand-making, Sameshima's 'Documentary Paintings' spectacularize ephemera usually tucked away in archival boxes, drawers, or closets, forcefully arguing for their continuing importance to sexual life.

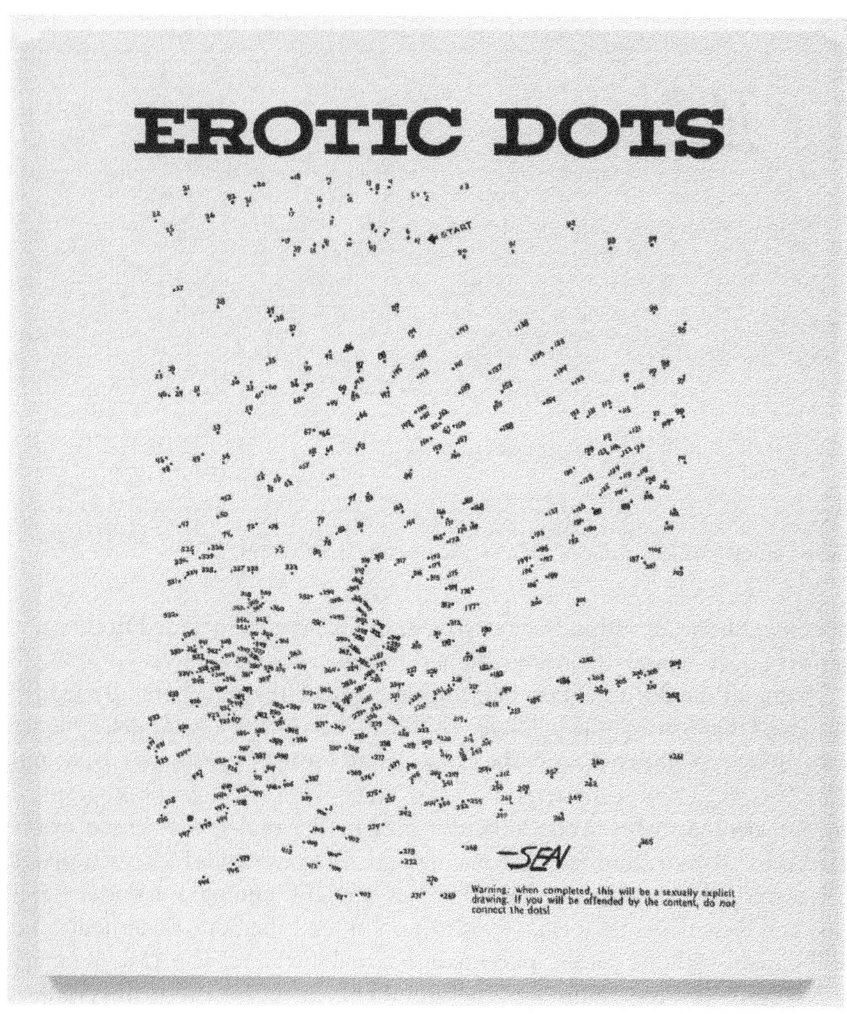


Dean Sameshima, *Numbers 1*, 2015, acrylic on canvas, 66 x 55 in.    **5.7**

As if to signal this series' relation to the ones that came before it, Sameshima includes another painting of Sean's erotic dots (figure 5.7). Entitled *Numbers 1* (2015), it is a self-conscious recalling of that 2007 exhibition of hanky-code paintings. In *this* painting Sameshima leaves in all identifying information, including Sean's signature and the small printed warning at the bottom right of the original design. Disarticulated from the color-coded system of the hanky code (nearly all of the paintings in the 'Documents' series invoke the facticity of the objects' original color scheme—black and white), *Numbers 1* delineates a further opening out of Sameshima's practice. It demands that this

**5.8**   Dean Sameshima, *The Zone #1*, 2017, acrylic on canvas, 22 x 38 in.

document be read; within the assortment of documents included in this new series of documentary paintings. Sameshima amasses an archive.

Some of the documentary paintings reproduce the membership cards of sex clubs that Sameshima belonged to during his time in Los Angeles (figure 5.8)—Exxile, Nighthawk, and The Zone (*Exxile* (2016), *Nighthawk* (2017), and *The Zone #1* (2017), respectively). Two of these were sex clubs photographed by Sameshima in his 'Wonderland' series in the mid-1990s. These works return to 'Wonderland' and reconsiders the terms under which such places are memorialized—this time not through 'straight' photographs of site, but through the enlargement and reproduction of the ephemeral documents that still remain with the people who made a sexual life there. The 'Documentary Paintings,' like the 'Numbers' before them, have an explicitly political purpose, in that Sameshima hopes they aid in combatting what he identifies as a growing 'conservatism in the gay community,' allied with a politics of respectability.[44] Claiming a history indelibly tied to the places that centered sexual encounter is only one part of this strategy. The second part is what we might have the audacity to imagine for our sexual futures.

In this way we might productively read *Numbers 1* alongside *The Zone #1*. Both present scenes of sexual possiblity. In *The Zone #1* the logo of the sex club, a typographic stylization of handwriting, is enjoined by the more bureaucratic registered trademark symbol. Unlike the other membership cards in the 'Documentary Paintings' series, all of which feature Sameshima's handwritten name, this painting only represents the card's front, and as such is mostly blank. The name of the sex club indexes the differences between The

Zone, which remains open today, and its competitors in 1995; namely, that it was one of the few sex clubs zoned *legally*.[45] Its compliance with regulations was pitched in near-glowing terms in a review in Scott O'Hara's *Steam* magazine:

> you won't find alcohol on the premises, but there are soda machines and free coffee (both decaf and regular!). You won't find glory holes (which local authorities have banned), but you will find a maze and semi-private booths. You won't find showers or tubs, but there is plenty of raunchy (and very art-directed) graffiti in both restrooms.[46]

The Zone's logo (also very art-directed), enlarged and dissociated from any context that would identify it to someone who didn't already know what The Zone was (no address or any other information appears on its front), could be read as a meditation on the act of painting itself. The blank canvas that confronts the artist is a portal of possibility. Like *Bodily Fluids* before it, *The Zone #1* builds upon the useful polysemy of its namesake—demanding that sexual practice be considered alongside urban planning and artistic mappings. Just as the erotic dots were an encomium on sexual becoming, this blank canvas that's not quite blank is an unambiguous call for an emergence out of an archival, temporal collapse.

## Notes

1 'I once—and quite literally—became a character from one of my own books. My second novel, *Numbers*, was set mainly in Griffith Park, its protagonist a young man named Johnny Rio, who spends his idle time seeking adventures in the park. I was idling in the same park one afternoon—still anonymous—when a stranger braked his car to tell me that someone had written a book about me. "Who?" I asked, befuddled. "His name is John Rechy," he said, "but I don't think that's his real name because nobody would write a book like that under his own name." As he left, he called back, "Goodbye, Johnny Rio."' John Rechy, 'Real People as Fictional Characters: Some Comic, Sad, and Dangerous Encounters,' lecture, Los Angeles Institute of the Humanities, Los Angeles, CA, 2007.

2 California Penal code 647(a), enacted 1872. Amended by Stats., 2016.

3 Tony DeBlase identified Sean's 'Erotic Dots' activities as 'a unique and popular feature of early issues [of *Drummer*].' Fledermaus (Tony DeBlase), 'Getting Off,' *Drummer*, 11:100 (1986), p. 6. My thanks to Gayle Rubin for drawing my attention to this particular article. The Erotic Dots also appeared in Jeanne Barney's *NewsLeather* after her acrimonious split with John Embry, publisher of *Drummer*.

4 Douglas Crimp, 'Mourning and Militancy,' in *Melancholia and Moralism: Essays on AIDS and Queer Politics* (Cambridge, MA: MIT Press, 2002), p. 140.

5 Robert Payne (John Embry), 'John Rechy, Author of the "Sexual Outlaw," Talks About S&M with Robert Payne,' *Drummer*, 3:16 (1977), pp. 8–11, 70–1.

6 Ibid., pp. 9–10.

7 Writers outside of leather communities were also unconvinced by Rechy's literary efforts; a review of Rechy's novel, published in the Philadelphia-based homophile magazine *Drum*, called it a 'homosexy potboiler,' assessing its literary merit as 'dreadful.' 'Review: "Numbers" by John Rechy,' *Drum*, 28 (January 1968), p. 11. The uncredited reviewer—potentially publisher Carl Polak—goes on: '*Numbers* is the non-story of ten non-days in the non-life of its non-hero, Johnny Rio' (p. 11).

8 Here I make reference to the novelist Serge Doubrovsky's coinage of 'autofiction,' which emerged almost a decade after Rechy's novel. While I acknowledge this historical anachronicity, the impulse to mix autobiographical content with literary language and conceit had existed for sometime before it had a name—as evidenced by Rechy's early novels. Serge Doubrovsky, *Fils* (Paris: Galilée, 1977).

9 Paranoid/reparative: Eve Kosofsky Sedgwick, 'Paranoid Reading and Reparative Reading; or, You're So Paranoid, You Probably Think This Introduction Is about You,' in Eve Kosofsky Sedgwick (ed.), *Novel Gazing: Queer Readings in Fiction* (Durham, NC: Duke University Press, 1997), pp. 1–40; Heather Love, 'Truth and Consequences: On Paranoid and Reparative Reading,' *Criticism*, 52:2 (2010), pp. 235–41; symptomatic/surface: Stephen Best and Sharon Marcus, 'Surface Reading: An Introduction,' *Representations*, 108 (2009), pp. 1–21; suspicion and entanglement/encounter: Rita Felski, *The Limits of Critique* (Chicago: University of Chicago Press, 2015).

10 Sebastian Michaels in *Numbers* is 'A small, slender, grayish-blond man in his 50's […] a famous writer of fine, serious, often beautiful, books.' John Rechy, *Numbers* (New York: Grove/Atlantic, 1967), p. 161. He and his dinner guests are modeled off of Christopher Isherwood and his circle. In this way Rechy cheekily follows Isherwood's personal advice to the author that, when modeling fictional characters off of persons in one's life, one can 'question their morals, call them liars, expose them as thieves—as long as you describe them as attractive.' Rechy, 'Real People as Fictional Characters.' Also see Ricardo Ortiz, 'Sexuality Degree Zero: Pleasure and Power in the Novels of John Rechy, Arturo Islas, and Michael Nava,' *Journal of Homosexuality*, 26:2–3 (1993), pp. 111–26; and Ricardo Ortiz, 'John Rechy and the Grammar of Ostentation,' in Sue-Ellen Case et al. (eds.), *Cruising the Performative: Interventions into the Representation of Ethnicity, Nationality, and Sexuality* (Bloomington, IN: Indiana University Press, 1995), pp. 59–70.

11 Rechy, *Numbers*, pp. 235–6.

12 Ibid.

13 Ibid.

14 The framing of Johnny Rio's interest in sex as pathological is not mine, but rather Rechy's. 'Johnny was driven,' Rechy writes early in *Numbers*, 'back to Los Angeles not unlike the apocryphal criminal driven to return to the scene of his crime.' Rechy, *Numbers*, p. 23.

15 Ibid., p. 240.

16 For more on sex normativity, see Gayle Rubin, 'Thinking Sex: Notes for a Radical Theory of the Politics of Sexuality,' in Carol Vance (ed.), *Pleasure and Danger: Exploring Female Sexuality* (London: Pandora, 1984), pp. 267–93.

17 Rechy, *Numbers*, p. 240.

18 Ibid., p. 255.
19 Thomas Moore, 'Seductive Darkness: An Interview with Dean Sameshima,' *The Fan Zine*, 28 April 2014, http://thefanzine.com/seductive-darkness-an-interview-with-dean-sameshima (accessed 10 October 2017).
20 Bettina Boxall, 'A Look Ahead,' *Los Angeles Times*, 27 October 1997.
21 For more on this series, see Susette Min, 'Remains to Be Seen: Reading the Works of Dean Sameshima and Khanh Vo,' in David L. Eng and David Kazanjian (eds.), *Loss: The Politics of Mourning* (Berkeley, CA: University of California Press, 2003), pp. 229–50. Indeed, a work from this series graces the cover of the anthology in which that essay appears.
22 Ibid.
23 'Appropriation is something I started to do in undergraduate school as well and it worked well for me because I was (and still am) a super shy person and I wanted to start to bring actual people into my work, actual bodies. Because in the beginning, my work was empty of people. I never wanted to put a demographic stamp on the sites I was photographing. The only real traces were from the tea-room drawings and texts I rephotographed from the walls of public toilets. I thought maybe it was time I start showing people what I was expecting to find in these spaces.' Moore, 'Seductive Darkness: An Interview with Dean Sameshima.'
24 Ibid.
25 Although I will be focusing on works made in 2007, in truth the series began the year before with a sequence of connect-the-dot paintings in white, black, and gray.
26 Richard B. Woodward, 'For Young Artists, All Roads Now Lead to a Happening Berlin,' *The New York Times*, 13 March 2005.
27 Florida Legislative Investigation Committee, *Homosexuality and Citizenship in Florida* (Tallahassee, FL, 1964).
28 Laura Allsop, 'What He Loved: Dean Sameshima,' *Art Review*, 10 (2007), p. 34.
29 Many artists working for gay and leather publications worked under mononymic pseudonyms. Perhaps the most famous is Tom of Finland (Touko Laaksonen), discussed earlier, but there was also Etienne/Stephan (Dom Orejudos), discussed in the first chapter, A. Jay (Al Shapiro), and others whose birth identities are not known or are generally kept out of public record, including Rex, Domino, The Hun, Bud, etc.
30 Ana Finel Honigman, 'Dean Sameshima talks to Ana Finel Honigman,' *Saatchi Online Magazine* (2007).
31 A few examples: Peaches' 2006 song entitled 'Hanky Code'; the short film anthology by experimental film collective Periwinkle Cinema called *Hanky Code: The Movie* (2015); and the Los Angeles-based artist collective Die Kränken's 'LA/ATX Pocket Expo: The New Rules of Flagging,' a component of their recent exhibition, 'Sprayed with Tears' at ONE in 2017, and discussed in this book.
32 This language has been changed in subsequent versions of the Pleasure Chest's hanky code to 'Asian Bottom' and 'Asian Top.'
33 John Kuo Wei Tchen, 'Asian,' in Bruce Burgett and Glenn Handler (eds.), *Keywords for American Cultural Studies*, 2nd edn (New York: New York University Press, 2014), p. 26.

34 Zora Neale Hurston, 'How it Feels to be Colored Me,' *World Tomorrow*, 11 (1928), pp. 215–16.

35 Bennett, 'The Exhibitionary Complex,' pp. 73–102; Brian O'Doherty, *Inside the White Cube: The Ideology of the Gallery Space* (Berkeley, CA: University of California Press, 1999).

36 Allsop, 'What He Loved: Dean Sameshima,' p. 34.

37 In one interview Sameshima was invited to name a 'Cutest Boy.' He chose Hidetoshi Nakata, a Japanese midfield footballer, who eventually played for Italian clubs. Sasha Bergstrom-Katz, 'Interview with Dean Sameshima,' *ArtSlant*, https://www.artslant.com/ny/articles/show/2050 (accessed 10 October 2017). For more on Asian-American queer sexual and affective constellations, see Hoang, *A View from the Bottom*.

38 Focusing on a Rembrandt van Rijn self-portrait in the Rijksmuseum in Amsterdam, the installation artist Jessica Stockholder discusses the tricky relationship between figure/ground, handily condensing nearly one hundred years of debate in the realms of abstract and representational painting. Although the artists are separated by centuries and geographies, Stockholder's description of the Rembrandt self-portrait could easily apply to Sameshima's *Bodily Fluids*, as well as to the descriptions of the cruising grounds of Griffith Park detailed by John Rechy: 'The figure is a thing lost in the background, perhaps one and the same with the background, even while emerging as figure. The little dabs that serve to illuminate the figure, which allow us to see it, are themselves figures on the flat surface of the painting.' Jessica Stockholder, *Figure-Ground Relations* (Rotterdam: Witte de With, 1993), p. 6.

39 Jean-Luc Nancy, *Being Singular Plural*, trans. Robert D. Richardson and Anne E. O'Byrne (Stanford, CA: Stanford University Press, 2000).

40 Berlant and Edelman, *Sex*, p. 125.

41 For more on Crimp's work with *October* and his eventual split, see 'Close Encounters: Douglas Crimp with Jarrett Earnest,' *The Brooklyn Rail*, 4 October 2016, http://brooklynrail.org/2016/10/art/douglas-crimp-with-jarrett-earnest (accessed 10 October 2017).

42 Sigmund Freud, 'Mourning and Melancholia,' in *A General Selection from the Works of Sigmund Freud*, ed. John Rickman (New York: Anchor Books, 1989), pp. 125–6.

43 Douglas Crimp, 'Mourning and Militancy,' *October*, 51 (winter 1989), p. 10. [AQ]

44 Although living and working from Berlin, his political intents seem aimed squarely at the U.S.: 'Pay attention. Do your research. Know your history. Because Trump is happening!' Carrie M. King, 'Know your history: Dean Sameshima,' *Exberliner*, 9 March 2017, http://www.exberliner.com/whats-on/art/dean-sameshima-647-a (accessed 10 October 2018).

45 Boxall, 'A Look Ahead.'

46 Dave Kinnick, 'L.A. Scene,' *Steam*, 1:1 (1993), p. 32.

*Archive*: The Carter/Johnson Leather Library; Viola Johnson's pin sash

An illustration in the 1955 *Girl Scout Handbook: Intermediate Program* depicts two teenage girls examining a sash filled with badges (figure 6.1). The girl wearing the sash looks down, her head bowed as she speaks to her companion. Lifting the sash away from her body with her right hand, she points with

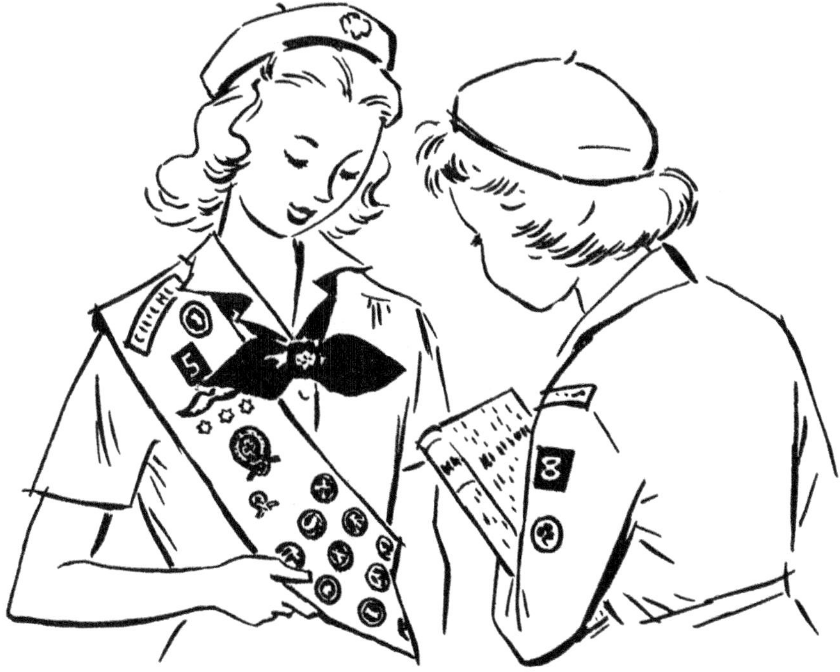

Illustration from the *Girl Scout Handbook: Intermediate Program*, © 1953/1955 by Girl Scouts of the United States of America. Used by permission of the Girl Scouts of the U.S.A.     **6.1**

her thumb to a particular circular badge on the edge of her sash. Her fellow scout looks on, cradling a book in her arms. These two girls are from different troops—5 and 3—and this drawing therefore illustrates the benefits of inter-troop interaction while underscoring a sense of individual accomplishment and pride. The drawing appears in a section of the handbook concerning the wearing of uniforms and special insignia, specifying the regulations concerning the construction and usage of the sash:

> *The badge sash* is a four-inch band of Girl Scout cloth and is worn over the right shoulder and fastened on the left hip. If you wear a uniform with short sleeves or the alternate uniform, or if you have no uniform, you may wear your proficiency and rank badges on a badge sash.[1]

The text goes on to say that proficiency badges, usually worn above the cuff of a long sleeve uniform, 'show that you are prepared to use what you have learned to serve others as well as yourself.'[2]

These lessons were not lost on Viola Johnson, who patterned her leather pin sash after a similar object from her past: the sash she owned as a Girl Scout in Roselle, New Jersey during the 1960s (figure 6.2). The choice of the pin sash as a form for keeping and displaying pins, buttons, and badges tied to motorcycle clubs and leather groups, events, and titles is an innovation in leatherwear of Johnson's own devising.[3] Having no uniform equivalent in the gay male leather scene, Johnson's pin sash reflects both her past affiliation with the Girl Scouts of the U.S.A., an organization that privileges uniform protocol as much as many leather communities, as well as her gendered dif-

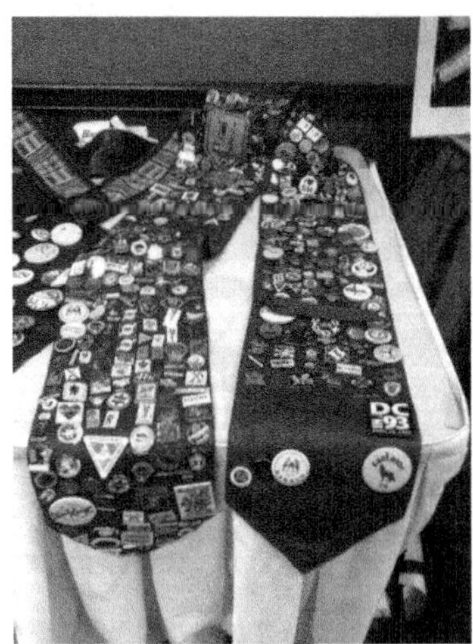

**6.2**    Viola Johnson, pin sash [on display at Northeast Master/slave Conference in Silver Springs, Maryland, 2011]

ference from a (largely) male leather scene, who commonly use leather and denim vests for the same purpose.

Johnson related the reactions to her pin sash during an interview I conducted with her in 2011 at the Northeast Master/slave Conference in Silver Springs, Maryland:

> Well, some people thought this was the greatest thing going, some people thought it was amusing. The old leathermen went [looks askance and pauses] … 'OK!,' because it was enough to honor them without trying to copy them. Only a few women crawled out of the old rat holes at the same time. We in many ways honored the men, we knew our boundaries, we were on the bar stools, we just left early enough so that they knew we knew the proper protocols.[4]

At once deeply related to gay male signifying forms, and marking a distinct departure from them, Johnson's pin sash underlines the continual 'process of differentiation' that historian Joan Wallach Scott values in the labor of history writing.[5] Now they are more common—studded leather sashes have become a hallmark of pageant events such as International Mr. Leather, but not until well after Johnson had hers made.[6] On her sash Johnson collects and displays a heterogeneous assortment of discrete objects, each a repository of histories of desire and difference. The hundreds of pins on Johnson's sash tell divergent tales, some directly experienced by Johnson and some not, but often recalling specific people, events, or places nevertheless. In this regard Johnson's pin sash can be seen as a mnemonic—or memory device—for both a general sense of leather history, as well as her own subjective experiences as a black leatherwoman, whose life in leather has been defined by the politics of intersectional oppressions and identities.[7]

Pins are ubiquitous in leather communities as a specific form of visual communication.[8] The practice developed out of the motorcycle clubs of the 1950s, whose members would disseminate their group's identifying colors (a broad umbrella term including cloth patches, metal pins, banners, emblems, and decorative arrangements of studs on the backs of white denim or leather vests).[9] Some colors are event-specific, commemorating a conference or a run, a days-long excursion filled with socializing, ceremony, and contest. Examining a leatherperson's pins is also a way to assess their history of contacts, travels, and affiliations. As historian Robert Bienvenue succinctly puts it, 'in a crowd of leathermen, one does a certain amount of reading from their vests and jackets.'[10]

Collecting these pins is tied, for Johnson, to the concept of service. Johnson's autobiography, *To Love, To Obey, To Serve: Diary of an Old Guard Slave*, which details her experiences as a black lesbian submissive, makes clear that service remains an important guiding life principle.[11] As a self-described slave, Johnson's notion of service spans from the scene of sexual enactment to her duties as the custodian of her mobile library (the Carter/Johnson Leather Library) and to leather history more generally.[12] Such a broad definition encompasses service to her mistress(es) and to a general leather public. Indeed, what the *Girl Scout Handbook* says on the concept of service aligns neatly with Johnson's own feelings of the subject:

> Have you ever thought that service is proof that you are important? It is citizenship in action. Service shows that you have grown up enough to think of someone besides yourself. Service is your way of making a contribution to your community. Service is being able to help someone else because of the skills you have learned.[13]

Enjoining the concept of a participatory national citizenship with an appeal to aid others, the *Girl Scout Handbook* entreats its young charges to occupy the beating heart of liberal democracy. Johnson's pin sash, sited within her mobile library/archive, exemplifies how such a call can be repurposed and perverted without losing the affective charge of care that ostensibly undergirds it.

Containing over 9,000 books, papers, magazines, posters, clothing items, photos, and sex toys, the primary purpose of the Carter/Johnson Leather Library (named for Johnson and her long-time partner Jill Carter, and from here on abbreviated to C/JLL) is to travel to LGBTQ and pansexual leather events across the country and provide attendees with access to the 'collective history of various communities who have chosen to live and love differently.'[14] Running and displaying her trove of personal and collected materials is an extension of Johnson's long-standing life mission of service to others, an expression of her leathersexuality, potentially reformatting the library and archive as a site where the logics of organization, collection, and display can be subsumed into the expansive circuits of pleasure so central to the mind–body mechanics of leathersex. Unlike the Leather Archives & Museum in Chicago, Johnson's library and pin sash is less formalized, more improvisatory, and most importantly, more mobile.[15]

One of Viola Johnson's special skills is that she makes anyone visiting the C/JLL feel like the most important person in the room.[16] Many who know her call her 'Mama Vi.' Reinforcing such kinship, Johnson responds in kind to many of her protégés, calling them her 'kinklings.' Currently, she is refashioning herself into 'Grandmom,' solidifying her position as an elder within leather communities. When folks call Johnson 'Mama' or 'Grandmom' they collapse two related, yet distinct, operations of caregiving: the interpersonal and therapeutic support that Johnson offers, and the care she gives the books, magazines, pins, and objects that enter into the collections of the C/JLL. Indeed, this is a collapse that is proposed by Johnson herself, as she lectures visitors about care for historical items ('stuff' is Johnson's preferred term) while referring to herself as 'Mom' and 'Grandmom.'

When Johnson brings the C/JLL to a leather event or conference she generally gives an introduction to the library, and this event is open to all attendees. Slotted alongside demonstrations on knot-tying and spanking, Johnson's standard introduction recounts two comings-out—her acceptance of her leathersexuality, and her origins as a collector, librarian, and archivist.

The drive to collect, and to thus preserve the visual and material culture of leather communities, is fueled by Johnson's experience with libraries, most particularly her childhood public library in Roselle, New Jersey. She describes this place as a 'safe space,' and a home for social interactions:

> When I was a kid, there was a little library in my town. The library in Roselle was open from nine to nine. Not only was it a wonderful space, but it was a safe space. We literally used to go to the library on Saturday, ride our bikes over at nine in the morning and not come home until well after dark. We all met there. We stayed there. We partied there, as long as the music wasn't loud, we could have our transistor radio. And if we needed something, a librarian went to get it. I once remember I was in fourth grade in Mrs. Henderson's class, and I had gone diving into Greek myths. A lot of them are written well over the head of a nine year-old. I asked her for a copy of one of the myths, written so that I could understand it. Three weeks later it was there. It is what I have tried to do with [the C/JLL]. The intent is to recreate the library of my youth, kinky-style.

But this gesture of generosity, perhaps embodied most clearly by the fond recounting of the librarian who fetches books that a patron most desires, is mitigated by another recollection of the Roselle public library:

> History [is] my first love, black poetry [is] my second. So the preservation of history is very important to me, and it went from fact to anecdote because of one teacher that I had in eighth grade who said that history isn't a collection of dates, but a collection of people. Find out the story, and understand the meaning and the reason, and *then* you will understand history. By the end of that eighth grade year they fired him. He talked about book burning and the danger of an idea. He made us read, in history class, *Farenheit 451* … as eighth graders! […] It was one of the reasons he got fired. He made us think about the power of an idea, and how dangerous it was to have one face. […] I can't remember if it was '69, '70, or '71, somewhere in there. There was a historical society that, with the permission of the library, burned *Huck Finn*. […] Taking it out of the fact that for its time it showed an incredibly loving and understanding relationship. But 'nigger' was in it. It's gotta go! Oooooh! The other one they burned was *Lady Chatterley's Lover*. And that safe space was defiled. […] It was

> stuff that shouldn't have been read. Shouldn't be in a library, so let's destroy it. That safe space got defiled for me.

In this story Johnson keenly observes that repression and censoring of ideas runs counter to liberal democracy, as emblematized by the material and symbolic violence of the book-burning. Ray Bradbury's *Farenheit 451*, Mark Twain's *Huckleberry Finn*, and D. H. Lawrence's *Lady Chatterley's Lover* all contain, either in their narratives or their histories of reception, parallels to the cultural erasure that Johnson frets about: Bradbury's text literally concerns book-burning, and the continuing importance of history rendered through the possibility of traumatic loss; Twain's representations of blackness and the interracial intimacies of friendship between the book's two central characters has been a perennial flashpoint for the boundaries of censorship (one that Johnson perhaps reads too charitably); and *Lady Chatterley's Lover* has been historically banned for its descriptions of non-normative, interclass sexual contact. It is this social and ideological performance of book-burning that commences Johnson's drive to collect and preserve. The threat is not quite the death drive that Derrida sees as constituitive of the *mal d'archive*, but something more communal—the ever-present possibility of cultural erasure.[17] Johnson's formative relationship to history, archive building, and books connects concepts of safety, trauma, and history to the public and shared social space of the library.

Yet the book-burning outside the Roselle public library, an event that Johnson cites as a primary reason for her self-described 'obsession' with collecting historic material, was not directly experienced by her. Instead, Johnson encountered the charred remains of the book-burning two days *after* the event, and after a 'four or five year' absence from Roselle. She was a witness not to the event itself, but to its residue and meanings in the wake of the event. And perhaps in the nexus between the material remains and the possibility of future book-burnings, Johnson was able to fully appreciate the enormity of cultural loss. Johnson's indirect experience of the book-burning is what Christina Sharpe articulates as 'wake work,' a mode 'inhabiting and rupturing this episteme with our known lived and un/imaginable lives.'[18]

Like the book-burning, many of the events commemorated on the pins attached to Johnson's pin sash were not experienced by her directly. Instead, many of the pins were gifted to her, or bought on online auction platforms such as eBay. Her experience of these events, in short, is transmitted second- or third-hand—and Johnson performs the role of the removed witness—what we might call a historian—as she relates these stories to others. The traumatic memory of the Roselle library book-burning is foundational to the creation of the C/JLL, whose motto is 'Never again landfill. Never again flames.' Johnson directly correlates these words with a particular pin on her sash—an oblong, horizontal, red and gold pin, which simply reads 'NEVER.' An adverb without a subject (or verb), 'NEVER' modifies whatever Johnson needs it to. While Johnson was not able to recall the origin of the pin, she has clearly resignified it, enframing it within the mission of the C/JLL. Collecting, as a practice, is for Johnson a recuperation or preservation of losses, an important counterbalance to the resources disappeared through landfill, fire, or illness/ the AIDS pandemic.

But if 'NEVER' indicates a negation at the heart of Johnson's archival project, the experience of being in the C/JLL is one of absolute affirmation. I have witnessed a variety of activities take place in the C/JLL. Gifts are constantly given to Johnson, most commonly books and the occasional magazine, and in this process sometimes a trade of goods or services is negotiated. I witnessed a vesting ceremony in which a slave was formally welcomed and recognized as part of a Master's 'family' through the gift of a studded vest. That particular event had many of the trappings of a normative marriage ceremony—including a dedicated photographer, and a ritual that ended with a kiss and clapping. Some visitors to the C/JLL recognize specific texts or people from their pasts, and become visibly emotional—joyful, nostalgic, and/or mournful. While I was in the C/JLL Johnson once gave an especially stirring pep talk to a self-published author, looking him square in the eyes and telling him, 'You don't get to fade away!' People gather at reading tables, exchanging information and anecdotes, tips on particular techniques, and holding meetings. Leather authors give talks and sign books for their public, often gifting Viola Johnson a copy (if she doesn't already own one … and she usually does).

The C/JLL is also, importantly, a space set up and run by people of color. All the library assistants—members of Johnson's extended family, folks she calls sons and daughters—are people of color. In this regard, the C/JLL is an important intervention in leather communities whose coded language of Master/slave could otherwise marginalize people of color; yet, within Johnson's library, people of color are the primary stewards of a rich array of historical source material, and the very gatekeepers of knowledge. Each library assistant has a named role (e.g. 'Robi, Prince of Pack-n-Load' or 'Pulse, Technology Jinn'), but despite these ad hoc titles, everyone winds up doing a little of everything. Because the C/JLL is a mobile library, much of the packing, unpacking, set-up, space-planning, and off-site digitizing is performed collaboratively by Johnson with this crew of family/volunteers.

The result is the creation of a multi-faceted and multi-functional space, one that affirms the place of women and people of color in broader leather communities. Although Johnson collects, orders, freights, and presents the history of pansexual, gay, and lesbian leather communities, she doesn't call herself a historian, but rather a griot. Here's how she described the consecration of the C/JLL prior to welcoming its visitors:

> We opened the space as we always do, with an evocation to those whose stories
> we would share, to come and be with us […] In West African tradition the
> storyteller/griot is the second most honored person of the tribe. The griot/
> storyteller is charged with remembering the history of the tribe and sharing
> those stories with the generations to come.[19]

It is within this invocation of West African performatics that Johnson most
clearly understands her role.[20] Johnson's pin sash is one of the most significant objects in this regard, as one can point to nearly any pin on her sash, and
this is enough for Johnson to launch into a story or three. The library and
Johnson's personal effects, such as her pin sash, are not mute—they do not
collect dust—but are rather animated by Johnson's raconteurish presence.

During one introduction to the C/JLL, I watched as Johnson picked up
her pin sash, heavy with hundreds of pins, to illustrate a particular point
regarding memory and material culture. She gave the sash to a large, built
leatherman, helping him to put it on. She continued without missing a beat:

> Do me a favor, take a walk. Not only is he wearing my personal history, he is
> wearing evidence of the clubs that have called me friend. Clubs that don't exist
> anymore. He is wearing the personal friendship pins of men and women that
> have called me friend, many of whom are long since dead. He is the walking
> living embodiment of those memories.

Johnson remembers the first pin she gave as her own token—a small pin of
the outline of the state of New Jersey. Gathered from tourist bureaus, Johnson
resignified this pin to stand in for herself, effectively collapsing her identity
with where she grew up. In doing so she was following established convention
in leatherwear. Colors, patches, and pins would often feature elements of
flags, geographical outlines, or place emblems. Pride of place was therefore
worn on the vest, displayed on the banner, and reiterated in dozens of metal
pins. The New Jersey state pin, if encountered by a person who did not know
Johnson, might only be a generic signifier, indicating New Jersey broadly as a
place. But to those who received the pin directly from Johnson, or who knew
this to be Johnson's personal pin, the pin would conjure Johnson specifically.

Johnson was not the only person to carry and give out a personal pin; it is
a practice she learned from another leatherman. When I asked her about one
of the smallest and most abstract pins on her sash, she recounted that it was
one of the first pins she was ever given:

> God, somewhere in the [early] 80s, as the group that is now Threshold […] long
> before it was Society of Janus South, when it was The Group. I had been given a
> few pins and had learned to exchange—someone gives you one you exchange
> one. […] So Jill [Carter] and I moved to California, and the man that had actu-
> ally founded The Group was a man named Billy Larkin. Wonderful man, Billy

was Bob Hope's lead writer. He wanted something that would tell the world
who he was, without telling the world who he was … he designed this little pin.
It is a top, and … it is a tush.

Like the New Jersey pin, Larkin's personal emblem—a child's top—comes
to mean one thing to a non-leather viewer, yet in the presence of someone
attuned to the language of leathersex, the gestalt of the form can be apprehended as a double entendre on dominant and submissive sexual positions.
By relying on the multiplicity of the form's meanings, Larkin could wear his
personal leather pin to work, in Hope's writing room, and have his sexuality
at once displayed and also occluded to most he encountered. Such visual
codings in fashion, at once revealing and concealing, are a central feature of
twentieth-century LGBTQ visual cultures.[21]

At the leather events that the C/JLL travels to, a small selection of pins
and buttons are frequently displayed in a box adjacent to Johnson's sash.
These pins and buttons are some of Johnson's most prized. She tells me that
they are gathered in this box, away from the sash, because she is afraid of
losing them. Some have previously been on her sash and were taken off in
the intervening years, and others have only ever been in the box. Near the
bottom of the display box is a black button with white lettering that reads,
'The L.A.P.D. FREED the Slaves April 10, 1976' (figure 6.3). The button
commemorates a raid conducted by the Los Angeles Police Department on
a 'slave auction' held in the leather-friendly Mark IV bathhouse. The event
was one in which people voluntarily auctioned themselves off to be a slave-
for-a-day to the highest bidder. The auction functioned as a fundraiser for
*Drummer* magazine and the Gay Community Services Center. The button,
produced in the wake of the L.A.P.D.'s raid, sends up the sensationalism of
local and national news media coverage, extolling, tongue firmly in cheek,
the police department's great deed. Like the book-burnings in front of the
Roselle public library, it was not an event that Johnson was present for, and
yet it is one she recognizes as important—too important to be on the pin
sash itself. During our interview Johnson reiterated that the events of the
Mark IV raid revealed the processes through which leather communities
became organized in the face of bogus and egregious actions on the part of
law enforcement. She further indicated that the response to the Mark IV
raid was prototypical for subsequent responses mobilized in the 1980s by
U.K. pansexual leather communities in the wake of Operation Spanner, a
large-scale bust of leatherfolks that resulted in the criminalization of sadomasochistic practice.[22]

I take this button to be emblematic, in that it reveals the stakes of the
histories that Johnson collects, displays, and interprets on her body and
in the C/JLL, because the event it references illustrates how community

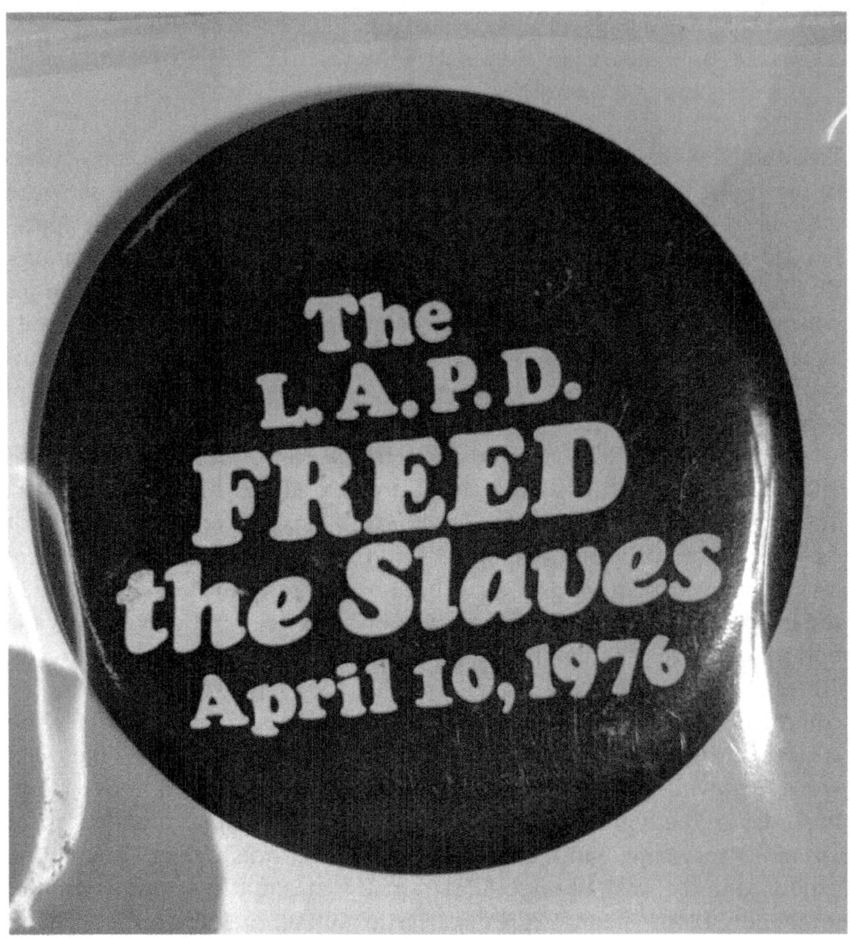



**6.3**    'The L.A.P.D. Freed the Slaves' [button], 1976

organizers—editors, clergy, parade directors, filmmakers, artists—helped to define the visual terms by which leather communities would be seen and discussed, thereby situating them within larger LGBTQ, municipal, and national conversations. These representations often circle around contested meanings attached to dress, leveling critiques in sartorial languages of domination and submission—both in terms of the visual vocabulary of leathersexuality (chains and leather harnesses) as well as in the visual language of power central to a state enacting violence against LGBTQ leatherfolks (handcuffs and chains).

Coordinating the research I conducted in the C/JLL with my discussion of the Mark IV raid button with Johnson evinces the kind of reading that can occur with nearly any pin on Johnson's pin sash. In doing so, I hope to enter into the space of the griot, recalling the outlines of a particular historical event, while also illuminating the subjective terms under which this event is understood within Johnson's biography and larger collecting, archiving, and writing practices.

The Mark IV, like many other bathhouses in Los Angeles and San Francisco, was essentially a private club. Those who entered paid a small fee for membership, a locker or room, and a towel, and were given access to the sauna and pool area, as well as rows of small rooms for fucking.[23] However, unlike other contemporaneous bathhouses, the Mark IV also maintained a dungeon and provided leather restraints (for an extra fee) to those patrons who required them.[24] This made the Mark IV baths available to some of the sexual needs of the leathermen.

Sometimes the Mark IV baths played host to fundraising events for organizations such as the Gay Community Service Center or the Homophile Effort for Legal Protection (H.E.L.P.). Institutions such as H.E.L.P. were necessary because the L.A.P.D., then under the management of Police Chief Ed Davis, was notorious for targeting gays and lesbians in public, semi-public, and private settings. A virulently homophobic man, Davis believed that gay people could transmit gay germs to others, infecting them with homosexuality.[25] In a response to an invitation to participate in the 1975 Christopher Street West parade, Davis wrote to the organization's president: 'As you no doubt expected, I am declining your invitation to participate in the celebration of "GAY PRIDE WEEK" … I would much rather celebrate "GAY CONVERSION WEEK."'[26] Under Davis's regime the vice squad (a specialized unit of undercover cops enforcing moral/vice laws) zealously targeted gays, lesbians, leatherfolks, sex workers of all genders and orientations, as well as drug dealers. Such behavior earned him the nickname Crazy Ed among these targeted communities.[27]

On the evening of the slave auction the L.A.P.D. officially—according to police testimony—assembled a team of 65 police and vice squad officers to conduct the raid, but some of those present at the raid claimed (and later on even the police department acknowledged) that the count approached closer to 105–108 policemen.[28] The L.A.P.D. set up command posts in a nearby park, on the roof of a neighboring building, and in a van on street level. At least four vice officers roamed inside the event, outfitted with leather gear rented from the costume department of Universal Studios.[29] That the police relied on Hollywood costume departments to go undercover is indicative of both their resourcefulness and the movie studio's tacit complicity in their activities. One wonders what items, exactly, the police rented, and what or how much they knew about leather dress. A briefing of all personnel was held at 6 p.m. on 10 April and it was then that a quota of 40–50 arrestees was established. The L.A.P.D. notified local news media of the impending raid and brought along a commercial photographer to document it. The raid included two buses to transport those arrested and two helicopters. Some reports maintain that arrestees were to be charged in accordance with nineteenth-century slavery laws, when essentially those arrested were charged with 'pandering'—a law deployed by vice officers when targeting sex workers. Of the initial forty detained, only four were actually charged with 'pandering': John Embry (publisher of *Drummer*), Jeanne Barney (editor of *Drummer*), Val Martin (a porn star who served as emcee at the auction), and Doug Holliday.[30] Entrapment was a common procedure used by vice officers, and the Mark IV raid was not singular in this regard.[31] Police handcuffed the forty they chose to arrest with nylon handcuffs, then a new carceral technology intended for riots, and paraded the arrested men and woman in front of television and newspaper media, ostensibly to humiliate and out those arrested. All of those detained during the raid sat in the police bus while the L.A.P.D. went through the baths confiscating sex toys and paraphernalia. One Associated Press photograph shows a Los Angeles policeman holding shackles, as though they were foreign to his own profession.

In the following days, news stories about the Mark IV raid appeared on the front pages of local and national news outlets. Papers in California, New York, Texas, and Idaho all reported on the event.[32] The *Orange County Register*, regarded as a conservative paper sympathetic to the motives of Police Chief Davis's policies and politics, screamed the headline 'Police Free Gay "Slaves."'[33] A month later *Drummer*'s cover featured the headline 'Drummer goes to a Slave Auction' (figure 6.4). A representation of the button reading 'The L.A.P.D. Freed the Slaves, April 10, 1976' can be found inside the 'o' of the word 'Auction' in that headline. Inside, an article written by *Drummer*'s publisher, John Embry, detailed the events of the night.[34] Further into the magazine, a page of cartoons drew attention and poked fun at the overlap of signs related to incarceration, slavery, and the L.A.P.D. One of these cartoons shows two leathermen at an MGM Studio auction (figure 6.5). The man at the information booth looks nervously at the two leather-clad men and states that there are no slaves from *Ben-Hur* available—the joke is that these men showed up to the wrong auction. Although there are no explicit references to the Mark IV raid in the cartoon, its inclusion speaks obliquely to differing deployments of slavery, as well as the Universal Studios costume department where L.A.P.D. officers outfitted themselves in preparation for the raid.

In the coming months *Drummer* would feature more cartoons that referenced the Mark IV raids, caustically reflecting the core issues of police power and brutality in marked opposition to consensual sadomasochistic practice and fashion. One depicts a leatherman in his home being raided by two members of the L.A.P.D. He informs them that just as they have been keeping files on him—archly pointing to the surveillance tactics of the

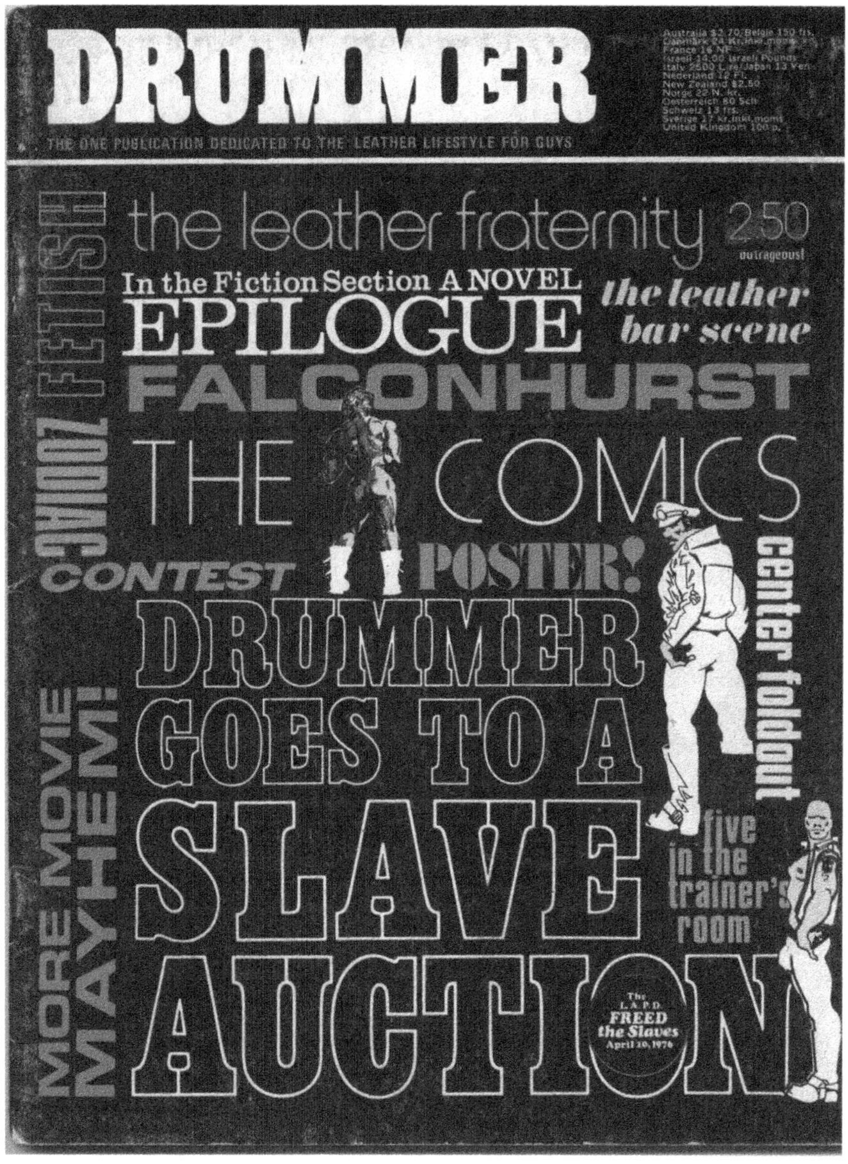


*Drummer*, 1:6 (1976) [cover]  **6.4**

L.A.P.D.—so, too, has he been keeping his own archive. Three uniforms hang in his closet, police uniforms from New York and Los Angeles, as well as an S.S. uniform. Besides acknowledging a persistent fetish within leathersex's signifying economy (uniforms of all kinds, including Nazi uniforms), the

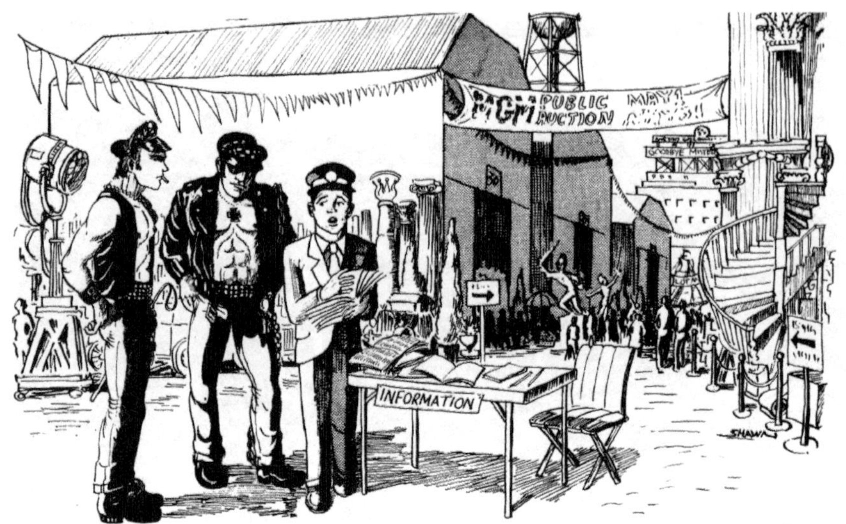



N-NO SIR, WE'RE NOT AUCTIONING OFF ANY OF THE SLAVES FROM "BEN-HUR"

**6.5**   'Drumbeats' [illustrations by Walt Handelsman, Shawn, and Sean], *Drummer*, 1:6 (1976), 29

association of the repressive tactics of the L.A.P.D. with the genocidal behavior of Nazis provides a forceful critique of authority. In another issue, *Drummer* published an interview with a gay vice officer, pairing that story with a how-to uniform guide, including locations where L.A.P.D. gear and clothing could be purchased.

Less than two weeks after the Mark IV raid, a second slave auction was held to raise money to pay for the legal fees accrued as a result of the raid. Pat Rocco emceed the event, along with Sharon Cornelison, president of Christopher Street West. Trouper's Hall, a small venue used for community musicals and revues, hosted the event, which included an opening dance number entitled 'Free the Slaves' and a skit called 'Crazy Ed Goes to the Baths' (featuring 'forty two faggots and a drag queen').[35] Some of the people directly involved in the legal proceedings defending the four arrested agreed to be auctioned off. Many of these people were not leathermen, and so were participating in a form of sociality that was otherwise unfamiliar to them. Al Gordon, for example, who was chief legal counsel, and who, although straight, was a leading pro bono lawyer to L.A.'s gay community, was auctioned off with a large 'slave' sign placed around his neck (he was purchased by his wife).[36] The Reverend Troy Perry, founder and leader of the Metropolitan Community Church, hanged an effigy of Ed Davis in a performative exorcism of bigotry. Transgender activist Christine Jorgensen gave a rousing speech and wore a 'Free the Slaves' button. Those who chose to be auctioned off arrived on stage through a 'prison door' manned by a leatherwoman in police uniform, making direct reference to the incarceration of those arrested. Unlike the participants in the initial Mark IV slave auction, many of the people who produced and attended the Trouper's Hall slave auction were not leather community members.[37] However, they played a vital role in formulating the leather community's response to the Mark IV raid and their participation represented an alliance (even if only temporary) between leather communities and broader gay and lesbian political communities in Los Angeles.[38]

The L.A.P.D. did not raid this second slave auction, partly because in the Los Angeles press the Mark IV raid had become a source of public outrage and ridicule. Letters sent to the editor of *The Los Angeles Times* by Angelinos expressed contempt for Davis's gross waste of time, energy, and money (estimated at \$150,000) on the raid.[39] Some who complained wrote about a rape and murder that happened only blocks away from the site of the Mark IV raid while the police were busy arresting consenting adults.

Seen in this context, Johnson's 'L.A.P.D. Freed the Slaves' button indicts the raiders, rather than promoting the aims of the raid. Another button and T-shirt produced at the same time reversed the joke, its text more succinct— 'Free the Slaves'—demanding that the L.A.P.D. free those whom they had arrested. These two messages, 'The L.A.P.D. Freed the Slaves' and 'Free the Slaves,' while seemingly contradictory, carry within them an implicit valuation of the otherwise burdensome language of chattel slavery. Produced specifically for the Trouper's Hall slave auction, these buttons and shirts were consistently worn by those present at the Mark IV arraignments and trials. Such accessories showed visible support for the release of the four persons ultimately tried, and silently made fun of authority on authority's own turf, thereby structuring a community response around the first Mark IV slave auction.

Buttons like Johnson's were also worn by supporters that year during an impromptu performance at the 1976 Gay Freedom Day parade. Briefly captured on film by Pat Rocco, Barney and another man are cuffed and chained to two men wearing L.A.P.D. uniforms who are 'walking' them down the sidewalk (figure 6.6). Every few feet the four performers stop and the two policemen make out to the applause of those watching. Staged in front of a broader gay and lesbian community, but perhaps more importantly the actual L.A.P.D. security forces holding the sidelines of the parade, this performance powerfully reformulates abusive state power relationships vis-à-vis the signifying sexual economy of leathersex, while also suggesting that the L.A.P.D.'s own form of sexual gratification is, in reality, the unwilling and wrongful imprisonment of others.

As a person of color, and one invested in the terminologies of servitude and slavery, in both leather and black poetic contexts, the display of the

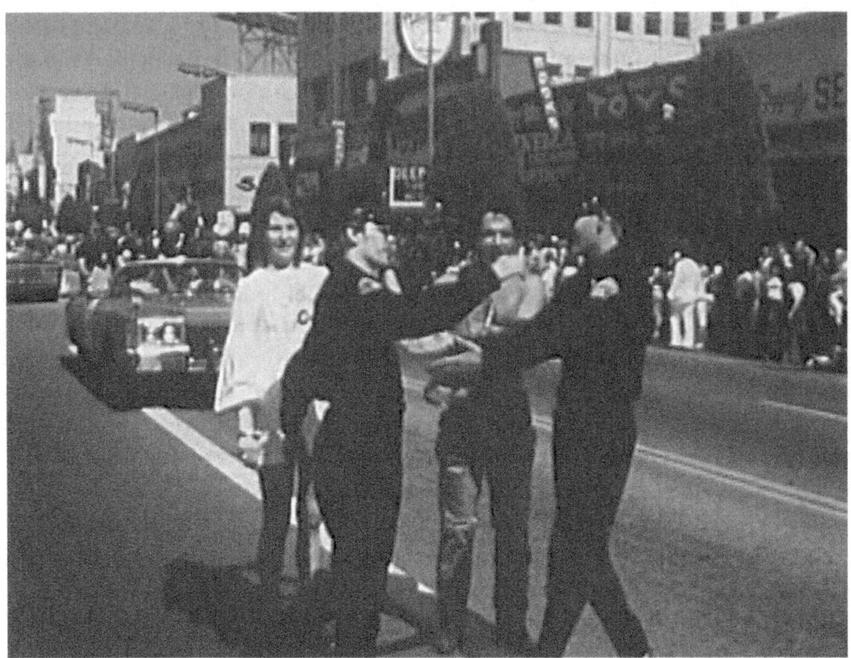

**6.6**    Pat Rocco, video still from *We Were There* showing Mark IV protest performance, 1979

button could be laden with potentially conflicting meanings for Johnson. Yet Johnson privileges its intent to indict wrongful action on the part of the L.A.P.D., and in doing so she also refuses to minimize slave auctions as a historical trauma.[40] Johnson has been a vocal proponent of the ways that terminologies of slavery can be productively negotiated within leather communities, and particularly by people of color in submissive roles. In a column for *Black Leather in Color*, a magazine produced by and for leatherfolks of color, Johnson describes her own relationship to the terminology of slavery:

> When I first tried to write this article I was having a lot of trouble with it. Sure my Mistress and I play with ethnic stereotypes. At times we don't just play with them, we stomp all over them […] I started to talk about the incredible S.S. fantasy that [Mistress] Mir and I had played out, and the conversation came to a screeching halt. My friends suddenly turned into the Sex Police. The berating barrage of 'How could you actually do that,' [*sic*] and 'You must be kidding,' coupled with 'Are you nuts. Don't you have more pride than that?,' was more than I could take.
> I LOST IT!!!
> What about all the other ethnocentric games we play? Even cop and speeder takes on ethnic connotations if the fantasy place is in the south.[41]

Johnson's point here, in part, is that racial/ethnic play is more pervasive than in scenes where extreme race play seems more obvious, as she surmises that cop/speeder role-play could potentially be more racially charged in the present moment than U.S. and global chattel slavery.

While it may not be unsurprising that a magazine dedicated to central concerns and erotic lives of leatherfolks of color would delve so deeply, and with such nuance, into this topic, it is also sadly unsurprising that leaders from the national publication of note for gay leatherfolks, *Drummer*, and those who attended the first slave auction, who were largely white, were reluctant to address the relationship of leather language of mastery and servitude with the history of chattel slavery. Despite their silence in directly addressing this topic, the traces of these conversations can sometimes be found in the pages of *Drummer*. In the initial reporting on the Mark IV raid for *Drummer* magazine, John Embry notes that the money raised by the slave auction could be funneled to a charity of the slave's choosing, provided 'that it be a GAY charity—none of this "Toys for Tots" shit that the Uncle Toms of the Leather crowd seem to be so fond of.'[42] Making reference to a particularly racist, and romanticized, white projection of black slaves, Embry's comment betrays what he otherwise failed to address with any criticality in his publication. Here Embry uses a racist taxonomy to pejoratively call out what would later be termed 'homonormative' practices by gay leathermen. Johnson's button clarifies a yawning absence regarding a critical race consciousness in the broader literature of leathersexuality, while also performing a rebuke of state-sanctioned violence and carceral authority.

The pin sash is a collection of people, to paraphrase Johnson's eighth grade teacher, and places, and events. And in displaying it, Johnson serves others— for her, a radical intimacy of empowerment and relation. Johnson and her pin sash are mutually informing, creating a dynamic filled with extemporaneous riffing, well-rehearsed storytelling, and moments of profound silence, mourning, and amnesia. It seems, then, that Johnson and her sash work in concert with one another, as well as upon one another. Within the context of the C/JLL these moments of intimacy have the capacity to shift lived worlds and our notions of history in a manner that might not happen otherwise in a more official or sedentary archive or museum. One may be able to 'read' Johnson through her pin sash, but the myriad objects fastened to it have also shaped and marked Johnson's leather consciousness. I have only discussed one of these pins/buttons in great detail, but Johnson's pin sash is ultimately a garment with multiple centers, with an organization that reflects the vying and multiple places where leather history might be enacted and understood.

Notes

1 Girl Scouts of the U.S.A., *Girl Scout Handbook: Intermediate Program* (New York, 1955), p. 31.
2 Ibid., p. 81.
3 Viola Johnson, interview with author, 4 September 2011. The interview was recorded during the Master/slave Northeast Conference held at the Crowne Plaza Hotel in Silver Springs, MA. The interview came at the end of three days spent researching and occasionally volunteering in the Carter/Johnson Library. The interview lasted approximately two hours, and Johnson's pin sash was physically present at the table to refer to and riff off of. As oral history is not a common tool in art history—my avowed discipline—my methodology for conducting this interview was informed primarily by two sources—Marjorie Hunt's *Smithsonian Folklife and Oral History Interviewing Guide* and a pamphlet produced by the Oral History Project at the Leather Archives & Museum in Chicago, where one transcription of my oral history interview with Viola Johnson currently resides. The other resides in the Carter/Johnson Leather Library. Verbal permission to use the content of the interview in my dissertation and any subsequent publication was given to me by Viola Johnson after the interview. Accessible audio no longer exists due to digital obsolescence. Both Hunt and the LA&M pamphlet address oral histories as a community imperative—providing pragmatic and theoretical tools when interviewing the 'bearers of tradition,' to use Hunt's evocative phrasing. Because of the nature of the interview—covering sexual history and aspects of leather culture—the LA&M pamphlet was especially helpful in navigating some of the more particular aspects of interviewing a leatherperson—for example, ensuring that you are dressed 'appropriately' for the interview, with respect to the display of club colors. Marjorie Hunt, *Smithsonian Folklife and Oral History Interviewing Guide* (Washington DC: Smithsonian Institution, Center for Folklife and Cultural Heritage, 2003); Leather Archives & Museum Oral History Project, 'Guidelines for Doing Oral History Interviews for the LA&M' [pamphlet], (Chicago: Leather Archives and Museum, n.d.), web. http://leatherarchives.org/pdf_files/ohbrochure.pdf (accessed 10 October, 2018).
4 All quotes from Viola Johnson in this chapter, unless otherwise noted, are from the interview with the author, 4 September 2011.
5 Joan W. Scott, 'After History?,' in Joan W. Scott and Debra Keates (eds.), *Schools of Thought: Twenty-Five Years of Interpretive Social Science* (Princeton, NJ: Princeton University Press, 2001), p. 95.
6 Begun in 1979, the International Mr. Leather contest emerged out of similar pageants conducted in Los Angeles and elsewhere (such as *The Advocate*'s Groovy Guy contest). Winners would typically get leathergear and other prizes. Starting in 1981, the winner would be given a title sash (the earliest ones made out of ribbon material or thin leather), which by 1985 became body-length, studded objects. For more on IML and its history, see Bean, *International Mr. Leather*.
7 The notion of intersectionality was first developed by gender and legal scholar Kimberlé Crenshaw, and has since been extrapolated by many others. Crenshaw

was focused on the legal case of a black woman who was subject to multiple and intersecting *oppressions*—and over time the term has come to be understood as the intersecting *identities* of particular subjects. Kimberlé Crenshaw, 'Demarginalizing the Intersection of Race and Sex: A Black Feminist Critique of Antidiscrimination Doctrine, Feminist Theory and Antiracist Politics,' *The University of Chicago Legal Forum*, 1 (1989), pp. 139–67. For an overview as to more recent permutations of the term, see Patricia Hills Collins and Sirma Bilge, *Intersectionality* (Cambridge: Polity Press, 2016). For the term's applicability to fashion discourse, see Susan B. Kaiser, *Fashion and Culture Studies* (London: Bloomsbury, 2013), pp. 72–4.

8  Rubin, 'The Valley of the Kings' (Ph.D.), p. 301.

9  Robert Bienvenu, 'The Development of Sadomasochism as a Cultural Style in the Twentieth-Century United States,' Ph.D. diss., Indiana University, 1998, p. 225.

10  Ibid.

11  Viola Johnson, *To Love, to Obey, to Serve: Diary of an Old Guard Slave* (Fairfield, CT: Mystic Rose Books, 1999).

12  The beginnings of the C/JLL are recounted in Johnson's book—as she travels the nation judging leather contests she notes how surprised she is with 'how little the New Guard knows of its own history' (Johnson, *To Love*, p. 328).

13  Girl Scouts, *Girl Scout Handbook*, pp. 85–6.

14  'Homepage,' the Carter/Johnson Leather Library, http://www.leatherlibrary.org/home.html (accessed 31 May, 2018).

15  The Leather Archives & Museum also travels to many of the events that the C/JLL does—but the LA&M's set-up when traveling is nowhere near as extensive as Johnson's.

16  This is a personal judgment, one based in my observations of folks entering, leaving, and browsing the stacks of Johnson's library.

17  Derrida, *Archive Fever*.

18  I use wake to invoke Christina Sharpe's *In The Wake: On Blackness and Being* (Durham, NC: Duke University Press, 2016), which surmises 'wake work' as a mode of 'inhabiting and rupturing this episteme with our known lived and un/imaginable lives' (p. 18).

19  Viola Johnson, 'Floating World, A Personal Recollection,' *The Carter/Johnson Leather Library Newsletter*, 1:8 (2012), http://www.leatherlibrary.org/newsletter/Vol1/CJLL_Newsletter-Vol1Issue8.html (accessed 10 October 2017).

20  My use of the term 'performatic' comes from performance studies scholar Diana Taylor's *The Archive and the Repertoire: Performing Cultural Memory in the Americas* (Durham, NC: Duke University Press, 2003).

21  Valerie Steele (ed.), *A Queer History of Fashion: From the Closet to the Catwalk* (New Haven, CT: Yale University Press, 2013).

22  For more on Operation Spanner, see The Spanner Trust, 'The History of the Spanner Case,' http://www.spannertrust.org/documents/spannerhistory.asp (accessed 31 May 2018); Jeffrey Weeks, *Invented Moralities: Sexual Values in an Age of Uncertainty* (Cambridge: Polity Press, 1995); and William N. Eskridge, Jr., *Gaylaw: Challenging the Apartheid of the Closet* (Cambridge, MA: Harvard University Press, 1999).

23  In one of the continuing ironies of working on minority and stigmatized sexual populations who, consequently, are under ongoing surveillance, the most complete description of the bathhouse comes from the L.A.P.D. press release regarding the Mark IV raid: 'Those attending were admitted to the Mark IV by presenting their ticket and being buzzed through two electronically controlled doors. Inside was a complex of rooms. There were 32 small cubicles, each containing a mattress. These locked from the inside, and many were occupied by two nude males. There was a larger room with mattresses on the floor to accommodate groups of men. A jail/dungeon occupied a portion of the premises. It was apparent that this facility was not hastily constructed for this event. It consisted of jaillike [*sic*] bars and had chains and handcuffs attached to the walls. On the floor was an apparatus commonly known as stocks. It was hinged and contained sufficient holes to contain four ankles, four wrists, and one head.' Los Angeles Police Department, Press Release, 11 April 1976, pp. 1–2.

24  Ibid.

25  Susan Fraker with John Barnes, 'California: Of Human Bondage,' *Newsweek*, 26 April 1976, p. 35.

26  E. M. Davis (L.A.P.D. Chief of Police), letter to Sharon Cornelison (president, Christopher Street West Association), 23 May 1975, in *Christopher Street West Gay Pride Celebration*, event program, 1976, ONE National Gay and Lesbian Archives at the USC Libraries.

27  For example, a fundraiser for those arrested in the Mark IV raid included a skit, along with a second slave auction, entitled 'Crazy Ed Goes to the Baths.' '"Free the Slaves" Benefit Show & Dance & Slave Auction,' event program, 23 April 1976, ONE Archives, Pat Rocco Collection.

28  '107 Officers Used in Mark IV Raid, Police Papers Reveal,' *NewsWest*, 25 June 1976, p. 3.

29  Ibid.

30  The felony charge eventually leveled against the defendants was connected to prostitution, rather than outdated laws on slavery.

31  James Spada, 'I Was a Gay Vice Cop,' *Drummer*, 2:13 (1977), pp. 6–8.

32  Fraker and Barnes, 'California: Of Human Bondage,' p. 35; 'Mark IV Raid Receives Wide News Coverage Across Nation,' *NewsWest*, 30 April–14 May 1976.

33  An image of *The Register* appears in a photo-spread in *Drummer*, 1:6 (1976), p. 13.

34  John Embry, 'Drummer Goes to a Slave Auction,' *Drummer*, 1:6 (1976), pp. 12–14.

35  '"Free the Slaves" Benefit Show.'

36  Faderman and Timmons, *Gay L.A.*, pp. 217–18.

37  Lee Young, 'Gay "Spirit" Invoked by Raid, Court Action,' *NewsWest*, 30 April 1976.

38  This was not an across-the-board response from gay/lesbian political communities—as one column in *Drummer* magazine stated, 'The Gay Rights chapter of the ACLU chose not to support the Mark IV case.' It also condemned *The Advocate*, the direct competitor of *Drummer* publisher John Embry's mainstream gay magazine *The Alternate*, for using 'the bust to divide and deride.' 'In Passing,' *Drummer*, 3:20 (1977), p. 98.

39 'In Passing,' *Drummer*, 2:15 (1977), p. 82; Herbert E Selwyn et al. 'Letters to the Times: Police Arrests at "Slave Auction",' *The Los Angeles Times*, 16 April 1976, p. C4.

40 For more on slave auctions and cultural trauma, see Weiss, *Techniques of Pleasure*.

41 Johnson, 'The Love That Dare Not Speak Its Name,' pp. 8–9. *Black Leather in Color* had a distribution of 3,000 in eighteen markets, ten 'with the largest people of color demographics.' 'Fact Sheet,' 1 June 1994, Leather Archives & Museum. Johnson was a regular contributor to *Black Leather in Color*, and the magazine often directly addressed the language of slavery that accompanies leathersex.

42 Embry, 'Drummer Goes to a Slave Auction,' p. 12; The Kiwi Collective, 'Race and Sex … Who's Panicking?,' *Black Leather in Color* (fall/winter 2000), pp. 25–6.

# 7    Attached to history

*Artwork*: Nayland Blake, *FREE!LOVE!TOOL!BOX!*, 2012

'Dust,' writes Carolyn Steedman, 'is about circularity, the impossibility of things disappearing, or going away, or being gone.'[1] A pulverized, dry matter, agitated dust suspends in clouds and eventually settles in thin, even coats. Sure, dust may be vacuumed, wiped, and thrown away in good turn, in deference to cleanliness and in obeisance to a persnickety order, but dust never really departs in an existential sense. It always winds up somewhere else. The endurance of this fugitive material—one of the touchstones for Steedman's enriching meditation on cultural history, archives, and materiality—is a testament to and a refutation of the figuration of death so often positioned as the foundational antagonist and driver of archival enterprises. It points to all we don't know, all that is too granular to see, and so we give it a generic name. And this is meant to be enough. With dust the question is not whether the world of old exists (it does—in tiny bits, everywhere), but how legible it is to the ones who wish to read the motes. The world—the past—is stranger than we know, and this is chief among dust's many lessons.

How the dust of the past, in particular the fugitive histories of marginalized peoples, is attended to—disposed, loved and adored, or treated with indifference—is central to the installation devised by Nayland Blake at Yerba Buena Center for the Arts in San Francisco. Entitled *FREE!LOVE!TOOL!BOX!*, Blake's installation evinces how the artists (and we) might be attached to leather histories. In Blake's case the attachment is at once figurative and literal. Figurative in the sense of Blake's querying regarding our investment in historical narratives and archival objects, and literal in the sense that the artist was attached (via ribbons tied to staples running down the artist's arms and back) to one of their works. It is my contention that this literal attachment reveals the unruly flow of affect described and mobilized by queer theorists, including Eve Kosofsky Sedgwick, who writes, 'Affects can be, and are, attached to things, people, ideas, sensations, relations, activities, ambitions, institutions, and any number of other things, including other affects.'[2] That such affects might be, in turn, descriptive of a 'queer utopian memory' (as per José Esteban Muñoz) suggests a loosely connected chain of affects and events circling around queer histories and their contemporary retellings.[3] Both Blake's installation and their public performance elegantly refute James Penney's critique of queer theory's 'passionate investment in one's own affective history [while] discourag[ing] interest in locales, times and experiences other than one's own.'[4] Indeed, it seems that these interests are the very grounds upon which Blake's investments are founded.

Dust may seem to be an odd opening onto some of these questions, but its very ubiquity suggests otherwise. Once you start to notice dust, you'll see it everywhere, projecting its existence into places occluded from the eye. I imagine, for instance, errant dust nestled in the grooves of some of the nearly three thousand vinyl records that comprise *Ruins of a Sensibility* (1972–2002), a DJ-booth/participatory sculpture (figure 7.1). The records in question are both popular (Madonna's 1983 debut album) and relatively obscure (a cast recording of *The Threepenny Opera* staged by Richard Foreman). They line the walls in mounted bins, similar to how one might encounter them in a record store. A large painting in the style of Jackson Pollock hangs above the bins—its whorls and tendrils of enamel paint—yellow, white, red, and lots of black—applied in loose arcs around the center of the masonite board. This painting was collaboratively made by a young Blake and their father (whom

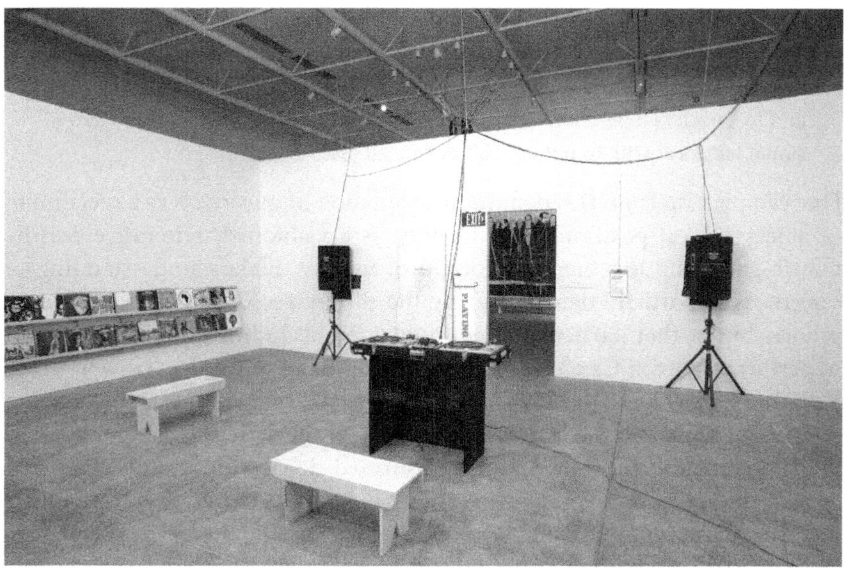

Nayland Blake, *Ruins of a Sensibility*, 1972–2002 in *FREE!LOVE!TOOL!BOX!*, 2012,    **7.1**
installation view, Yerba Buena Center for the Arts, San Francisco

the artist is named after) in 1963–64, when the artist was three or four years of age. This painting on the wall signifies thrice over: it winks at the perpetual complaint against certain strands of modernist abstract art ('My kid could do that!'—well, they did!); it suggests familial transmission and genealogical connection through creativity; and it serves as a visual map of the larger work, whose wild and unpredictable form is only truly activated when viewers interact directly with it.

*Ruins of a Sensibility* was first shown as part of a summer group show curated by the artist for their gallerist, Matthew Marks. In this initial context, the sculpture connected curatorial labor with the work of a DJ, who orders and chooses music from a carefully gathered collection. Broadcast through the gallery, the impromptu selections of gallery staff (who were tasked with DJing) created a running soundtrack for the works on display by other artists. Queen Latifah's 'Ladies First' might precede Richard Strauss's 'Thus Spake Zarathustra' or 'Annie I'm Not Your Daddy' by Kid Creole and the Coconuts—all is up to the DJ.

Blake's eclectic choices as both a record collector and a curator are central to what the artist identifies as a queer practice. They speak directly to this in their essay in the exhibition catalog for the 1995 exhibition 'In a Different Light' (which they co-organized with curator Larry Rinder):

> From the margins, queers have picked those things that could work for them and recoded them, rewritten their meanings, opening up the possibility of viral reinsertion into the body of general discourse. Denied images of themselves, they have changed the captions on others' family photos. Left without cultural vehicles, they have hijacked somebody else's. They have been forced to trespass and to poach. To be queer is to cobble together an identity, to fashion provisional tactics at will, to pollute and deflate all discourses.[5]

One can pick up from this definition a valuation of queerness as a reclaiming of abject subject-positions, and identity as a fashioned, reiterative performance gathering together the flotsam of history. Blake's understanding of queerness is partially determined by the discourses of feminist and queer scholarship at that particular time—informed by Judith Butler's discussion of performativity in *Gender Trouble* and Sedgwick's advice on 'How to Bring Your Kids Up Gay.'[6] The other influence on Blake's thinking was the ongoing AIDS pandemic and the 'provisional tactics' of the activism that attended to it. The pandemic subsumed and transformed debates in feminist, gay and lesbian, and critical race studies regarding the politics of identity—suggesting lines of commonality and difference between generations over the use of doggedly anti-assimilationalist politics which we now know as 'queer.'[7]

At YBCA, *Ruins of a Sensibility* served as one of five 'stations' structuring *FREE!LOVE!TOOL!BOX!* Blake's installation synthesized the political and visual histories of its site with the personal histories of the artist and the exhibition's viewers. The South of Market area of San Francisco—once home to many leather bars and stores, as well as light industry, Filipino populations, and street people—was rezoned and redeveloped to make way for the Moscone Convention Center (opened in 1981) and Yerba Buena Gardens, including the San Francisco Museum of Modern Art, designed by Mario Botta (opened in 1993 and 1995, respectively), displacing hundreds of residents and businesses in the process.[8] Blake spent these years living and working in San Francisco (1984–96) and thus knows this history intimately.

Beyond the dust I imagine among the records of *Ruins of a Sensibility*, dust was something of a visual keyword in Blake's exhibition. The sculptural assemblage *Maypole Way* (2012)—another of the five stations of the exhibition—included two black fabric flags, each decorated with the word 'DUST,' rendered in the bold, heavy-serifed typography one might find outside a country-western bar (figure 7.2). These letterforms appropriated and ana-grammatized the graphic identity of The Stud, a South of Market leather bar that opened in 1966 and is still in operation today in nearby Folsom (as of this book's writing). Blake made their first 'DUST' flag in 1987, exhibiting it within a few blocks of the original Stud (figure 7.3).[9] As Blake explains, 'The main thing that distinguishes the Stud as a bar is that for as long as [it] has been open, the old Stud has been better [...] so for successive generations, evidently, The Stud has been in decline for decades.'[10] Wryly remarking on a 'then' of queerness that was always, somehow, better than the current moment, the flags' appearance in *Maypole Way* can be read as elegiac. Blake's 'DUST' flags hang on a makeshift chandelier, whose messy geometry is com-posed of cascades of paper chains, ribbons, an 'old man' fright mask, electrical cords, and a string of industrial lights ensconced in plastic bags—all held into a loose mass by neon zip ties. Filling the volume of YBCA's cavernous main exhibition hall, this chandelier stretched from the ceiling to the floor, where a winding paper chain eventually terminated in a red, dildo-like protrusion on a low wooden footstool.

These flags, or to be more precise the text on the flags, gesture toward important characteristics of Blake's installation—and indeed, of their decades-long practice: the use of archival history as an artistic material, and an emphasis on flexible and recombinant forms. These notions of flexibility are due, perhaps, in no small part to the then and still-changing sexual landscape of San Francisco; spurred on and thwarted by development, political change, and the languages and protocols of leathersex. Blake's 'DUST' flags imply that in the transformation of 'STUD' to 'DUST' there have been losses and gains, mutually informing. Lost: a sense of cultural specificity occasioned by institutions such as leather bars, which by dint of urban redevelopment and 'renewal,' or through the vicissitudes of a growing and tenacious pandemic,

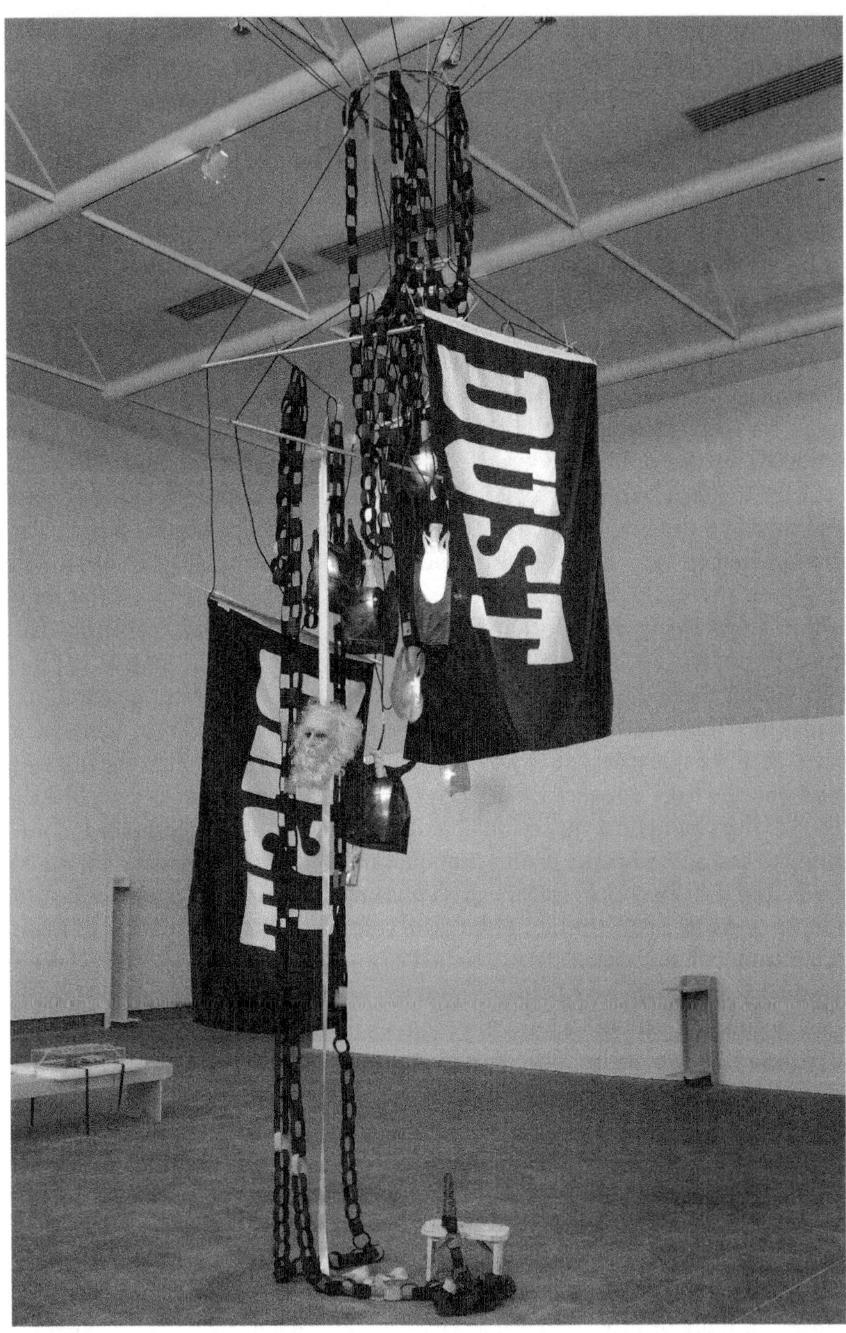


**7.2**    Nayland Blake, *Maypole Way*, 2012 in *FREE!LOVE!TOOL!BOX!*, 2012, installation view, Yerba Buena Center for the Arts, San Francisco

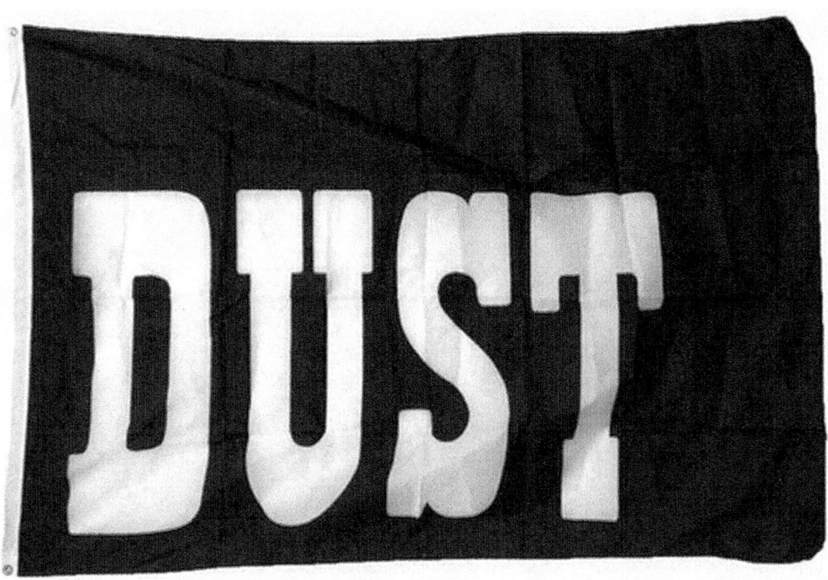

Nayland Blake, *Dust*, 1988, cotton flag, 48 x 72 in.                    **7.3**

have disappeared or mutated. Gained: new forms, cobbled together—as Blake says of identity above—from the pieces of the past, and a growing (if belated) reflection on the importance of place. In this way Blake's 'DUST' flags align with the chief features of dust—its circularity and its doggedness, acting as a continual reminder of presence.

Like Man Ray's famous title for a photograph of dust collecting on Marcel Duchamp's *The Large Glass*, dust breeds. In one part of the exhibition a small, red, logographic candle spelling out the word 'LOVE'—a long-time possession of the artist's—rests on a small shelf alongside a battery-operated LED candle. Black rubber copies of this 'LOVE' candle are also scattered throughout the exhibition space, making something solid and kinky out of an object otherwise consigned to immolation. Through repetition, objects like the 'LOVE' candle or the 'DUST' flags become semiotically 'sticky,' to borrow Sarah Ahmed's evocative description of how objects can be 'saturated with affect.'[11]

White, black, and baby-blue ribbons are threaded through the negative space of the original candle's 'O'—a hole, an opening—and attached to a large nylon banner. On the banner a phalanx of ruggedly handsome men gather and pose; a small pile of rubble rests at their feet. This image is a reproduction of a mural painted by the leather artist Chuck Arnett for the inside of the first leather bar in the South of Market area, The Tool Box (figure 7.4).[12] The photograph reproduced by Blake was initially taken by leatherman and part-owner

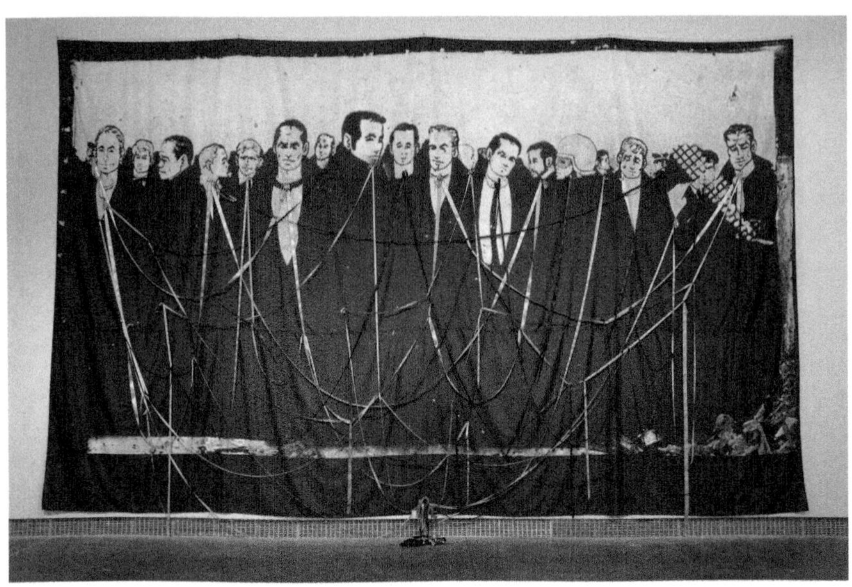

7.4    Nayland Blake, *Tool Box Again*, 2012 in *FREE!LOVE!TOOL!BOX!*, 2012, installation view, Yerba Buena Center for the Arts, San Francisco

of The Tool Box, Henri Leleu, after the bar had been mostly demolished in the early 1970s. Blake has attached a ribbon to each one of these drawn men's necks, and together they hang in a loose network across the vast black space of the lower half of Arnett's design. Entitled *Tool Box Again* (2012), this work is situated as the first station, and thus the exhibition's starting point.

For the fifth and final station, *Rest Area* (2012), Blake constructed a series of MDF shelving loaded with objects left by both the artist and their audience (figure 7.5). Sunglasses, cards, photomat strips, drawings, wigs, clothes, gift bags—all accumulated on the shelves during the three-month run of the exhibition. *FREE!LOVE!TOOL!BOX!*'s flexible form is bound up in social contracts such as these—whether a viewer participates as a DJ interacting with *Ruins of a Sensibility*, leaves a tchotchke or two on *Rest Area*, or takes a video in a small side room kitted out with emergency blankets and ad hoc glory holes (*Video Studio*, 2012). During the exhibition Blake also reconfigured the gallery, adding and subtracting items, and subtly changing the architecture of the exhibition. Perhaps the most visible of these changes was the repurposing of a group of long, low, wooden benches. These were initially installed leaning against the walls of the exhibition, and eventually were  reconstituted as additional wall shelving.

*FREE!LOVE!TOOL!BOX!* owes much to the language of 'stations' proposed by Molly Nesbit, Hans Ulrich Obrist, and Rirkrit Tiravanija for the

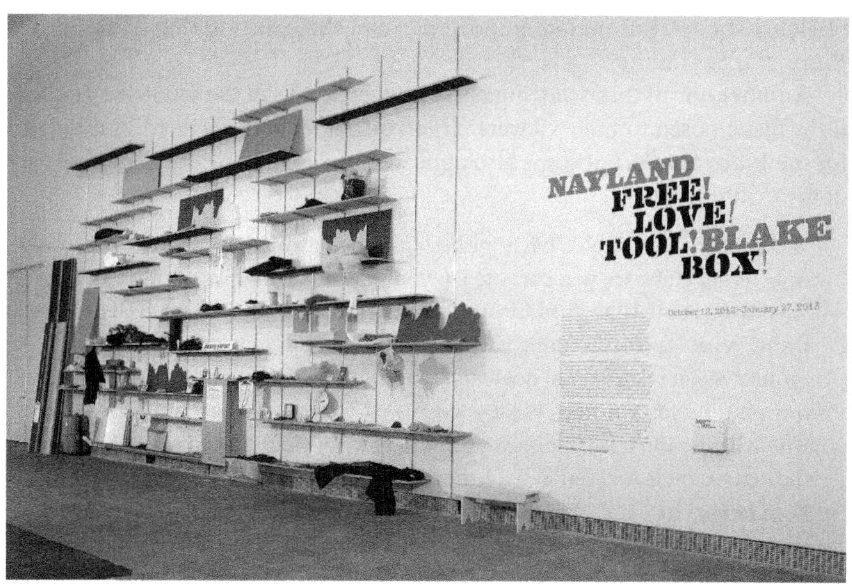


Nayland Blake, *Rest Area*, 2012 in *FREE!LOVE!TOOL!BOX!*, 2012, installation view, Yerba     **7.5**
Buena Center for the Arts, San Francisco

trio's ongoing, international exhibition and publication platform *Utopia Station* (2002–). Nesbit et al. identify the station as a 'flexible' structure, a 'field of starting points' which allow one to 'stop, to contemplate, to listen and see, to rest and refresh, to talk and exchange.'[13] Indeed, one could view *FREE!LOVE!TOOL!BOX!* as a such a field of starting points, for it gives a viewer a set of references leading down a number of pathways, some quite literal. For example, painted arrows with the words 'Private club, 835' appear at every threshold of the exhibition space, each signed by the preparator who painted it. They are loose recreations of the historical signage that served as the only marker to the entrance of New York's famed leather bar and sex club, The Mineshaft (1976–85). To strengthen this association, over one of these doorways Blake placed a replica of the skeletal awning that hung above the club's entrance in the Meat Packing district of New York. This area, once home to many of New York's leather bars and other important cruising grounds for gay men such as freighter trucks and waterside piers, is now the location of the High Line and the Whitney Museum of Art. Although historically there was only one Mineshaft, in Blake's exhibition multiples exist. In discussing these hand-painted signs with Blake and the curatorial and production departments at YBCA, I found out that many of the exhibition's preparators were queer themselves. Each signed replica is a kind of artistic and familial genealogical transmission—this one more obviously queer, but no less important, than the painting that hangs above *Ruins of a Sensibility*.

Another one of these starting points can be found in the sequence of questions Blake posed to their viewers. These questions were printed in didactics for the *Video Studio*, but some also appeared in a workbook, published as part of the exhibition:

> Where do you feel safe? What is the best thing about your body? What is liberation? What clubs are you part of? Do you want to change our world? Where would you start? Who lived in your home before you did? What happened to them? What was the last thing you created? Where did you do it? Ever have sex for fun? What is sex? What does your community think about sex? When was the last time you felt free? What good is a party? Did you ever put on a show with friends? What is your most powerful piece of clothing and why? Who set the best example for you? What behavior is your least favorite? Have you ever been helped by pain? When and how? What is the more important thing to pass on? Describe a beautiful thing from your past. What was queer life like before Stonewall? What was queer life like before AIDS? Ever have trouble picking a bathroom? What is your favorite costume? What is your favorite uniform? Ever know anyone into leather?

As profound as they are innocuous, these questions point to the trickiness of identity and the dilemmas of navigating the world as a queer, kinky, old/young, (anti)social, (un)liberated, (un)creative, (non)sexual person. 'Ever have trouble picking a bathroom?' points to the lived experience of many trans folks, for whom choosing a gendered restroom produces anxiety ('trouble') over considerations of safety and bodily integrity. And although what someone considers a costume versus a uniform is mostly a matter of personal inclination, one's answers reveal a great deal about class, sexuality, and the imagination. Modified by the last question, these questions about costumes and uniforms take on a particularly kinky cast. Some viewers will not be able to answer all, or even most, of the questions Blake poses, and in this way they are not imagining a single viewer but a heterogeneous queer audience—diverse in gender expression, class and family background, sexual expression, age, and ability

I can't answer the question 'What was queer life like before AIDS?,' for example, because I don't remember it—I was born more than a full year after the CDC's *Morbidity and Mortality Weekly* reported five cases of pneumonia among 'previously healthy' gay men in Los Angeles.[14] Because I can't imagine an answer to this question myself, I am curious about the person who might be able to offer an answer. Blake's questions thus identify and gently ask a viewer to address the gaps in their own knowledge. Among these questions is only one statement: 'Describe a beautiful thing from your past.' This might serve as an informal subtitle for much of *FREE!LOVE!TOOL!BOX!*—an exhibition that germinates these 'beautiful things' of the past—even of the artist's past works—blooming them, viscerally and intellectually, within an embodied present.

* * *

Written and sung by Dory Previn (her husband André shared writing credit), the theme song from *The Valley of the Dolls* (1968) presents a narrator confused by her circumstances. The opening notes are accompanied by a spoken-word narration, given by one of the film's stars, Barbara Parkins: 'You've got to climb Mount Everest to reach the Valley of the Dolls, it's a brutal climb to reach that peak…' Themes of trial and tribulation, with little hope for easy resolution, coalesce in this title song for a film, based on a 1966 novel of the same name, about three women navigating show business and their incipient drug habits. The narrator of the song frantically asks questions that interrupt themselves ('When did I get, Where did I / How was I caught in this game?') and it is only in the swell of the chorus that her auto-interrogation turns existential: 'Is this a dream, am I here, where are you / What's in back of the sky, why do we cry?' Some of these questions are, of course, impossible to answer. The song, melancholic about a loss that is never quite named, serve as the soundtrack to the final few minutes of Nayland Blake and Lolita Wolf's piercing demonstration and performance, part of *FREE!LOVE!TOOL!BOX!*'s public programming.

As the song begins Blake stands motionless. They wear a pink costume mixing military and bourgeois feminine signifiers. Ribbons, stapled to Blake's back and arms, are anchored to a mural-sized painting behind them. The artist walks slowly to the right until the ribbons pull at their skin. They then move left, experiencing the same taut effect. Their collaborator, Lolita Wolf, who only moments before had aided in piercing Blake's body, stands off to the side, hands on hips, smiling. Blake gathers the slack of the attached ribbons into their right and left palms and pushes forward and back, as if in parody of some gym exercise (figure 7.6). As Blake moves forward the ribbons lift away from the wall in unison, a chorus of affinitive relations. As the music begins its denouement, Blake walks to their left, ending the performance with their back to *Tool Box Again*, their right hand filled with the ribbons that keep them attached to their work.

This simple performance was inflected by the events that directly preceded it, which prepared the bodies and minds of Blake's gathered audience for this moment. Before Blake's performance even began, attendees were treated to a lecture by art historian Richard Meyer, who spoke about the historical context and significance of Chuck Arnett's mural. Meyer described its importance in terms of the queer visual cultures of the 1960s—a history I'll also be sketch-

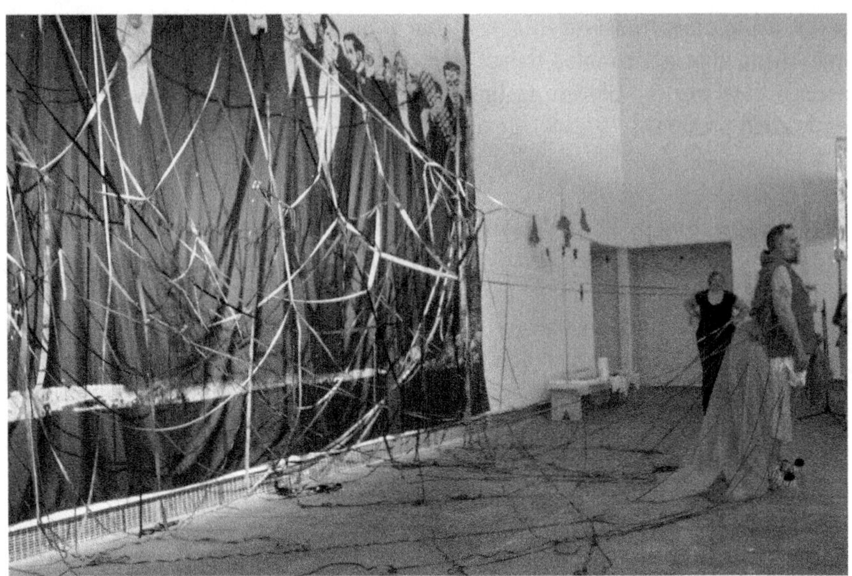

**7.6**    Nayland Blake and Lolita Wolf, 'Decorative Piercing' demonstration and performance, 2012 in *FREE!LOVE!TOOL!BOX!*, 2012, Yerba Buena Center for the Arts, San Francisco

ing out—but, tellingly, he began, not in San Francisco, but by reflecting on urban space, and the strange and sometimes affirming juxtapositions that occur by happenstance in the fabric of a densely populated city. His example was the proximity of a well-known gay sex club to the offices of the College Art Association in New York, the primary professionalizing organization of artists and art historians in the United States. Suggesting that queer histories exist in proximity to, but are often invisibilized within, canonical histories of art and visual culture, Meyer pointed out that like an 'archivist of queer history,' Nayland Blake also turned their attention to the overlooked and the marginalized aspects of queer culture.[15] Giving credence to Blake's project, and by implication asking what kinds of histories and worlds abut one another in everyday life, Meyer's lecture provided critical context for the embodied connections made between Blake themselves and a lost artifact of leather history.

This particular history, and its intersection with popular culture, is at the center of *Tool Box Again*. In reproducing an image of Chuck Arnett's Tool Box mural in its ruined state, Blake makes a statement about the denigrated status of queer history, as well as queer history's intersections with straight culture. Arnett's mural became as iconic as it did in large part because of its appearance as the splash image for a story entitled 'Homosexuality in America' in a 1964 issue of *LIFE* magazine (figure 7.7).[16] Filled with sad

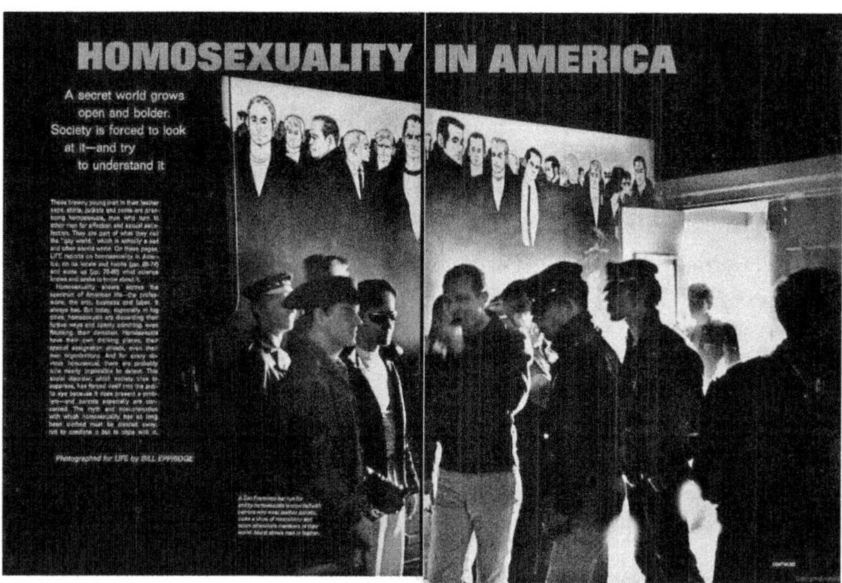

Paul Welch with photographs by Bill Eppridge, 'Homosexuality in America,' *LIFE*, 56:26    **7.7**
(26 June 1964), 66–7

and sordid details of lives marked by police entrapment and deviant sexual behavior, the *LIFE* magazine story might best be characterized as a piece of sensationalistic garbage. Still, historian Martin Meeker identifies that this particular story and its accompanying photographs were the occasion for a 'particularly innovative exchange between the mass media, the homophile movement, and [the] gay male community itself,' one that would reveal the lineaments of a world, no matter how jaundiced the lens, that was often not visible or spoken about in national discourse.[17]

As depicted in *LIFE*, Arnett's Tool Box mural forms the literal backdrop for a social world that the article's author, Paul Welch, only sees as a social problem. He describes the interior of The Tool Box as featuring 'murals of masculine-looking men in leather jackets.'[18] This much is readily apparent from the photograph taken by Bill Eppridge, but Welch also describes the other decorations of The Tool Box: 'A metal collage of motorcycle parts hangs on one wall. A cluster of tennis shoes—favorite footwear for many homosexuals with feminine traits—dangles from the ceiling. Behind it a derisive sign reads: "Down with sneakers!"'[19] Because Welch's article constantly identifies effeminacy as a defining characteristic of (always white and male) homosexuality, the décor and attitude of leathermen presents something of a bugbear—one that he is never able to square. In Welch's article leathersexuality, particularly its reliance on tropes of normative masculinity, is variously positioned as highly mannered and as an insidious, and potentially covert, new development in the signs and lifeways of (white, male) homosexuals.

Arnett's mural revels in the representational space that Welch would later find so troublesome, depicting a line of men, many of whom look out at the bar patron. They represent a variety of types in the genus of post-WWII masculinities: most are bikers, but there's a police officer and a businessman or two among the gathered crowd. A male and female on the far right of the mural are making toward the door—having found themselves in the wrong bar. Using only black and white, Arnett slices his composition horizontally, the bottom two-thirds entirely black, and the top third the zone where faces and bodies are graphically articulated. This makes sense within the spatial logics of the darkened bar. Men's bodies would enliven the otherwise blank bottom of the mural, while the faces were meant to stare out—watching over, cruising over—the bar patrons. This gave the men who frequented The Tool Box something to literally look up to, an aspirational image of cultivated masculinity.

The photograph that Bill Eppridge took of The Tool Box is telling, and as Meeker notes, 'performed a great deal of cultural work.'[20] It was almost theatrically staged by Eppridge and Welch, in dialog with the president of the local Mattachine Society, Hal Call, and the owner of The Tool Box, Bill Reque.[21] In Eppridge's photograph men gather in the space in front of Arnett's mural, illuminated by the bright light flooding in from the front door of the bar at the right. This detail indicates that the picture was taken during the day, not at the usual cruising time. Bar patrons and employees populate the photograph—in addition to Chuck Arnett, who was a bartender at The Tool Box, there is Bill Tellman, a fellow leather artist and one-time lover of Arnett, Mike Caffee (another bartender), and choreographer Carlos Carvajal, among others. The men of The Tool Box loosely mimic, in dress and in their position, the figures in Arnett's mural—and Eppridge's photograph collapses the space of pictorial representation with self-presentation in what Meyer dubs a 'call-and-response.'[22] Due, in part, to the popularity of this mural, Arnett would go on to design murals and decorative elements like leather banners, cards, and matchbooks for The Stud (1968), the Red Star Saloon (1972), The No Name (1973), and The Ambush (1974).

*FREE!LOVE!TOOL!BOX!* features a copy of this issue of *LIFE* magazine, cementing a relationship with past mainstream (mis)understandings of homosexuality. It appears under a plexiglass box on a bench facing *Tool Box Again* (figure 7.8). Resting on top of the issue of *LIFE* is a closed copy of *$TUD*, a collection of short erotic stories written by Samuel Steward under the penname Phil Andros. The stories in *$TUD* concern a cultured hustler and his various intimates.[23] Etienne did the illustration for the book's jacket, which

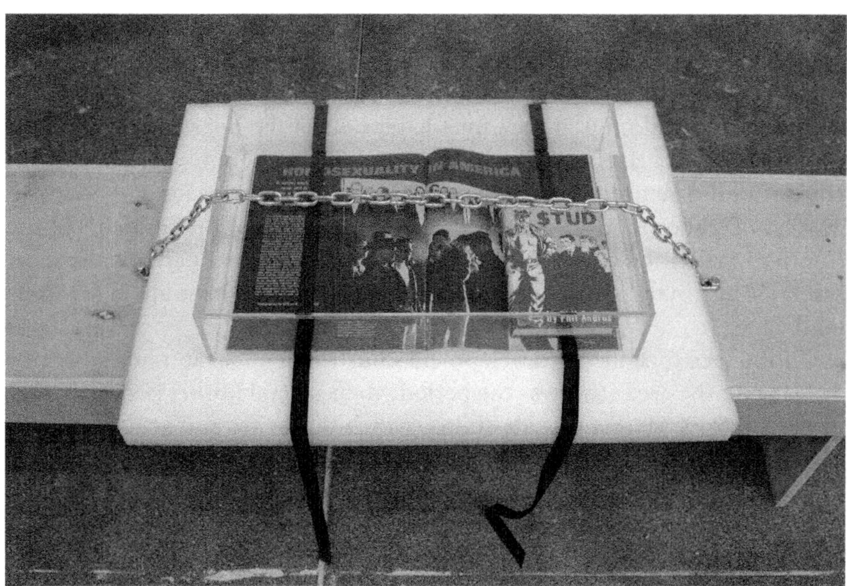

Nayland Blake, *FREE!LOVE!TOOL!BOX!*, 2012, installation view, Yerba Buena Center for    **7.8**
the Arts, San Francisco

in Blake's evocative placement continues the line of men in Arnett's mural. A metal chain locks the ad hoc plexiglass vitrine onto the bench. While this sculptural assemblage of reading material gives a potential viewer the tools to recognize the source of Blake's appropriation, it importantly denies the pleasure of looking through either volume. In an iconoclastic reclaiming of historical representation Blake counters a viewer's inclination to read Welch's story by cutting off his text with a black ribbon running along the right edge of the blocked text. What one *is* able to 'read' (in addition to Eppridge's photograph and the cover illustration of *$TUD*) is the tone of the *LIFE* story by picking up on particular words: 'sordid … furtive … deviation … disorder … suppress…'

While Blake stresses the cultural and visual importance of Chuck Arnett's mural in the bench-vitrine sculpture, it is the conditions of ruination and continuity that the artist stresses in *Tool Box Again*, and their performative activation of it. When The Tool Box was demolished in 1975—after being closed for nearly four years—the wall with Arnett's mural was left standing and exposed to the elements, an act which made the mural, in effect, public.[24] The Tool Box's demolition was a small part of a larger municipal project to rezone and redevelop the South of Market area. In 1966 the San Francisco Board of Supervisors approved a plan to begin acquiring land from the area's many light industry and working-class tenants.[25] The group Tenants and Owners in Opposition to Redelopment (TOOR) was one of many grassroots activist groups resisting development from the ground; and even though TOOR could not ultimately halt the demolition of buildings in the immediate wake of the Board of Supervisors' decision, they at least delayed and threw political light onto a process which cut out and disenfranchised many of the people who made the South of Market neighborhood their home. The 1977 eviction of the residents of the International Hotel (most were Filipino Americans) was perhaps the most symbolic loss in the midst of the larger, seismic changes in South of Market's landscape.[26]

In the face of stalled redevelopment construction, cheap rentals became available in the area. This was the period when several leather bars took root in the South of Market neighborhood, which the writer and activist Marcus Hernandez (Mister Marcus) dubbed the 'Valley of the Kings' (in contrast to Polk Street, which was the 'Valley of the Queens,' and the Castro, which was the 'Valley of the Dolls').[27] Although redevelopment aided in the enlargement of the South of Market area as a leather hub, the move of leathermen and their cultural institutions, such as bars and clubs, was initially occasioned by a long string of police crackdowns on waterfront bars that put the lives and well-being of leathermen at risk. The opening of The Tool Box in 1962 was a signaling beacon away from such threats of surveillance and incarceration, and its location in the working-class South of Market area of San Francisco meant that leatherfolks could be assured some measure of privacy. Fe-Be's and The Stud opened later, in 1966, and began to sediment a core of leather social life around Folsom Street.[28]

Redevelopment, as Gayle Rubin points out, posed distinct problems for leather communities in the South of Market area, as 'the potential for conflict and violence along these ruptured territorial membranes [was] immense.'[29] By the time Nayland Blake arrived in San Francisco in 1984, South of Market had been irrevocably changed by this rezoning and privatization, which Margot Weiss identifies as a 'neoliberal redistribution project.'[30] The Moscone Convention Center was opened in 1981, displacing thousands of residents and hundreds of businesses in the process.[31] The second wave of South of Market's development, inclusive of Yerba Buena and the San Francisco Museum of Modern Art, happened apace of sex panics in the wake of the ever-growing HIV/AIDS pandemic.[32] The year that Blake arrived in San Francisco the city was in a full-tilt campaign to close down bathhouses, operating under the misguided notion that such an action would be of benefit to public health.

While Blake was living in San Francisco they began to make work that directly reflected this history, borrowing signifiers from the leather communities they began to associate with. *Restraint: Ankle, Wrist, Ankle* (1988) is an early example of Blake's direct quotation of the material cultures of leathersex

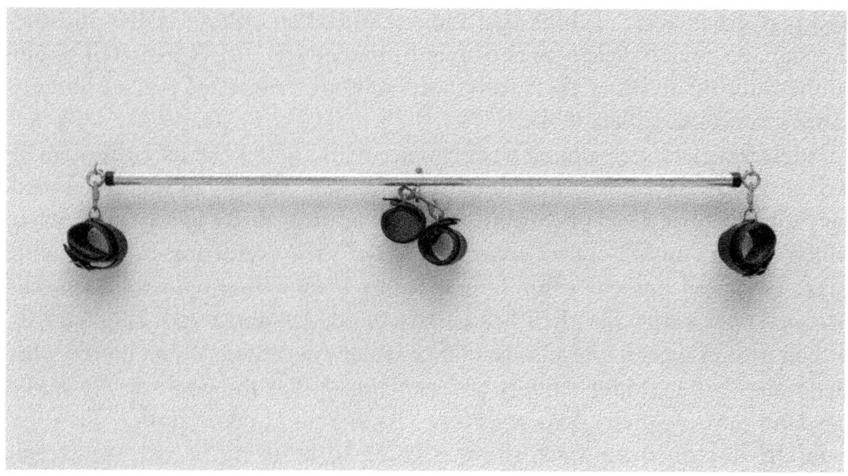

Nayland Blake, *Restraint: Ankle, Wrist, Ankle*, 1988, mixed media. Courtesy the artist and    **7.9**
the Hammer Museum, Los Angeles. Gift of Councilman Joel Wachs. © 1988 Nayland
Blake

(figure 7.9). The sculpture is essentially a spreader bar—the ankle/wrist/ ankle ordering of the title indicates which limb is to be restrained where. It shares a certain sensibility with Cady Noland's rail sculptures from the same time—*Push Papers* (1986), for example, or *The American Trip* (1998)—and so is also in dialog with conversations circulating in sculptural practice around assemblage and national ideologies. But whereas Noland's works assemble together items that pressurize nationalist violence, Blake's *Restraint: Ankle, Wrist, Ankle* (and other works from the same series) explores the dimensions of *pleasure* to be found in confinement. One doesn't have to be harnessed into a Blake sculpture to understand this. Positioned within the space of the gallery or museum (the object is now in the permanent collection of the Hammer Museum in Los Angeles), where touching is verboten, the sculpture's utility is evacuated in the service of a speculative erotics.

In the following years Blake developed a series of assemblages—which they called 'kits'—incorporating leather gear and utilitarian implements (such as knives) on stainless steel carts. The included objects strongly implied activation but were never used in performance, making the 'kits' dynamos of potentiality.

During this time Blake was serving on the board and curatorial committee of the non-profit arts venture that became New Langton Arts, which opened in 1975 in the heart of South of Market. For Blake, leather culture was not only related to the machinations of redevelopment in the city in which they lived, but was also related to their growing appreciation of performance and performance art: 'I think that the rise of leather culture in the mid-60s through the 70s paralleled the rise of performance art. […] You can talk about leather culture as being the anonymous folk-art version of the supposedly more respectable gallery work.'[33]

Blake's decorative piercing performance with Lolita Wolf took the form of a demo, what the BDSM wiki identifies as 'an opportunity to watch a skilled performer utilize best practices while performing a discipline,' and what Margot Weiss usefully calls 'working at play.'[34] The performance began with Blake being led into the exhibition space by Wolf—wearing a child's jacket oriented backwards over their head, like a hood, decorated with long tendrils of hair as if exaggerated eyelashes. Once Blake was seated, Wolf chatted with the audience—building rapport and explaining that the goal was 'to make Nayland part of [their] own sculpture.' As any good demo leader, she then carefully described the tools she was going to be using (a '3M brand 35w Staple gun') and her credentials ('I got trained by people who were professional piercers and nurses').[35] After cleaning and preparing Blake's back and arms, Wolf began to staple Blake's skin. She kept cleaning solution and paper towels nearby on the bench. At one end of the bench was the assemblage of *LIFE* magazine and the Samuel Steward book; at the other a skeletal wire tree from which dozens of pink and black ribbons dangled. These were folded and bound up in little bundles, pink strings hanging from them like tinsel on a Christmas tree.

After the first few staples Wolf invited the audience to have a try—carefully supervising each of the two volunteers who tried their hand at the task. One of these volunteers verbally checked in with Blake, asking them how they were doing. Answering with a stoic nod, Blake otherwise remained resolutely passive throughout this part of the performance. Once the stapling was finished Wolf began to remove the bundled ribbons from the tree, tying each one to a staple on Blake's back and arms. She then invited the audience to take the ribbons and attach them to *Tool Box Again*. At this point several volunteers from the audience came forward, unwound the ribbons and carefully attached them to the resurrected mural.

The performance realizes what Kathleen Chapman and Michael du Plessis identified as a trait inherent to queercore music and subcultural practices—a community that Blake also interfaced with while living in San Francisco—that 'unastonishing assumption that identities are tactical, relational, and distinct, that is, social, historical, and necessarily collective.'[36] From the first moment to the last Blake's performance was about connection to others—first carefully led into the space by their friend, and then lovingly connected to a queer artistic past by a gallery full of strangers.

In the final minutes of their performance, as Blake moved to Previn's theme from *Valley of the Dolls*, they revealed the actions of their audience as a tangled web of connection—to the past (Arnett's Tool Box mural), to each other, and to the artist and their co-performer. These connections tugged on Blake's skin, pulling it indelibly away from the viscera of their body, demarcating the kinds of movements they could make. Animating this web of connections was the *work* of Blake's installation, which drew together objects from a generalized archive of leather history, and insisted on our affective and physiological attachments to them in the present.

A final note, and a return to dust—because if we know anything it is that dust always returns: Unlike The Tool Box, which is now long gone, The Stud is still around. Although always on the precipice of closure, it has survived the many rezonings and redevelopments of South of Market, weathering the 'dot com boom and bust' of the 1990s and its attendant spike of residential and commercial rental prices. It now hangs on at a moment of unparalleled and exorbitant economic disparity in San Francisco. It has done this, primarily, by changing its administrative shape—by shuffling through several owners, and in 2016 becoming a cooperatively owned bar. The motley group of queer people who now own and operate The Stud—one of whom worked as a preparator for *FREE!LOVE!TOOL!BOX!*—are committed, in a deep way, to keeping queer spaces in San Francisco open and available against the nearly insurmountable tide of exponential property taxes. For them, for me, and perhaps for you, too, the dust of history appears not as motes floating through the air, but as the enriching soil out of which we continue to grow. Tethered to Blake's sculptural assemblages, a flag that proclaims 'DUST' and points back to a bar that remains open against all odds does not represent the demise and pulverization of historical memory, but its points of survival and regeneration.

## Notes

1 Steedman, *Dust*, p. 164.
2 Eve Kosofsky Sedgwick, *Touching Feeling: Affect, Pedagogy, and Performativity* (Durham, NC: Duke University Press, 2003), p. 19.
3 Muñoz, *Cruising Utopia*, p. 35.
4 James Penney, *After Queer Theory: The Limits of Sexual Politics* (London: Pluto Press, 2014), p. 30.
5 Blake, 'Curating In a Different Light,' pp. 12–13.
6 Annamarie Jagose, *Queer Theory: An Introduction* (New York: New York University Press, 1996), p. 83. See also Judith Butler, *Gender Trouble: Feminism and the Subversion of Identity* (London: Routledge, 1990); and Sedgwick, *Tendencies*.
7 Blake, 'Curating In a Different Light,' p. 25; for more on the contexts of queer theory's emergence, see Kadji Amin, 'Haunted by the 1990s: Queer Theory's Affective Histories,' *Women's Studies Quarterly*, 44:3/4 (2016), pp. 173–89.
8 For an in-depth history of this, see Chester Hartman (with Sarah Carnochan), *City*

for Sale: The Transformation of San Francisco, rev. edn (Berkeley, CA: University of California Press, 2002); and Rubin, 'The Miracle Mile,' pp. 247–72.

9 Nayland Blake, 'Roski Talks: Nayland Blake,' USC Roski School of Art and Design, 21 March 2017, https://www.youtube.com/watch?v=NyYE1WP_wZU 29:00- (accessed 10 October 2018)

10 Ibid.

11 Sarah Ahmed, The Cultural Politics of Emotion, 2nd edn (New York: Routledge, 2004), p. 11.

12 Rubin, 'The Miracle Mile.'

13 Molly Nesbit, Hans Ulrich Obrist, and Rirkrit Tiravanija, 'What is a Station?,' E-Flux (2003), http://projects.e-flux.com/utopia/about.html (accessed 10 October 2017).

14 The Centers for Disease Control, 'Pneumocystis Pneumonia—Los Angeles,' Morbidity and Mortality Weekly Report, 30:21 (1981), pp. 1–3. Of course June of 1981 was not the beginning of HIV/AIDS, only its first emergence in popular and scientific consciousness in the United States.

15 Richard Meyer, 'SF Queer Subculture & Art History,' lecture, Yerba Buena Center for the Arts, 19 December 2012, https://www.youtube.com/watch?v=-PbD_-B4Bek (accessed 10 October 2017).

16 Welch, 'Homosexuality in America,' p. 68.

17 Martin Meeker, Contacts Desired: Gay and Lesbian Communications and Community, 1940s–1970s (Chicago: University of Chicago Press, 2006), p. 151. Meeker is not the only one to have written about Arnett's mural, but his analysis is the most detailed and sustained. See also Rubin, 'The Miracle Mile,' pp. 247–72; and Jack Fritscher, 'Artist Chuck Arnett: His Life / Our Times,' in Mark Thompson (ed.), Leatherfolk: Radical Sex, People, Politics, and Practice (Boston, MA: Alyson Publications, 1991), pp. 106–18.

18 Welch, 'Homosexuality in America,' p. 68.

19 Ibid.

20 Meeker, Contacts Desired, p. 163.

21 Ibid.

22 Meyer, 'SF Queer Subculture.'

23 For more on Samuel Steward and his biography, see Justin Spring, Secret Historian: The Life and Times of Samuel Steward, Professor, Tattoo Artist, and Sexual Renegade (New York: Farrar, Straus, and Giroux, 2010).

24 Meyer, 'SF Queer Subculture.' Meyer states that the Tool Box mural 'unwittingly became a public work of art, that is no less visible to passing motorists and pedestrians, than, say, the Harrison Street sign behind the detritus strewn lot on which the bar once stood.'

25 Rubin, 'The Miracle Mile,' pp. 247–72.

26 For more on the International Hotel, see Estella Habal, San Francisco's International Hotel: Mobilizing the Filipino American Community in the Anti-Eviction Movement (Philadelphia, PA: Temple University Press, 2007); Randy Shaw, 'Tenant Power in San Francisco,' in James Brooks et al. (eds.), Reclaiming San Francisco: History, Politics, Culture (San Francisco: City Lights Books, 1998),

pp. 287–300; and James Sobredo, 'From Manila Bay to Daly City: Filipinos in San Francisco,' in the same volume, pp. 273–82. Also see Curtis Choy's documentary *The Fall of the I-Hotel* (1983).

27 Rubin, 'The Miracle Mile,' p. 258.

28 Ibid.

29 Ibid., p. 266.

30 Weiss, *Techniques of Pleasure*, p. 42.

31 Ibid., p. 41.

32 Historians Allan Berubé and Gayle Rubin have both ably written about the moral panics that place sex—and venues where sex is centralized—in the crosshairs of restrictive moral building codes and laws. For more, see Allan Berubé, 'The History of Gay Bathhouses,' in Dangerous Bedfellows (eds.), *Policing Public Sex: Queer Politics and the Future of AIDS Activism* (Boston, MA: South End Press, 1996), pp. 187–220; and Gayle Rubin, 'Sites, Settlements, and Urban Sex: Archaeology and the Study of Gay Leathermen in San Francisco 1955–1995,' in Robert A. Schmidt and Barbara L. Voss (eds.), *Archaeologies of Sexuality* (London: Routledge, 2000), pp. 62–88.

33 Jesse Pearson, 'Nayland Blake,' *Vice*, 1 October 2008, https://www.vice.com/en_us/article/4w4dk9/nayland-blake-125-v15n10 (accessed 10 October 2017).

34 'Demonstration,' *BDSM Wiki* (31 March 2014), http://bdsmwiki.info/Demonstration (accessed 10 October 2017); Margot D. Weiss, 'Working at Play: BDSM Sexuality in the San Francisco Bay Area,' *Anthropologica*, 48 (2006), pp. 229–45.

35 Lolita Wolf and Nayland Blake, 'Decorative Piercing,' performance, Yerba Buena Center for the Arts, 19 December 2012, https://www.youtube.com/watch?v=o68oQju8gEo (accessed 10 October 2017).

36 Kathleen Chapman and Michael du Plessis, 'Queercore: The Distinct Identities of Subculture,' *College Literature*, 24:1 (1997), p. 46.

*Archives*: Museum of Modern Art (NY), Outfest UCLA Legacy Project
*Artwork*: A. K. Burns and A. L. Steiner, *Community Action Center*, 2010

Here are three descriptions of the same film, reproduced in their entirety:

> *L.A. Plays Itself*, shot in 16mm, begins with tedious, aimless scenes of a man driving around the streets of Los Angeles, accompanied by a long, poorly recorded and almost totally incomprehensible soundtrack. The words that can be understood are spoken by a young man who has come to Los Angeles and has been warned to beware of the unkindness of strangers. A man cruising in the car (played by Halsted himself) picks the boy up and takes him home, where he physically beats him and subjects him to protracted sexual abuse. After this vision of sex as cruel abasement, however, the tone of the movie changes; the second half is shot in the woods and features two handsome young men who engage in several homosexual acts in a forest and under a waterfall.[1]

> Halsted classic. Evolution from nature to industry and sexual revolution. A hiker finds a nude blonde man in a small stream and they make beautiful love together. Then comes a bulldozer and development. Now it's L.A. with its adult movies and sex for sale on the street. Fair. HIS version deleted S&M.[2]

> Theme is how sexual behavior has deviated with the industrial revolution and the destruction/desecration of nature.[3]

It would appear from these accounts that three distinct, yet similar, films are being described.[4] This is because *L.A. Plays Itself* is comprised of two 25-minute acts, creating, in the words of its director Fred Halsted, 'a simplistic structure to work against a detailed complexity.'[5] Shot in 16mm in 1969 and 1970, and finally released in 1972, one act focuses on the natural grandeur of the Malibu hills and details a sexual encounter between a hiker and a nude blonde man playing in and around a stream. The other features Halsted cruising up and down Selma Avenue in Los Angeles, then whipping, beating, and finally fisting Joey Yale, Halsted's long-time lover, in a two-story domestic interior. Kenneth Turan and Stephen Zito's review (the first description reproduced above) is nearly contemporaneous with the release of Halsted's film. In it the leather act is described as preceding the nature act. That order is reversed in the second description reproduced above, which comes from a 1989 pornographic video guide. The last, and briefest description is also the most interpretive in that it elides the distinction between the leather and nature segments, understanding the film as a contiguous whole, with an equally contiguous argument about sexuality and industrial modernism. The discontinuity between these descriptions might simply stem from the fact that Halsted's film was edited differently for the two different formats, 16mm film and VHS, respectively. But this is not precisely the case, as the film copy housed in the Museum of Modern Art's collection conforms to the order of the VHS, not to the order of the 16mm film described by Turan and Zito.[6] Similarly, the copy of *L.A. Plays Itself* in the Outfest UCLA Legacy Project (a joint effort of the LGBTQ film festival, Outfest, and the UCLA film archive) also places the nature act first. But this copy also contains a credit sequence in the middle of the film—suggesting that even if the film was assembled one way on the reel, it could potentially be assembled otherwise. To discuss *L.A. Plays Itself* is then to describe a moving target whose editing history, as well as archival contexts, are key factors to its interpretation. Without these, one is left with generally accurate but factually incorrect assessments of the film, like the one that appeared in *Bookforum* in 2011, whose author praises the film as 'non-narrative' and 'non-linear' but reinforces the belief that in the earliest screenings Halsted's film 'ended with a scene of a penetrative act so violent, it was called perverse even in the porn community.'[7] In fact, this 'penetrative act so violent' (one can only assume the author means Halsted's fisting of Yale) was first seen in the middle of the film, with long, languorous shots of the Malibu landscape immediately following it.

As for Halsted, he described *L.A. Plays Itself* as 'a sadomasochistic, fist-fucking faggot film.'[8] In this respect Halsted centers what would have initially been the experiential and temporal center of his film. In the pages that follow I'll re-center Halsted's own conception of his film, which has enthused later artists, most especially A. K. Burns and A. L. Steiner who, together, along with a group of queer friends and kin, made a 69-minute pornographic film entitled *Community Action Center* (2010), after seeing *L.A. Plays Itself*. Beyond the fact that both films are now held in MoMA's film collections, they share other similarities: an interest in subverting dominant pornographic tropes, intentional play with the personae of the performers, and an implicit relation to 'switching' as both formal and sexual strategy. Burns and Steiner ultimately use *L.A. Plays Itself* as one piece of a larger feminist and queer assemblage, revealing how viewing Halsted alongside a more heterogeneous pornographic archive can instantiate sexual possibility in the face of assimilative pressures.

Media scholar and activist Cindy Patton and artist William E. Jones have already written meaningfully about *L.A. Plays Itself*, and my work here is indebted to their insights and research.[9] Patton examines the film alongside Wakefield Poole's sun-drenched *Boys in the Sand* (1971), using both to illuminate the then-circulating discourses around sex and public health. Jones, on the other hand, offers a biographical portrait of the filmmaker, tracing his familial roots back to a radical, pacifist, Christian sect called the Doukhobors. Both Jones and Patton mention, to varying degrees, that the film was screened in alternate orderings during the first few years of its exhibition, but neither of them greatly invests in this fact.

The two orderings of *L.A. Plays Itself* result in two similar, but ultimately different films. It was archival research that revealed this to me in the first place, as I sought to track down contemporaneous reviews of Halsted's film. Because none of the extant copies of the film I'm aware of retain Halsted's initial ordering, in order to understand how the initial film might have played, I decided to view a pirated copy of *L.A. Plays Itself* out-of-order.[10] How one describes Halsted's film is largely dependent upon the order one sees it in, and I'm using description in this chapter to reveal such an experiential divide. Description perseveres as one of art history's most fundamental tools; Michael Baxandall calls it the 'mediating object of explanation,' and by examining *L.A. Plays Itself* through others' descriptions of it, and in turn offering my own, I argue for the consideration of its various orderings as a way of revealing how the film orders experience and makes meaning.[11] Halsted's description of his film as a 'sadomasochistic, fistfucking faggot film' is foundationally different from the video guide that describes the same film as an 'evolution from nature to industry and sexual revolution,' and yet both are true. Both also generate particular affects—Halsted's is atmospherically political, deploying graphic language and the otherwise derogatory term 'faggot' to jolt a reader and film viewer out of easy identification with his film. The video guide's description is more more soothingly narrative, and together they represent two ways we might think about what *L.A. Plays Itself* was in its historical moment, and how it is now positioned within the archives where it resides. While discussing the experience of seeing *L.A. Plays Itself* in its initial ordering, I keep in mind Joan Wallach Scott's cautionary advice to not treat experience as incontrovertible historical evidence, as it 'is not individuals who have experience, but subjects who are constituted through experience.'[12] I would argue that the same holds true for description, for it is via the modality of description that experience as a historical category is perhaps most apparent. Description, then, when closely examined and engaged as a process of meaning-making, is intimately tied to the pleasures and anxieties offered by archives and what might be said of their contents.

Halsted made his 'sadomasochistic, fistfucking faggot' remark to Paul

Alcuin Siebenand, a Ph.D. student writing his dissertation on 1960s and 1970s pornographic films made in Los Angeles. Over the course of four interviews, during which Fred Halsted began to shoot *Sextool* (and potentially as he was reordering *L.A. Plays Itself*), Siebenand was able to get some answers from Halsted concerning his process, thoughts on sex, and relation to other filmmakers. Halsted's responses indicate that he saw his films as different from those made by his contemporaries, such as Wakefield Poole, whom he knew Siebenand was also interviewing.[13] One of these contemporaries, the filmmaker Pat Rocco, eventually bought a 16mm print of *L.A. Plays Itself*, and it is this print that is now part of the OutFest Legacy Project at UCLA. Rocco, who was well-known in Los Angeles and the West Coast for his film loops of naked youths in idyllic natural surrounds and political events, is perhaps the most direct influence on the segment of Halsted's film set in the Malibu canyons. But *L.A. Plays Itself*'s leather act, with its raw and graphic sex and gritty cruising scenes, marked out Halsted's departure from Rocco's aesthetic.

For the first three years of its exhibition life (1972–74) *L.A. Plays Itself* was screened in the same order—first the leather act, then the nature act. This is documented in both Turan and Zito's review (quoted above) and in Jonas Mekas's 1972 review in the *Village Voice* of the film's initial New York screening.[14] During this period the film was never screened in more than one location simultaneously, indicating that perhaps only one print existed. It wasn't until a Cineprobe screening at MoMA in 1974 that contemporary descriptions of the film indicate a reordering of the two acts. This important turning point in the film's ordering underscores the need for a flexible understanding of the meanings of *L.A. Plays Itself*. The modern/industrial narrative put forth by the 1986 porn video guide—'evolution from nature to industry and sexual revolution'—doesn't appear until after the reordering of the film. Similarly, one has to wonder, is the 'beautiful love' described in the video guide experienced differently when it appears directly after a scene of fistfucking? By examining *L.A. Plays Itself* in tandem with Halsted's extra-filmic, business and personal enterprises in the years between 1969 and 1975, it is my hope to arrive at a reading that privileges both the early flexibility of this film alongside the seeming inflexibility of the roles that Halsted and Yale seemed to inhabit during this time, especially Halsted's public persona as a top.

I should also note that while *L.A. Plays Itself* is my chief concern, the film was (and still is) often screened along with another film, *Sex Garage* (1971), which Halsted described to Siebenand as his 'greatest.' This pendant film only compounds the issue of ordering, because it was screened in various programs either before or after *L.A. Plays Itself*. Thus one could add another host of meanings to the structure of *L.A. Plays Itself*.[15] I have chosen not to integrate *Sex Garage* into my analysis here, and admit this as a possible failing. But because *Sex Garage* and *L.A. Plays Itself* were not always screened together, and ultimately because they were conceived as two unique films, I am confident that there is important work to be done in considering *L.A. Plays Itself* on its own terms.

Halsted identified 'switching' as a major theme of *Sextool*, the feature film that he made after *L.A. Plays Itself*, a film he was busy editing as he screened *L.A. Plays Itself* at MoMA.[16] Initially devised as a strategy for distribution, Halsted thought that switching between straight, gay, and trans characters and sex scenes in *Sextool* would help him broaden his potential audience. Ever the business hustler, his intention to bridge gay and straight audiences by providing a little something for everyone was indicative of an ethics of sexual pluralism (albeit filtered through capitalist opportunism).[17] I home in on switching because it is descriptive of the process of reordering *L.A. Plays Itself*—a film he was likely switching around as he made his remarks—as well as describing the fundamental flexibility of the seemingly dyadic sexual roles discussed in this book's introduction.[18] Halsted also boasted of his ability to 'turn' or change another's preferred sexual role. Referencing the practice of hanging a ring of keys on the left or right side of the body to indicate top or bottom sexual proclivities, Halsted crowed, 'That key business is all just playing games. You can take any of them and turn them around. At least I can.'[19] For Halsted, switching was not really an intrinsic characteristic of leathersexuality (as I have argued elsewhere in this book). It may be merely coincidental that Halsted's discussion of switching occurred at the same time that his film was 'mainstreamed' into MoMA's permanent collection—but I don't think so.

Halsted saw his film as expressive of an auteurist point of view: 'Everything in the film has been done deliberately. One the one hand schematic, on the other ambivalent. Am I for impersonal sex or against it? For the city or against it?'[20] Considering Halsted's two orderings of his film animates these questions. For example, the 'evolution from nature to industry and sexual revolution' would only be possible if the nature act precedes the leather act; while ostensibly the apprehension of the film as a piece of underground cinema (Mekas) might hinge on its initial ordering.[21] To really understand this, first *L.A. Plays Itself* must be described in depth. In the description that follows, I provide a critical exegesis of *L.A. Plays Itself* as it would have appeared in its initial ordering. Although it might strain the limits of a reader's attention, I think this is a useful exercise precisely because the film remains largely unavailable to a general public, and if one sees the film in MoMA or at UCLA the experience will differ greatly.

* * *

*L.A. Plays Itself* begins with scenes of cruising. Here we are on Selma Avenue below the Out-Of-Town newsstand, at the corner of Hollywood and Las Palmas, in Griffith Park, and on Santa Monica Blvd. Non-diegetic Moog-synth and flute music (by the electronic duo Tonto's Expanding Headband) is interspersed with sound samples—motorcycles and voices chattering.[22] Fred Halsted, who plays himself, walks up and down the streets—his point of view collapsing with the camera (a kind of autofictional conceit), and so we are invited to inhabit his cruising gaze.[23] He gets in his car and begins to drive. The camera lingers on a billboard advertising Donald Cammell and Nicholas Roeg's 1968 film *Performance* (figure 8.1). Mick Jagger, that film's lead, is depicted twice on the billboard, once as a long-haired rocker and again as a greased-back businessman. The tagline is: 'Underground Meets Underworld.'

The billboard for *Performance* in this early montage introduces Halsted's recurrent tactic of intercutting shots of an urban environment overloaded with visual signifiers, while also winkingly placing *L.A. Plays Itself* in the context of underground film production. The split in how Jagger is represented rhymes with Halsted's film, as does the film's tagline. Indeed, it is within the framing of underground film that *L.A. Plays Itself* was initially

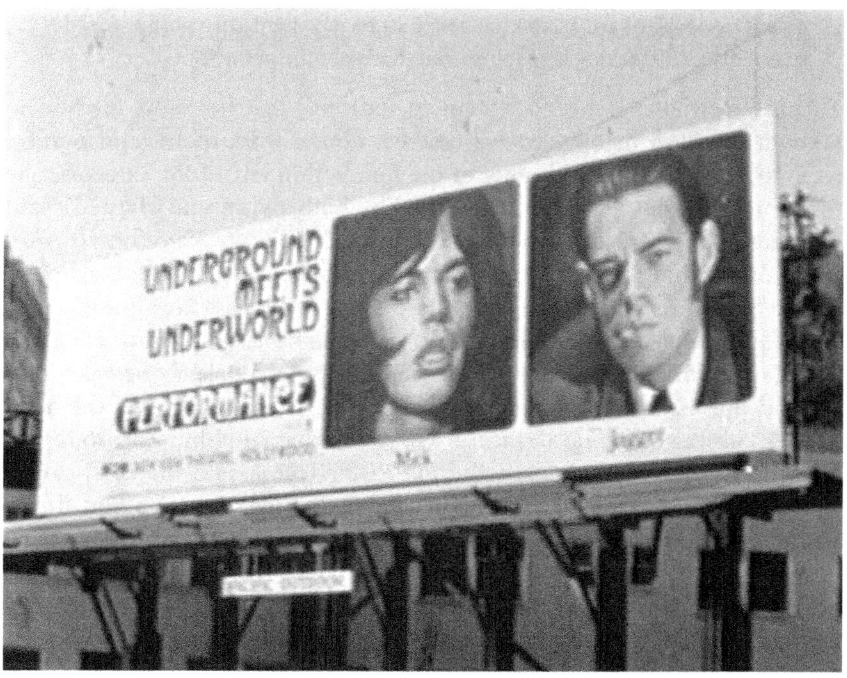


Fred Halsted, still from *L.A. Plays Itself*, 1972, DVD transfer (originally 16mm)    **8.1**

presented to audiences in New York, Los Angeles, San Francisco and Seattle by the film's publicist, Stuart Byron, who was also a film critic for the *Village Voice* and the *Real Paper*. *L.A. Plays Itself* and *Sex Garage* first opened in New York on 11 April 1972 at the 55th Street Playhouse—a venue known for screening experimental and pornographic films.[24] Following this screening, the films opened on 11 June 1972 at the Paris Theater in Los Angeles.[25] These openings were often presaged by a screening or two for an audience of critics and gay rights activists. The multi-page press package given out by Byron at press screenings contained no fewer than two dozen quotations from a pantheon of cultural figures such as Norman Mailer, Allen Ginsberg, Dennis Altman, Frank O'Hara, Leo Braudy, and Halsted himself. In these and other materials, Byron was making a concerted effort to present *L.A. Plays Itself* and *Sex Garage* in the context of poetry (Ginsberg, O'Hara), avant-garde fiction (Mailer), and Surrealist experimental film (Braudy on Jean Renoir). This publicity strategy aligns with Halsted's own aims for the film:

> On my first films [*L.A. Plays Itself* and *Sex Garage*] I screened them with big name critics. Up to that time porno was always considered something you made money off of, but something you were never proud of, something you did secretly. Well, I just barged into fucking New York and said this is a film, cinema, a work of art. It also happened to be gay, hard-core porno. A sado-masochistic, fistfucking faggot film, but that's not the point.[26]

Taken as a whole, Halsted's statement indicates that he wants his film to be understood in many ways (as cinema, film, a work of art, and porno), so as to avoid the pigeon-holing of the film within any of the categories he mentions. This positioning of the film (by both Byron and Halsted) paid off when Jonas Mekas reviewed the film for the *Village Voice* on 20 April 1972. After complaining about the smoke-filled 55th Street Playhouse, Mekas lauded *L.A. Plays Itself*, reviewed along with Rosa von Praunheim's *It is Not the Homosexual Who is Perverse but the Society in which He Lives*, as the first works in an emergent genre that struck a balance between film art and pornography. To make this argument Mekas compares the films to Jack Smith's *Flaming Creatures* (1963), Barbara Rubin's *Christmas on Earth* (1963), Kenneth Anger's *Scorpio Rising* (1963), and the even earlier Jean Genet film, *Un Chant d'Amour* (1950)—setting Halsted's film firmly within an already decade-old canon of experimental films, mostly made by homosexual filmmakers.[27] Mekas doesn't connect *L.A. Plays Itself* to other pornographic films—Wakefield Poole's *Boys in the Sand* had only recently been released and broke new ground as a gay pornographic film with relatively wide distribution—indicating, perhaps, that Mekas saw Halsted's film as rising to the level of film art, while Poole's did not. Even though Mekas makes clear his preference for Praunheim's film over Halsted's, he acquiesces that 'There is something about the first cries, first loves, first journeys abroad, first almost everything—and they are inimitable and they are total and very very real and they sum up once and for all everything that there is on the subject.'[28] Mekas gives Halsted's film credit as a first in this genre, and by this virtue, somewhat unassailable.

*L.A. Plays Itself*'s opening in Los Angeles couldn't have been more different. Instead of being compared to the films of Anger, Smith, Rubin, and Genet, some critics saw the film and filmmaker's claim to art as mere 'pretention.'[29] One reviewer roundly dismissed Halsted's efforts: 'Halsted seems to think that his film is both art and social commentary. Forget it; it isn't even good pornography.'[30] Stuart Byron attributed these criticisms of *L.A. Plays Itself* to the fact that the film was done in a 'butch' rather than 'femme' aesthetic.[31] Byron may have been right, and this criticism, which collapsed Halsted's persona with his film, suggests that a different kind of pornographic aesthetic was dominant on the West Coast. Fellow Angelino filmmaker Pat Rocco was a purveyor of such a 'femme' aesthetic, and his thoughts on Halsted and *L.A. Plays Itself* are instructive:

> A very unusual man, who has done many diverse things in filmmaking. I had a private screening of *L.A. Plays Itself* before it was released. It seemed a very disjointed film to me, and I was quite surprised at its success. I don't see what people like in this film, but then tastes differ. I liked the scene by the waterfall, but the rest seemed rather odd.[32]

Rocco posits his reaction as a difference in 'taste'—that he preferred the nature act over the leather act is unsurprising given the content of his own films. But more importantly, Rocco seems to confirm Byron's hypothesis that those in Los Angeles could not make sense of Halsted's film or even of the man himself at that early moment in his career.[33]

Joseph Bean, who lived in Los Angeles and eventually became the executive director of the Leather Archives & Museum, recounts the opening of *L.A. Plays Itself* and confirms its success based on a very specific criterion—sexual excitation: 'it seemed pretty unremarkable to me, frankly. I was doing Joey at a sex club regularly, watching Fred do scenes at the same club, and pretty much untouched by the content [of *L.A. Plays Itself*] in any but the intended way (that is, arousal).'[34] Already then, a dynamic was set up in the film's reception—most likely a symptom of larger cultural conversations happening long before Halsted's film was screened—that critics in Los Angeles lukewarmly accepted the film as pornography, while critics in New York accepted it as art. Halsted was more partial to the latter interpretation. In considering an opening city for his next feature, *Sextool*, Halsted remarked that he wanted to open in New York rather than Los Angeles because 'L.A.

is a fucking cowtown,' further commenting that he had 'never been a hit in L.A.'[35]

Following the initial cruising scene the film cuts to a shot of an exterior of a porn theater. A voice-over begins to read a prose passage, seemingly disconnected from the action of the film and difficult to understand. The images came quickly: a sidewalk filled with people, a hitchhiker, more porno advertisements. Then Halsted's voice comes in, 'What you reading?' A close-up of a blonde trick's face (Joey Yale) is followed by extreme close-ups of his blonde mop, mouth, and hairless chin. Voice and image are rarely synched, and so the soundtrack remains somewhat disconnected from the action. A voice with a thick Texas drawl answers that he's reading something he found on a Greyhound bus on his way from Houston, Texas. (It should be mentioned here that it is rumored that Joey Yale's part was played by three different actors: one for the voice, one for the body and sex scenes, and one for the eventual fisting scene.)[36] We see Yale at the bottom of a set of stairs, undoing his fly and taking off his shirt and pants (figure 8.2). The conversation continues audibly, but visually the film thrusts the viewer back onto the streets with a short montage of a Kentucky Fried Chicken billboard, graffiti reading 'Gay Power,' street traffic, industrial waste, a billboard for Skippy peanut butter, and more shots of street hustlers.

Halsted was a vocal proponent of gay rights, although not within the terms of the nascent gay rights movement. He wrote of 'the love of men for men' as 'the oldest continuing culture,' and that for him 'the issue [was] not gay pride or gay equality but rather the obvious fact of GAY SUPERIORITY!'[37] Meanwhile in the voice-over Halsted tells Yale's character to be careful of the guys on the street. 'They have dirty pants,' Halsted says—his tone fatherly, concerned. The blonde pick-up replies devilishly, 'Lots of people like dirty pants.' Agreeing, Halsted warns his charge that he's got to keep his wits about him, and that he has to watch out for such people.

The film cuts back to an interior where we see black boots climbing a set of stairs, and the music now supplies a discernible beat. Soon, Yale is crawling up the stairs naked while Halsted (the man wearing the black boots) whips him from above with his belt. While being whipped Yale begins to lick Halsted's boot. Newsclippings of articles about the Manson family murders are montaged in with the action, giving the proceedings a sinister air. One of the headlines reads 'New Weird Cult.'

By the time that *L.A. Plays Itself* and *Sex Garage* were first screened, the Tate and LaBianca murders were almost three years past. The presence of the clippings reveals something about the extended timeline in which *L.A. Plays Itself* was made. Conceived of in 1969, most of the footage was shot in that year and in 1970—with editing taking place over the next year and a half.[38] By the time Halsted screened the film in Los Angeles, where the Manson

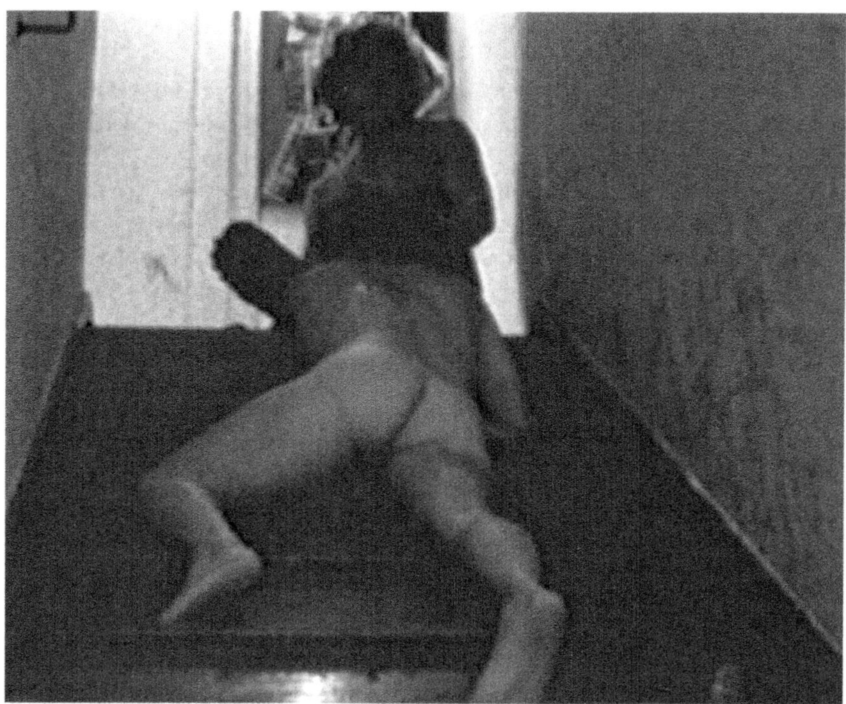

Fred Halsted, still from *L.A. Plays Itself*, 1972, DVD transfer (originally 16mm)          **8.2**

murders had taken place, he knew that these intercut headlines could be viewed skeptically:

> At the gay lib screenings last week, some S&M people also complained about the intercuts to newspaper headlines. I say simply that these are thoughts that might go through my head during the sexual act and nothing else. It's no more valid to see that scene as suggesting that violence in bed leads to violence outside of it than it is to see it suggesting the opposite—that Theodore Reik and others are correct in suggesting that those who are brave enough to relieve their aggression in bed are <u>less</u> likely to do something like murder Sharon Tate.[39]

This quote tells us a few important things about how Halsted understood his film: the first is that self-identified leatherfolks received the montaged sequences of leathersex and headlines concerning the Tate/LaBianca murders as a suspect visual stratagem—one that ultimately left the consensual nature of Halsted and Yale's filmed sex scenes (a negotiation between one and another) and murder (a non-consensual extermination of the other) confused. Perhaps more important is the implication that the montage is meant to represent Halsted's own subjectivity and thought process during sex. Thus the film, as conceived of by Halsted, is an outlet for both the artist's self and society's ills.

Once more the action shifts to the street, as the camera and we, by extension, cruise by newsstands and watch a bulldozer in the cityscape demolishing a building. The interruption is only momentary, as we are soon back inside where Halsted is now kicking his blonde trick with his boot. We see Yale from the back: a white handprint outlined in a wash of red is clearly visible on his backside, evidence of his having been recently and smartly slapped. Halsted kicks him into the bedroom where a dirty mattress pathetically rests directly on the floor. With the camera angled low to the ground, some rope, drugs and a bottle (of beer?) can also be spotted before the action moves again outside. Fast cuts reveal details of bugs pinned to a board, comic books, a leather jacket with a metal pin of an upraised fist, a black-and-white illustration of masculine eyes, and Halsted in the driver's seat.

Throughout this half of *L.A. Plays Itself*, short, montaged sequences are interspersed with the primary narrative; these iterate, in miniature, the larger themes of Halsted's film.[40] In this particular instance the disparate images—bugs, comics, a metal pin of an upraised fist, an illustration, and Halsted himself—condense and expand a sense of time and space (we're indoors then outdoors, between drawing and film, organic and synthetic life), while also foreshadowing events to come. The footage of bugs will be central to the nature act of *L.A. Plays Itself*, and so this moment represents the introduction of a leitmotif—one that Halsted strategically used to convince Yale to acquiesce to being in the film (more on this shortly). The comic book imagery works as a visual rhyme to the schlocky reading material described on the voice-over soundtrack—both could be found in Greyhound bus stations. Connected to the earlier graffiti of 'Gay Power,' the raised fist of the metal pin comes from a specific iconography tied to emergent gay liberation efforts. A brooding and dark illustration precedes the image of Halsted himself, and this Kuleshovian effect in editing directs the viewer to connect Halsted's visage with that of the mysterious drawing. Montages such as this (many more appear throughout the film) break a viewer out of a passive viewing experience and serve as an opportunity to reinforce the persistent themes and images of *L.A. Plays Itself*.

Dialog from earlier in the film is repeated as the film cuts from Halsted and Yale's bodies writhing in mid-level darkness to comic books, and back again. Halsted has a rope around the Texan's neck, feet, and arms. Yale is hog-tied. Halsted puts his boot on Yale's upraised ass. Yale's body lies atop newspapers strewn about the floor.

To be clear, the sex is not represented as an equal and loving exchange of power, and perhaps this is why the gay liberation and 'S&M people' were so perturbed by Halsted's film. Yale struggles and uncomfortably squirms throughout this act, making a viewer wonder if the exchange is consensual at all. But I would contend that these meanings are largely constructed by Halsted's editing, both visual and sonic. Indeed, the soundtrack, which changes abruptly from dialog to the atonal compositions of Tonto's Expanding Headband, goes a long way in destabilizing the images, as beats are hard and arrhythmic, interspersed with motorcycle muffler sounds replayed at alternate speeds. The effect is one of speed, uncertainty, and imbalance.

Halsted once more cuts to the outside world. In an urban landscape Halsted is driving in his red El Camino, with a motorcyclist in tow. We then view more cruising shots in Griffith Park intercut with a sequence of images of a dog, tongue out and slobbering. Dumb animal desire is equated with the men milling outside of park restrooms. The voice-over between the blonde pick-up and Halsted continues with the young Texan complaining that he only has two dollars. Halsted replies with 'you got some attributes,' at which point he offers to show the young man 'the ropes.' Of course, we have already seen Halsted showing this young man a bit of rope. Back in the two-story flat, the Texan writhes onscreen; Halsted whips and beats him. Halsted ties his young charge to the bed and he is made to perform oral sex on Halsted. Images of rusty nails and spurs are intercut with this blowjob—again evincing danger and mythic figurations of masculinity.

Halsted then cuts to an extreme close-up of his own face; he breaks the fourth wall and stares directly into the camera with a 'pornographically penetrating' gaze.[41] The intensity of this direct address is unmatched. It insinuates that Halsted is not content with vigorously topping Yale unless he is topping his viewer as well.

In a harsh, bright light—daylight is finally coming into the apartment—Halsted lubes up his hands and body with oil and begins to masturbate. Images of comic books and Kentucky Fried Chicken repeat (of course, one of the terms used to describe Yale's type—the young gay man—was 'chicken'). Multiple times the camera quickly zooms in and out on a sign reading 'Lips.' The sign, which is also in the shape of lips, is the concrete poetry of sexual consumption, imitating oral sex through Halsted's repeated zooming. While the music builds, the camera cuts with ever-increasing speed, approximating the physicalized gesture of masturbation and climax, between the image of Halsted masturbating and the following: a patch of a fist, pins, needles and clothespins, wax dripping on wood and hardening, cruising in a park, a dog slobbering, a drum circle, a biker. Halsted cuts back to his ejaculation, before finally returning to Yale, still tied up on the bed.

Here *L.A. Plays Itself* archly conforms to what Richard Dyer calls 'the basis of gay porn film,' which 'is a narrative sexuality, a construction of male sexuality as the desire to achieve the goal of a visual climax.'[42] Fisting is situated as the moment of visual climax. This underscores a point Halsted makes later in his interview with Siebenand:

> I am interested in the subtle aspects of sex. The mind-fucking aspects of sex. I like to make sex films because it gives me an opportunity to state my views, a minority viewpoint, a personal viewpoint. That is the only reason I make these films. I don't do it for money. Nobody else makes gay films the way I do. I have certain ideas about sexuality. I don't particularly view sex as fun. To me sex is not fun. To me sex is not enjoyable. To me sex is an emotional release. I am just speaking for me. Some people like it, some don't. Mine is personal cinema. I don't fuck to get my rocks off. In the best scenes I have ever had, I haven't come. I am not interested in coming. I got out of that years ago. I am interested in getting my head off, my emotions off—and if I get my dick off, my rocks off, it really doesn't matter that much to me, that is very down on the scale. I am interested in emotional satisfaction and intellectual satisfaction—mine.[43]

Halsted begins to rub his own semen on his fist and forearm. He moves to the bed and begins to play with the blonde pick-up's ass, before he puts first his fingers and then his fist into its crevice. His hog-tied trick struggles against the invading fist, and we soon see Halsted's arm elbow-deep in Yale's ass as the music grows louder and harder. The fisting sequence lasts about a minute. Shot in extreme close-up, close up, this virtuosic fucking is strangely abstracted, the body shown in fragments, never whole. Shot in this way it is certainly conceivable that the ass is not Yale's, and at points it is difficult to tell what is forearm, ass or thigh (figure 8.3).

In its first public exhibition the final fisting scene 'elicit[ed] audience gasps because of its anatomical difficulty.'[44] While there are shots in which Halsted's fist is undeniably inside of the blonde pick-up's ass, others are not quite so clear. Regardless, there is no footage of the hand in the process of being inserted into the ass. The hand is outside, and then it is inside. This is an elision of real time and reel time, as anyone familiar with fisting knows that it takes a significant amount of time to accomplish, as the sphincter must be relaxed to accommodate a fist. The action of fisting rhymes with this segment's closing shot: a sign of a hand holding a football helmet aloft.

The second act begins with a different sign, this one reading 'Population 2.5 million.' The score is now plunky Japanese music, providing a denouement from the previous act. There are long establishing shots of the mist and mountains of the Malibu hills—Halsted identified the location as 'two canyons north of Malibu' that were slated for rezoning.[45] Minutes pass by as the camera focuses on the total vista of the landscape, and small passages within it. Bugs and flowers are constantly in Halsted's framing of the coastal mountains, and soon a hiker wanders through the landscape (figure 8.4).

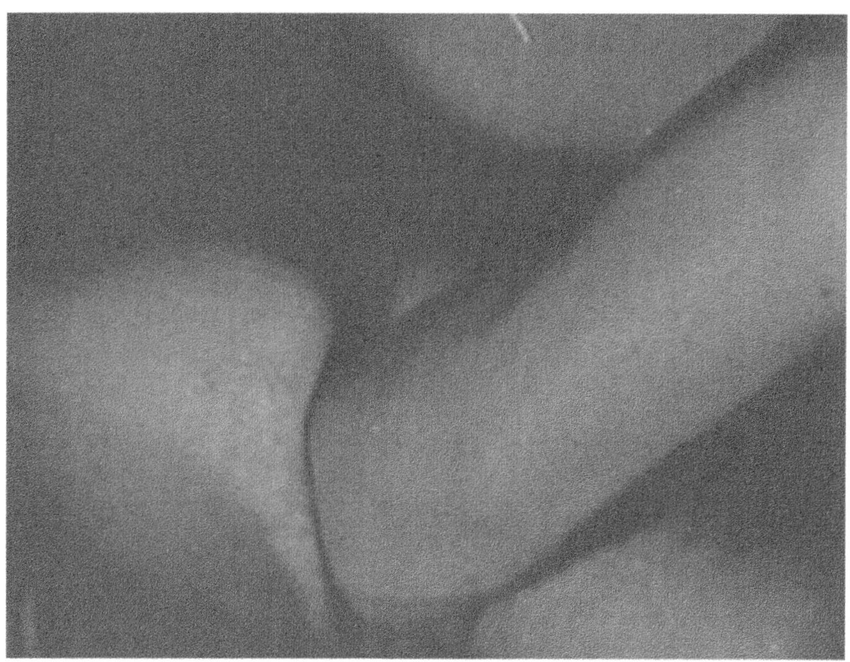

Fred Halsted, still from *L.A. Plays Itself*, 1972, DVD transfer (originally 16mm)    **8.3**

Halsted often claimed that *L.A. Plays Itself* was about bugs.[46] This was the ruse under which Halsted apparently seduced Yale into participating in the film's making, as he elaborated in a 1981 interview with *Skin* entitled, appropriately, 'Halsted and Yale: Who's on Top?':

> **JOEY:** Our films always take longer than anybody else in the industry to produce. But when Fred first told me about this film, he told me it was a film about nature, wildlife, and bugs. He did not tell me it was a sex film, when he first approached me with the idea of being in it—
> **FRED:** —he was so in love with me at that point I could do anything with him—
> **JOEY:** —so he basically told me a bunch o' lies—
> **FRED:** —there *are* bugs in it!
> **JOEY:** I know, there *are* bugs, and it's all full of nature in the film.[47]

Although they were dead, pinned and labeled, it is worth remembering that bugs also appeared in the first act of the film. It must have been remarkable to Yale, then, that at no point in time was he filmed outside in nature. One has to wonder what kind of experience Yale had while filming, as it was certainly counter to what he was told.

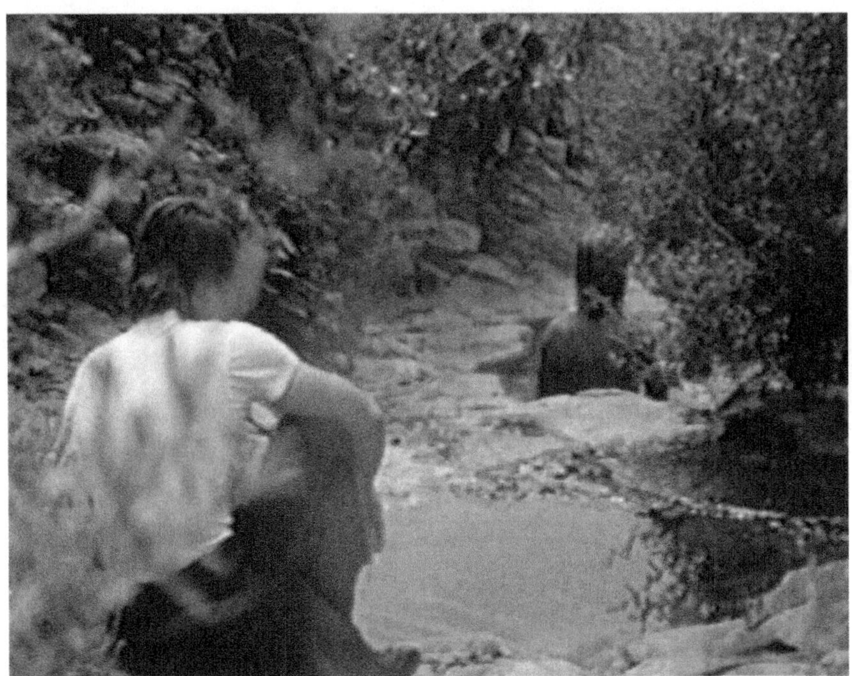

**8.4**    Fred Halsted, still from *L.A. Plays Itself*, 1972, DVD transfer (originally 16mm)

A voice-over explains that the 'city is where it's happenin.' We know this already, having just come from there. But this same voice also bemoans that it has 'filled up with so many New Yorkers [...] taking over everything.' Another voice asks, in an unrelated string of dialog, 'What's wrong with sniffing flowers?' The answer from Halsted: 'At least I ball humans!'

Of these voices, Halsted's California twang is distinctive, but his interlocutor doesn't have the distinctiveness of the Texan drawl that appeared in the first act. Although Halsted does not appear in this act of the film, his voice ties the two acts together. When he exclaims that he 'ball[s] humans,' he is only confirming what we already know because we have in fact witnessed it. He doesn't just ball humans, he also handballs—or fists—them.

Meanwhile, on screen a male hiker happens upon a naked blonde man playing by a small body of water. At this point the score shifts from Japanese shamisen music to Beethoven's *Pastoral Symphony* as the two men begin to talk. The blonde quickly offers the hiker a blowjob. The hiker unbuckles his belt and the blonde, described in Stuart Byron's press release as 'Elf in Stream,' begins to suck his dick.[48] Their interaction is slow and sweet. The two men touch each other's bodies and hold each other's hands as they exchange blowjobs. As they do the music shifts back again to the Japanese score.

After the leathersex in the film's first act, the action here seems genuine to the point of being disingenuous, saccharine, or naïve. This seemed to be a conscious strategy on the part of Halsted, who thought the second act had a palliative function: 'I knew a large part of the audience would walk out [during the fisting scene] so I immediately cut to the flowers to calm them down. Everyone told me to rearrange the scene. They said show the flowers first, the S&M second. That's the traditional way!'[49]

Although Halsted began making this film in 1969, the second act would have visually echoed Wakefield Poole's *Boys in the Sand* for contemporary viewers, in its use of idyllic natural settings and sex, recalling most especially that film's first scene starring Casey Donovan and Peter Fisk. Setting sex in nature was not exclusive to Poole; it was a well-worn convention in short film loops that were distributed via mail-order catalog to viewers' homes during the 1960s. Halsted's film played in the same venues in which Poole's films were screened the year before. After the blowjob the two men romp and splash around in the water. This is the scene by the waterfall that Rocco singles out as being worthy of his attention.

Halsted said that time in his film was meant to be ambiguous, taking place in 'a day, a month, a year.'[50] This is evidenced by the dialog in *L.A. Plays Itself*, which helps to denaturalize time as a linear progression. The action of the hiker and the elf happens in an ambiguous and elastic timeframe. Sexual play is interspersed with non-sexual play, and climax (here: ejaculation) is put off until after the characters have had a swim. Even after ejaculation they continue to fuck, perhaps suggesting repeated encounters over a longer period of time. Footage of frogs coupling is playfully intercut into the sequence of light-hearted fun.

Halsted follows this with a sequence of close-ups of bodily contact. As the camera shows wider shots the activity becomes clear—the hiker is fucking the elf. They fuck in many positions, each carefully and aesthetically considered, and the action is always slow and sensual—never fast or rough. Shots of butterflies and nature are intercut as the orchestral music swells. The camera lands on the hiker's tattoo, which reads 'U.S.N. Never Again!,' identifying him as a member of the Navy. The two men switch positions as images of nature are overlaid in the manner of a double-exposed photograph. Nature becomes a patterned veil—obscuring and, in consequence, making the unobstructed image all-the-more precious (figure 8.5). The hiker then ejaculates in extreme close-up.

These overlain filmic images perhaps inspired the paintings that Halsted created after he completed *L.A. Plays Itself*. A gardener, pornographic film director, business owner, writer, and actor, Halsted was also an artist. Although representative of only a small part of his creative output, Halsted had at least one gallery show in 1977, at the Paideia Gallery on La Cienega in

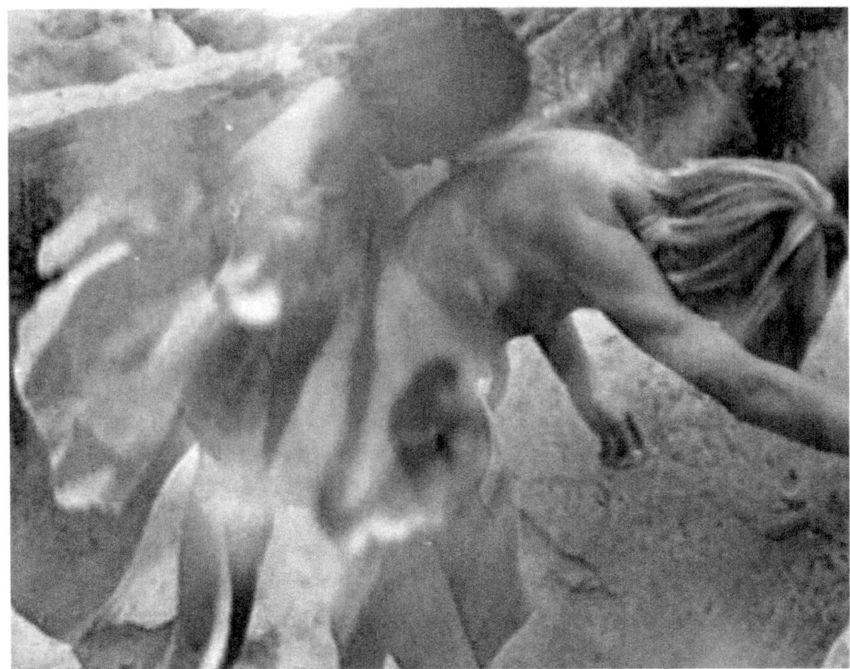

**8.5**    Fred Halsted, still from *L.A. Plays Itself*, 1972, DVD transfer (originally 16mm)

Los Angeles.[51] The show was reviewed in the *Los Angeles Times*, and it seems that the critic lets the knowledge of Halsted's status as pornographic film director inform his analysis, stating, 'The artist forces the spectator to slowly enter into the secret places his uneven paintings provide.'[52] The paintings themselves consisted of amorphous shapes of muddy colors laid atop one another. Their abstract patterning might be seen as a material extension of the overlain images in *L.A. Plays Itself*. The painted abstractions appear by turns cave-like and colonic.

Quickly the score shifts to a deep rumbling, and images of lizards, spiders, and bulldozers are interspersed with the fucking onscreen. Sequences of bulldozing, detailing large mechanical plows with hard-hatted riders, are overlain onto the sexual action. Some of these overlain shots appear upside-down, further denaturing the two characters' fucking within their environs. The sexual activity toggles between oral sex and anal penetration. Bulldozing accompanies shots and counter-shots of sexual activity and dirt. This sequence of overlays lasts a few minutes and builds to a kind of release. During this sequence Halsted's shots become more and more densely layered and less decipherable. Finally, the camera slowly zooms out from an American flag standing on the highest mesa of a strip mine teeming with bulldozers; construction workers and cars are queued up to drive out of the frame.

It is telling that Halsted ends his film here, as he was melancholy about the implications of urban encroachment and development:

> Even in the Forties, when I was a kid, Southern California, to me, was still a paradise, a paradise that's now been largely lost. Cesar Chavez is one of my heroes, but I would argue that even for a migrant worker—even for the Okies and Chicanos and blacks—L.A. was a better place then than now. The air was pure, you were five minutes from unspoiled mountains and beachfronts. Every cent of profit from this film is going to the Theodore Payne Foundation, which hopes to buy up Decker Canyon, where the second half of the film was largely shot. If not, it's going to be sold to some subdivider who'll put up another shopping center.[53]

Evident here is not only Halsted's disdain for commercial interests replacing an 'unspoiled' and 'pure' paradise, but also his relative cognizance of social justice movements, as he references Cesar Chavez and vows to support the preservation of nature through a gesture of philanthropy.[54] Yet Halsted shows a penchant for nostalgic memory and naïve utopianism, especially in regards to his assertion that things were better for Chicana/os and black people during his childhood. It is not factually true that the 1940s were a better time for Chicana/os and black people in Los Angeles—especially considering the Zoot Suit riots and racial tensions that accompanied the redevelopment of Compton as a black subdivision in the city.[55] His politics, rendered here as anti-consumerist and anti-development, are nonetheless important, and somewhat at odds with his own self-positioning as an entrepreneurial harnesser of capital. Left with the image of the flag waving over the strip mine, Halsted communicates a cynical take on the contemporary American landscape as *the* final statement of *L.A. Plays Itself.*

* * *

When the screening order of the two acts of *L.A. Plays Itself* is reversed from how I have described it above (as in the ordering of prints of the film that belong to UCLA and MoMA) the film takes on different meanings. For example, as reordered, the opening shot of the film is the green Los Angeles city limits sign. The sign confirms that the city is indeed an important character (as is also confirmed in both the title credits, and the end credits in which Los Angeles is acknowledged as playing 'itself'). The city limits sign places a viewer in relation to a *specific* urban context.[56] The slow and ponderous nature scenes would then complicate a rendering of Los Angeles as a sprawling West Coast metropolis. In this reading, the 'natural' sex that takes place outside is not rural sex, but sub-urban or para-urban sex, a form of public sex that could also be taking place in the infamous cruising grounds of Griffith Park, the easternmost outpost of the Santa Monica mountains.

The shot of the American flag and the strip mine at the end of the nature act would then serve to connect the acts together. Instead of ending with the indictment that urban encroachment is a ruination of the natural utopia of Decker Canyon, this ordering of the film indicates that such encroachments partly *facilitate* the expansion of cruising grounds and new forms of fucking: parks, docks, auto-body shops, as well as fisting. In this light, the actions of the bulldozers are a visual prelude to the plowing that Yale receives.

There is also a formal connection of cars going from right to left and out of frame, echoed in the establishing shot of the second act as Fred Halsted gets into his El Camino and drives away. Unlike the first ordering of the film in which driving away signaled the beginning, here driving away is much more tightly related to liminal separation between work and play: just like the strip-miners, Halsted might be interpreted as having just gotten off of work, and as beginning to enjoy his leisure time with a bit of cruising.

The leather act finishes with an image of a sign on which an arm holds a football helmet aloft, rhyming with the previous shots of deep and vigorous fisting. In the second ordering of *L.A. Plays Itself* this is last thing an audience would see, an everyday/commercial image which has been imbued with new sexual charge through Halsted's fast-paced and wildly signifying editing. The film ends by teaching audiences to read sexual meaning into everyday (ostensibly) non-sexual signs—to recognize that fucking is everywhere at all times. Halsted perverts Americana itself, football being a distinctly American sport in origin. Instead of filing out of the theater like cars, an audience leaves prepped to read the profusion of visible signs already populating their everyday worlds.

Returning to the descriptions at the beginning of this chapter, the orderings of *L.A. Plays Itself* inform the parameters within which the authors cited were able to describe the film's content or meaning. For example, the 'evolution from nature to industry and sexual revolution' would only be possible if the nature act precedes the leather act; while ostensibly the apprehension of the film as a piece of underground cinema might hinge on its initial ordering.[57] *L.A. Plays Itself*'s editing history accentuates the notion of switching as a dynamic strategy of signification. This can be extended to include the ways in which Halsted and Yale represented their relationship in the popular press, and in Halsted's short-lived *Package* magazine. Instead of positing *L.A. Plays Itself* as mere documentation of Halsted and Yale's relationship, I pick up on this notion of switching as one around which the meanings of leathersex hinge at the moment of *L.A. Plays Itself*'s subsequent screening at the Museum of Modern Art.

* * *

Recommended for 'Adults Only,' the Cineprobe screening of *L.A. Plays Itself,* *Sex Garage* and clips of *Sextool* took place at the Museum of Modern Art in New York City on Tuesday, 23 April 1974. The screening was sponsored by MoMA's film department, under the supervision of curator Adrienne Mancia. Initially the Cineprobe series intended to 'provide exposure for the independent filmmaker, a category including both radically experimental filmmakers and directors of more conventional films which do not receive commercial distribution.'[58] Already in its seventh season of programming in 1974, the Cineprobe series that year included St. Clair Bourne's documentary on black churches entitled *Let the Church Say Amen!*, Leo Hurwitz and Paul Strand's *Native Land*, Jan Lenica's feature-length animation *Adam II*, Ralph Bakshi's *Coonskin*, and work by Barry Gerson. That same year MoMA hosted programs celebrating D. W. Griffith's centennial and the poet and filmmaker James Broughton. It also began a two-year series of screenings on the 'History of Film to 1970.'

MoMA's programmatic desire to historicize the medium of film fit hand-in-glove with the exhibition programming of the 1970s, which sought to revisit and canonize the insitution's early exhibition history. This happened both under the museum's aegis and outside of it—an example of the latter being *Good Old Modern*, written by Russell Lynes in 1973, which offered an 'intimate portrait' of the museum and remains an important and early attempt to narrate MoMA's institutional and exhibition histories.[59] A cursory glance at the exhibition program of MoMA in the 1970s reveals an institution that sought to project an 'aura' around its collections to all visitors, a strategy that inspired Carol Duncan and Allan Wallach to critique the museum's layout and ordering as a 'late Capitalist ritual' in 1978.[60] They describe MoMA as a cathedral and a labyrinth that 'organizes ritual activity'—one ultimately akin to a 'walk through a hall of mirrors in which isolation, fear, and numbness appear as exciting and desirable states of being. Thus MoMA would reconcile you to the world, as it is, outside.'[61] Their critical assessment rhymes with Brian O'Doherty's series of essays for *Artforum*, eventually published in book form as *Inside the White Cube* (1976), which places the 'neutral' white space of the gallery in a historical, social, and political context, recognizing the deep biases of 'modernism' and the white cube as a space for display and encounter.[62] Molly Nesbit writes of the 'pernicious seduction' of overviews of modern art, like the one proffered by Alfred Barr in his famous 1936 diagram of modern art movements and influences—an important model for organizing the museum's permanent collection, one that rested on a 'definition that closed more than it opened, that confused art with models and often seemed to censor discussion.'[63]

This process of self-canonization took place alongside moments of deep institutional soul-searching, catalyzed by the Art Workers Coalition's Art Strike in 1970. Art historian Julia Bryan-Wilson cites this, and other examples, as evidence that MoMA fashioned its own image as 'actively, progressively *supporting* artistic and political avant-gardes, not just putting up with them.'[64] Halsted's screening might be another illustration of this effort.

In a *Variety* article published the day after Halsted's Cineprobe screening, MoMA's assistant curator of film, Larry Kardish, reiterated that although an earlier screening of *Sex Garage* was cited for obscenity the museum believed in Halsted's talent and wanted to give him more exposure.[65] In recognition of this institutional support Halsted regifted his $100 honorarium and the 16mm prints of his films to MoMA.[66] This gesture of generosity was both in earnest and a clever way to ensure that his films entered into the permanent collection of the museum, a fact that Halsted leveraged in his publicity campaigns for subsequent films.

*Screw* magazine, a heterosexual pornographic weekly aimed at men, which had two years previously reviewed both *L.A. Plays Itself* and *Sex Garage* as 'classics of the '70s and the homosexuals' *Gone With the Wind*,' remarked giddily upon the Cineprobe screening, writing, 'the Museum of Modern Art will be validating [our] prophesy.'[67] That prophecy was that gay pornographic film would attain a level of recognition that was unknown to its practitioners at the time. More daily and weekly newspapers remarked upon Halsted's MoMA screening than in 1972 when the films were first screened, and nearly every obituary and article regarding Halsted and/or Yale post-1974 mentioned MoMA's ownership of *L.A. Plays Itself* and *Sex Garage*. Such claims to credibility gave Halsted the ability to procure larger arthouse/pornographic cinemas for screening his next feature *Sextool* in his quest to appeal to a diverse (read: not exclusively gay) audience.[68]

In short, the MoMA screening was a big moment for Halsted, and he knew it.[69] And this is most likely when Halsted reordered *L.A. Plays Itself*. Although no direct documentation exists (director's notes or even written anecdotes) as to why Halsted made this strategic move, it suggests that Halsted was trying to make a narrative that would be most palatable for MoMA's audience and film curators. Unlike the 'gay libbers' who anxiously worried about the optics of hardcore representations of leathersex, Mancia clearly believed that Halsted's films offered an example of experimental and underground aesthetics from within the genre of pornography. By switching the two acts and ordering the film so that the nature act would be followed by cruising and fist-fucking in the big city, *L.A. Plays Itself* wittingly reflected larger narratives regarding industrialization, Modernism, post-industrial urbanism, and capital that were so central to MoMA's developmental and teleological curatorial narratives. In effect, MoMA's acquisition of Halsted's films allowed the institution to confirm its status as the primary narrator of the story of modern art and as a supporter of outlaw experimental practices.

Earlier pornographic filmmakers in Los Angeles, such as Pat Rocco, did not enjoy the same level of critical success on the East Coast, even when their work contained similar elements to Halsted's. A compilation of Rocco's shorts, *Man Happenings* (1968), which were first screened at the Park Theater under the marquee title 'A Pat Rocco Happening,' featured films that highlighted male nudity in the context of natural surrounds, as well as in 'the city of the future,' Los Angeles.[70] Incorrectly riffing off the performance-based format of happenings, which Allan Kaprow defined as 'events that, put simply, happen,' Rocco eschewed the happening's abstract and non-linear aspects in favor of narrative representation.[71] In *Boy on the Run*, an inmate escapes from a precinct jail, running all the way to the seclusion of Griffith Park. There he strips down, and suddenly starts to pogo. The zaniness of this scene, what cultural theorist Sianne Ngai recognizes as 'incessant doing,' operates in contradistinction to the short's pornographic set-up.[72] As the actor's penis bounces up and down, alternately slapping his stomach and upper thighs, one is reminded of the ways in which Rocco's films both welcome and push against eroticizing their subjects. Thomas Waugh, in his signal text 'Men's Pornography: Gay vs. Straight,' calls this type of pornographic film, appropriately, a 'danglie'—historically bookended at one end by the easement of censorship laws and, at the other, the introduction of hardcore.[73] As if in response to the excesses of this pure joy of jumping naked in the park (perhaps a stand-in for the other kinds of activities men enjoyed while naked in the park), the short film ends when the actor puts his clothes back on and returns, willingly, to the precinct jail. Another film from this anthology, *Discovery*—originally titled *A Disneyland Discovery*—narrates the meeting of two men in the Disneyland theme park, countering what Jane Kuentz identifies as 'a compulsive heterosexuality in the service of reproduction [that] is [Disney's] chief fetish.'[74] Rocco's film explores the park's many attractions solely through the eyes of its two male protagonists. Disney is both the site of the innocent fun of 'going on many rides' together, and of homoerotic dalliance, as the two men abscond to Tom Sawyer's Island (at least this is what Rocco claims; the landscape looks much more like Griffith Park) where they make out, and run, hand-in-hand, in the nude (figure 8.6).[75] For efforts such as this Rocco was dubbed 'a romanticist, not a pornographer.'[76] Indeed, this is something that Rocco himself asserted many times, preferring the label of 'soft-core' to 'hardcore' and 'pornographic.'[77] One writer breathlessly described the actors featured in Rocco's films as 'shiny-eyed wet-lipped small-assed teen-aged, passionate tender silky haired muscled smooth skinned small-hipped, long-tooled kids,' and conveys the basic plot of a Rocco flick as 'they meet, they look, they lust,

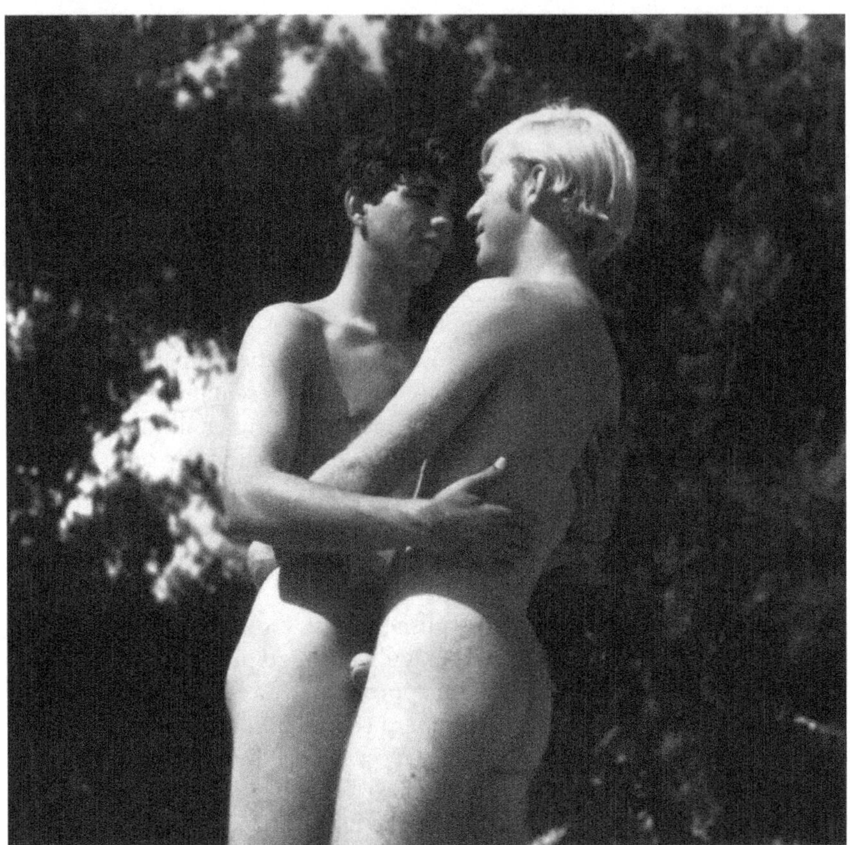

**8.6**    Pat Rocco, still from *(Disneyland) Discovery*, 1968

they tender, they kiss, they strip, they eye each other's equipment…'[78] Even when he did include harder figurations of sex, often using the leatherman as a type, as in 1968's *The Sailor and the Leather Stud* or *Viva Leather*, Rocco undercuts them with music choices that point to leather aesthetics as merely a camp charade.[79]

Rocco's aesthetic is important to note because Halsted's film represented a clear break from it. Rocco himself delineated a sea change in the making and exhibition of pornographic films, relaying that 'when gay films turned from "soft" to "hard" in about 1971, I chose not to go along with the trend, and turned to making documentaries of events in the gay community.'[80] Although Rocco's date matches the release of Wakefield Poole's *Boys in the Sand*, Halsted's *L.A. Plays Itself* was another nail in the coffin. Curious, then, but not incomprehensible is the fact that Rocco's disavowal rests alongside his ownership of Halsted's film. Understood in the context of Rocco's papers and films, *L.A. Plays Itself* signals another kind of cut—not reflective of a broader history of ideas concerning modernity's relationship to urbanity, but of an internal divide limned in the history of gay pornographic film.

Rocco donated his collection of films, which included his own films and compilations, full-length Disney films and trailers, and other pornographic titles including the print of *L.A. Plays Itself,* to the UCLA Film and Television Archive in the early 1980s.[81] The timing of UCLA's acquisition is contemporaneous with a growing awareness of the then recently named Acquired Immune Deficiency Syndrome. By 1983 AIDS was the cause of over 3,000 deaths, many of them gay men. This fact radically recasts Derrida's oft-quoted pronouncement regarding archives, that 'if there is no archive without consignation in an *external place* which assures the possibility of memorization, of repetition, of reproduction, or of reimpression, then we must also remember that repetition itself, the logic of repetition, indeed the repetition compulsion, remains, according to Freud, indissociable from the death drive.'[82]

In Rocco's papers, housed at ONE archives, are clippings of articles detailing the goings-on at the UCLA Film and Television Archive (then known only as the UCLA Film Archives), proving that Rocco had been aware of the archive's collecting efforts since 1977.[83] Joining similarly minded institutions such as the Museum of Modern Art, the George Eastman House, and the Library of Congress, UCLA's archive was at that time one of the few places in the United States where films were collected, catalogued, and preserved, often by the transfer of nitrate film onto non-flammable safety film. Although largely reliant on donations from the big film studios, UCLA's archive also accepted relatively smaller-scale donations such as Rocco's. His donation must have appealed on many fronts: his collections of clips and trailers provide adequate snapshots of studio production and publicity efforts, and his own films evidence of a particular cultural milieu that would have been understood as being under existential threat—especially his newsreel-like documentaries on gay liberation activities, protests, and parades. As per the language of the archive, its heterogeneous collection demonstrated that a film (like a television or radio program) was at once 'an art object, ideological force, social document, product of mass culture, commodity of the market place, and a source of entertainment.'[84]

It is the UCLA print of *L.A. Plays Itself* that confirms the changeable ordering of Halsted's 'sadomasochistic, fistfucking faggot' film. Shortly after the end of the nature act (which is placed first in the film's sequence) is a credit title card, the kind found most often at the end of a film. It is a vestigial remnant of Halsted's initial ordering, one that did not find its way into MoMA's print.

* * *

In 2011 A. K. Burns and A. L. Steiner's *Community Action Center* (2010) became the second expressly pornographic object acquisitioned into the Museum of Modern Art's film collection. The 69-minute video is handily described by the artists as a 'sociosexual' work inspired by both '1960's and 1970's feminist video art and [the] porn-romance-liberation films' of Fred Halsted, Jack Smith, and Wakefield Poole, among others.[85] In its conception and early exhibition history, *Community Action Center* (*CAC*) sought to represent these disparate, yet related, historical moving image traditions from a contemporary lesbian feminist perspective, all while considering the limitations of 'community' as a practice, one ultimately inclusive of the sociality of fucking. *CAC* is a rumination, in the words of its makers, on the 'cultural realness of a homo-grown lesbian sexuality.'[86] In exhibiting this video, Burns and Steiner ask if a pornographic viewing public in the present can constitute a community, and if so, what is one's responsibility to such figurations?[87]

One of the grounds on which Burns and Steiner claim their particular politics is through the regulation of the video's distribution and exhibition. Prescribing that the video cannot be viewed unless it is by an audience of three or more people, Burns and Steiner take their video out of the viewing economy of the couple or single viewer. The artists harken back to a previous model of viewership, one tied to the viewing conditions of porn theaters, placed in contra to the conditions occasioned by the rise of home-viewing technologies (such as VHS) in the 1970s and 1980s, which arguably did much to privatize pornographic viewership.[88] In an era when pornographic theaters are few and far between, and the opportunities for communally viewing porn are likewise severely limited, viewership has moved to large online video-hosting services such as *XTube* and *Pornhub*, accessed via the small screens of laptops and smartphones. While much of *CAC*'s significance is located in what art historian Kelly Dennis has identified as 'the power of the image to move our own flesh,' such movement must also fundamentally be understood in this context to be group work.[89] The viewer of *CAC* necessarily engages in the difficult work of community while sustaining Thomas Waugh's simple, yet surprisingly difficult, exhortation to support 'the full rights of sexual outlaws to act out their individual (consensual) desires.'[90]

Just as Halsted called his film 'a sadomasochistic, fistfucking faggot film,' A. L. Steiner has called *CAC* 'a small archive of an intergenerational community built on collaboration, friendship, sex, and art.'[91] But this description belies the difficulty of describing the 'flaming sense and sensibility' of this immodest archive.[92] Writing about *CAC* thus means at once acknowledging language's failure to capture the vast multiplicities embedded in the profusion of bodies and their un/scripted sexual performances, and investing in such failures as only one way in which creative practices such as film or art-making might aid in 'corrupting hegemonic discourses.'[93]

To take up the affect of distanced criticality is therefore to miss the heart of the video's ethic.[94] Maggie Nelson writes of watching a screening of *CAC* in Los Angeles, where many of the performers who appeared in the video were based at the time, and finding affinities with 'watching people hit each other during sex without it seeming violent, the scene of someone jerking off with a chunk of purple quartz down by the water, and the slow sewing of feathers onto a girl's butt.'[95] She notes that other viewers found the whole video distasteful, or were 'seriously grossed out by the sex.'[96] This, too, limns Burns and Steiner's tricky claim to community—for such a person to be brought fully and truly into the fold of the video's polymorphously perverse world-making efforts requires an expanded definition of community that recognizes difference, dissensus, and antagonism as key components or possibilities.

One approach would be to examine the extra-textual sources gathered by Burns and Steiner into a 'Cliffs Notes' zine published alongside the video.[97] Using the zine as an interpretive tool—an object whose 'power to bring about change is located in, rather than despite, its unpredictability'—the artists are able to bring into virtual dialog a broad array of sometimes antagonistic source-material.[98] Far from merely providing 'a reference point' for the video, the zine enacts a similar kind of gathering as the video does with the bodies of its participants.[99] Moving promiscuously between genre and gender, both the video and zine enact a queer politics out of the history of feminist and gay/lesbian theory and aesthetics.[100] Viewing 'the entire body as a sex organ,' *CAC*, its related archival printed matter, and its early exhibitionary contexts together perform a critical pedagogy connecting community and queer fucking.[101] Before getting into the intricacies of video, zine, and exhibition history, though, I want to pause to consider a few theoretical notions of community that might be helpful in understanding the sociality at play in *CAC*.

* * *

The complexity of community thus relates to the difficult interaction between the tendencies originally distinguished in the historical development: on the one hand the sense of direct common concern; on the other hand the materialization of various forms of common organization, which may or may not adequately express this. Community can be the warmly persuasive word to describe an existing set of relationships, or the warmly persuasive word to describe an alternative set of relationships. What is most important, perhaps, is that unlike all other terms of social organization (*state, nation, society,* etc.) it seems never to be used unfavourably, and never to be given any positive opposing or distinguishing term.[102]

As usual, Raymond Williams displays an extraordinary gift for at once revealing the etymology of a term while also exposing its particular vulnerabilities. In the case of community he points out the fact that the term has never been 'used unfavorably,' implying a positive affective bias inherent in the term's usage. Williams is aware of this romanticizing, as he iterates not once, but twice, that the term is 'warmly persuasive.' Queer theorist Miranda Joseph extends the line of this thought across her book *Against the Romance of Community*, which details how discursive understandings of community are 'imbricated in capitalism' even as they attempt to offer 'hope in a difficult world.'[103] This is true of both 'existing sets of relationships' (normative), *and* an 'alternative set of relationships' (non-normative) that Williams describes. Regardless of what purposes the group that composes a community is organized around—identity is a common, sticky wicket—the application of the terminology of community has an ultimately similar effect. The fact that community is often positioned as immune to critical examination is good enough reason to bear down upon it. Popular conceptions of community have been the grounds upon which categorical containments of what is or is not obscene have historically been determined, as evidenced by the amorphous renderings of community in U.S. Supreme Court case law regarding the censorship of sexually graphic materials.[104] Under these juridical circumstances community comes to variously metonymically stand in for nation, non-profit group, couple, and, in some circumstances, even individual, each of whom possesses a sense of morality drawing a circle around what is acceptable.[105]

But how to locate what *binds* a community? Williams names these forces as 'common concern' and 'common organization.' While it may at first appear easy to pinpoint what constitutes a 'common concern' or 'common organization,' in reality the common is a set of complex modes of identification that are anything but. An example would be a remark made by philosopher Jean Luc-Nancy in an essay he wrote concerning the Bosnian War: 'What I have in common with another Frenchman is the fact of *not being the same Frenchman as him*, and the fact that our "Frenchness" is never, nowhere, in no essence, in no figure, brought to completion.'[106] In other words it is the *difference* between two like-named or constituted people which actually holds them in common. That 'Frenchness,' which is another way of ascribing a national commonality or identity, is 'never, nowhere [...] brought to completion' speaks to the ongoing process of making, reiterating, and redefining communities as the spacing between similarities and not only their adjoinings.

When applied to sex the two definitions of community offered above take on particular relevance—as the limits of theoretical suppositions of community are reconciled with bodily practices. Fucking is indeed a common way we organize our bodies in relation to others, and yet this common organization is ephemeral, predicated on the difference and shifting dynamics between participating bodies. When discussing (and thus attempting to name) a community, there are necessarily elisions. While a fist-fucker is not necessarily in the same community as a person into rope bondage, both share the commonality of non-normative sexual practice. That we can't 'bring to completion' these different yet related sex practices is ultimately a useful strategy in interrupting the flow by which such communities are called into the service of capitalism or normative models of familial organization. Admitting as much could be the foundation of a coalitional political power and will, even if this power is not ultimately directed through the usual channels of civil protest and legislative imperatives. As discussed in my introduction, the terminology of leather exemplifies this model of community as it indicates an utter diversity of sexual practices, contained within the 'warmly persuasive' ideology of community.

In *The Inoperative Community* Jean-Luc Nancy attunes to the fact that community structures the individual, and not the other way around—in spite of, and perhaps because of, community's rhetorical and theoretical 'excess.'[107] Here the individual is generically historicized as 'merely the residue of the experience of the dissolution of community,' effects that are naturalized 'as origin and as certainty.'[108] Nancy rethinks the whole foundation of the immanent individual, viewing it as the *product* of community rather than *a priori* to it, concentrating on what ideological formulations of community do within larger national and philosophical discourses.[109] He works against building a strictly codified definition of community, or even a historiography of community (à la Foucauldian genealogy), and so runs the risk of leaving unchallenged the 'warmly persuasive' quality of community.[110] As John Paul Ricco notes, in this regard, community, like queer theory, is 'always coming never arriving.'[111] Indeed, after reading Nancy's *The Inoperative Community*, one would be forgiven for being mostly unsure about what community may actually be, and this unfixity, similar to the archival turn in scholarship that Kate Eichhorn critiques, may push community's linguistic significance toward catachresis.[112]

At its most basic, though, Nancy's definition of community can be summed up as 'being in common,' with a stress placed on the 'in':

> Being *in* common has nothing to do with communion, with fusion into a body, into a unique and ultimate identity that would no longer be exposed. Being *in* common means, to the contrary, *no longer having, in any form, in any empirical or ideal place, such a substantial identity, and sharing this* (narcissistic) *'lack of identity.'*[113]

Nancy proposes a reorientation of the terms by which community is understood; by stressing the active process of 'being *in* common' he indicates that community is always in negotiation. Therefore community is a process-based verb, not a static noun. Historically, Nancy's rendering of 'being *in* common' had a particular political relevance, as his text was foremost a reaction against national discourses that sought to produce fascist subjects and nations, with political ideologies that deny or erase a subject position in favor of 'ideal places' and 'substantial identities' servicing sustained efforts to subjugate others. His philosophy can be aligned with the concerns of postcolonial thought, which seek, in part, to destabilize and question assumed commonalities.[114] Yet Nancy's move away from 'communion' and 'fusion' could also complicate notions of identity, which, like community, is a 'warmly persuasive' foundation on which we formulate many kinds of analyses—particularly within the realm of queer studies. Think again of Nancy's description of his relationship to another Frenchmen, a relationship that might be based on a 'lack of identity.' When others are subject to an overdetermined identity, community loses the 'in' of 'being-in-common'—rendering individual people within such formations as simply 'being common.'[115]

This insight has a direct correlation to leather communities in the 1970s, which, for a variety of reasons, never organized politically in the manner of women's liberation or gay liberation movements as a coherent identity category, or codified their existence within a set of demands and rewards inside of a public, political realm. In short, leather communities of the 1970s didn't lose their 'in' until later, when they started to organize around a politics based on a national sense of identity via organizations such as the GMSMA and the NLA.[116]

* * *

The 'in' of 'being-in-common' is at the heart of *Community Action Center*, which opens with a mixed-gendered wrestling/birthing/orgy scene. The participants make prodigious use of traditional artists' materials (paint and clay), fruits and vegetables (repurposed as bodily protrusions, a pregnant belly, a phallus, an ass), and household items ('pervertibles' repurposed for penetration: a recurring motif of *CAC*) (figure 8.7). 'Trans-genre' performer Justin Vivian Bond serves as the voice-over, reading an excerpt from Jack Smith's text 'Normal Love.' Functioning at once as work, practice, and play, this first scene sets up the terms for what occurs throughout *Community Action Center*—sexual experimentalism, (mis/re)use of heterogeneous materials, and expansive sex within elastic relationships. *Community Action Center* is a collaborative video work that makes claims to being a center for a much broader political engagement. John Paul Ricco could have been speaking about *CAC* when he wrote, 'queer sexual drive and erotic attraction in its aimless wandering, inadvertent detours and unexpected encounters, is dedicated to the accidental, transitional, minor and that which goes and comes in passing.'[117] The 'action' in *Community Action Center* is exemplary of this

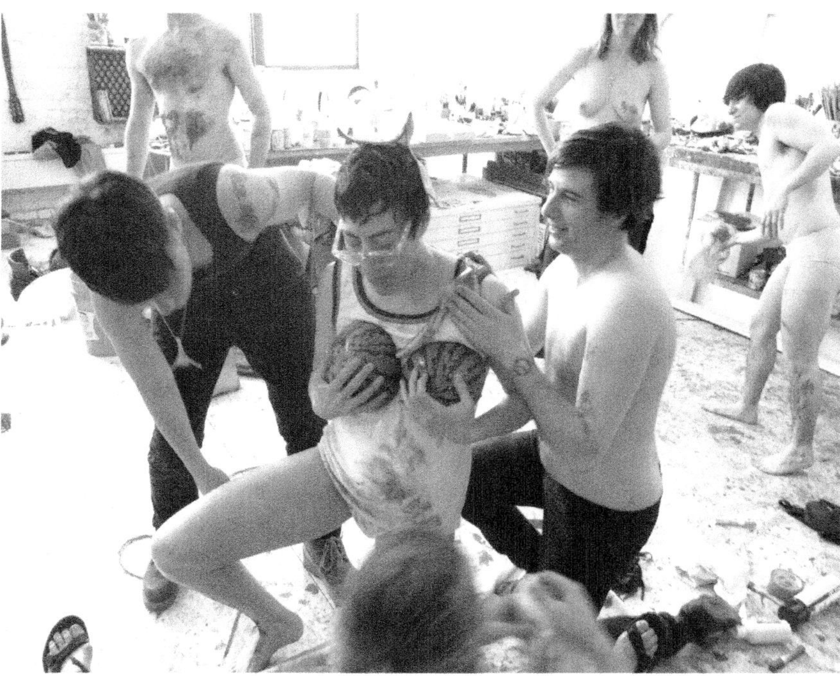

A. K. Burns and A. L. Steiner, production still from *Community Action Center*, 2010    **8.7**

'going and coming in passing,' as the term, like community, remains multiply meaningful—it is the action of the political protest, the action that is called for by a director on a film set, and that which also describes, in a euphemistic dodge of more graphic terminology, the frenzied motions of pornography.[118] There is no attempt made by Burns and Steiner to control or specify what is meant by 'action' or 'community,' implying that all definitions are already bound up in one another.

Here's a brief run-down of the scenes that follow: a leatherdyke dominates a pony-tailed woman in an old train depot; two glam, short-haired, androgynous people make out behind a mylar curtain; a trans, queer person penetrates themselves with a crystal, and later finger-fucks themselves using honey as a lubricant; a topless butch cracks a belt at the upper terminus of a stairwell, while someone licks her boots adoringly; the pony-tailed woman is tied up and pierced/threaded multiple times, resulting in a fan of feathers on her ass and face; the topless butch from a previous scene is fisted with her own menstrual blood; food is erotically fed to a supine woman and then ritualistically hacked with an axe; a witch fashions and bites the phallus of an arriving pizza delivery boi; the leatherdyke and the pony-tailed woman from an earlier scene resume fucking until both come, one spraying ejaculate; and finally a woman soaps up her breasts, washing a car with them and her long … green … garden hose.

Burns and Steiner also appear in their own video, and like the rest of the cast, use pseudonyms in the tradition of erotically evocative pornographic credits. Steiner is credited as Juggz, perhaps because her large breasts are used to wash a car in the video's ultimate scene. Burns is credited as Pansy Hanks, a name that short-circuits her role in the video as the belt-cracking butch at the top of the stairs (figure 8.8). These names point to each figure's erotic signifying practices, and are, by turns, titillating and funny. They are moaners and groaners.

Similar to the practices of earlier underground queer filmmakers such as Jack Smith, Andy Warhol, and the Kuchars, a viewer familiar with the particular folks appearing in *Community Action Center* would recognize not only the off-camera identities of the actors, but the ways in which they are knitted together relationally through friendship, intimate relationships, and political engagement. Because of the agreements the artists made with their collaborators, their identities cannot be revealed in any text written about *CAC*. All of these actors have their own artistic practices, which, if a viewer is already familiar with them, bear on, broaden, and thicken an experience of watching them at play in *Community Action Center*. While I cannot be more

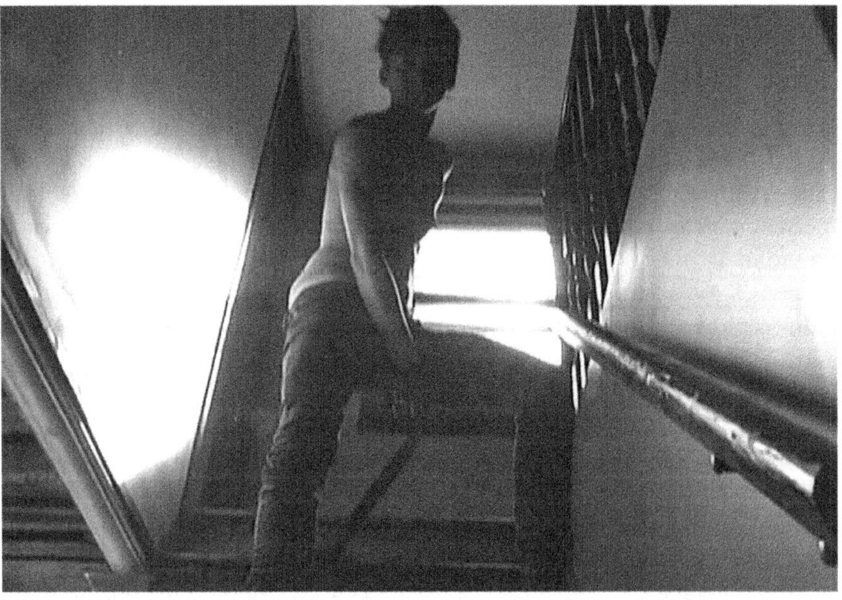

**8.8**    A. K. Burns and A. L. Steiner, video still from *Community Action Center*, 2010. SD single-channel video, 69 min.

specific about the intricacies of these community bonds and relations, this is essentially the 'local' component of the community described in *CAC*, an interrelated group of queer people making work in and around Los Angles in the years encompassing the making and immediate exhibition of Burns and Steiner's video, roughly, 2007–12.

This extends, also, to the funding structure of the video. Burns and Steiner campaigned and solicited donations from larger queer communities to pay the actors and crew, as well as to tour *CAC* to LGBTQ centers across the nation. Crowdfunding, which has rightly elicited criticism for asking communities to bring to bear financial resources that could otherwise be provided by states and/or local governments were they not so beholden to a neoliberal model of privatization, is also a process by which this community's economic support systems are made visible.[119] This is an enduring interest of both Burns and Steiner, who are co-founders and participants of W.A.G.E. (Working Artists and the Greater Economy), a group that advocates for the fair pay of artists, writers, and performers within the larger economic system of the artworld. *CAC* therefore evinces what Katja Diefenbach calls 'militant connectionism.'[120]

Because this book examines the ways in which contemporary artist projects reformat source material from leather communities of the past, I want to focus on two particular scenes in *CAC*, as they quote directly from or approximate Fred Halsted's *L.A. Plays Itself*. One short scene is an almost shot-by-shot remake of a sequence from *L.A. Plays Itself* – even the characters' names, Jacques Strap and Universal Twink, seem knowing winks to Halsted and Yale's publicly cemented roles. In this scene, a young, butchy top—Burns—whips her belt at the top of a set of stairs, while a long-haired bottom—Universal Twink—crawls up the stairway, eventually licking Strap's boots. This scene is a direct and knowing quotation of the stairwell scene from *L.A. Plays Itself*, which kicks off the sexual encounter between Halsted and Yale in the film's leather act. That Burns and Steiner should quote Halsted's film so consciously is an outgrowth of *CAC*'s genesis, which artists note was a response to viewing *L.A. Plays Itself* in MoMA's screening room.[121]

Unlike the soundtrack of the garbled southern 'yokel' that plays over Halsted's original, here a voice reads the line 'When you're hungry you eat, when you're tired you go to sleep' in chant-like repetition. The advice, simple and direct, formats the onscreen action of consensual humiliation and whipping as a needs-based activity, not just the expression of a sexual quirk. Positioning these sexual dynamics as being as vital as food and sleep allows Burns and Steiner to make an explicit argument for the importance of leathersexuality and its history of representations. In reconstructing Halsted's staircase sequence, the artists are involved in a process of rearticulating the terms and conditions under which leathersexuality might be understood in

2010. Because the bodies represented in *CAC* are largely gender non-binary and/or overtly lesbian (gay male bodies are few and far between), Burns and Steiner's quotation has the effect of broadening the scope of sexual relations beyond what appears in *L.A. Plays Itself*.

When Halsted originally shot his scene, it was a fresh and original approach to a gay pornographic genre solely defined by twinky pornographic danglie 'loops' featuring men in natural settings. If there was sex in these loops, it was tame by comparison to what Halsted produced. In *CAC*, Burns and Steiner bracket the sadomasochism of this particular scene with a crystal penetration performed near a bubbling brook—at once pushing the reference to Halsted toward further revision. In my estimation such appropriations honor the variety of queer visual traditions while also widening its field to incorporate more bodies, more identities, and more pleasures.

This relationship to Halsted, specifically, and a notion of a shared feminist queer past, more broadly, is corroborated in Burns and Steiner's 'Cliffs Notes' zine. The zine, publicly and readily accessible from a number of online sites, provides a 'small archive' of the source material the artists pulled from—including the 'Who's on Top?' interview between Joey Yale and Fred Halsted quoted earlier in this chapter. Alongside Halsted and Yale's interview are excerpts from Monique Wittig's *The Lesbian Body*, Jack Smith's *Normal Love*, Jean Genet's *Querelle*, Angela Carter's *The Sadeian Woman*, Leo Bersani's *Homos*, *The Joy of Lesbian Sex*, and the Wikipedia entry on 'The Feminist Sex Wars.' Visual collages featuring photographs and diagrams of vaginas and vulvic-shaped formations, fisting, book covers, and erotic drawings accompany these texts. Burns and Steiner pull from a constellated assortment of related sources, relying on all of them equally to create their 'guidebook.' Although Wittig's and Halsted's notions of sex might be incommensurate, Burns and Steiner force these diverse queer and feminist sources to rest alongside one another, and so ask a viewer to make sense of their distinctiveness, building up an archive of being-with and in difference.

Take this passage from Wittig's *The Lesbian Body* that the artists reproduce in their 'Cliffs Notes' zine. It is a joyous listing of anatomies that values the entirety of a body's geography as the potential site for erotic desire and affirmation:

THE MOUTH THE LIPS THE JAWS THE EARS THE RIDGES OF THE EYEBROWS THE TEMPLES THE NOSE THE CHEEKS THE CHIN THE FOREHEAD THE EYELIDS THE COMPLEXION THE ANKLE THE THIGHS THE HAMS THE CALVES THE HIPS THE VULVA THE BACK THE CHEST THE BREASTS THE SHOULDERBLADES THE BUTTOCKS THE ELBOWS THE LEGS THE TOES THE FEET THE HEELS THE LOINS THE NAPE THE THROAT THE HEAD THE INSTEPS THE

GROINS THE TONGUE THE OCCIPUT THE SPINE THE FLANKS THE
PUBIS THE LESBIAN BODY.[122]

Wittig's ecstatic lists of body parts rhyme with leathersex's de-genitalization
of sexual pleasure. And in including this particular passage from Wittig,
instead of one of the many others that pepper Wittig's text, the artists insist on
the lesbian body, in particular, as an emblematic site for the expansive sexual
possibilities leathersex offers.

The second scene to make reference to *L.A. Plays Itself* is more oblique,
and is split into two parts. This scene not only attempts to re-embody
Halsted's work but works more intently to play with, and reformat, the
rigid roles established in *L.A. Plays Itself* between top and bottom. The two
sequences between the characters listed in the credits as Leatherdyke and
Working Girl (played by actors under the pseudonyms of Max Hardhand and
Stargëizer respectively) serve as internal bookends to the action of *CAC*—the
post-premiere and penultimate scenes. The first is structured like the cruising
segment of Halsted's *L.A. Plays Itself*. Leatherdyke leans against the wall of
an automotive shop and cruises a young woman walking past her, following
her across the train tracks, and upon finding a small shack/depot begins to
engage a consensual scene of domination and submission, using slapping
and restraints to iterate a top/bottom relationship (figure 8.9). When these

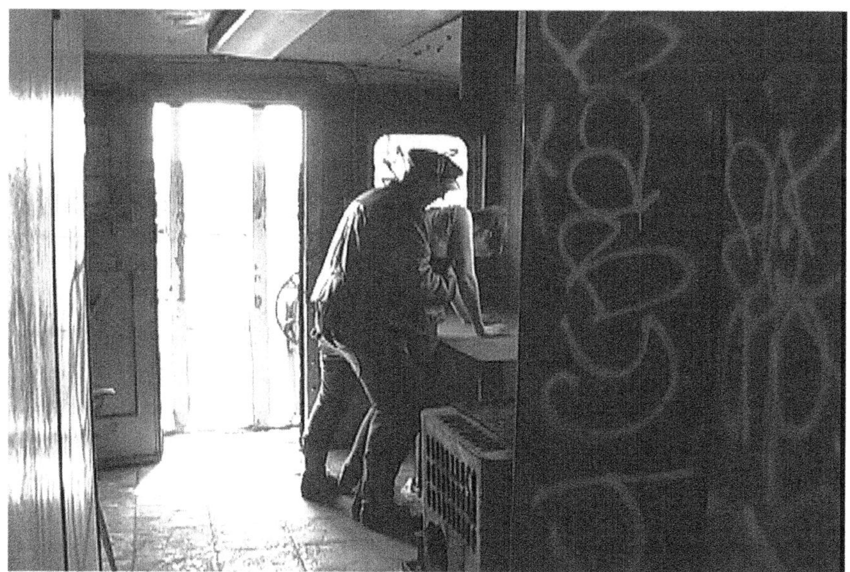

A. K. Burns and A. L. Steiner, video still from *Community Action Center*, 2010. SD single-    **8.9**
channel video, 69 min.

characters return toward the end of *CAC*, Burns and Steiner expand the roles established earlier in the video. This second scene at first appears to be an intensification of the power relationship previously established, but in a series of quick cuts the two characters trade places, fucking and being fucked by each other. Female orgasmic possibility and genital pleasure are highlighted as both characters come (unlike *L.A. Plays Itself* in which only Halsted comes). Working Girl ejaculates sprays of watery fluid, serving as a liquidy segue into the final carwash scene. The sounds that come from these two actors while both reach climax are some of the only diegetic sounds in *CAC*, enlivening the embodiment of female orgasm with sonic realism. In this sequence, Burns and Steiner move beyond the burden of their pornographic source material to create a scene that honors and homes in on the female orgasm, something Halsted was categorically uninterested in.

Thus far, I've discussed *CAC*'s relation to both 'community' and 'action,' but what of 'center'? *CAC* engages the process of centering, an ideological repositioning born out of the second-wave feminist tactic of consciousness-raising, refiguring that which had historically been marginalized and trivial (such as the lived experiences and artistic productions of women) as newly central and significant.[123] Yet 'center' also implies the administrative logics of the community center, a place of identification, validation, and social responsiveness. As social and architectural structures, community centers remain undertheorized, and their historical emergence relatively obscure.

An early twentieth-century text by the urban planner and sociologist Clarence Arthur Perry traces how the earliest community centers in the United States were school buildings repurposed outside of school hours for 'recreational, social, civic, or cultural,' purposes.[124] During World War I and its aftermath the U.S. bore witness to a burgeoning community centers movement, which at least one commentator remarked shared a social and moral purpose with the 'get-together' efforts of urban labor unions and the rural Grange movement.[125] This modern understanding of social responsibility in bridging socio-economic divides with a space for people to meet and share in fellowship was later grafted onto the dire needs of lesbian and gay people, running concurrent with the gay liberation efforts of activists in the U.S. In Los Angeles, this meant the establishment of the Gay Community Service Center in 1971, which eventually provided a 'hotline, information, referral, counseling, housing, education, and employment services,' all free or nearly free.[126] By 1972 'The Center' had served 75,000 people, with staff comprised mostly of volunteers as well as a skeleton crew of paid employees living on a 'survival stipend.'[127] The Center's founders imagined a place that would 'protect and serve' the 'individuals … of the homosexual community,' in part through a 'broadly based community outreach program directed toward increasing public awareness of the nature of homosexuality and the problems and needs of those individuals expressing their possibility of the human condition.'[128]

While not necessarily bound to the task of shedding light on problems faced by self-identifying members of LGBTQ community, I'd contend that *CAC* has the potential to transform the spaces it is shown in into temporary LGBTQ community centers, under the general condition of 'increasing public awareness' of queer people's lives, pleasures, and affinities. To expand upon this theory I want to briefly discuss the three contexts in which *CAC* was initially exhibited. These three exhibitions—in New York, Berlin, and Toronto, respectively—mark *CAC* as a shifting and evolving project, constantly reconceptualized and reformatted by Burns and Steiner. The artists took an expansive approach to installing *CAC*, incorporating video and two-dimensional collage, as well as sculpture and performance. As such the video is supposed, in its early exhibition history, to share more in common with traditional logics of museum and gallery display than the more temporal mode of film programming. The artists name the gallery as an important space for exhibition, serving as a necessary foil for the activity represented in *CAC*. As the artists write in their 'Cliffs Notes' zine, 'Using the gallery to exer/ exorcise the mystical and discreet lost spaces of homosocial configuration, the artists have created a reason and a space to reflect on the cultural realness of homo-grown lesbian sexuality.'[129]

*CAC*'s initial exhibition at Taxter & Spengemann gallery in New York in 2010 was marked by the competing needs and desires of the artists and the gallery. Burns and Steiner wanted to use the basement space, but the gallery, wanting to showcase the video more visibly, placed it in its main showroom instead.[130] To the artists the use of marginalized or unkempt spaces was an important component structuring the possible reception of the video—as such spaces would be more likely to be reminiscent of the improvisatory and run-down locales represented throughout the video, as well as to historical spatializations of the backrooms in leather bars and sex clubs. The clean-swept space of a Chelsea gallery communicates quite the opposite: tidiness and professionalization. In response to this positioning of *CAC* as comfortably fitting within the 'white cube' of the gallery, Burns and Steiner hosted a 'Casual Separatist Friday,' in which the gallery became a woman-separatist space. Mashing up the formats of lesbian separatist spaces such as the Michigan Womyn's Music Festival with corporately sanctioned 'casual Friday'—a carnivalesque respite that undergirds higher expectations for professionalism Monday through Thursday—reifies the strategems and mélange of source material filtered through *CAC* and its accompanying zine.

Concurrent with the end of their run at Taxter & Spengemann in New York, Burns and Steiner also opened *CAC* at Horton Gallery in Berlin. Upon entering the gallery a viewer was greeted with a large, sprawling, wheat-pasted wall-collage—a hallmark of A. L. Steiner's solo work—featuring Xeroxed black-and-white photographs taken on set, as well as appropriated posters of a play about the commercially successful pornographic film *Deep Throat* (1972), and several color *CAC* movie posters (figure 8.10). In execution, the wallpapering of the gallery walls conveys a deep polysemy (similar to the archive presented in Burns and Steiner's 'Cliffs Notes') from the activist street tactics of wheat-pasting, to the histories of key pornographic films such as *Deep Throat* and their contemporary reiterations. Placed in front of the wall-collage is a deconstructed duratrans lightbox, the kind most often used to advertise upcoming films outside cinema multiplexes. This particular element is more closely aligned with A. K. Burns's sculptural practice.[131] Placed on a wooden palette, the elements of the lightbox (frame, image, plexi, light, cord) are disassembled and placed in new relationships—the most striking is a fluorescent tube that pierces/penetrates the *CAC* poster, illuminating it while also poking a hole where there was no hole before. Penetration and the repurposing of utilitarian objects to achieve sexual pleasure is a key motif of the action in *CAC*, and the artists' sculptural assemblage represents an extension of these onscreen tactics.

To get to the screening room, a viewer passed through a curtain, vulvic in design with handstitched ruffles, made from the dropcloths used in *CAC*'s initial orgiastic, food-filled scene. Splattered but dry, the curtain carried the

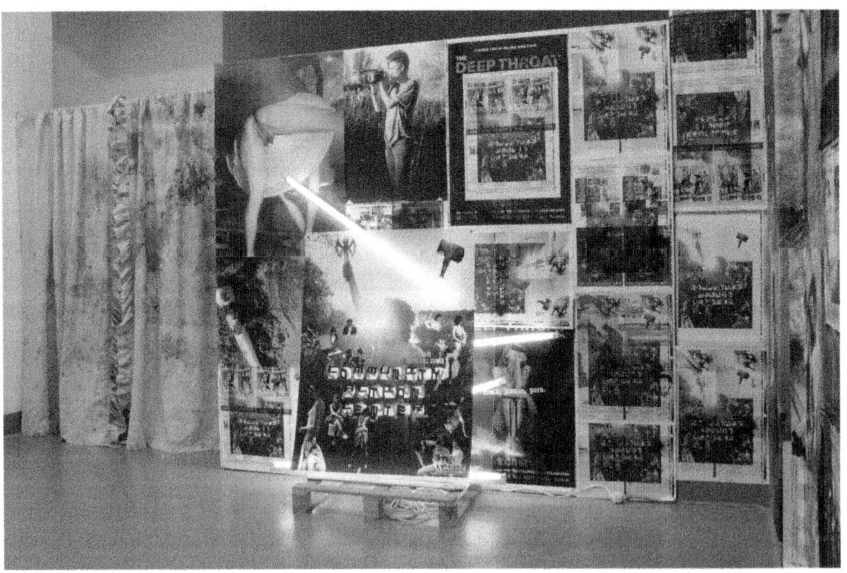

**8.10**   A. K. Burns and A. L. Steiner, installation view of *Community Action Center*, 2010 at Horton Gallery, Berlin

traces of food and bodily substances left upon it, and reoriented the ground of action as a soft barrier. By insisting that a gallery audience touch the surface on which cast members of *CAC* had played and fucked, Burns and Steiner draw together actor and viewer and consistently renegotiate the terms under which *CAC* is understood and sensually, haptically felt.

Finally, a year later, the artists developed an exhibition for the Feminist Art Gallery (FAG) in Toronto—a garage/gallery space conceived of and run by fellow artists and community activists Deirdre Logue and Allyson Mitchell. In this space, much smaller than the previous two venues *CAC* was exhibited in, the artists repeated the gesture of wheat-pasting a collage of images. However, the sculptural element here was a plushy green Laz-E-Boy recliner, pierced by a vertical stripper pole (figure 8.11). The sculpture was made functional during the opening event, when it was used by a pole-dancer outfitted in a bathing suit covered with Bud Light beer logos. The video was not projected here (the space was too small), but rather shown on a diminutive wall-mounted screen with attached headphones (an exception to the exhibition format mandated by the artists). The vulvic dropcloth/curtain was also present here, and so was the curtain made from black faux-leather from the original Taxter & Spengemann installation. Finally, the artists added the element of a public reading library, featuring books by Judith Butler, bell hooks, Pat Califia, Kate Bornstein, Henry Abelove, Gertrude Stein, and several anthologies of feminist, lesbian-separatist, and queer writings.

Photographs posted on Facebook of the *CAC* opening in Toronto show the artists and attendees sitting in the gallery's anteroom, the ruffles of the black leather curtain framing the scene. They gather in conversation—perhaps before or immediately following the screening of the video. Above them hang examples of Allyson Mitchell's knitwork—a crocheted target rug featuring a saccharine image of a bow-tied cat, the text 'Dyke Pussy,' and a seventies flower emblem heraldically flanked by crossed labyrises.

The labyris, the double-headed axe, is featured as a primary symbol in *Community Action Center*'s poster, as it is held aloft by one of the actors in the video. This poster was a recurrent element on the wheat-pasted walls of both the Berlin and Toronto exhibitions. The labyris appears again in the 'Cliffs Notes' to *CAC*, as part of an excerpt from Monique Wittig and Sande Zeig's *Lesbian Peoples: Material for a Dictionary*.[132] Wittig and Zeig's text lists the labyris as the 'name given to the double-headed axe of the ancient amazons and to the representation of this arm as the emblem of amazon empires.' As a symbol of empowerment, its use reinforces a specific kind of feminist world-making, one that privileges the symbolic resonance of matriarchal societies. Although the labyris isn't featured prominently in *CAC* until its final frames, the fact of its recurrence in the supporting materials (zine and poster) marks it as an important and enduring symbol of the heterogeneous queer archives

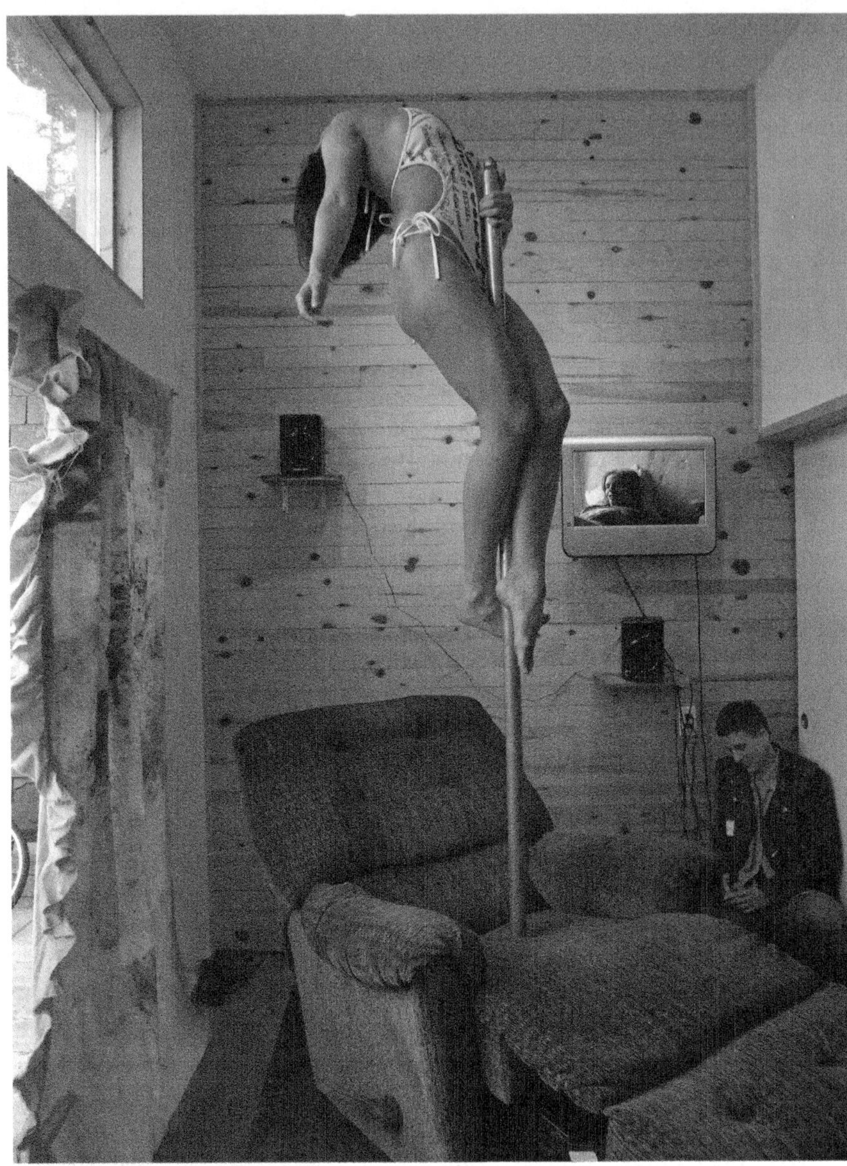

**8.11**    A. K. Burns and A. L. Steiner, installation view of *Community Action Center: The Exhibition(ist)* at Feminist Art Gallery (F.A.G.), Toronto, Canada. Live performance by Cat Nimmo

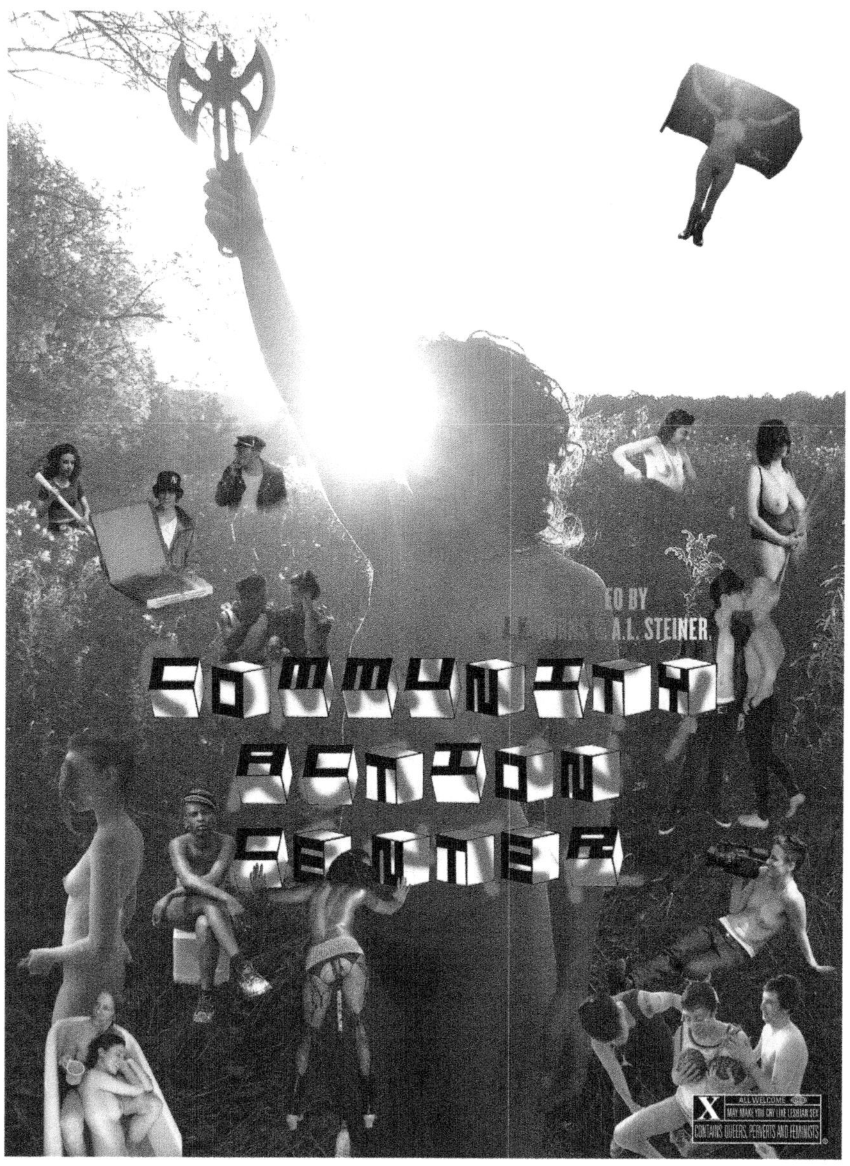


A. K. Burns and A. L. Steiner, *Community Action Center* film poster, 2010. Offset full-color poster, 13 x 18 in.    **8.12**

tapped in the making of the video and all its related materials. In the *CAC* poster the labyris is an emphatic vertical extension of the actor's body (figure 8.12). If the axe represents physical power (weapon) and the significance of writing our own histories (via its attachment to matriarchal mythology), Burns and Steiner's visual message is ultimately a call to action—to imagine and inhabit a feminist queer world. For an axe is nothing without the fist that holds it aloft.

## Notes

1 Kenneth Turan and Stephen F. Zito, *Sinema: American Pornographic Films and the People Who Make Them* (New York: Praeger, 1974), pp. 192–3. What Turan and Zito describe as 'tedious' and 'aimless' is evidence of their total lack of awareness regarding a 'cruising' gaze. A lot is, in fact, going on—the viewer is invited to cruise the many bodies captured by Halsted's lens, deciding for themselves which they would or wouldn't attempt to pick up. If a viewer is not attuned to this, as it seems Turan and Zito are not, the early montages of the film just look like snippets of street life. Furthermore there is a fundamental misunderstanding in this review of the sadomasochistic content as 'sexual abuse.'

2 *The Blue Guide to Adult Male Films & Stars* (Ogdensburg, NJ: FD Enterprises, 1989), p. I-56. This guide also gives *L.A. Plays Itself* a rating of 88 (out of 100 points possible). The breakdown goes as follows: 22 for technique, 23 for the cast, 23 for the plot, and 20 for eroticism. These categories are further defined by this guide. 'Technique: The quality of the sound, the picture, the set or background and/or the props, etc. Cast: The attractiveness of the actors, their appropriateness for the role and their performance. Plot: Reflects the believability of the story line and the flow of the action Eroticism: The subjective judgement of the reviewer as to the general excitement of the material.' Although the scoring is fairly uniform, it's interesting that *L.A. Plays Itself* gets high marks on the casting and believability of the story-line and its lowest mark for its ability to arouse a viewer.

3 *Al's Male Video Guide* (New York: Midway Publications, 1986), p. 140. This entry is in reference to the VHS release of *L.A. Plays Itself*.

4 The title of this chapter is taken from the article 'Deep Fist At The Modern,' *Screw*, 29 April 1974, p. 11.

5 Stuart Byron, 'L.A. Plays Itself,' *The Real Paper*, 13 June 1973, p. 17. I am using the term 'act' as a way of describing the 'macrostructure' of the almost half-hour segments, as opposed to the 'microstructure' of shots, aligning with David Bordwell's use of the same term. David Bordwell, 'The Hook: Scene Transitions in Classical Cinema' (January 2008), http://www.davidbordwell.net/essays/hook.php (accessed 10 October 2017). Bordwell points out that this macrostructure comes from the physical limitations of reel size, and so the structure of classical cinema traditionally had three or four acts tracing the set-up of characters and their wants and desires, the things that block these desires, and the resolution (whether in the character's favor or not). This is only one way to read 'act';

the word has a useful polysemy. Act also implies something about the process of behaving in front of a camera (acting), as well as the process of doing something—or in the case of *L.A. Plays Itself* the sex act itself. Sexual play is also called action. I also want to assert that 'act' here has a philosophical performative genealogy as well—especially in the use of J. L. Austin's performative theories of language by Judith Butler. Judith Butler, 'Performative Acts and Gender Constitution: An Essay in Phenomenology and Feminist Theory,' *Theatre Journal*, 40:4 (1988), pp. 519–31.

6 Early research indicated that there might be a few more 16mm prints of *L.A. Plays Itself*: one residing with the Bijou Theater in Chicago, and another belonging to *Hustler* publisher Larry Flynt. The long-time owner of the Bijou, Steve Toushin, can't seem to find his copy of the film, and Flynt's archives do not exist in a form accessible to scholars. Therefore this chapter looks at the two confirmed prints accessed through my research—leaving room for future scholars to extend and abut the arguments I make.

7 Sam Biederman, '*Halsted Plays Himself* by William E. Jones,' *Bookforum*, 26 September 2011, https://www.bookforum.com/review/8399 (accessed 10 October 2018).

8 Siebenand, 'The Beginnings of Gay Cinema,' pp. 200–1.

9 Cindy Patton, *L.A. Plays Itself / Boys in the Sand: A Queer Film Classic* (Vancouver, BC: Arsenal Pulp Press, 2014); and William E. Jones, *Halsted Plays Himself* (Los Angeles: Semiotext(e), 2011).

10 The DVD I used was created by William E. Jones, reconstructed from both film and VHS sources. That DVD, a copy of a copy I received from artist Ivan LOZANO as I was beginning research for this book, is a deeply meaningful object to me—evincing the power of extended virtual networks of engaged cultural workers of all kinds, reminiscent of the zine and tape sharing at the foundation of the Riot Grrrl movement. Kate Eichhorn's discussion of Riot Grrrl zine networks has inspired my thinking in this regard. Kate Eichhorn, *The Archival Turn in Feminism* (Philadelphia, PA: Temple University Press, 2013).

11 Michael Baxandall, *Patterns of Intention: On the Historical Explanation of Pictures* (New Haven, CT: Yale University Press, 1985), p. 1.

12 Joan W. Scott, 'Experience,' in Judith Butler and Joan W. Scott (eds.), *Feminists Theorize the Political* (London: Routledge, 1992), p. 26.

13 One of the fabulous things about Siebenand's dissertation is that he specifically asks each filmmaker about the other filmmakers and producers he's interviewing—therefore one gets a clear sense of how each filmmaker positions himself (all the directors Siebenand talks to are male) in relation to his peers.

14 Jonas Mekas, 'Movie Journal,' *The Village Voice*, 20 April 1972, p. 75.

15 I do not spend time in this chapter describing and discussing *Sex Garage* in the same way I do *L.A. Plays Itself*. *Sex Garage* is a black-and-white short that contains straight sex (between a man and women), gay sex (between two men), self sex (male masturbation) and man–machine sex. In the ultimate scene a man penetrates a motorcycle tailpipe. More thinking has to be done in regards to the effect of the sequencing of *Sex Garage* and *L.A. Plays Itself*. For example,

when screened first, *Sex Garage* may be a doorway for straight viewers—the first kinds of sex are straight sex—and this would go along with Halsted's repeated statements of wanting to appeal to a broader audience, discussed elsewhere in this chapter. The ending act, fucking a tailpipe, is indeed shocking, but may prepare an audience for the final fisting sequence of *L.A. Plays Itself.* Even today the films are screened together in the scant exhibition programs in which they appear. As with the two parts of *L.A. Plays Itself, Sex Garage* and *L.A. Plays Itself* were ordered differently before and after 1974. *Sex Garage* is, however, infamous on its own, as Halsted and the 55th Street Playhouse were charged with obscenity because of its exhibition. Addison Verrill, 'N.Y. Hits Abuse-Abasement Pic,' *Variety*, 19 April 1972, pp. 1, 22. This same incident is described by Turan and Zito: 'The police shutdown of *L.A. Plays Itself* had an amusing aspect. The undercover police who made the arrest went into the theater, saw a few minutes of hardcore sex, and lodged a complaint against the film. What they saw, however, was another film by Halsted, a short called *Sex Garage*, which depicted a variety of unusual sexual activities, including a man making love to his motorcycle.' Turan and Zito, *Sinema*, p. 193. But *Sex Garage* and *L.A. Plays Itself* were not always screened together. Take, for instance, the screenings held in the fall of 1974 at The Mini, a coffee lounge/ sex club on 7th Ave. in New York, which only screened *L.A. Plays Itself.* See listings in *New York Times*, 16 October 1974 and 5 November 1974. Although not within the purview of this chapter, it would also be interesting to compare *L.A. Plays Itself* with Uwe Brandner's German film *I Love You, I Kill You*, also from 1972, which debuted at Cannes, and is much more classically narrative than Halsted's film.

16 Siebenand, 'The Beginnings of Gay Cinema,' pp. 194–5. The whole quote is: '*Sextool* is based on several different specific sex scenes. In the sex scenes I want complete diversity. I let my imagination run amok. That is why my star is Charmaine Lee Anderson. I go from her with lipstick and bubbles to some of the roughest sex scenes you will ever see. She is a transsexual and I cut from her to a Crisco greased-up bicep. And this switching is thematic of the film.'

17 Konstantin Berlandt, 'An S&M Film the Whole Family Can Enjoy,' *Village Voice*, 2 June 1975, pp. 69–70.

18 '*LA Plays Itself* pretty much appealed to one audience. It was more or less autobiographical, so I didn't try to appeal to a broad audience … I am intending [*Sextool*] to be an encyclopedia of sex…' Siebenand (quoting Halsted), 'The Beginnings of Gay Cinema,' p. 194.

19 Ibid., pp. 218–19. The brackets are Siebenand's.

20 Stuart Byron, 'A Commonplace Press Handout on "L.A. Plays Itself" and "The Sex Garage",' 1972.

21 *The Blue Guide to Adult Male Films & Stars*, p. I-56.

22 This chapter could just as easily be about the use of music in Fred Halsted's movies. Here he utilizes the state-of-the art synthesizer sounds of Tonto's Expanding Headband, an experimental electronic duo comprised of the musicians Robert Margouleff and Malcolm Cecil. The name of the group was epony-

mous with the instrument they co-created, dubbed Tonto, an acronym for 'The Original New Timbral Orchestra.' In *L.A. Plays Itself* Halsted also uses Western classical and East Asian orchestral scores during the nature act. As I intimated in an earlier footnote, elsewhere in Halsted's oeuvre he pulls from new wave, punk, and disco. These soundtrack choices not only mimicked the diegetic sounds that might have been filmed at the director's leather bar, Halsted's, where some of his filmic action is set, but opens up a space for multiple readings of lyrical content. For example, in 'Pumping (my heart)' by Patti Smith, which appears in *A Night at Halsted's* (1982), Smith righteously yells 'My fists, start pumping,' a couplet that could just as easily describe fist-fucking.

23 We know that Halsted 'plays himself' not only from the end-credits but also from promotional materials given out to coincide with the premiere of *L.A. Plays Itself* at the 55th Street Playhouse in New York. While everyone else seems to have a typological role—Joey is the 'Blonde pick-up in L.A.' and Jim Frost is the 'Motorcycle hiker'—only Fred Halsted and the city of Los Angeles play themselves.

24 *The New York Times*, 9 April 1972, p. D15.

25 'Independent Theater Guide,' *The Los Angeles Times*, 28 June 1972, p. F14. The Paris was located at 8163 Santa Monica.

26 Siebenand, 'The Beginnings of Gay Cinema,' pp. 200–1.

27 Mekas, 'Movie Journal,' p. 75. For more on underground film, see Parker Tyler, *Underground Film: A Critical History* (New York: Grove Press, 1970).

28 Mekas, 'Movie Journal,' p. 75.

29 'L.A. Plays Itself,' *Variety*, 12 April 1972, n.p.

30 Ibid.

31 Byron, 'Brothers Under the Skinflick,' p. 57.

32 Siebenand, 'The Beginnings of Gay Cinema,' p. 75. The scene Rocco makes reference to, and that I discuss later in this chapter, looks as though it was ripped straight from a Rocco movie. Many of Rocco's films featured young, slim, hairless men in natural settings—posing and occasionally kissing, rarely fucking.

33 Even today, film scholars view *L.A. Plays Itself* as lacking a certain finesse: 'Another thing that set him apart from this group was his pride in how little he knew about the process of filmmaking. While the work of Poole et al. had somewhat respectable production values, or at least aspired to them, Halsted's films are ragged collages of imagery, with ambient (i.e., sometimes incomprehensible) audio, confusing double exposures, and nonlinear narratives, to put it mildly.' Gary Morris, 'Private Rituals Made Public: The Lost Erotica of Fred Halsted,' *Bright Lights Film Journal*, 49 (August 2005), http://brightlightsfilm.com/private-rituals-made-public-lost-erotica-fred-halsted (accessed 10 October 2017).

34 Here's the full quote: '*LA Plays Itself*. That's another story. I was being in a new wave of sex flicks at the time that Fred Halsted and Joey Yale began making that whole series of movies, and I always went to the "grand openings." Of course, some of their grand openings had trouble happening for various reasons, but *LA Plays Itself* and *Sex Garage* opened together and I saw them in their opening at a little theater on a northerly curve of Sunset Boulevard where such things

happened back then, I think I have this sorted out correctly in memory. The openings tended to be at that little theater, including Fred's and I'm pretty sure the *Sex Garage* double bill was there … Anyway, it seemed pretty unremarkable to me, frankly. I was doing Joey at a sex club regularly, watching Fred do scenes at the same club, and pretty much untouched by the content in any but the intended way (that is, arousal).' Joseph Bean, email correspondence with author, 12 September 2009.

35 Siebenand, 'The Beginnings of Gay Cinema,' pp. 200, 202.

36 'There were three people involved and not two in the last sequence of *LA.*' Siebenand, 'The Beginnings of Gay Cinema,' p. 54. For other directors the veracity of the actors actually fisting didn't matter either. To Bob Mizer, founder of the *Athletic Model Guild,* a magazine and mail-order catalogue that trafficked in posing-strap and beefcake images of naked and near-naked youths, 'The people interested in fistfucking don't even care about the faces of the people involved' (Siebenand, 'The Beginnings of Gay Cinema,' p. 53). Regardless, Yale was not Texan, but rather from Indiana.

37 Fred Halsted, 'Editorial,' *Package,* 1:1 (1976), p. 3. Halsted also believed that with the onset of birth control, heterosexuals were becoming functioning homosexuals, due to their ability to engage in purely recreational sex. Siebenand, 'The Beginnings of Gay Cinema,' p. 226.

38 Fred Halsted, 'Personal Training,' *Package,* 1:4 (1976), p. 16.

39 Byron, 'A Commonplace Press Handout,' p. 6.

40 For more on montage, see David Bordwell, 'The Idea of Montage in Soviet Art and Film,' *Cinema Journal,* 11:2 (1972), pp. 9–17. I think Maya Deren's conception of montage is more appropriate to this particular film; in a roundtable published in *Film Culture* (with Parker Tyler, Arthur Miller, Dylan Thomas, and moderated by Willard Maas), she delimits 'horizontal' and 'vertical' forms of montage. To Deren, 'horizontal' montage suggests merely a narrative action, while 'vertical' montage—even though 'the incidents themselves might be quite disparate'— is the territory of dreams and poetry. Such 'vertical' montages are held together by an emotional resonance. Willard Maas, 'Poetry and the Film: A Symposium,' *Film Culture,* 29 (1963), pp. 55–63.

41 Michael Kearns, 'Fred Halsted. Not a Comeback, A Return,' *FREEP,* 30 December 1977–5 January 1978, p. C-1.

42 Dyer, 'Male Gay Porn,' pp. 27–9.

43 Siebenand, 'The Beginnings of Gay Cinema,' pp. 205–6.

44 Verrill, 'NY Hits Abuse-Abasement Pic,' pp. 1, 22.

45 Ernest Peter Cohen, 'Interview: A Sadistic Homosexual Pornographer on Gay Liberation,' *Gay Activist,* 11 (April 1972), p. 11. Halsted saw this choice of location with an anti-development political lens, telling Cohen that the two canyons are 'now zoned for a shopping center and condominiums. So these locations you've seen, the birds and the animals you've seen, within a year will be dead.'

46 'I needed a young boy, and it was about bugs and stuff.' Fred Halsted, 'Fred Halsted,' *Drummer,* 1:4 (1976), p. 48.

47 Jeremy Hughes, 'Halsted & Yale—Who's On Top?,' *Skin,* 3:1 (1981), p. 8.

48  Bryon, 'A Commonplace Press Handout.'

49  Cohen, 'Interview,' p. 11.

50  Byron, 'Brothers Under the Skinflick,' p. 57.

51  Ibid.

52  H.J.S., [untitled review], *Los Angeles Times*, 10 June 1977, p. H5.

53  Byron, 'A Commonplace Press Handout.'

54  No records exist as to whether or not the profits actually did go to the Theodore Payne Foundation.

55  For more on the Zoot Suit riots, see Rodolfo Acuña, *Occupied America: A History of Chicanos*, 7th edn (Boston, MA: Longman, 2011); and Eduardo Obregón Pagán, *Murder at the Sleepy Lagoon: Zoot Suits, Race, and Riot in Wartime L.A.* (Chapel Hill, NC: University of North Carolina Press, 2003). For more on the development of Compton in the 1940s, see Emily E. Straus, *Death of a Suburban Dream: Race and Schools in Compton, California* (Philadelphia, PA: University of Pennsylvania Press, 2014).

56  The exception to this, of course, would be those intimately familiar with the stretch of Selma Ave. that Halsted films—a strip that included light industry, sex workers, and gay men who cruised in that area.

57  *The Blue Guide to Adult Male Films & Stars*, p. I-56.

58  'Cineprobe series begins seventh season as forum for independent filmmakers' [press release], Museum of Modern Art, September 1974, pp. 1–2.

59  Russell Lynes, *Good Old Modern: An Intimate Portrait of the Museum of Modern Art* (New York: Atheneum, 1973).

60  Carol Duncan and Allan Wallach, 'The Museum of Modern Art as Late Capitalist Ritual: An Iconographic Analysis,' *Marxist Perspectives*, 1:4 (1978), pp. 28–51.

61  Ibid., p. 37.

62  O'Doherty, *Inside the White Cube*.

63  Molly Nesbit, 'MoMA: The Problem,' *ANY: Architecture New York*, 22 (1998), pp. 16–17.

64  Julia Bryan-Wilson, *Art Workers: Radical Practice in the Vietnam War Era* (Berkeley, CA: University of California Press, 2009), p. 192.

65  'Sado-Maso Sex Makes Art Museum,' *Variety*, 24 April 1974.

66  Ibid.

67  'Deep Fist at the Modern,' p. 11.

68  Berlandt, 'An S&M Film,' p. 69. Halsted ambitiously projected to gross five million dollars with the theatrical release of *Sextool*. Of gay theaters, Halsted had this to say: 'I've always been ashamed to play at gay theaters … because they're toilets and because the audience is only gay.'

69  Filmmakers were often present for their Cineprobe screenings, and indeed MoMA made it a habit to collect audio from the interactions between the film-makers and their audiences. While MoMA did, in fact, record the exchange between Fred Halsted and his audience, that audiotape has since been lost. No transcripts or accounts of the screening exist to draw upon.

70  *Man Happenings* (dir. Pat Rocco, 1968/2007). These films were mostly made on a shoestring budget of anywhere between $100–500. Letter from Pat Rocco to Tod

Jonson, 5 March 1985, box 5, folder 12, Pat Rocco Papers [1934–], ONE Archives, University of Southern California Libraries..

71 Allan Kaprow, 'Happenings in the New York Scene' (1961), in *Essays on the Blurring of Art and Life* (Berkeley, CA: University of California Press, 1993), p. 16.

72 Sianne Ngai, *Our Aesthetic Categories: Zany, Cute, Interesting* (Cambridge, MA: Harvard University Press, 2012), p. 181.

73 Thomas Waugh, 'Men's Pornography: Gay vs. Straight,' *Jump Cut*, 30 (March 1985), pp. 30–5.

74 The Project on Disney (Jane Kuentz et al.), *Inside the Mouse: Work and Play at Disney World* (Durham, NC: Duke University Press, 1995), pp. 68–9.

75 Jim Kepner, Pat Rocco [interview], 27 April 1983, https://www.cinema.ucla.edu/sites/default/files/Rocco.pdf, n.p. (accessed 10 October 2017).

76 *Somebody* [review], *Variety* clipping, n.d. box 6, folder 5, Pat Rocco Papers [1934–], ONE Archives. Jim Kepner agreed in this assessment when conducting an interview with Rocco, remarking that the films had a 'romantic idealism that the Disney films had at their best, and the MGM musicals of the '30s and '40s had at their best.' Jim Kepner, Pat Rocco [interview].

77 'It must be said that my films were all "soft-core" and non pornographic. No explicit sex was actually seen, but it was often implied.' Pat Rocco to Tod Jonson, 5 March 1985, box 5, folder 12, Pat Rocco Papers [1934–], ONE Archives.

78 Author unknown, 'homo films' [manuscript], n.d. box 5, folder 12, Pat Rocco Papers [1934–], ONE Archives. All grammatical errors original to the text.

79 Richard Whitehall writing for the *Open City Newspaper* describes that film thusly: 'The best, for those who aren't too busy window shopping for genetelia [*sic*], is "the Sailor and the Leather Stud" if only because the sight of the stud unlacing himself out of his leather cocoon [stripping down to, and beyond, leather briefs no less] is very funny. And all the while the Max Steinerish music is surging to the sort of climax which leads one to expect the parting of the Red Sea at the very least.' Richard Whitehall, 'Prick Flicks,' *Open City Newspaper*, 19 December 1968, n.p.

80 Letter from Pat Rocco to Tod Jonson, 5 March 1985, box 5, folder 12, Pat Rocco Papers [1934–], ONE Archives.

81 Ibid.

82 Derrida, *Archive Fever*, p. 14.

83 Pat Rocco, UCLA Film Archives clippings, 1977–??, box 5, folder 7, Pat Rocco3 Papers [1934–], ONE Archives.

84 Ibid.

85 A. K. Burns and A. L. Steiner, 'Cliffs Notes on Community Action Center' (2010), http://akburns.net/wp-content/uploads/2015/06/zine_CAC_sm.pdf (accessed 10 October 2017).

86 Ibid.

87 This sentence is in reference to Linda Williams's summary of her 2008 book *Screening Sex*. Her full sentence is: 'Nevertheless, as I have argued recently in *Screening Sex* with respect to narrative art films, there is such a thing as hard-core

art film that is hard-core in its explicitness, yet not pornography in a primary desire to arouse.' Williams, 'Pornography, Porno, Porn,' pp. 26–7.

88 For more on this, see Lucas Hilderbrand, *Inherent Vice: Bootleg Histories of Videotape and Copyright* (Durham, NC: Duke University Press, 2009); Chuck Kleinhans, 'The Change from Film to Video Pornography: Implications for Analysis,' in Peter Lehman (ed.), *Pornography: Film and Culture* (New Brunswick, NJ: Rutgers University Press, 2006), pp. 154–67; and Zabet Patterson, 'Going On-Line: Consuming Pornography in the Digital Era,' in Linda Williams (ed.), *Porn Studies* (Durham, NC: Duke University Press, 2004), pp. 104–24.

89 Kelly Dennis, *Art/porn: A History of Seeing and Touching* (Oxford: Berg, 2009), p. 1.

90 Waugh, 'Men's Pornography,' pp. 30–5.

91 Siebenand, 'The Beginnings of Gay Cinema,' pp. 200–1; Burns and Steiner, 'Cliffs Notes on Community Action Center.'

92 David Velasco, 'Queer Eyes,' *artforum.com*, 11 March 2012, https://www.artfo rum.com/film/id=30482 (accessed 10 October 2017).

93 Elijah Adiv Edelman, 'The Cum Shot: Trans Men and Visual Economies of Ejaculation,' *Porn Studies*, 2:2–3 (2015), pp. 150–60.

94 David Velasco, writing for *Artforum*, puts it similarly: 'Indeed, to have a properly "critical" response to *CAC* would mean suspending one's sexual response, and this would only jettison the work's most valuable contributions and, in a way, engage the work in bad faith.' Velasco, 'Queer Eyes.'

95 Maggie Nelson, *The Argonauts* (Minneapolis, MN: Graywolf Press, 2015), p. 115.

96 Ibid., p. 116.

97 Burns and Steiner, 'Cliffs Notes on Community Action Center.'

98 Eichhorn, *Outrage in Order*, p. viii.

99 Johnny Micheff, 'Community Action Interaction,' *dis Magazine*, 2010, http:// dismagazine.com/discussion/9725/community-action-interaction (accessed 10 October 2017).

100 I will have more to say on pornographic tropes, but in lieu of an extended dis-cussion, see a list of some of the characters that appear in their film, and their related pornographic generic tropes: 'There's Pony the radikal fairy, Stargëizer the hard-working girl, Pansy Hanks the universal twink, Jacques Strap the dom, Juggz the carwasher, Kasimir Solaj the pizza delivery boy, Stevie Lijks the witch, Max Hardhand the leatherdaddy, the poets, the Puritan, the eater, the feeder, the crooners, the transglamslammers, and the group art orgiast. The list goes on and on.' Michef, 'Community Action Interaction.'

101 Ibid.

102 Williams, *Keywords*, p. 76.

103 Joseph, *Against the Romance of Community*, p. ix.

104 See the following court cases: *Roth v. United States*, No. 582, Supreme Court of the US, 24 June 1957; *MANual Enterprises v. Day*, No. 123, Supreme Court of the US, 25 June 1962; *Jacobellis v. Ohio*, No. 11, Supreme Court of the US, 22 June 1964; *Memoirs v. Massachusetts*, No. 368, Supreme Court of the US, 21 March 1966; *Miller v. California*, No. 70–73, Supreme Court of the US, 21 June 1973.

Each of these cases put to the test what was 'obscene' or 'pornographic,' and thus acceptable for circulation through the U.S. Mail, or subject to state or federal regulation. Yet each also revolves around a sense of who is included/excluded from the 'community' that deems the objects under question to be un/acceptable. This notion of community is legally inconsistent across these cases, and open, at least in my own view, to broader interpretation than the courts oftentimes allowed.

105  Anderson, *Imagined Communities*.

106  Nancy, *Being Singular Plural*, p. 155.

107  Jean-Luc Nancy, *The Inoperative Community*, trans. Peter Connor et al. (Minneapolis, MN: University of Minnesota Press, 1991), pp. 25–6.

108  Ibid., p. 3.

109  For further uses of Nancy's ideas within a contemporary art historical framework, see Nicolas Bourriaud, *Relational Aesthetics*, trans. Simon Pleasance et al. (Dijon: Les Presses du Réel, 2002); Sandhini Poddar, *Being Singular Plural* (New York: Guggenheim, 2012); and Miwon Kwon, *One Place After Another: Site-Specific Art and Locational Identity* (Cambridge, MA: MIT Press, 2004).

110  Because I've made a passing reference to Foucault here, I might well expand on what I intend. I refer to the term 'genealogy' as Foucault used it in *Discipline and Punish*, closely related to his earlier concept of archaeology, as a method of apprehending historiographical power shifts without relying on the primacy of the intent of any particular individual. Indeed, these shifts occur, almost subconsciously, on a sociocultural and juridical level, and Foucault often picks out emblematic examples. The most famous and most widely understood of these is Foucault's discussion of Jeremy Bentham's panopticon prison, which Foucault uses to point toward a linkage between vision and power. Foucault's original title, *Surveiller et Punir* ['Monitor/Surveil and Punish'], reinforces this alliance between a surveilling gaze and an enactment of power. Foucault, *The Archaeology of Knowledge*; and Foucault, *Discipline and Punish*.

111  John Paul Ricco, *The Logic of the Lure* (Chicago: University of Chicago Press, 2002), p. 141.

112  Eichhorn, *Outrage in Order*, p. viii.

113  Nancy, *The Inoperative Community*, p. xxxviii. Emphasis original.

114  For more on this point, as well as an elucidating summary of Nancy's *The Inoperative Community*, see Tilottama Rajan, 'On (Not) Being Postcolonial,' *Postcolonial Text*, 2:1 (2006), http://postcolonial.org/index.php/pct/article/view/403/822 (accessed 10 October 2017).

115  Others have taken up this rendering of 'being common' as a point of political empowerment. I am thinking here most specifically of José Esteban Muñoz's work on a 'brown commons.' José Esteban Muñoz, 'The Wildness of the Commons,' keynote, *WE WHO FEEL DIFFERENTLY*, New York, New Museum, 5 May 2012.

116  In many ways, this is the transition mapped by Weiss, *Techniques of Pleasure*.

117  Ricco, 'The Art of the Consummate Cruise.'

118  This is a reference to Linda Williams's explication of pornography as a 'frenzy of the visible.' Williams, *Hard Core*.

119  Jen Harvie, *Fair Play – Art, Performance, and Neoliberalism* (New York: Palgrave Macmillan, 2013), pp. 172–3.

120  Amelia Jones, Cheri Gaulke, A. L. Steiner, and Terry Wolverton, 'Dyke Talk, or "Political Lesbianism" and Queer Feminist Art (History),' in Amelia Jones and Erin Silver (eds.), *Otherwise: Imagining Queer Feminist Art Histories* (Manchester: Manchester University Press, 2016), p. 164. The idea of 'militant connectionism' comes from Katja Diefenbach, 'Fizzle Out in White: Postporn Politics and the Deconstruction of Fashion,' in Tim Stüttgen (ed.), *Post/Porn/ Politics Reader: Queer Feminist Perspectives on the Politics of Porn Performance and Sex Work as Cultural Production* (Berlin: b.books, 2009), pp. 25–32.

121  A. K. Burns, interview with author, 12 May 2012.

122  Wittig as quoted in Burns and Steiner, 'Cliffs Notes on Community Action Center,' p. 15.

123  See especially Lucy Lippard, *From the Center: Feminist Essays on Women's Art* (New York: E. P. Dutton, 1976); Ann Reynolds, 'Circa 1970: Towards a Feminist Public,' in Rhea Anastas (ed.), *Witness to Her Art* (Annandale-on-Hudson, NY: Bard Center for Curatorial Studies and D.A.P. Press, 2006), pp. 27–33; and Meg Linton and Sue Maberry (eds.), *Doin' It in Public: Feminism and Art and the Woman's Building*, vols. I & II (Los Angeles: Otis College of Art and Design, 2011).

124  Clarence Arthur Perry, *First Steps in Community Center Development* (New York: Department of Recreation, 1916), p. 3.

125  C. J. Bushnell, 'The Community Center Movement as a Moral Force,' *International Journal of Ethics*, 30:3 (1920), p. 327.

126  Finding aid, 'L.A. Gay and Lesbian Center Records,' ONE Archives, prepared by Michael P. Palmer (2007), http://pdf.oac.cdlib.org/pdf/calaong/2007–010_gcsc. pdf (accessed 10 October 2017).

127  Ibid.

128  'Articles of Incorporation of The Gay Community Services Center,' 22 July 1971, in 'L.A. Gay and Lesbian Center Records,' ONE Archives, box 1, folder 1, p. 1. Of course, as will be explored later in this book, such unity of purpose did not mean that there was not significant turbulence in the community center's early years— a series of protests, both official and unofficial, marked the center's fourth year of operations, evidencing struggles over 'worker control, patriarchal management systems, racism, sexism, classism, and the like.' Ed Culp, 'Letter and Chronology of Recent Events at the Gay Community Services Center,' 29 March 1975, in 'L.A. Gay and Lesbian Center Records,' ONE Archives, box 1, folder 24, p. 1.

129  Burns and Steiner, 'Cliffs Notes on Community Action Center,' p. 2.

130  A. K. Burns, interview with author, 12 May 2012.

131  Burns confirmed that the wall collages and sculptural elements in the Horton Gallery, and all subsequent installations, were conceived and completed almost separately within the Burns and Steiner collaboration. A. K. Burns, interview with author, 12 May 2012.

132  Monique Wittig and Sande Zeig, *Lesbian Peoples: Material for a Dictionary* (New York: Avon, 1979).

# Conclusion: surrogates, envelopes

It may sound obvious, but what I mean is: sex is sex. What I don't mean is sex is sea birds eating the entrails of live turtles. Of course, you could consider that was sex by construing it as a sadistic metaphor. But then, you see, then it would not be horrid, it would be *yummy*.

Parker Tyler[1]

Nearly a decade ago when I asked Monica Majoli about her series of watercolor and gouache paintings of rubbermen—figures encased in fetish rubberwear (figure 9.1)—she described them to me as 'surrogates' for herself, 'envelopes' for thoughts and feelings.[2] It was not immediately clear to me what she meant by calling her large works on paper 'surrogates' and 'envelopes,' though I left our conversation with a sense of her deep commitment to the subjects (people) she paints. She echoed her sentiment elsewhere, writing, 'as I continued to paint I slowly realized that I was identifying, uncomfortably so, with the masochist in the compositions.'[3] Her evocative descriptions of her practice and its effects on her own identifications continued to unsettle me, and I now realize that this is because I was engaged in a similar process. At the time when I met Majoli I didn't identify as a leatherman, but my close study and enthusiastic drive to gather research material suggested that I was invested to a great degree, both professionally and personally. As Majoli's work was an act of surrogacy and self-discovery, so too, over the years, has her work become a 'surrogate' and 'envelope' for my own relationship with leather communities and sexuality.

For some, this admission may severely undercut the credibility of anything I might now say about Majoli's paintings—but this would be to ignore the insights and work of our feminist, POC, and queer forebears who locate a sustained critique of culture within the personal that supports, augments, and countervails notions of personal responsibility, desire, and need. Audre Lorde famously wrote of how 'personal visions help lay the groundwork for political action,' and Rita Felski, following her, speaks of affinity as a pleasurable 'puzzle for investigation,' rather than a reason for dismissal from

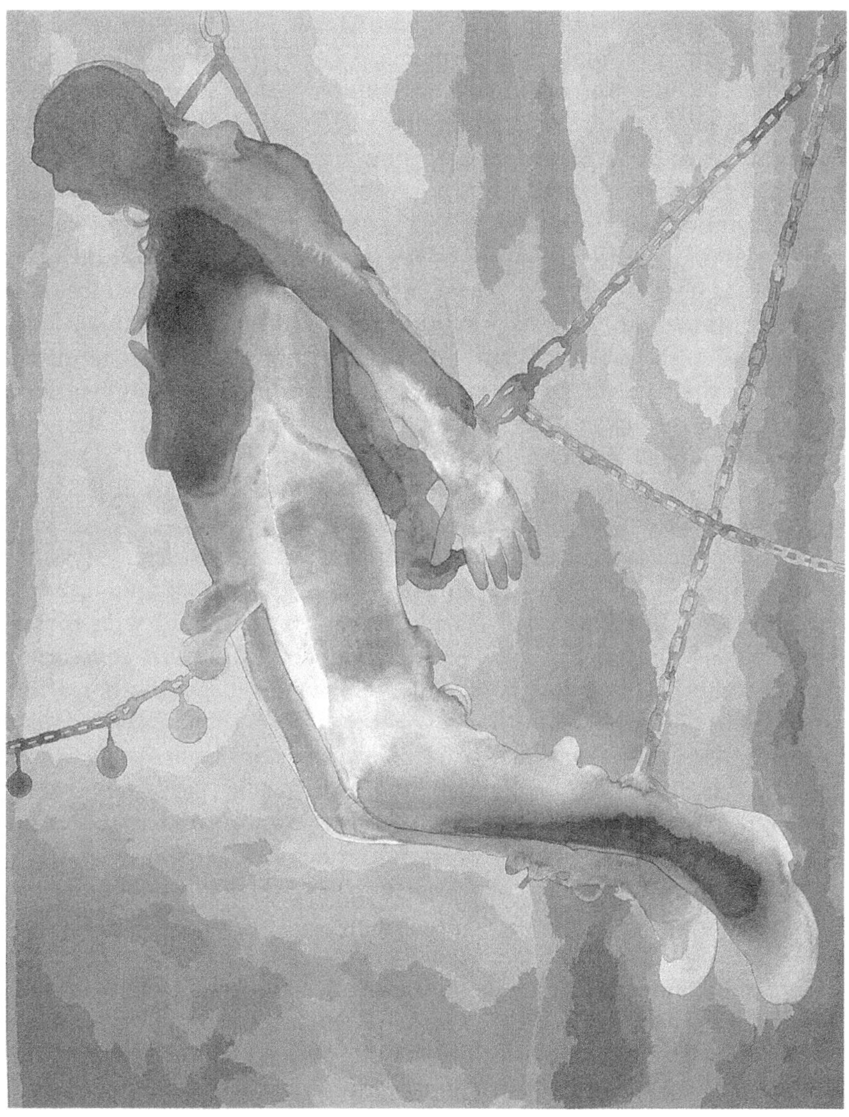

Monica Majoli, *Hanging Rubberman #2*, 2003, watercolor and gouache on paper,
64 x 51 in.



**9.1**

consideration or criticality.[4] In concluding this book with a rumination on Majoli's work I hope to also turn a lens back on myself, on the archive I've assembled while writing this book, and on the transformative capacities that accompany identification with another within and outside the scene of sex—a practice some might call love.

Years after my initial conversation with Majoli, I happened to be reading Roland Barthes's assemblage of fragments, *A Lover's Discourse*. The occasion was a book group convened by a friend who hoped to stage an adaptation of *The Pillow Book*, an eleventh-century collection of poems, stories, and essays authored by Sei Shōnagon describing court life in Heian Japan. While dutifully reading one particular passage of Barthes's text, it immediately called to mind Majoli's notion of surrogacy; in it, Barthes begins with an urge, a common desire. 'I want to be the other,' he writes, 'I want the other to be me, as if we were united.'[5] He imagines himself with the amorous other 'enclosed in the same sack of skin'; this new 'garment' a 'smooth envelope of that coalescent substance out of which my amorous Image-repertoire is made.'[6] Barthes's conceit of the Image-repertoire, while never fully explained, is essentially the internal archivization of every pang of desire, amorous intention, and self-shattering moment within and outside of the other's/ lover's embrace. The term names the constitutive force around which Barthes organizes his aleatory exegesis on love.

It is also an apt term for describing Majoli's oeuvre, which, at the time of this writing, encompasses four distinct series of works spanning nearly three decades. In paintings of friends, unknown men encased in rubber, ex-girlfriends, and most recently, gay porn models, Majoli has consistently plumbed the reconstitutive possibilities of loving others. She bores into what Barthes describes as the 'raving energy' of love, robbing it of some of its reckless velocity along the way. Her paintings are labored, made over months, sometimes years, with methodical intentionality, suggesting that the same intensity might be required from a viewer. Majoli's preferred medium changes with each new body of work, and so her series are not only distinguishable by content, but also by their materiality, which no doubt influences other decisions regarding scale, color, framing, and the like.

I want to address, most specifically, the first two of these series—a group of untitled paintings of gay male orgies and close-up body parts (1990–98), and the subsequent series of 'Rubbermen' (1999–2007)—as complementary projects that limn what it is to love another—friend and/or stranger. This is done through the primary relational position of the masochist, which is the anchor of Majoli's Image-repertoire. Here, self and other(s) are encased, bound together in difference.

Majoli's first works, completed in the 1990s, are diminutive panel paintings, rendered in layers of oil glazes, not dissimilar to the process used by many Northern Renaissance painters. As a series, these paintings are split in their focus. Some render vulnerable parts of the body—a nape, an exposed wrist, a sternum—in close-up (figure 9.2). In these paintings the skin proves to be a flimsy covering for the viscera beneath; veins and arteries channel atop muscle and bone in a biological burlesque. Blood has spilled out, coagulated,

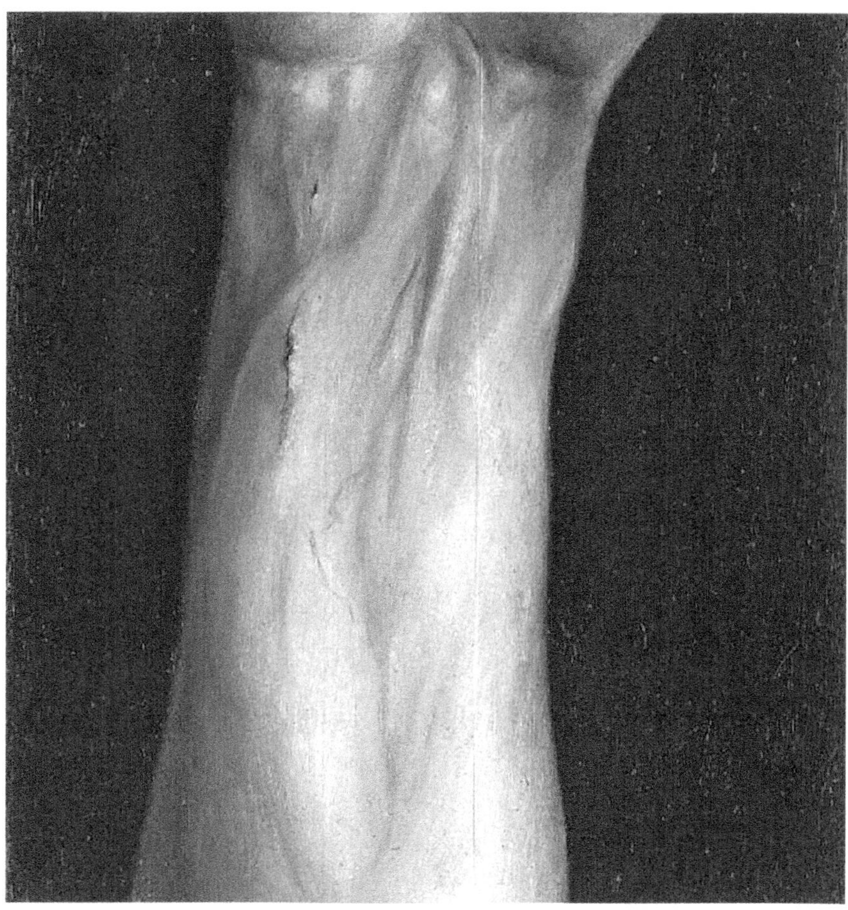

Monica Majoli, *Untitled (wrist)*, 1990, oil on panel, 5.5 x 6 in.    **9.2**

and scabbed over a vertical cut in *Untitled (wrist)* (1990). Nearby scars indicate that each new wound is a version of older ones. Figured against a black background, Majoli presents this fragmented body part at nearly life-size, terminating the image at the top of the panel, the point at which the wrist ends and the soft, fleshy padding of the palm begins. The cleft of the palm corresponds to a subtle conjoining of veins near the bottom of the panel, creating a vulvic enclosure within the rounded limits of the arm.

Other works in this series depict orgies of men, often wearing leather, sometimes pissing on each other (figure 9.3). A blonde-headed figure reappears with some frequency in these paintings, and this is Majoli's friend, Paul Wood.[7] Of these paintings Majoli writes:

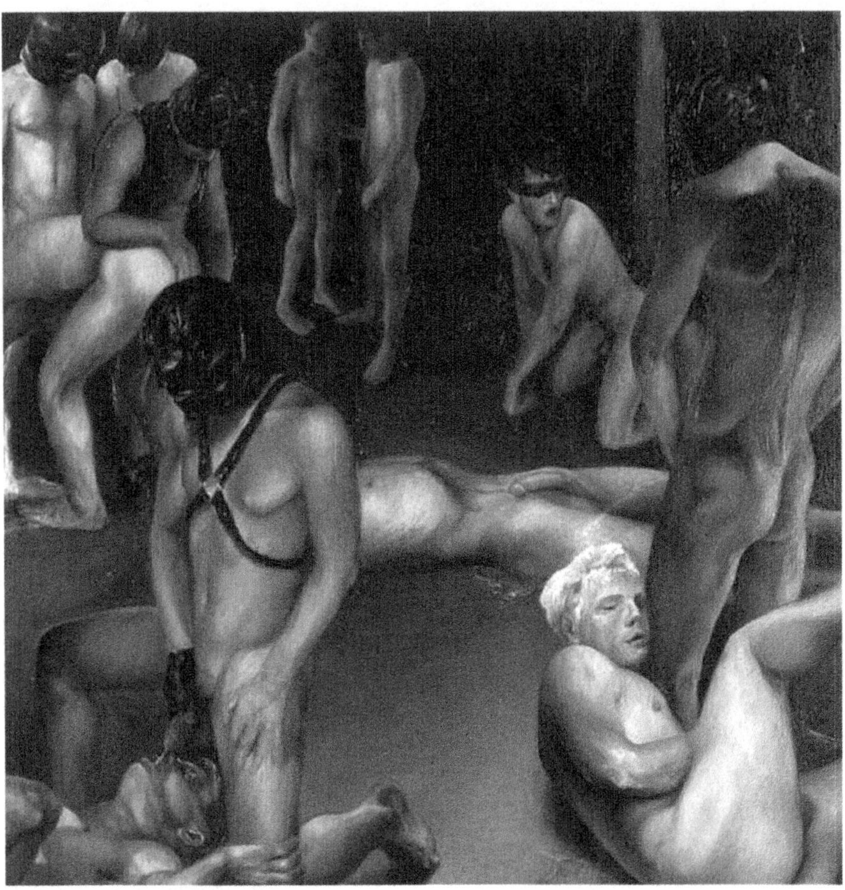

**9.3**     Monica Majoli, *Untitled (piss orgy)*, 1990, oil on panel, 12 x 12 in.

The male sex scenes began when a close friend of mine started to go to underground piss parties and became increasingly involved with S/M sex. I had always been fascinated by his anonymous encounters with men. I envied the nonverbal quality and the absolute sexual abandon of his experiences. AIDS confused all this—and I began to wonder about this decision to pursue this despite the consequences.[7]

Wood seroconverted after Majoli began to paint his sexual experiences, and this transformation in the life of her friend instantiated a crisis for Majoli as well, newly rendering these paintings as premature memorials to the future loss of her friend. As Majoli relayed in our initial interview, 'The impetus behind doing those paintings was that I felt he wouldn't be alive. I really thought he might be gone in a year's time, I had no idea. Part of the reason was to memorialize him. It seems an odd thing to memorialize someone in this way.'[8] Reading these diminutive paintings, personal in both their scale and subject, as memorials *and* as documents of Wood's lived experiences is to acknowledge both his life and Majoli's sense of future survivorship—an asynchronous temporality central to those who care for those living with HIV/AIDS, and other terminal or long-term degenerative conditions. Despite her anxieties, to memorialize Wood as she does in another painting in the same series, *Untitled* (1990), is to acknowledge and validate the ways in which her friend found pleasure. In this regard, Majoli's paintings of Wood's experiences are profound treatises on friendship, empathy, and the creative possibilities of sexual life.

During the making of the series her artistic collaboration with Wood continued to grow, and soon Majoli began to ask him to pose as he recollected his experiences, taking photos of his reenactments. These photos served as referents, guiding the making of future works in the series. Painting figures from source photographs is not a process unique to Majoli, but in this context the process places emphasis on Wood's somatic and performance-based retellings of a (recent) past. In this way Majoli's early oil paintings are thrice mediated images, encompassing a retelling (Wood relating), a restaging (Majoli posing Wood) and a rerepresentation (Majoli painting) of another's experience.

Wood's orgiastic recountings enabled Majoli to first imagine, and then realize, her own masochistic fantasies. Her process was relayed to me as an uncomfortable identification—one that ruptured and reconfigured her sense of self and art. Reflecting her growing self-awareness as well as the devastating dissolution of an intimate partner relationship, the final examples of these early works are a sequence of arresting self-portraits wherein the artist handles, fucks, and adores sex toys in the absence of the lover.

Although I typically abjure psychoanalytic readings of artists' intentions, moving away from the kind of overdetermined and flat appraisal of artworks that Mieke Bal terms 'biographism,' Majoli readily invites this mode of thinking about her work by speaking and writing candidly about her motivations and her attractions to her painted others.[9] And while it is true that 'all bodies are vulnerable to the affect of others,' Majoli merits the label of 'vulnerability artist,' which queer theorist José Esteban Muñoz bestowed upon performance artist Nao Bustamante for her capacity to erect 'strange monument[s] to the sad beauty of reparation.'[10] This reparation—whose model resides in the psychoanalytic work of Melanie Klein—is a productive force that reshapes and resignifies one's subjectivity in relation to an other, or to a group of others, a schematic that rhymes with the scene of the piss orgies Majoli paints.[11]

Leo Bersani, in writing about psychoanalytic (mis)understandings of (gay male) homosexuality and sadomasochistic practice, insightfully suggests that a 'certain rhythm of mastery and surrender' is knitted into the very structures of the epistemic project of Freudian psychoanalysis.[12] This would seem then to call for an analysis of sadomasochistic practice as suspended between these two dyadic positions, the co-constituitive forces of sadistic mastery and masochistic surrender. But for Bersani, and also for the philosopher Gilles Deleuze, masochism remains primary in discussions of sadomasochism.[13] Deleuze, in reviewing the literature of Leopold von Sacher-Masoch, makes categorical distinctions between the forces that animate the Austrian writer's work and those that animate the nearly torturous sex described at length in the novels of the Marquis de Sade.[14] He suggests that sadism and masochism are foundationally distinct, and thus should not be brought together in the creation of a 'sadomasochistic entity.'[15] From a literary perspective he couldn't be more right; but within the sexual practice of leather he couldn't be more wrong. I'll have more to say about this below. Bersani likewise privileges the subjectivity-annihilating capacities of masochism—where one is put entirely at the service of someone else's will—remarking that the masochist is ultimately 'unfindable as an object of discipline.'[16] The sadist, on the other hand, is more than findable, being 'fully complicit with the culture of death.'[17]

But this understanding of sadism and masochism, which sees one as productive and the other as destructive (and never the twain shall meet), is a futile attempt to divide that which is already enmeshed. In Majoli's paintings of herself—especially those where she uses dildos to penetrate herself—the masochist and sadist positions are presented within a single figure, suggesting their interdependence and interchangeability.

This shuttling between the seemingly dyadic positions of sadism and masochism within the singular is a central idea in Majoli's subsequent series, the large gouache and watercolor 'Rubbermen.' Comprised of both large and small-scale works, Majoli's 'Rubbermen' are best understood as a sequence of single-figure compositions. In the largest works, rubbermen hang from ropes and chains in an ambiguous space; in the smallest they strip their rubber suits from their bodies and play with their cocks against the ground of the paper. Never are they with others—rather their relationality is implicitly restated within the relationship of art viewing; viewer and image become sadist and masochist.

Like the previous orgy paintings, this series begins with Majoli's connection with another person, this time a near-stranger named Peter Tolos, who was well-known under the pseudonym Rubber Bear within rubber fetish communities. Tolos was respected for his facility with industrial rubber, both within rubber communities as the publisher and editor of the magazine *Rubber Rebel* (1993–96), and outside of them as a technical expert on Hollywood movie sets that required rubber-oriented special effects. Majoli initially found his work in an issue of *Rubber Rebel* magazine that she had collected. Shortly thereafter she contacted him to inquire about the photographs that appeared in the magazine—many of which Tolos had set up and shot himself. During their meeting Majoli purchased a small stack of these photographs, and these were used as inspiration for the 'Rubbermen' compositions. Soon after their meeting Tolos died of a heart attack. In attempting to move away from paintings that speculatively mourned the death of her close friend, Majoli's new series was returned, unexpectedly, to the scene of mourning—this time for someone she didn't know as well. What remained of this relationship was a small archive: some magazines and a few photographs.

Throughout this book I have tried to pay attention to the various things that happen to dead people's stuff. Whether it gets displayed as art, collected into institutional or personal archives, or thrown away has a lot to do with how the past is understood and valued. Death is the kind of event that can radically reorient interpretations of such archival materials—especially if the death is sudden, unexpected, or violent. I wonder, then, what will become of these photographs once Majoli is no longer living? How will they be interpreted? More than compositional devices, these photographs would best be considered affective touchstones of a newly formed relationship that changed the course of Majoli's life and work.

With *Rubber Rebel* magazine, Tolos sought to communicate to an audience whose desires he projected as largely contiguous with his own. In his first editorial, Rubber Bear cast his net fairly wide, calling forth his readership generically as 'those of us with bizarre tastes, wants, and fantasies.'[18] Like other leather publications such as *Drummer* and *DungeonMaster*, *Rubber Rebel* offered its subscribers the opportunity to buy specialized gear and gave its readers a forum for the expression of a particularized fetish. There is some indication that at the time he was publishing *Rubber Rebel* the fetish was *too* niche, as Tolos spends significant editorial column space imploring readers for their submissions.

A complex photo essay printed in *Rubber Rebel*'s second issue (figure 9.4) is exemplary of the sophistication and playfulness of Tolos's editorial work. The photo essay is dedicated to the erotics of 'layering' several rubber garments one atop the other.[19] If this causes a reader of *Rubber Rebel* pause or anxiety, Rubber Bear preemptively assures them, 'You are in there, somewhere, consumed and engulfed in the rubber you love.'[20] The photo essay follows the involved sequence of layering a single rubberman. It begins with a man donning rubber shorts. In short order he has added three full-body rubber suits. He is outfitted with a bondage mask, complete with breath-constricting gags, before he is taken to a backyard pool for a dip. There he 'revels in his rubber solitude,' before being buttoned into a Russian diving suit.[21] While enclosed in the 'green rubberized fabric' of this suit he 'feels one with this diving ghost as he moves his constricted body.'[22] Finally, he puts on a silver proximity suit,

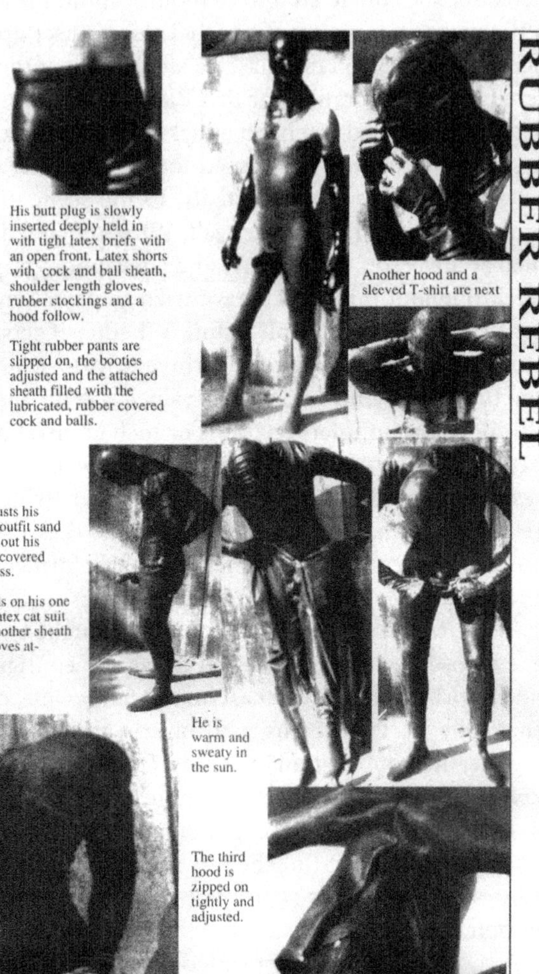


**9.4**    Peter Tolos (AKA Rubber Bear), 'Layering,' *Rubber Rebel*, 1:2 (1993)

typically used by firemen for extreme heat environments. There is pleasure in this as Tolos writes that 'he comes as he places the shimmering helmet over his diving mask.' In this way he is 'deep in rubber, encased in ecstacy.'[23]

Certain photographs in this editorial spread were used to make the earliest works in Majoli's 'Rubbermen' series—a suite of fifteen small watercolor and

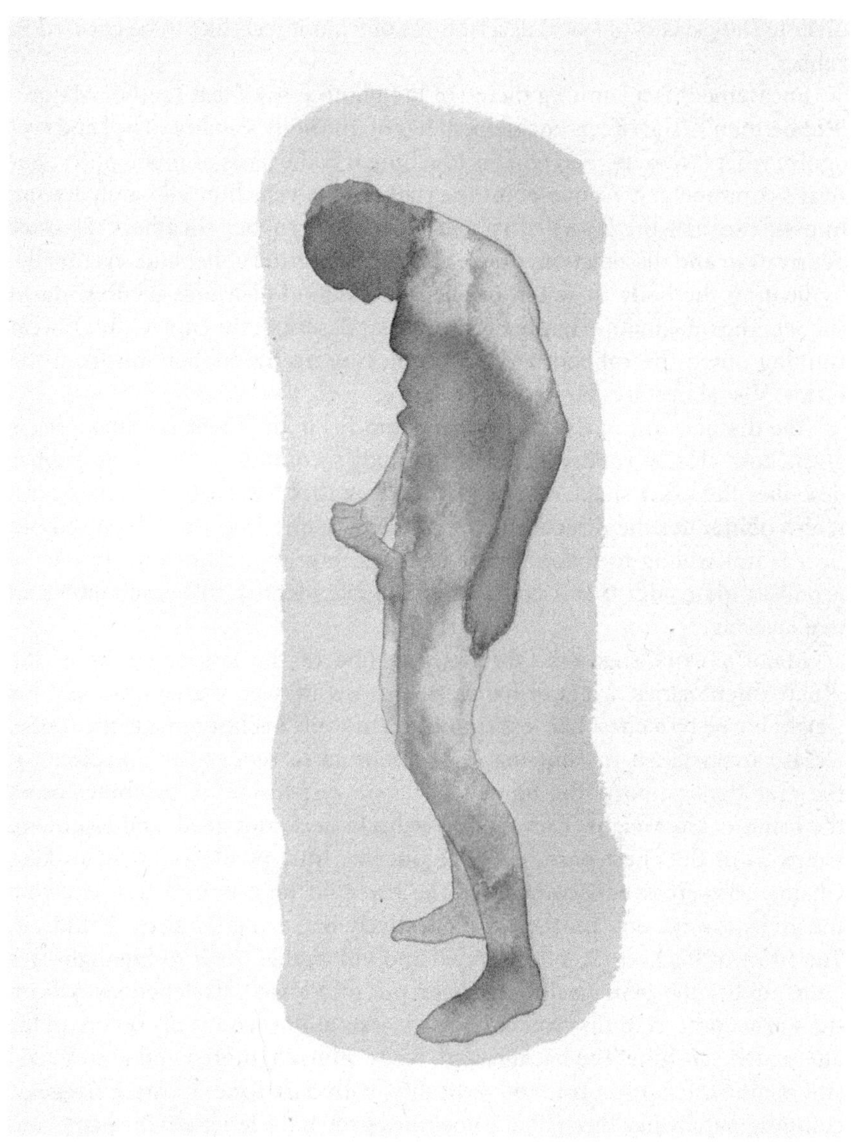

Monica Majoli, *Rubbermen* (11 of 15), watercolor and gouache on paper, 1999–2000,    **9.5**
14 x 10 in.

gouache works on paper (figure 9.5). But beyond the hide-n-seek pleasure of finding formal correspondences between Majoli's paintings and her source material, Tolos's photo essay offers an interpretive guide for Majoli's series— from his evocative somatic conjuring of the 'ghost' of a generic Russian diver to the psycho-physical descriptions of what it feels like to be encased in rubber.

Encasement is a running theme of the photo essay's text (and of Majoli's 'Rubbermen'). The effects encasement has on the body's ability to feel and recognize what it touches and what is touching it is the basis of much of Rubber Bear's commentary. At one point the rubberman 'rubs himself barely feeling himself through the layers of rubber gloves and rubber sheaths.'[24] Sensory deprivation and dissociation, exacerbated by layers of rubber and, eventually, by floating the body in water, is one of the stated pleasures of dressing in rubber. The imagination ignites: Rubber Bear describes the (not-visible) sweat running down the rubberman's body, slicking up his rubber suit from the inside. Visual opacity clarifies erotic desire.

The dissociation of the rubberman from his body might not make sense given how closely rubber hews to the body's contours—but while rubber describes the exact shape of a body (in a way that few other materials can), it also obliterates the direct sense of connection one feels to it. Even Rubber Bear is not willing to follow the self-obliterating implications of this, as he promises his reader that a cohesive and stable identity still exists under all that layering.

Majoli's work suggests otherwise. In one of the largest works in the 'Rubbermen' series, a figure hangs suspended in a gray-green morass, his weight borne by a chest harness connected to some anchor outside the frame. Great care is taken in *Hanging Rubberman #2* to render the intricacies of the gear that supports the figure's virtuosic suspension. A carabiner bears the brunt of the weight from the upper back, neck and head, and elsewhere straps from the chest harness flange out like little phalluses about to kiss. Chains criss-cross and connect to the backs of boot-bound feet, drawing the limbs toward one another, and effectively hog-tying the man in mid-air. The front of his body is left extended and vulnerable. As if to highlight this vulnerability the man's balls have been put into a vice, stretched away from the warm comfort of his crotch. His cock rests almost comically on top of his attenuated scrotum. The background, while 'blurred, muted and abstracted,' still retains the faintest trace of verticality, with dark tones creating irregular columns, patchy like birch, that sometimes stretch the length of the paper and sometimes dissolve before reaching either the bottom or top of the composition. Studies for *Hanging Rubberman #2* reveal the background to be a dense forest of trees.

Here medium and subject matter are brought into direct coordination: Majoli has described the series as exploring a 'fluid, disembodied consciousness encased within a confining structure.'[25] This sense of ambiguous fluidity is perhaps most evident in the material vacillation between the transparent (watercolor) and the opaque (gouache) media Majoli uses. But it is also present in the varied applications of these media within the limits of the represented body and outside of it. Within the body different shades of green—sea-soaked algae and dull mints—bleed into one another. Outside the body colors are stacked and layered in jagged forms reminiscent of the abstract and jagged edges of a Clyfford Still painting. Taken together these aspects dramatize the disjuncture between 'exterior and interior dimension[s].'[26]

Rubber as an eroticized material has circulated within leather literature for some time—with possible origins in the UK in the late 1950s.[27] In 1972, Larry Townsend mentions the existence of 'rubber publications' and suppliers in *The Leatherman's Handbook*.[28] Although he admits to thinking less of his brothers in rubber, Townsend eventually acquiesces that the practices of men into leather and men into rubber are 'very much the same,' further stating that 'it is mostly a matter of the fetish being focused on one material instead of the other.'[29] Townsend coordinates difference and affinity under the umbrella of leathersex.

Understanding suspension—the activity depicted in *Hanging Rubberman #2*—is also key to interpreting the 'Rubbermen' as a surrogate for Majoli's masochist identification. *Hanging Rubberman #2* presents a scenario outlined in an article by Jack Fritscher that appeared in *Drummer*, entitled 'Bondage: Blest be the Tie That Binds.'[30] The dialogic tone of the article is supplemented with a suite of photographs taken by Fritscher and David Sparrow. Some of these photos feature Fritscher, bound, hooded, and suspended from the ceiling.[31] Although he does not wear rubber, these photographs are striking in their visual similarity to Majoli's composition (a photograph from the same article also features in a painting by Dean Sameshima). Photographed against a flat, white wall, the bound figure appears to hang in a void-like space, not dissimilar to Majoli's hanging rubberman. Straps splay off from the line of the body, visually rhyming with Fritscher's exposed cock. For Fritscher, as well as for Majoli, this is key: 'Vulnerability. That's what most bondage masters want, because the master is going to make the guy even more vulnerable.'[32] This vulnerability is matched in Majoli's oeuvre—from the early exposed body parts to later paintings of ex-girlfriends reflected in the dark mirrors of the artist's bedroom.

Other leather writers have discussed suspension as an important practice in leathersex. Tony DeBlase, for example, wrote about suspension, and the technical equipment needed to do it right in the pages of *DungeonMaster*.[33] As with much of what he wrote for *DungeonMaster*, his concerns are primarily technical and safety-oriented. He warns that precaution must be taken when suspending someone from an exposed beam, a ceiling, or a tree branch: 'Raise him slowly, make certain that the restraints are not cutting too much, and this his body is being strained only in the ways that you had intended it to be.'[34] DeBlase highlights that the radical vulnerability described by Fritscher must be met by an equal dose of preparation and care from the sadist. This sadist, it should be noted—caring and careful—is far from the sadist discussed in Deleuze and Bersani's writings.

Townsend and DeBlase, for as much as they are different in their approach and general assessment of leather, share in the belief that to be an empowered and effective sadist, one must first occupy the masochist's position. Or as Townsend writes, 'the M component is there in all of us, whether manifestly displayed or not.'[35] In his view the experience of being a masochist is always embedded within the practice of sadism, and serves as the stop-gap between erotic possibility and nonconsensual, sociopathic cruelty. This would suggest that a viewer of Majoli's 'Rubbermen' is meant to both identify with the encased figure and the absent sadist, understanding these positions as profoundly relational, and equally caring, loving, and sexy.

In this sense Majoli's 'Rubbermen' are emblematic of the larger aim of this book, which has been to discuss artistic practices that relate the tensions in archival research and the objects one finds there to questions of identity and its politics. Over time I have deeply internalized Majoli's work and its operations, which is to say that, for me, Majoli's 'Rubbermen' have become surrogates for my own sexuality. She has modeled for me what interrogating interest and affinity might do to an otherwise stable subject-position—a method for making oneself vulnerable via the social and cultural accouterments that otherwise bind, suspend, and tie one up. While the outlines of these nodes of power and pleasure seem distinct, their effects are more nebulous—as subtle as the watery collision of two similar, yet distinct shades of gray-green. That I emerge from my encounters with Majoli's 'Rubbermen' less certain of the boundaries of my own desires is, for me, a mark of their success.

When I visit Majoli again, years later, we are in her studio looking at new work: large woodblock prints of famous, mononymous, gay porn models named Roger and Ted. On the floor and on large worktables are piles of gay pornographic magazines: *Blueboy* and *Inches*. The years of the issues Majoli has collected signal a change in the aesthetics of the gay pornographic body, from the hairy men of the 1970s and early 1980s to the plucked-smooth, twinky and hunky bodies of the 1990s.

By dint of necessity Majoli has become a collector of the histories she is interested in. Somewhere in her studio she still keeps the *Rubber Rebel* magazines and the small group of photographs she bought from Rubber Bear. Although this is true to a greater or lesser degree of any artist or writer with a significant research practice, for those who study subjugated knowledges and communities the task of gathering sources can be both methodologically fraught and pleasurable. We gather and store our stuff so that we can make the arguments we need—the instantiation of archives is only one response to a profound sense of unease we have about the past and its peculiar effects in the present. Looking across the stacks of magazines in Majoli's studio is a visual reminder of the unceasing physical labor and spatial tetris-ing of gathering, collecting, and archiving. In the end only a few images will be good enough for Majoli to work with.

I can relate. Over the course of a decade I have collected and archived an array of magazines, documents, and ephemera, now divided out in hundreds of manila folders. Each is carefully labeled. I have carried these folders with me on planes, ferrying them back and forth between home and work. The edges of the folders have become worn and cloth-like over the years, but their contents remain protected. Some are Xeroxes of Xeroxes, others original documents. The chapters in this book tell only a fraction of the stories housed in this evolving and ever-more unruly professional, yet also distinctly personal, archive.

It is a point of connection and pride when I visit with long-time pillars of leather communities, as each has their own collection of similar materials, and I am always in awe of their (dis)ordered array. Some of these archives are stored away in closets or attics, and a few have their own dedicated space where items are carefully placed in archival boxes in climate-controlled rooms. Some, like Viola Johnson, take their archives on the road, but most choose for the sake of ease to keep them sedentary. Such archives change shape slowly over the years—with additions and expurgations here and there. They can also change suddenly with a person's death—relegated to the trash, divided up among friends and (chosen) family, or stewarded into institutions where someone like myself might one day access their contents. Some, such as Jeanne Barney's archives discussed in the first chapter, are woefully split asunder, perhaps never to be reassembled again.

Majoli's evocative description of herself as a surrogate, a carrier who embodies multiple presences within her practice, is an enduring descriptive model for the archival histories I have attempted to write throughout this book—at once aware of the original contexts of particular sources, while also attentive to the ways contemporary artists have shifted and amplified their contextual, archival placements.

When Leo Bersani writes that 'to be a woman in a man's body is certainly an imprisoning definition, but at least it leaves open the possibility to wonder, as Freud did, about the various desiring positions a woman might take,' he is referring to Freud's supposition regarding the psychically gendered character of male homosexuality.[36] But these words could equally, and perversely, describe Majoli's process in making her 'Rubbermen,' and as such they clarify the political stakes of Majoli's experiments with surrogate subjectivity. The 'Rubbermen' present only one avenue through which desiring positions might multiply beyond handy transcriptions of gay or lesbian identities, and into something more manifold and compound; more queer and less sure.

And here a question remains: Who, after all, is the encased lover? To answer that we would need a discourse that valued the gifts of surrogacy and the conditions of loss in equal measure. History is one word for it, love another.

## Notes

1 Parker Tyler, *Screening the Sexes: Homosexuality in the Movies* (New York: Da Capo Press, 1993), p. 311.
2 Monica Majoli, interview with author, 17 November 2009.
3 Monica Majoli, 'Letter to Florence,' *Air de Paris*, n.d., http://www.airdeparis.com/past/majoli.htm (accessed 10 October 2017).
4 Audre Lorde, 'The Master's Tools Will Never Dismantle the Master's House,' in Cherríe Moraga and Gloria Anzaldúa (eds.), *This Bridge Called My Back: Writings by Radical Women of Color* (New York: Kitchen Table Press, 1983); Rita Felski, 'After Suspicion,' *Profession* (2009), p. 32.
5 Roland Barthes, *A Lover's Discourse: Fragments*, trans. Richard Howard (New York: Hill and Wang, 1978), pp. 127–8.
6 Ibid.
7 Majoli, 'Letter to Florence.'
8 Majoli, interview with author, 17 November 2009.
9 Bal, 'Autotopography.'
10 José Esteban Muñoz, 'The Vulnerability Artist: Nao Bustamante and the Sad Beauty of Reparation,' *Women and Performance*, 16:2 (2006), pp. 191–200.
11 Muñoz, 'The Vulnerability Artist'; also see Sedgwick, 'Paranoid Reading and Reparative Reading.'
12 Bersani, *Homos*, p. 98.
13 Ibid., p. 95.
14 Gilles Deleuze, 'Coldness and Cruelty,' in *Masochism* (New York: Zone Books, 1991), pp. 15–138.
15 Ibid., p. 32.
16 Bersani, *Homos*, pp. 99, 97.
17 Ibid.
18 Rubber Bear (Peter Tolos), 'Editorial: Why Gear? A Personal Fantasy,' *Rubber Rebel*, 1:1 (1993), p. 1.
19 Rubber Bear (Peter Tolos), 'Layering,' *Rubber Rebel*, 1:2 (1993), pp. 4–8.
20 Ibid., p. 4.
21 Ibid., pp. 6–7
22 Ibid., p. 7.
23 Ibid., p. 8.
24 Ibid., p. 5.
25 Monica Majoli, 'Identity, Intimacy and Mortality,' *Corpus*, 4:1 (2006), p. 47.
26 Ibid.

27 The earliest fetish rubber catalogs I've been able to find are the Richwear/Sealwear catalogs from 1959.
28 Townsend, *The Leatherman's Handbook*, pp. 230–1.
29 Ibid., p. 230.
30 Jack Fritscher, 'Bondage: Blest Be the Tie That Binds,' *Drummer* 3:24 (1978), pp. 16–23, 76.
31 Jack Fritscher, 'Mondo Bondage 1978,' http://jackfritscher.com/PDF/Drummer/Draft_Issues/024/Mondo%20Bondage%201978-B.pdf (accessed 10 October 2017).
32 Fritscher, 'Bondage,' p. 21.
33 Fledermaus (Tony DeBlase), 'The Safety Valve,' *DungeonMaster*, 1:4 (1980), p. 6.
34 Ibid.
35 Townsend, *The Leatherman's Handbook*, pp. 28–9.
36 Bersani, *Homos*, p. 106.

# Select bibliography


'107 Officers Used in Mark IV Raid, Police Papers Reveal,' *NewsWest*, 25 June 1976, p. 3.

Acuña, Rodolfo, *Occupied America: A History of Chicanos*, 7th edn (Boston: Longman, 2011).

Agamben, Giorgio, *Remnants of Auschwitz: The Witness and the Archive* (New York: Zone Books, 1999).

Ahmed, Sarah, 'In the Name of Love,' *borderlands*, 2:3 (2003), http://www.borderlands.net.au/vol2no3_2003/ahmed_love.htm (accessed 10 October 2017).

*Al's Male Video Guide* (New York: Midway Publications, 1986).

Allsop, Laura, 'What He Loved: Dean Sameshima,' *Art Review*, 10 (2007), p. 34.

Alpers, Svetlana, 'The Museum as a Way of Seeing,' in Ivan Karp and Steven D. Lavine (eds.), *Exhibiting Cultures: The Poetics and Politics of Museum Display* (Washington DC: Smithsonian Institution Press, 1991), pp. 25–32.

Alphen, Ernst van, 'Archival Obsessions and Obsessive Archives,' in Michael Ann Holly and Marquard Smith (eds.), *What is Research in the Visual Arts? Obsession, Archive, Encounter* (Williamstown, MA: Sterling and Francine Clark Art Institute, 2008), pp. 65–84.

American Psychological Association, *Diagnostic and Statistical Manual of Mental Disorders*, 5th edn (Washington DC: American Psychological Association, 2013).

Anderson, Benedict, *Imagined Communities: Reflections on the Origin and Spread of Nationalism* (London: Verso, 1991).

Andrews, Nigel, 'Tom of Finland—A Lugubrious Biopic,' *Financial Times*, 10 August 2017, www.ft.com/content/b2ee4372-7dd8-11e7-ab01-a13271d1ee9c (accessed 10 October 2017).

Appadurai, Arjun, 'Archive and Aspiration,' in Joke Brouwer and Arjen Mulder (eds.), *Information is Alive* (Rotterdam: V2 Publishing/NAI Publishers, 2003), pp. 14–25.

Austin, J. L., *How to Do Things With Words*, 2nd edn, ed. J. O. Urmson and Marina Sabisà (Cambridge, MA: Harvard University Press, 1975).

Baim, Tracy, and Owen Keehnen, *Leatherman: The Legend of Chuck Renslow* (Chicago: Prairie Avenue Productions, 2011).

Bakewell, Elizabeth, William O. Beeman, and Carol McMichael Reese, *Object, Image, Inquiry: The Art Historian at Work* (Santa Monica, CA: J. Paul Getty Trust, 1988).

Bal, Mieke, 'Autotopography: Louise Bourgeois as Builder,' *Biography*, 25:1 (2002), pp. 180–202.

Baldwin, Guy, 'Old Guard: Its Origins, Traditions, Mystique and Rules,' *Drummer*, 150 (September 1991), pp. 23–5.

Barney, Jeanne, 'S&M: Out of the Closets and Onto the Campus,' *Drummer*, 1:1 (1975), p. 9.

Barthes, Roland, 'Death of an Author,' in *Image – Music – Text*, trans. Stephen Heath (London: Fontana, 1977), pp. 142–8.

——. *A Lover's Discourse: Fragments*, trans. Richard Howard (New York: Hill and Wang, 2010).

Bean, Joseph, 'Busy Building, Growing Community, … and Thank You!,' *The Leather Archives & Museum Newsletter*, 12 (summer 2000), p. 6.

——. 'Executive Director's Report,' *The Leather Archives & Museum Newsletter*, 4 (April 1998), pp. 1–2.

——. *International Mr. Leather: 25 Years of Champions* (Chicago: Leather Archives & Museum, 2004).

——. 'The Ongoing Adventures of Mr. Bean!!,' *The Leather Archives & Museum Newsletter*, 6 (fall 1998), pp. 1–3.

——. 'We've Got the Keys!! Say, "Hello, Honey, We're Home!",' *The Leather Archives & Museum Newsletter*, 9 (fall 1999), pp. 1–2.

Bennett, Tony, 'The Exhibitionary Complex,' *New Formations*, 4 (spring 1988), pp. 73–102.

Bergstrom-Katz, Sasha, 'Interview with Dean Sameshima,' *ArtSlant* (n.d.), https://www.artslant.com/ny/articles/show/2050 (accessed 10 October 2017).

Berlandt, Konstantin, 'An S&M Film the Whole Family Can Enjoy,' *Village Voice*, 2 June 1975, pp. 69–70.

Berlant, Lauren, *Desire/Love* (New York: Punctum Books, 2012).

Berlant, Lauren, and Lee Edelman, *Sex, or The Unbearable* (Durham, NC: Duke University Press, 2014).

Bersani, Leo, *Homos* (Cambridge, MA: Harvard University Press, 1995).

Berubé, Allan, 'The History of Gay Bathhouses,' in Dangerous Bedfellows (eds.), *Policing Public Sex: Queer Politics and the Future of AIDS Activism* (Boston: South End Press, 1996), pp. 187–220.

Best, Stephen, and Sharon Marcus, 'Surface Reading: An Introduction,' *Representations*, 108 (2009), pp. 1–21.

Blake, Nayland, 'Curating In a Different Light,' in Nayland Blake, Lawrence Rinder, and Amy Scholder (eds.), *In a Different Light* (San Francisco: City Lights Books, 1995), pp. 9–43.

——. 'Tom of Finland: An Appreciation,' *Out/Look* (fall 1988), pp. 36–45.

Blanchot, Maurice, 'From Dread to Language,' in *The Station Hill Blanchot Reader: Fiction and Literary Essays*, trans. Lydia Davis, Paul Auster, and Robert Lamberton (Barrytown, NY: Station Hill Press, 1998), pp. 343–58.

Blouin, Francis X. (ed.), *Archives, Documentation, and Institutions of Social Memory: Essays from the Sawyer Seminar* (Ann Arbor, MI: University of Michigan Press, 2006).

*The Blue Guide to Adult Male Films & Stars* (Ogdensburg, NJ: FD Enterprises, 1989).

Boime, Albert, 'Curriculum Vitae: The Course of Life in the Nineteenth Century,' in

*Strictly Academic: Life Drawing in the Nineteenth Century* (Binghamton, NY: State University at Binghamton, University Art Gallery, 1981), pp. 5–15.

Bordwell, David, 'The Hook: Scene Transitions in Classical Cinema,' January 2008, http://www.davidbordwell.net/essays/hook.php (accessed 10 October 2017).

Bourriaud, Nicolas, *Relational Aesthetics*, trans. Simon Pleasance et al. (Dijon: Les Presses du Réel, 2002).

Boxall, Bettina, 'A Look Ahead,' *Los Angeles Times*, 27 October 1997.

Bryan-Wilson, Julia, *Art Workers: Radical Practice in the Vietnam War Era* (Berkeley, CA: University of California Press, 2009).

Burns, A. K., and A. L. Steiner, 'Cliffs Notes on Community Action Center' (2010), http://akburns.net/wp-content/uploads/2015/06/zine_CAC_sm.pdf (accessed 10 October 2017).

Burton, Antoinette (ed.), *Archive Stories: Facts, Fiction, and the Writing of History* (Durham, NC: Duke University Press, 2005).

Bushnell, C. J., 'The Community Center Movement as a Moral Force,' *International Journal of Ethics*, 30:3 (1920), pp. 326–55.

Butler, Judith, *Gender Trouble: Feminism and the Subversion of Identity* (London: Routledge, 1990).

——. 'Performative Acts and Gender Constitution: An Essay in Phenomenology and Feminist Theory,' *Theatre Journal*, 40:4 (1988), pp. 519–31.

Byrne, Romana, *Aesthetic Sexuality: A Literary History of Sadomasochism* (London: Bloomsbury Academic, 2013).

Byron, Stuart, 'Brothers Under the Skinflick,' *Village Voice*, 20 July 1972, p. 57.

——. 'A Commonplace Press Handout on "L.A. Plays Itself" and "The Sex Garage",' 1972.

——. 'L.A. Plays Itself,' *The Real Paper*, 13 June 1973, p. 17.

Caddigan, Jack, and James Alexander Brennan, *The Rose of No Man's Land* (Boston: Jack Mendelsohn Music, 1918).

Califia, Pat, 'Beyond Leather: Expanding the Realm of the Senses to Latex' (1984), in *Public Sex: The Culture of Radical Sex* (Pittsburgh, PA: Cleis Press, 1994), pp. 190–8.

——. 'A Secret Side of Lesbian Sexuality,' *The Advocate*, 27 December 1979.

The Centers for Disease Control, '*Pneumocystis* Pneumonia—Los Angeles,' *Morbidity and Mortality Weekly Report*, 30:21 (1981), pp. 1–3.

Chapman, Kathleen, and Michael du Plessis, 'Queercore: The Distinct Identities of Subculture,' *College Literature*, 24:1 (1997), pp. 45–58.

Cohen, Ernest Peter, 'Interview: A Sadistic Homosexual Pornographer on Gay Liberation,' *Gay Activist*, 11 (April 1972), p. 11.

Comay, Rebecca (ed.), *Lost in the Archives* (Toronto: Alphabet City Media, 2002).

The Commission on Obscenity and Pornography, *The Report of the Commission on Obscenity and Pornography* (New York: Bantam Books, 1970).

Cook, J'aivette, 'Leather & Race: Where Do We Fit In?,' *Black Leather in Color*, 3 (fall 1994), p. 17.

Crimp, Douglas, 'Mourning and Militancy,' in *Melancholia and Moralism: Essays on AIDS and Queer Politics* (Cambridge, MA: MIT Press, 2002), pp. 129–50.

——. 'Mourning and Militancy,' *October*, 51 (winter 1989), p. 10.

Cvetkovich, Ann, *An Archive of Feelings: Trauma, Sexuality, and Lesbian Public Cultures* (Durham, NC: Duke University Press, 2003).

——. *Depression: A Public Feeling* (Durham, NC: Duke University Press, 2012).

Davis, E. M. (L.A.P.D. Chief of Police), letter to Sharon Cornelison (President, Christopher Street West Association), 23 May 1975, in *Christopher Street West Gay Pride*, www.leatherpage.com/columns/davolt/rd041203.htm (accessed 10 October 2017), *Celebration* [program] (1976), ONE Archives.

de Certeau, Michel, *The Writing of History*, trans. Tom Conley (New York: Columbia University Press, 1988).

Dean, Tim, *Unlimited Intimacy: Reflections on the Subculture of Barebacking* (Chicago: University of Chicago Press, 2009).

'Deep Fist At The Modern,' *Screw*, 29 April 1974, p. 11.

Dehner, Durk, 'Afterword' to F. Valentine Hooven, III, *Tom of Finland: Life and Work of a Gay Hero* (Berlin: Bruno Gmünder, 2012).

Deleuze, Gilles, 'Coldness and Cruelty,' in *Masochism* (New York: Zone Books, 1991), pp. 15–138.

——. *Foucault*, trans. Seán Hand (Minneapolis, MN: University of Minnesota Press, 1988).

'Demonstration,' *BDSM Wiki* (31 March 2014), http://bdsmwiki.info/Demonstration (accessed 10 October 2017).

Dennis, Kelly, *Art/porn: A History of Seeing and Touching* (Oxford: Berg, 2009).

Derrida, Jacques, 'Archive Fever: A Freudian Impression,' trans. Eric Prenowitz, *Diacritics*, 25:2 (1995), pp. 9–63.

DeVun, Leah, and Michael Jay McClure, 'Archives Behaving Badly,' *Radical History Review*, 120 (fall 2014), pp. 121–30.

Diefenbach, Katja, 'Fizzle Out in White: Postporn Politics and the Deconstruction of Fashion,' in Tim Stüttgen (ed.), *Post/Porn/Politics Reader: Queer Feminist Perspectives on the Politics of Porn Performance and Sex Work as Cultural Production* (Berlin: b.books, 2009), pp. 25–32.

Duncan, Carol, and Allan Wallach, 'The Museum of Modern Art as Late Capitalist Ritual: An Iconographic Analysis,' *Marxist Perspectives*, 1:4 (1978), pp. 28–51.

Dyer, Richard, 'Male Gay Porn: Coming to Terms,' *Jump Cut*, 30 (March 1985), pp. 27–9.

Edelman, Elijah Adiv, 'The Cum Shot: Trans Men and Visual Economies of Ejaculation,' *Porn Studies*, 2:2–3 (2015), pp. 150–60.

Eichhorn, Kate, 'Introduction: Radical Archives,' *Archive Journal* (November 2015), www.archivejournal.net/essays/radical-archives (accessed 10 October 2017).

——. *Outrage in Order: The Archival Turn in Feminism* (Philadelphia, PA: Temple University Press, 2013).

Elkins, James, *Pictures and Tears: A History of People Who Have Cried in Front of Paintings* (New York: Routledge, 2004).

Embry, John, 'Drummer Goes to a Slave Auction,' *Drummer*, 1:6 (1976), pp. 12–14.

Eskridge, William N., Jr., *Gaylaw: Challenging the Apartheid of the Closet* (Cambridge, MA: Harvard University Press, 1999).

Faderman, Lillian, and Stuart Timmons, *Gay L.A.: A History of Sexual Outlaws, Power Politics, and Lipstick Lesbians* (New York: Basic Books, 2006).

Fairbanks, Harold, 'Fred Halsted [obituary],' *The News*, 9 June 1989, p. 19.

Featherstone, Mike, 'Archive,' *Theory Culture Society*, 23:2–3 (2006), pp. 591–6.

Felski, Rita, 'After Suspicion,' *Profession* (2009), pp. 28–35.

——. *The Limits of Critique* (Chicago: University of Chicago Press, 2015).

Ferguson, Kathy E., 'Theorizing Shiny Things: Archival Labors,' *Theory & Event*, 11:4 (2008).

Fledermaus (Tony DeBlase), 'Getting Off,' *Drummer*, 11:100 (1986), p. 5.

——. 'The Safety Valve,' *DungeonMaster*, 1:4 (1980), pp. 5–6.

——. 'Sandmutopia,' *DungeonMaster*, 6 (September 1980), p. 10.

Flinn, Andrew, Mary Stevens, and Elizabeth Shepherd, 'Whose Memories, Whose Archives? Independent Community Archives, Autonomy and the Mainstream,' *Archival Science*, 9 (2009), pp. 71–86.

Florida Legislative Investigation Committee, *Homosexuality and Citizenship in Florida* (Tallahassee, FL, 1964).

Forbes, Dennis, and Fred Bisonnes, 'Tom of Finland – An Appreciation,' in *Tom of Finland: Retrospective* (Los Angeles: Tom of Finland Foundation, 1988), p. 5.

Foucault, Michel, *The Archaeology of Knowledge*, trans. Alan Sheridan Smith (New York: Harper & Row, 1972).

——. *Discipline and Punish: The Birth of the Prison*, trans. Alan Sheridan (New York: Vintage, 1995).

——. 'Friendship as a Way of Life,' in *Foucault Live (Interviews, 1961–1984)*, ed. Sylvère Lotringer, trans. John Johnston (New York: Semiotext(e), 1989), pp. 135–40.

——. 'Lives of Infamous Men,' in *Power*, vol. 3 of *Essential Works of Foucault, 1954–1984*, ed. James D. Faubion, trans. Robert Hurley (New York: New Press, 2000), pp. 157–75.

——. 'Nietzsche, Genealogy, History,' in *Aesthetics, Method, and Epistemology*, vol. 2 of *Essential Works of Foucault, 1954–1984*, ed. James D. Faubion, trans. Robert Hurley (New York: New Press, 1998), pp. 386–7.

——. 'Sex, Power and the Politics of Identity,' in *Ethics: Subjectivity and Truth*, vol. 1 of *Essential Works of Foucault, 1954–1984*, ed. Paul Rabinow, trans. Robert Hurley (New York: New Press, 2001), pp. 163–74.

——. 'Two Lectures' (1976), in *Power/Knowledge: Selected Interviews and Other Writings, 1972–1977*, ed. Colin Gordon (New York: Pantheon Books, 1980), pp. 78–108.

Fraker, Susan, with John Barnes, 'California: Of Human Bondage,' *Newsweek*, 26 April 1976, p. 35.

'"Free the Slaves" Benefit Show & Dance & Slave Auction' (event program, 23 April 1976), ONE Archives.

Freeman, Elizabeth, *Time Binds: Queer Temporalities, Queer Histories* (Durham, NC: Duke University Press, 2010).

Freud, Sigmund, 'Mourning and Melancholia,' in *A General Selection from the Works of Sigmund Freud*, ed. John Rickman (New York: Anchor Books, 1989), pp. 124–40.

——. 'A Note Upon the "Mystic Writing Pad"' (1925), in *The Standard Edition of the*

*Complete Psychological Works*, ed. and trans. James Strachey, vol. XIX (London: The Hogarth Press, 1961), pp. 227–32.

——. *Three Essays on the Theory of Sexuality (the 1905 edition)*, trans. Ulrike Kistner (New York: Verso, 2017).

Fritscher, Jack, 'Artist Chuck Arnett: His Life / Our Times,' in Mark Thompson (ed.) *Leatherfolk: Radical Sex, People, Politics, and Practice* (Boston: Alyson Publications, 1991), pp. 106–18.

——. 'Bondage: Blest Be The Tie That Binds,' *Drummer*, 3:24 (1978), pp. 16–23, 76.

——. 'Getting Off,' *Drummer*, 3:24 (1978), pp. 8, 72–3.

——. 'Mondo Bondage 1978,' http://jackfritscher.com/PDF/Drummer/Draft_Issues/024/Mondo%20Bondage%201978-B.pdf (accessed 10 October 2017).

Gedalof, Irene, 'Identities in Transit: Nomads, Cyborgs and Women,' *European Journal of Women's Studies*, 7:3 (2000), pp. 337–54.

Girl Scouts of the U.S.A., *Girl Scout Handbook: Intermediate Program* (New York, 1955).

Gonzalez-Day, Ken, 'Tom of Finland,' in Claude J. Summers (ed.), *The Queer Encyclopedia of the Visual Arts* (San Francisco: Cleis Press, 2004), pp. 330–1.

Gooch, Brad, *The Golden Age of Promiscuity* (New York: Knopf, 1996).

Guenther, Bob, 'Four Early Hanky Codes,' *Leather Times* [formerly *The Leather Archives & Museum Newsletter*], 23 (fall/winter 2004), pp. 3–5.

Habal, Estella, *San Francisco's International Hotel: Mobilizing the Filipino American Community in the Anti-Eviction Movement* (Philadelphia, PA: Temple University Press, 2007).

Halsted, Fred, 'Editorial,' *Package*, 1:1 (1976), p. 3.

——. 'Fred Halsted,' *Drummer*, 1:4 (1976), p. 48.

——. 'Personal Training,' *Package*, 1:4 (1976), p. 16.

Hanson, Dian, *Tom of Finland: The Comics, Vol. 1* (Cologne: Taschen, 2011).

Hartman, Chester, with Sarah Carnochan, *City for Sale: The Transformation of San Francisco*, rev. edn (Berkeley, CA: University of California Press, 2002).

Harvie, Jen, *Fair Play – Art, Performance, and Neoliberalism* (New York: Palgrave Macmillan, 2013).

Hebdige, Dick, *Subculture: The Meaning of Style* (London: Routledge, 1979).

Heise, Kenan, 'Dom Orejudos, 58, Ballet Dancer and Artist Known as "Etienne",' *Chicago Tribune*, 2 October 1991, http://articles.chicagotribune.com/1991–10–02/news/9103300004_1_ballet-choreographer-and-principal-dancer-fantasy-art (accessed 10 October 2017).

Hilderbrand, Lucas, *Inherent Vice: Bootleg Histories of Videotape and Copyright* (Durham, NC: Duke University Press, 2009).

Holly, Michael Ann, 'What is Research in Art History, Anyway?,' in Michael Ann Holly and Marquard Smith (eds.), *What is Research in the Visual Arts? Obsession, Archive, Encounter* (Williamstown, MA: Sterling and Francine Clark Art Institute, 2008), pp. 3–12.

Hong, James T., 'The Suspicious Archive, Part I: A Prejudiced Interpretation of the Interpretation of Archives,' *E-flux*, 75 (September 2016), www.e-flux.com/

journal/75/67172/the-suspicious-archive-part-i-a-prejudiced-interpretation-of-the-interpretation-of-archives (accessed 10 October 2017).

Honigman, Ana Finel, 'Dean Sameshima talks to Ana Finel Honigman,' *Saatchi Online Magazine* (2007).

hooks, bell, *All About Love: New Visions* (New York: Perennial, 2001).

Hooven, F. Valentine, III, *Tom of Finland: His Life and Times* (New York: St. Martin's Griffin, 1993).

——. *Tom of Finland: Life and Work of a Gay Hero* (Berlin: Bruno Gmünder, 2012).

Hudson, 'Tom of Finland – An Appreciation,' in *Tom of Finland: Retrospective II* (Los Angeles: Tom of Finland Foundation, 1991), p. 5.

Hughes, Jeremy, 'Halsted & Yale – Who's On Top?,' *Skin*, 3:1 (1981), p. 8.

Hurston, Zora Neale, 'How it Feels to be Colored Me,' *World Tomorrow*, 11 (1928), pp. 215–16.

'In Passing,' *Drummer*, 2:15 (1977), p. 82.

'In Passing,' *Drummer*, 3:20 (1977), p. 98.

Jagose, Annamarie, *Queer Theory: An Introduction* (New York: New York University Press, 1996).

Jarzombek, Mark, 'The Mapplethorpe Trial and the Paradox of Its Formalist and Liberal Defense: Sights of Contention,' *Appendix*, 2 (spring 1994), pp. 58–81.

Johnson, Viola, 'The Love That Dare Not Speak Its Name: Playing With and Against Racial Stereotypes,' *Black Leather in Color* (1994), pp. 8–9.

——. *To Love, to Obey, to Serve: Diary of an Old Guard Slave* (Fairfield, CT: Mystic Rose Books, 1999).

Jones, Amelia, et al., 'Dyke Talk, or "Political Lesbianism" and Queer Feminist Art (History),' in Amelia Jones and Erin Silver (eds.), *Otherwise: Imagining Queer Feminist Art Histories* (Manchester: Manchester University Press, 2016), pp. 160–74.

Jones, William E., *Halsted Plays Himself* (Los Angeles: Semiotext(e), 2011).

Joseph, Miranda, *Against the Romance of Community* (Minneapolis, MN: University of Minnesota Press, 2002).

Kant, Immanuel, *The Critique of Judgment*, ed. Nicholas Walker, trans. James Creed Meredith (Oxford: Oxford University Press, 2007).

Kaprow, Allan, 'Happenings in the New York Scene' (1961), in *Essays on the Blurring of Art and Life* (Berkeley, CA: University of California Press, 1993), pp. 15–26.

Kearns, Michael, 'Fred Halsted: Not a Comeback, A Return,' *FREEP*, 30 December 1977–5 January 1978, C-1.

Kepner, Jim, 'Pat Rocco' [interview], 27 April 1983, https://www.cinema.ucla.edu/sites/default/files/Rocco.pdf, n.p. (accessed 10 October 2017).

King, Carrie M., 'Know Your History: Dean Sameshima,' *Exberliner*, 9 March 2017, http://www.exberliner.com/culture/art/dean-sameshima-647-a (accessed 10 October 2017).

Kinnick, Dave, 'L.A. Scene,' *Steam*, 1:1 (1993), p. 32.

The Kiwi Collective, 'Race and Sex … Who's Panicking?,' *Black Leather in Color*, 8 (fall/winter 2000), pp. 25–6.

Kleinhans, Chuck, 'The Change from Film to Video Pornography: Implications for

Analysis,' in Peter Lehman (ed.), *Pornography: Film and Culture* (New Brunswick, NJ: Rutgers University Press, 2006), pp. 154–67.

Knight, Christopher, 'Review: Fun To Be Had in Works of Bob Mizer and Tom of Finland,' *The Los Angeles Times*, 5 December 2013, www.latimes.com/enter tainment/arts/culture/la-et-cm-review-bob-mizer-tom-of-finland-at-mocapdc-20131204-story.html (accessed 10 October 2017).

Krafft-Ebing, Richard von, *Psychopathia Sexualis* (Burbank, CA: Bloat Books, 1999).

Kwon, Miwon, *One Place After Another: Site-Specific Art and Locational Identity* (Cambridge, MA: MIT Press, 2004).

Linden, Robin Ruth, et al. (eds.), *Against Sadomasochism: A Radical Feminist Analysis* (East Palo Alto, CA: Frog in the Well Press, 1982).

Linton, Meg, and Sue Maberry (eds.), *Doin' It in Public: Feminism and Art and the Woman's Building*, vols. I & II (Los Angeles: Otis College of Art and Design, 2011).

Lippard, Lucy, *From the Center: Feminist Essays on Women's Art* (New York: E. P. Dutton, 1976).

Lodge, Guy, 'Film Review: Tom of Finland,' *Variety*, 11 February 2017, http://variety.com/2017/film/reviews/tom-of-finland-review-1201983671 (accessed 10 October 2017).

Love, Heather, 'Truth and Consequences: On Paranoid and Reparative Reading,' *Criticism*, 52:2 (2010), pp. 235–41.

Lucie-Smith, Edward, 'Tom of Finland,' in Dian Hanson (ed.), *Tom of Finland XXL* (Cologne: Taschen, 2009).

Lynes, Russell, *Good Old Modern: An Intimate Portrait of the Museum of Modern Art* (New York: Atheneum, 1973).

Lyotard, Jean-Francois, 'Critical Reflections,' trans. W. G. J. Niesluchawski, *Artforum*, 24:8 (1991), pp. 92–3.

Maas, Willard, 'Poetry and The Film: A Symposium,' *Film Culture*, 29 (1963), pp. 55–63.

Mains, Geoff, *Urban Aboriginals* (San Francisco: Gay Sunshine Press, 1984).

Majoli, Monica, 'Identity, Intimacy and Mortality,' *Corpus*, 4:1 (2006), pp. 46–53.

——. 'Letter to Florence,' *Air de Paris* (n.d.), http://www.airdeparis.com/past/majoli.htm (accessed 10 October 2017).

Manalansan, Martin F., 'The "Stuff" of Archives,' *Radical History Review*, 120 (fall 2014), pp. 94–107.

Mar, Alex, 'Paper Trail,' *New York Magazine*, 9 March 2013, http://nymag.com/nymetro/news/people/columns/intelligencer/9500/# (accessed 10 October 2017).

Marshall, Daniel, Kevin P. Murphy, and Zeb Tortorici, 'Editors' Introduction: Queering Archives: Historical Unravelings,' *Radical History Review*, 120 (fall 2014), pp. 1–11.

McNally, Anna, 'All That Stuff! Organising Records of Creative Process,' in Judy Vaknin, Karyn Stuckey, and Victoria Lane (eds.), *All This Stuff: Archiving the Artist* (Faringdon: Libri Publishing, 2013), pp. 97–108.

Meeker, Martin, *Contacts Desired: Gay and Lesbian Communications and Community, 1940s–1970s* (Chicago: University of Chicago Press, 2006).

Mekas, Jonas, 'Movie Journal,' *The Village Voice*, 20 April 1972, p. 75

Mercer, Kobena, 'Skin Head Sex Thing: Racial Difference and the Homoerotic Imagination,' in Bad Object Choices (eds.), *How Do I Look? Queer Film and Video* (Seattle, WA: Bay Press, 1991), pp. 169–210.

Meyer, Richard, *Outlaw Representation: Censorship and Homosexuality in Twentieth-Century American Art* (Oxford: Oxford University Press, 2002).

——. 'SF Queer Subculture & Art History,' lecture, Yerba Buena Center for the Arts, 19 December 2012, https://www.youtube.com/watch?v=-PbD_-B4Bek (accessed 10 October 2017).

Micheff, Johnny, 'Community Action Interatction,' *dis Magazine*, 2010, http://dismagazine.com/discussion/9725/community-action-interaction (accessed 10 October 2017).

Min, Susette, 'Remains to Be Seen: Reading the Works of Dean Sameshima and Khanh Vo,' in David L. Eng and David Kazanjian (eds.), *Loss: The Politics of Mourning* (Berkeley, CA: University of California Press, 2003), pp. 229–50.

Moore, Thomas, 'Seductive Darkness: An Interview with Dean Sameshima,' *The Fan Zine*, 28 April 2014, http://thefanzine.com/seductive-darkness-an-interview-with-dean-sameshima (accessed 10 October 2017).

Muñoz, José Esteban, *Cruising Utopia: The Then and There of Queer Futurity* (New York: New York University Press, 2009).

——. 'The Vulnerability Artist: Nao Bustamante and the Sad Beauty of Reparation,' *Women and Performance*, 16:2 (2006), pp. 191–200.

——. 'The Wildness of the Commons,' keynote, *WE WHO FEEL DIFFERENTLY*, New York, New Museum, 5 May 2012. Audio, https://wewhofeeldifferently.info/files/Ephemera/SYM_D2/4.%20Day%202%E2%80%94Jose%20Munoz%E2%80%94%20Keynote_1-2.mp3 (accessed 12 July 2019).

Musser, Amber Jamilla, *Sensational Flesh: Race, Power, and Masochism* (New York: New York University Press, 2014).

Nancy, Jean-Luc, *Being Singular Plural*, trans. Robert D. Richardson and Anne E. O'Byrne (Stanford, CA: Stanford University Press, 2000).

——. *The Inoperative Community*, trans. Peter Connor et al. (Minneapolis, MN: University of Minnesota Press, 1991).

Nault, Curran, 'Hanky Code 2.0: LA/ATX Pocket Expo—The New Rules of Flagging,' in David Evans Frantz (ed.), *Die Kränken. Sprayed With Tears* [exh. cat.] (Los Angeles: ONE Archives, 2017), pp. 51–7.

Nelson, Maggie, *The Argonauts* (Minneapolis, MN: Graywolf Press, 2015).

Nemerov, Alexander, 'Seeing Ghosts: *The Turn of the Screw* and Art History,' in Michael Ann Holly and Marquard Smith (eds.), *What is Research in the Visual Arts? Obsession, Archive, Encounter* (Williamstown, MA: Sterling and Francine Clark Art Institute, 2008), pp. 13–32.

Nesbit, Molly, 'MoMA: The Problem,' *ANY: Architecture New York*, 22 (1998), pp. 16–18.

Nesbit, Molly, Hans Ulrich Obrist, and Rirkrit Tiravanija, 'What is a Station?,' *E-Flux* (2003), http://projects.e-flux.com/utopia/about.html (accessed 10 October 2017).

Ngai, Sianne, *Our Aesthetic Categories: Zany, Cute, Interesting* (Cambridge, MA: Harvard University Press, 2012).

Nguyen, Tan Hoang, *A View from the Bottom: Asian American Masculinity and Sexual Representation* (Durham, NC: Duke University Press, 2014).

Nochlin, Linda, 'Why Have There Been No Great Women Artists?,' *ArtNews* (January 1971), pp. 22–39, 67–71.

O'Doherty, Brian, *Inside the White Cube: The Ideology of the Gallery Space* (Berkeley, CA: University of California Press, 1999).

Oosterhuis, Harry, 'Richard von Krafft-Ebing's "Step-Children of Nature": Psychiatry and the Making of Homosexual Identity,' in Vernon A. Rosario (ed.), *Science and Homosexualities* (London: Routledge, 1997), pp. 66–88.

Opel, Bob, 'Arnett: Lautrec in Leather,' *Drummer*, 1:4 (1976), pp. 18–20.

Ortiz, Ricardo, 'John Rechy and the Grammar of Ostentation,' in Sue-Ellen Case et al. (eds.), *Cruising the Performative: Interventions into the Representation of Ethnicity, Nationality, and Sexuality* (Bloomington, IN: Indiana University Press, 1995), pp. 59–70.

——. 'Sexuality Degree Zero: Pleasure and Power in the Novels of John Rechy, Arturo Islas, and Michael Nava,' *Journal of Homosexuality*, 26:2–3 (1993), pp. 111–26.

Osborne, Thomas, 'The Ordinariness of the Archive,' *History of the Human Sciences*, 12:2 (1999), pp. 51–64.

Pagán, Eduardo Obregón, *Murder at the Sleepy Lagoon: Zoot Suits, Race, and Riot in Wartime L.A.* (Chapel Hill, NC: University of North Carolina Press, 2003).

Paglia, Camille, 'Sex Quest in Tom of Finland,' in Dian Hanson (ed.), *Tom of Finland XXL* (Cologne: Taschen, 2009), pp. 81–2.

Patterson, Cynthia Lee, *Art for the Middle Class: America's Illustrated Magazines of the 1840s* (Jackson, MS: University of Mississippi Press, 2010).

Patterson, Zabet, 'Going On-Line: Consuming Pornography in the Digital Era,' in Linda Williams (ed.), *Porn Studies* (Durham, NC: Duke University Press, 2004), pp. 104–24.

Payne, Robert (John Embry), 'John Rechy, Author of the "Sexual Outlaw" Talks About S&M with R,bert Payne,' *Drummer*, 3:16 (1977), pp. 8–11, 70–1.

Pearson, Jesse. 'Nayland Blake,' *Vice*, 1 October 2008, https://www.vice.com/en_us/article/4w4dk9/nayland-blake-125-v15n10 (accessed 10 October 2017).

Perry, Clarence Arthur, *First Steps in Community Center Development* (New York: Department of Recreation, 1916).

Pettis, Ruth M., 'Gay and Lesbian Bookstores,' in *The GLBTQ Encyclopedia* (2007), www.glbtqarchive.com/literature/gay_lesbian_bookstores_L.pdf (accessed 10 October 2017).

Poddar, Sandhini, *Being Singular Plural* (New York: Guggenheim, 2012).

Pollock, Griselda, 'Artists Mythologies and Media Genius, Madness and Art History,' *Screen* 21:3 (1980), pp. 57–96.

Preston, John, 'What Happened?,' in Mark Thompson (ed.), *Leatherfolk: Radical Sex, People, Politics, and Practice* (Boston, MA: Alyson Publications, 1991), pp. 210–20.

The Project on Disney (Jane Kuentz et al.), *Inside the Mouse: Work and Play at Disney World* (Durham, NC: Duke University Press, 1995).

Rajan, Tilottama (ed.), 'Introduction: Imagining History,' *PMLA*, 118:3 (2003), special issue, 'Imagining History,' pp. 427–35.

——. 'On (Not) Being Postcolonial,' *Postcolonial Text*, 2:1 (2006), http://postcolonial. org/index.php/pct/article/view/403/822 (accessed 10 October 2017).

Ramakers, Micha, *Dirty Pictures: Tom of Finland, Masculinity, and Homosexuality* (New York: St. Martin's Griffin, 2000).

Rechy, John, *Numbers* (New York: Grove/Atlantic, 1967).

——. 'Real People as Fictional Characters: Some Comic, Sad, and Dangerous Encounters,' lecture, University of Texas, El Paso, TX, 2007, www.johnrechy.com/ so_realPeople.html (accessed 10 October 2017).

Reed, David, 'The Multimillion-Dollar Mystery High,' *Christopher Street*, 3:7 (1979), pp. 21–8.

Renslow, Chuck, 'From the Founder: On 25 Years of Leather History,' in Jakob VanLammeren and José Santiago Pérez (eds.), *Leather Archives & Museum: 25 Years* (Chicago: Leather Archives & Museum, 2016), pp. 17–18.

'Review: "Numbers" by John Rechy,' *Drum*, 28 (January 1968), p. 11.

Reynolds, Ann, 'Circa 1970: Towards a Feminist Public,' in Rhea Anastas (ed.), *Witness to Her Art* (Annandale-on-Hudson, NY: Bard Center for Curatorial Studies and D.A.P. Press, 2006), pp. 27–33.

Ricco, John Paul, 'The Art of the Consummate Cruise and the Essential Risk of the Common,' *FeedBack*, 4 February 2016, http://openhumanitiespress.org/feedback/ sexualities/the-consummate-cruise-2 (accessed 10 October 2017).

——. *The Logic of the Lure* (Chicago: University of Chicago Press, 2002).

Ridinger, Robert B. Marks, 'Things Visible and Invisible: The Leather Archives & Museum,' *Journal of Homosexuality*, 43:1 (2002), pp. 1–9.

Román, David, 'Visa Denied,' in Joseph A. Boone et al. (eds.), *Queer Frontiers: Millennial Geographies, Genders, and Generations* (Madison, WI: University of Wisconsin Press, 2000), pp. 350–66.

Ross, Johnny, *Golden Shower Chicken* (San Diego, CA: Greenleaf Classics, 1984).

Rubber Bear (Peter Tolos), 'Editorial: Why Gear? A Personal Fantasy,' *Rubber Rebel*, 1:1 (1993), p. 1.

——. 'Layering,' *Rubber Rebel*, 1:2 (1993), pp. 4–8.

Rubin, Gayle, 'The Leather Archives & Museum: Some Pre-History,' in Jakob VanLammeren and José Santiago Pérez (eds.), *Leather Archives & Museum: 25 Years* (Chicago: Leather Archives & Museum, 2016), pp. 25–32.

——. 'The Miracle Mile, South of Market and Gay Male Leather 1962–1997,' in James Brooks et al. (eds.), *Reclaiming San Francisco: History, Politics, Culture* (San Francisco: City Lights Books, 1998), pp. 247–72.

——. 'Samois,' *Leather Times* [formerly *The Leather Archives & Museum Newsletter*], 21 (spring 2004), pp. 3–6.

——. 'Sites, Settlements, and Urban Sex: Archaeology and the Study of Gay Leathermen in San Francisco 1955–1995,' in Robert A. Schmidt and Barbara L. Voss (eds.), *Archaeologies of Sexuality* (London: Routledge, 2000), pp. 62–88.

——. 'Thinking Sex: Notes for a Radical Theory of the Politics of Sexuality,' in Carol Vance (ed.), *Pleasure and Danger: Exploring Female Sexuality* (London: Pandora, 1984), pp. 267–93.

——. 'The Valley of the Kings,' *Sentinel USA*, 13 September 1984.

——. 'The Valley of the Kings: Leathermen in San Francisco, 1960–1990,' Ph.D. diss., University of Michigan, 1994.

'Sado-Maso Sex Makes Art Museum,' *Variety*, 24 April 1974.

Samois (eds.), *What Color is Your Handkerchief? A Lesbian S/M Sexuality Reader* (San Francisco: Samois, 1979).

Schwenk, Kim, 'Another World Possible: Radical Archiving in the 21st Century,' *Progressive Librarian*, 36:7 (2011), pp. 51–8, 110.

Scott, Joan W., 'After History?,' in Joan W. Scott and Debra Keates (eds.), *Schools of Thought: Twenty-Five Years of Interpretive Social Science* (Princeton, NJ: Princeton University Press, 2001).

——. 'Experience,' in Judith Butler and Joan W. Scott (eds.), *Feminists Theorize the Political* (London: Routledge, 1992), pp. 22–40.

——. *The Fantasy of Feminist History* (Durham, NC: Duke University Press, 2011).

Sedgwick, Eve Kosofsky, 'Paranoid Reading and Reparative Reading; or, You're So Paranoid, You Probably Think This Introduction Is about You,' in Eve Kosofsky Sedgwick (ed.), *Novel Gazing: Queer Readings in Fiction* (Durham, NC: Duke University Press, 1997), pp. 1–40.

——. *Tendencies* (Durham, NC: Duke University Press, 1993).

Shaw, Randy, 'Tenant Power in San Francisco,' in James Brooks et al. (eds.), *Reclaiming San Francisco: History, Politics, Culture* (San Francisco: City Lights Books, 1998), pp. 287–300.

Siebenand, Paul Alcuin, 'The Beginnings of Gay Cinema in Los Angeles: The Industry and the Audience,' Ph.D. diss., University of Southern California, 1975.

Sobredo, James, 'From Manila Bay to Daly City: Filipinos in San Francsico,' in James Brooks et al. (eds.), *Reclaiming San Francisco: History, Politics, Culture* (San Francisco: City Lights Books, 1998), pp. 273–82.

Spada, James, 'I Was a Gay Vice Cop,' *Drummer*, 2:13 (1977), pp. 6–8.

The Spanner Trust, 'The History of the Spanner Case,' http://www.spannertrust.org/documents/spannerhistory.asp (accessed 10 October 2017).

Spivak, Gayatri Chakravorty, 'The Rani of Sirmur: An Essay in Reading the Archives,' *History and Theory*, 24:3 (1985), pp. 247–72.

Spring, Justin, *Secret Historian: The Life and Times of Samuel Steward, Professor, Tattoo Artist, and Sexual Renegade* (New York: Farrar, Straus, and Giroux, 2010).

Staff, Patrick, and Tess Edmonson, 'Patrick Staff "The Foundation",' *Vdrome* (n.d.), www.vdrome.org/patrick-staff-the-foundation (accessed 10 October 2017).

Steedman, Carolyn, 'Culture, Cultural Studies and the Historians,' in Simond During (ed.), *The Cultural Studies Reader*, 2nd edn (London: Routledge, 1999), pp. 46–56.

——. *Dust: The Archive and Cultural History* (New Brunswick, NJ: Rutgers University Press, 2002).

——. 'Something She Called a Fever: Michelet, Derrida, and Dust,' *The American Historical Review*, 106:4 (2001), pp. 1159–80.

Stockholder, Jessica, *Figure-Ground Relations* (Rotterdam: Witte de With, 1993).

Stoler, Ann Laura, *Along the Archival Grain: Epistemic Anxieties and Colonial Common Sense* (Princeton, NJ: Princeton University Press, 2008).

Storer, Rick, 'LA&M Mortgage: GONE!!,' *Leather Archives & Museum Newsletter*, 22 (summer 2004), p. 10.

Straus, Emily E., *Death of a Suburban Dream: Race and Schools in Compton, California* (Philadelphia, PA: University of Pennsylvania Press, 2014).

Streitmatter, Roger, *Unspeakable: The Rise of the Gay and Lesbian Press in America* (New York: Faber & Faber, 1995).

Taylor of San Francisco, 'Signs: Their Meaning and Their History,' *DungeonMaster*, 16 (1982), pp. 6–7.

Tchen, John Kuo Wei, 'Asian,' in Bruce Burgett and Glenn Handler (eds.), *Keywords for American Cultural Studies*, 2nd edn (New York: New York University Press, 2014), pp. 26–9.

Tom of Finland, 'Tom of Finland Speaks at Calarts 1/2 & 2/2,' lecture, CalArts, 1988, www.youtube.com/watch?v=KmDfUkZC_wo (accessed 10 October 2017).

Townsend, Larry, *The Leatherman's Handbook* (New York: The Other Traveller, 1972).

Trooper, A., 'Malecall/Dear Sir:,' *Drummer*, 1:10 (1976), p. 4.

Truscott, Carol, 'San Francisco: A Reverent, Non-Linear, Necessarily Incomplete History of Its SM Community,' *Sandmutopia Guardian*, 8 (1990), p. 6–12.

Turan, Kenneth, and Stephen F. Zito, *Sinema: American Pornographic Films and the People Who Make Them* (New York: Praeger, 1974).

Tyburczy, Jennifer, 'Queer curatorship: Performing the History of Race, Sex, and Power in Museums,' *Women and Performance*, 23:1 (2013), pp. 107–24.

——. *Sex Museums: The Politics and Performance of Display* (Chicago: University of Chicago Press, 2016).

Tyler, Parker, *Screening the Sexes: Homosexuality in the Movies* (New York: Da Capo Press, 1993).

——. *Underground Film: A Critical History* (New York: Grove Press, 1970).

Vaidhyanathan, Siva, *The Anarchist in the Library: How the Clash between Freedom and Control is Hacking the Real World and Crashing the System* (New York: Basic Books, 2004).

VanLammeren, Jakob, 'Memory and the Power of Place: Meditations on Archives and Community at the LA&M,' in Jakob VanLammeren and José Santiago Pérez (eds.), *Leather Archives & Museum. 25 Years* (Chicago: Leather Archives & Museum, 2016), pp. 55–9.

Vazquez, Neil, 'At LA Pride Durk Dehner Talks Tom of Finland's Popular Resurgence,' *ArtSlant*, 7 June 2016, www.artslant.com/ny/articles/show/46019-at-la-pride-muse-durk-dehner-talks-tom-of-finlands-popular-resurgence (accessed 10 October 2017).

Velasco, David, 'Queer Eyes,' *artforum.com*, 11 March 2012, https://www.artforum.com/film/id=30482 (accessed October 10 2017).

Verrill, Addison, 'N.Y. Hits Abuse-Abasement Pic,' *Variety*, 19 April 1972, pp. 1, 22.

Walters, Margaret, *The Nude Male: A New Perspective* (London: Paddington Press, 1978).

Waugh, Thomas, 'Men's Pornography: Gay vs. Straight,' *Jump Cut*, 30 (March 1985), pp. 30–5.

Weeks, Jeffrey, *Invented Moralities: Sexual Values in an Age of Uncertainty* (Cambridge: Polity Press, 1995).

Weiss, Margot D., *Techniques of Pleasure: BDSM and the Circuits of Sexuality* (Durham, NC: Duke University Press, 2011).

——. 'Working at Play: BDSM Sexuality in the San Francisco Bay Area,' *Anthropologica*, 48 (2006), pp. 229–45.

Welch, Paul. 'Homosexuality in America,' *LIFE*, 26 June 1964, pp. 68–74.

White, Hayden, *Tropics of Discourse: Essays in Cultural Criticism* (Baltimore, MD: Johns Hopkins University Press, 1978).

Whitehall, Richard, 'Prick Flicks,' *Open City Newspaper*, 19 December 1968, n.p.

Williams, Linda, *Hard Core: Power, Pleasure, and the 'Frenzy of the Visible'* (Berkeley, CA: University of California Press, 1989).

——. 'Pornography, Porno, Porn: Thoughts on a Weedy Field,' *Porn Studies*, 1:1 (2014), pp. 24–40.

Williams, Raymond, *Keywords: A Vocabulary of Culture and Society*, rev. edn (Oxford: Oxford University Press, 1983).

Winzen, Matthias, 'Collecting—So Normal, So Paradoxical,' in Ingrid Schaffner and Matthias Winzen (eds.), *Deep Storage: Collecting, Storing, and Archiving in Art* (Munich: Prestel, 1998), pp. 22–31.

Witomski, T. R., '*Urban Aboriginals*, by Geoff Mains' [review], *DungeonMaster*, 26 (August 1984), p. 9.

Wittig, Monique, and Sande Zeig, *Lesbian Peoples: Material for a Dictionary* (New York: Avon, 1979).

Wolf, Lolita, and Nayland Blake, 'Decorative Piercing,' performance, Yerba Buena Center for the Arts, video, 19 December 2012, https://www.youtube.com/watch?v=0680Qju8gE0 (accessed 10 October 2017).

Woodward, Richard B., 'For Young Artists, All Roads Now Lead to a Happening Berlin,' *The New York Times*, 13 March 2005.

Zimmerman, Chris, 'De-TAILing Vi,' *The Leather Archives & Museum Newsletter*, 11 (spring 2000), p. 2.

Zinn, Howard, 'Secrecy, Archives, and the Public Interest,' *Midwestern Archivist*, 2:2 (1977), pp. 14–26.

<h1 style="text-align:right">Index</h1>